JOURNAL FOR THE STUDY OF THE OLD TESTAMENT
SUPPLEMENT SERIES
371

Ralph W. Klein

The Chronicler as Theologian

Essays in Honor of Ralph W. Klein

edited by

M. Patrick Graham,
Steven L. McKenzie
& Gary N. Knoppers

T & T CLARK INTERNATIONAL
A Continuum imprint
LONDON • NEW YORK

Copyright © 2003 T&T Clark International
A Continuum imprint

Published by T&T Clark International
The Tower Building, 11 York Road, London SE1 7NX
15 East 26th Street, Suite 1703, New York, NY 10010

www.continuumbooks.com

British Library Cataloguing-in-Publication Data
A catalogue record for this book is available from the British Library

Typeset and edited for Continuum by Forthcoming Publications Ltd
www.forthcomingpublications.com

Printed on acid-free paper in Great Britain by Bookcraft, Midsomer Norton

ISBN 0-8264-6671-0 (hardback)
    0-5670-8392-6 (paperback)

CONTENTS

PREFACE

This volume presents articles that deal in some way with the Chronicler as a theologian, illuminating the author's thought and message by means of certain critical texts or by identifying and tracing larger themes through the work. It follows *The Chronicler as Historian*[1] and *The Chronicler as Author*[2] and so is the third in a series to appear in the Journal for the Study of the Old Testament Supplement Series. All have endeavored to show the diverse approaches employed in Chronicles scholarship, and all have been nourished by the work of the Chronicles–Ezra–Nehemiah Section of the Society of Biblical Literature. The first of the three books 'explored the value of Chronicles for historical information about the pre-exilic period of Israelite and Judean history', while the second investigated 'the Chronicler's…work in terms of its literary sources, the techniques by which it was constructed and its perspective advanced, how early readers may have encountered it, and the value of several contemporary reading strategies for making its voice heard clearly once more'.[3]

This book has taken shape as a tribute to Ralph W. Klein, who has stimulated and nurtured the study of Chronicles through his own scholarship, beginning with his doctoral dissertation and the studies that followed it, and continuing through the leadership and encouragement that he has given a generation of Chronicles scholarship in America and beyond by virtue of his work in the Society of Biblical Literature, labor that gave birth to the society's Chronicles–Ezra–Nehemiah Section. He invited young scholars to join him on the program committee for that section; he solicited and nurtured their ideas and then he passed along to them the leadership of this body. His friendship, guidance, and wisdom have been

---

1. M.P. Graham, K.G. Hoglund and S.L. McKenzie (eds.), *The Chronicler as Historian* (JSOTSup, 238; Sheffield: Sheffield Academic Press, 1997).
2. M.P. Graham and S.L. McKenzie (eds.), *The Chronicler as Author: Studies in Text and Texture* (JSOTSup, 263; Sheffield: Sheffield Academic Press, 1999).
3. Graham and McKenzie, 'Preface', in *idem* (eds.), *The Chronicler as Author*, p. 7.

invaluable and always available. He has been generous with his time and attention, and he became a mentor to many. It is fitting then that the first essay of this book is a tribute to Ralph and was written by Robert Smith, a longtime friend of the honoree and one who knows him well, and it is followed by a select bibliography of Ralph's publications, prepared by Allen Mueller, Ralph's colleague at the Lutheran School of Theology at Chicago who directs the Jesuit-Kraus-McCormick Library there.

The second part of the volume offers five articles that deal with individual texts in Chronicles and are arranged in canonical sequence. The genealogies of 1 Chronicles 1 are treated by Gary Knoppers, who demonstrates the author's effort to set the history of Israel within the larger, international context of the history of other peoples. Gerrie Snyman's treatment of 1 Chron. 2.3–4.23 proceeds in a decidedly different way: by means of comparisons with modern African practices, he attempts to show how genealogies may be used to advance issues related to group identity and claims to land. In the third article Ehud Ben Zvi takes up the secession of the Northern Kingdom after the death of Solomon (2 Chron. 10–12) and finds that the Chronicler left unresolved the question of why God destroyed the unity of his people by allowing a powerful anti-Jerusalem party to arise and pull away the North. How the Chronicler rewrote 2 Kings 21 in order to make sense of Manasseh's reign (2 Chron. 33.1-20) and guide the understanding of exile and the need for conversion for later generations is the task Philippe Abadie assumes in his contribution. Finally, Mark Throntveit addresses a topic often debated in Chronicles scholarship—the relationship of Hezekiah to the other two luminaries in the history, David and Solomon—and concludes that Hezekiah is portrayed in terms of both!

The final part of this collection presents eight studies, arranged alphabetically by author, that address themes found in Chronicles or that deal in some way with the author's perspective on the life and history of Israel. Leslie Allen explicates the expression, 'God of your/our/his fathers', as the Chronicler's means to actualize earlier traditions for the exhortation and instruction of later audiences. In the second article of Part III, Chris Begg reviews the Chronicler's history of the ark from Saul to Josiah and invites the reader to consider whether the ancient author might have maintained hope for a restoration of this cult object to the temple in Jerusalem. Roddy Braun casts his net broadly to include Second and Third Isaiah, as well as Chronicles, Ezra and Nehemiah, in his study of how Cyrus was understood by these authors, concluding that the Chronicler was left with many uncertainties about the future of his people. John Endres's exploration of the topic of worship in Chronicles delineates the various forms and functions of worship and underscores its positive elements for the life of Israel. Isaac Kalimi distinguishes the portrayal of Jerusalem in Chronicles from that in other parts of the Hebrew Bible and affirms that for the Chronicler Jerusalem was the permanent capital of Israel and the eternal throne of God. Brian Kelly tackles an important theme in Chronicles and takes issue with prevalent scholarly opinion. He concludes that the Chronicler uses retribution to emphasize the *mercy* of God on sinful humans. Bill Schniedewind's study tracks the development of 'Name Theology' from its origins in the seventh century until the time of the Chronicler, who came to believe that God's name would come to reside in the Second Temple, just as it had in the First. Finally, John Wright undertakes an intricate investigation into the Chronicler's representation of God's presence and absence in the life of Israel, a study that is highly suggestive for later generations concerned with such matters.

In the course of introducing this volume, the editors would also like to express appreciation to those who have made the work possible. The authors of these essays have given generously of their expertise, time and energy to honor a friend and colleague. All have been collegial and conscientious, and it is our hope that their labor will serve to advance the study and appreciation of Chronicles. Next, thanks are due to Gillian T. Peabody (Pitts Theology Library) for her translation of Philippe Abadie's contribution, 'From the Impious Manasseh (2 Kgs 21) to the Convert Manasseh (2 Chron. 33): Theological Rewriting by the Chronicler', and to Lydia Dene (Pitts Theology Library), Justin M. Fuhrman (Candler School of Theology) and Myka Kenedy Stephens (Candler School of Theology) for their assistance with the checking of citations and certain other matters of copy editing. We are also grateful to Philip R. Davies and David J.A. Clines for the encouragement they offered in the production of these three volumes, for their inclusion in the *JSOT* Supplement Series and for the leadership they have afforded our discipline for a generation. Finally, to the editors of Continuum Press we offer our thanks for seeing this third volume through to its conclusion and our best wishes for the future of this and the other series of the Sheffield Academic Press that are now in their care.

M. Patrick Graham
Gary N. Knoppers
Steven L. McKenzie

ABBREVIATIONS

AAR	American Academy of Religion
AB	Anchor Bible
ABD	David Noel Freedman (ed.), *The Anchor Bible Dictionary* (New York: Doubleday, 1992)
ABS	Archaeology and Biblical Studies
ADPV	Abhandlungen des Deutschen Palästinavereins
AJBI	*Annual of the Japanese Biblical Institute*
AJS	*American Journal of Sociology*
ANET	James B. Pritchard (ed.), *Ancient Near Eastern Texts Relating to the Old Testament* (Princeton: Princeton University Press, 1950)
AnOr	Analecta orientalia
AS	Assyriological Studies
ATD	Das Alte Testament Deutsch
BAT	Biblischer Commentar über das Alte Testament
BEATAJ	Beiträge zur Erforschung des Alten Testaments und des antiken Judentums
BHS	*Biblia hebraica stuttgartensia*
Bib	*Biblica*
BibInt	*Biblical Interpretation: A Journal of Contemporary Approaches*
BibRes	*Biblical Research*
BK	*Bibel und Kirche*
BN	*Biblische Notizen*
BWANT	Beiträge zur Wissenschaft vom Alten und Neuen Testament
BZAW	Beihefte zur *ZAW*
CBC	The Cambridge Bible Commentary on the NEB
CBQ	*Catholic Biblical Quarterly*
C^{MT}	Chronicles, Masoretic Text
ConBOT	Coniectanea biblica, Old Testament
CRBS	*Currents in Research: Biblical Studies*
CTM	*Concordia Theological Monthly*
CurTM	*Currents in Theology and Mission*
DBSup	*Dictionnaire de la Bible, Supplément*
DJD	Discoveries in the Judaean Desert
DtrH	The Deuteronomistic History/Historian

ESHM	European Seminar in Historical Methodology
EVV	English versions
FAT	Forschungen zum Alten Testament
FOTL	The Forms of the Old Testament Literature
FRLANT	Forschungen zur Religion und Literatur des Alten und Neuen Testaments
FTS	Freiburger theologische Studien
GNB	Good News Bible
GTA	Göttinger theologische Arbeiten
HALAT	L. Koehler *et al.* (eds.), *Hebräisches und aramäisches Lexikon zum Alten Testament* (5 vols.; Leiden: E.J. Brill, 1967–95)
HAT	Handbuch zum Alten Testament
HBC	J.L. Mays (ed.), *Harper's Bible Commentary* (San Francisco: Harper & Row)
HCOT	Historical Commentary on the Old Testament
HCSB	W.A. Meeks (ed.), *The HarperCollins Study Bible; New Revised Standard Version; with the Apocryphal/ Deuterocanonical Books* (New York: HarperCollins)
HKAT	Handkommentar zum Alten Testament
HSAT	Die Heilige Schrift des Alten Testamentes
HSM	Harvard Semitic Monographs
HSS	Harvard Semitic Studies
HTR	*Harvard Theological Review*
IBC	Interpretation, a Bible Commentary for Teaching and Preaching
ICC	International Critical Commentary
IDB	G.A. Buttrick (ed.), *Interpreter's Dictionary of the Bible* (4 vols.; Nashville: Abingdon Press, 1962)
IDBSup	*IDB*, Supplementary Volume
IEJ	*Israel Exploration Journal*
Int	*Interpretation*
ISBE	Geoffrey Bromiley (ed.), *The International Standard Bible Encyclopedia* (4 vols.; Grand Rapids: Eerdmans, rev. edn, 1979–88)
JANESCU	*Journal of the Ancient Near Eastern Society of Columbia University*
JAOS	*Journal of the American Oriental Society*
JBL	*Journal of Biblical Literature*
JETS	*Journal of the Evangelical Theological Society*
JJS	*Journal of Jewish Studies*
JSNTSup	*Journal for the Study of the New Testament*, Supplement Series
JSOT	*Journal for the Study of the Old Testament*
JSOTSup	*Journal for the Study of the Old Testament*, Supplement Series

JSPSup	*Journal for the Study of the Pseudepigrapha*, Supplement Series
JTS	*Journal of Theological Studies*
LS	*Louvain Studies*
LThQ	*Lexington Theological Quarterly*
LXX	Septuagint
LWF	Lutheran World Federation
MT	Masoretic Text
NCB	New Century Bible
NEAEHL	E. Stern (ed.), *The New Encyclopedia of Archaeological Excavations in the Holy Land* (Jerusalem: Israel Exploration Society/Carta; New York: Simon & Schuster, 1993)
NEB	*New English Bible*
NIB	L.E. Keck *et al.* (eds.), *New Interpreter's Bible* (12 vols.; Nashville: Abingdon Press, 1994–)
NIV	New International Version
NovT	*Novum Testamentum*
NRSV	New Revised Standard Version
OBO	Orbis biblicus et orientalis
OBT	Overtures to Biblical Theology
OTL	Old Testament Library
OTP	James Charlesworth (ed.), *Old Testament Pseudepigrapha*
OTS	*Oudtestamentische Studiën*
RB	*Revue biblique*
ResQ	*Restoration Quarterly*
RSV	Revised Standard Version
SB	Sources bibliques
SBB	Stuttgarter biblische Beiträge
SBL	Society of Biblical Literature
SBLDS	SBL Dissertation Series
SBLSCS	SBL Septuagint and Cognate Studies
SBLSP	SBL Seminar Papers
SBT	Studies in Biblical Theology
SJC	Studies in Judaism and Christianity
SJCA	Studies of Judaism and Christianity in Antiquity
SJOT	*Scandinavian Journal of the Old Testament*
S^{MT}	Samuel, Masoretic Text
SNTSMS	Society for New Testament Studies Monograph Series
SR	*Studies in Religion/Sciences religieuses*
SSEA	Society for the Study of Egyptian Antiquities
ST	*Studia theologica*
TA	*Tel Aviv*
TANZ	Texte und Arbeiten zum neutestamentlichen Zeitalter
TBC	Torch Bible Commentary

TDOT	G.J. Botterweck and H. Ringgren (eds.), *Theological Dictionary of the Old Testament*
TLOT	E. Jenni and C. Westermann (eds.), *Theological Lexicon of the Old Testament* (3 vols.; Peabody, MA: Hendrickson, 1997)
TOTC	Tyndale Old Testament Commentaries
TynBul	*Tyndale Bulletin*
VT	*Vetus Testamentum*
VTSup	*Vetus Testamentum*, Supplements
WBC	Word Biblical Commentary
WMANT	Wissenschaftliche Monographien zum Alten und Neuen Testament
WTJ	*Westminster Theological Journal*
WW	*Word and World*
YNER	Yale Near Eastern Researches
ZAH	*Zeitschrift für Althebraistik*
ZAW	*Zeitschrift für die alttestamentliche Wissenschaft*
ZKT	*Zeitschrift für katholische Theologie*

LIST OF CONTRIBUTORS

PHILIPPE ABADIE
Catholic University of Lyon, France

LESLIE C. ALLEN
Fuller Theological Seminary, Pasadena, CA, USA

CHRISTOPHER T. BEGG
Catholic University of America, Washington, DC, USA

EHUD BEN ZVI
University of Alberta, Edmonton, Alberta, Canada

RODDY L. BRAUN
Gainesville, VA, USA

JOHN C. ENDRES
Jesuit School of Theology at Berkeley, CA, USA

M. PATRICK GRAHAM
Emory University, Atlanta, GA, USA

ISAAC KALIMI
Depaul Univerity, Chicago, IL, USA

BRIAN E. KELLY
Canterbury Christ Church University College, Canterbury, UK

GARY N. KNOPPERS
Pennsylvania State University, University Park, PA, USA

STEVEN L. MCKENZIE
Rhodes College, Memphis, TN, USA

ALLEN W. MUELLER
Jesuit-Krauss-McCormick Library, Chicago, IL, USA

WILLIAM M. SCHNIEDEWIND
University of California, Los Angeles, CA, USA

ROBERT H. SMITH
Pacific Lutheran Theological Seminary, Berkeley, CA, USA

GERRIE F. SNYMAN
Unisa, Pretoria, South Africa

MARK A. THRONTVEIT
Luther Seminary, St Paul, MN, USA

JOHN W. WRIGHT
Point Loma Nazarene University, San Diego, CA, USA

Part I

RALPH W. KLEIN

'*IOTA* SUBSCRIPT' AND RALPH W. KLEIN

Robert H. Smith

It was just like Ralph to begin a conversation not long ago by asking, 'Have you heard the one about the scholar on his deathbed?' Ralph continued, 'As he lay there dying, he lifted his eyes and said to those surrounding his bed, "If I had to do it all over again, I would devote my life to *iota* subscript!"' I laughed out loud, but Ralph's own laughter and delight in his story eclipsed my own.

Anyone who has had even minimal contact with Ralph can recall other jokes, anecdotes and shaggy dog tales that he loves to insert into the conversation. Of all the ones I can remember, the one about *iota* subscript leaps to the front of my mind on this occasion. Ralph enjoys that story largely, I am sure, because the tendency of his own life has been in a direction diametrically opposed to that of the dying scholar who apparently wished to know more and more about less and less.

Ralph's own doctoral work at Harvard under Frank Moore Cross Jr, was entitled, 'Studies in the Greek Texts of the Chronicler' (1966). His earliest publications continued the text-critical work he had begun at Harvard. In some early essays, for example, he examined the minutiae of the chronologies of Genesis 5 and 11 on the basis of the MT, the Samaritan Hebrew Pentateuch and the LXX. He displayed the original chronological scheme of those chapters and demonstrated how that original scheme was modified in the MT. In that early work and in all of his subsequent work Ralph has demonstrated that he cares deeply about details and that he is a master at noting the smallest individual features of texts. Nevertheless Ralph is not merely a gifted analyst and masterful collector of great masses of esoteric data. He possesses a powerful synthetic imagination.

He knows how to excavate biblical and textual data and then make them count in the ongoing discussions of the scholarly guild and also in the wider world of religious communities. He cares about communicating with a variety of audiences. His first published book was *Textual Criticism of the Old Testament: From the Septuagint to Qumran* (1974 [repr. 1978; Korean translation 1988]). It appeared in a series (Guides to Biblical Scholarship) designed to make accessible to students and lay people the ways in which modern scholarship has opened new vistas for understanding the significance of the biblical record. Ralph's book on textual criticism is a parade example of his ability to write on a complex subject with consummate clarity for the non-expert.

Ralph's earliest scholarly work dealt with the Chronicler, and his interest and expertise in the Chronicler have only increased over the years. Ralph initiated and chaired the 'Consultation on Chronicles–Ezra–Nehemiah' of the SBL (1985–86) and the 'Chronicles–Ezra–Nehemiah Group' (1987–90) and has been a leader in promoting the study of this part of Scripture. He is an active member (never a passive bystander) of the SBL, the Catholic Biblical Association, the International Organization for Septuagint and Cognate Studies, and the Chicago Society of Biblical Research.

Ralph has authored many articles and books, both for fellow scholars and for a wider audience of non-specialists, and they are listed in his bibliography. What his extensive bibliography does not show is his labor on behalf of the publications of others. He served as a member of the editorial board of the *Journal of Biblical Literature* from 1986–92. And he is currently a member of the editorial boards of the Chicago Society of Biblical Research (1985–) and the *Catholic Biblical Quarterly* Monograph Series (1986–). Since 2001 he has been Associate Editor of the *Catholic Biblical Quarterly*.

At the Lutheran School of Theology at Chicago (LSTC), Ralph served as Academic Dean for a dozen years (1988–99). Ralph filled the position with his customary energy, wisdom and humor. Colleagues never fail to mention Ralph's jokes, both good and bad, but they speak in hushed tones as they describe his awesome labors on behalf of the students and faculty, the curriculum and the wider life of that academic community. He accepted the work of Dean as a vocation and made it an integral part of his calling as scholar and teacher. For Ralph, being Dean meant being a teacher under a different form.

William Lesher, President at LSTC during the time that Ralph was Dean, comments that Ralph's weekly Dean's report was often the first message that faculty members found when they checked their email on Monday morning. The report carried a calendar of activities, a list of Dean's directives and a journal of personal notes that served to keep the community in touch. Lesher notes that Ralph 'was an impatient Dean, often out in front of the faculty, administrators and students with ideas, plans and actions. It was in the chapel, however, that the seminary community saw the fullest integration of Ralph's scholarship, his deep doctrinal piety, his contemporary insights and his human compassion.'

Another LSTC colleague describes Ralph as a 'consummate churchman'. Many Sundays find Ralph leading adult forums in his own Chicago congregation and in other congregations of the Metropolitan Chicago Synod and beyond. His churchmanship is anything but parochial. He served on the St Louis Task Force on Soviet Jewry (1977–78) and on the Seminary Series Dialogue Group of the National Conference of Christians and Jews (1978–83). For these and other contributions, he was the recipient of the Micah Award of the American Jewish Committee (1983). He was a member of the Consultation on Lutheran/Jewish Relations of the Evangelical Lutheran Church of America (1990).

Since 1974 Ralph has been the editor of *Currents in Theology and Mission*, a bi-monthly journal aimed at an audience of pastors and serious laity. The magazine carries articles and opinion pieces, book reviews and homiletical studies. The journal is not the official voice of any school, although its masthead notes that it is 'published by Lutheran School of Theology at Chicago in cooperation with Pacific Lutheran Theological Seminary and Wartburg Theological Seminary'. Nor is it the house organ of any department of a church body. It would be inadequate to describe *Currents* as designed to bridge the gulf between the world of academic theology and that of the local parish. In some respects it does that, but it ranges over a broad landscape of topics and reflects Ralph's own openness to the various voices speaking and needing to be heard in the churches. The contributors to the journal are not only scholars and teachers but also pastors and lay people at work in many different callings. The magazine has been a pet project of Ralph for over a quarter of a century. His continuing editorship is a sign of his commitment to serious conversation on serious issues in language that is always direct and engaging but never shrill or arrogant, always colloquial and clear and never stuffy or merely technical.

Never did Ralph want his life to be narrowly fixated even on such interesting matters as *iota* subscript or the *kaige* recension of the Greek text of the Old Testament, even though he speaks with authority on such matters. Ralph was born into a Lutheran parsonage in 1936. In spite of being adventurous and independent, and he surely is that, Ralph seemed destined to follow in his father's footsteps by becoming a Lutheran pastor.

He attended a Lutheran high school, a Lutheran college and a Lutheran seminary. But what his teachers noted early was his tremendous love of learning and his aptitude for research and writing. He earned the degree of Doctor of Theology at Harvard University Divinity School in 1966. He was ordained as a pastor in the Lutheran Church in the same year but did not take up the position of parish pastor. His ministry is that of teaching. He was called to join the faculty of Concordia Senior College in Fort Wayne, Indiana, in 1966. After two years in that institution he was called to serve as Assistant Professor of Old Testament Studies on the faculty of Concordia Theological Seminary in St Louis, Missouri, a school he served from 1968–74. In 1974 he participated in the founding of Christ Seminary-Seminex (St Louis) and served there first as Associate and then as full Professor (1974–83). Since 1983 he has been Christ Seminary-Seminex Professor of Old Testament at Lutheran School of Theology at Chicago.

Ralph was married to Marilyn Kieninger in 1962. Ralph and Marilyn have two daughters (Martha and Rebecca), and they boast very proudly, as they ought, of their grandchildren: Patrick and Daniel were born in 1998 and 2001, and triplets Luke, Seth and Jonah were born in 2001. When he finishes sharing the latest joke, Ralph loves to share pictures and stories of his grandchildren.

Ralph has been described in terms that seem almost contradictory: totally serious and yet wonderfully humorous, as disciplined as a Spartan and yet boyishly playful, fiercely demanding of himself and colleagues and yet profoundly gentle.

Ralph's colleagues await the completion of his work on 1 and 2 Chronicles, slated to be published in the Hermeneia commentary series, perhaps as early as 2006. We expect that much anticipated work to be a fitting capstone to a wonderfully productive career. But who knows what post-Chronicles work Ralph will undertake!

RALPH W. KLEIN:
A SELECT BIBLIOGRAPHY

Allen W. Mueller

Ralph Klein is currently a member of the editorial boards of the Chicago Society of Biblical Research (since 1985) and the *Catholic Biblical Quarterly* Monograph Series (since 1986) and was on the editorial board of the *Journal of Biblical Literature* from 1986–92. He has been the editor of *Currents in Theology and Mission* since 1974 and began to serve as an associate editor of the *Catholic Biblical Quarterly* in 2001. Ralph Klein was managing editor of *Preaching Helps* from 1974–86, and since 1977 he has been an abstractor for *Religious and Theological Abstracts* for the journals *Currents in Theology and Mission* and *Zeitschrift für die alttestamentliche Wissenschaft*. Ralph Klein has written numerous homiletical and exegetical pieces, as well as more than 190 reviews of books in the fields of biblical and theological studies. He has frequently addressed groups as diverse as the SBL, interfaith clergy groups, bishops' and pastors' conventions, and liturgical conferences. The following bibliography reflects both the focus and the breadth of Ralph Klein's scholarship.

1966
'Studies in the Greek Texts of the Chronicler' (ThD dissertation, Harvard Divinity School).

1967
'New Evidence for an Old Recension of Reigns', *HTR* 60, pp. 93-105.

1968
'The Day of the Lord', *CTM* 39, pp. 517-25.
'The Prophet of God in Society: Trinity XX/I Kings 21.17-25', in *The Concordia Pulpit for 1969* (St Louis: Concordia Publishing House), pp. 249-54.
'Supplements in the Paraleipomena: A Rejoinder', *HTR* 61, pp. 492-95.
'Wait Actively: Trinity XXI/Isaiah 30.15-19', in *The Concordia Pulpit for 1969* (St Louis: Concordia Publishing House), pp. 254-58.

1969

'Old Readings in 1 Esdras: The List of Returnees From Babylon (Ezra 2/Nehemiah 7)', *HTR* 62, pp. 99-107.

1970

'Jeroboam's Rise to Power', *JBL* 89, pp. 217-18.
'The Song of Hannah', *CTM* 41, pp. 674-87.

1971

'Job's Wife', *CTM* 42, pp. 399-401.
'Yahweh Faithful and Free: A Study in Ezekiel', *CTM* 42, pp. 493-501.

1972

'Aspects of Intertestamental Messianism', *CTM* 43, pp. 191-203 (repr. in V.L. Tollers and J.R. Maier [eds.], *The Bible in its Literary Milieu: Contemporary Essays* [Grand Rapids: Eerdmans, 1979], pp. 507-17).

1973

'The Church Needs the Old Testament', *Seminar* 5.6, pp. 4-6.
'Once More: Jeroboam's Rise to Power', *JBL* 92, pp. 582-84.
'The Text of Deuteronomy Employed in the Testament of Moses', in G.W. Nickelsburg (ed.), *Studies on the Testament of Moses: Seminar Papers* (SBLSCS, 4; Cambridge, MA: SBL), p. 78.

1974

'Archaic Chronologies and the Textual History of the Old Testament', *HTR* 67, pp. 255-63.
Textual Criticism of the Old Testament: The Septuagint after Qumran (Philadelphia: Fortress Press) (Korean translation: *Goo Yak BonMoon Bee Pyoung* [transliterated title] [Seoul, Korea: Emmanuel Publishing Company, 1988]).
'The Yahwist Looks at Abraham', *CTM* 45, pp. 43-49.

1975

'Apocalyptic: What Is It?', *Academy: Official Journal of the Lutheran Academy for Scholarship* 32.2, pp. 1-8.

1976

'Ezra and Nehemiah in Recent Studies', in F.M. Cross, W.E. Lemke and P.D. Miller (eds.), *Magnalia Dei: The Mighty Acts of God; Essays on the Bible and Archaeology in Memory of G. Ernest Wright* (Garden City, NY: Doubleday), pp. 361-76.
'Interpreting Old Testament Texts for Preaching: Ten Easy Steps', *Preaching Helps* 3, pp. 11-13.
'Samaria Papyri', in *IDBSup*, p. 772.
'Sanballat', in *IDBSup*, pp. 781-82.
'So You Want to Buy an Old Testament Commentary', *CurTM* 3, pp. 54-55.

1977

'The Ordination of Women in the Lutheran Church', *CurTM* 4, pp. 151-57.

1978

'Going Home: A Theology of Second Isaiah', *CurTM* 5, pp. 198-210.
'A Theology for Exiles: The Kingship of Yahweh', *Dialog* 17, pp. 128-34.

1979

Israel in Exile: A Theological Interpretation (OBT; Philadelphia: Fortress Press) (translated
        into Portuguese: *Israel No Exílio* [São Paulo: Edicioes Paulinas, 1990], and Japanese:
        Babiron Hoshu to Isuraeru [transliterated title] [Tokyo: Riton, 1997]).
'The Thrill of Discovery: Reflections on Frederick W. Danker's Contributions to New
        Testament Lexicography', *CurTM* 6, pp. 63-66.

1980

'Jeremiah 23:1-8: An Expository Article', *Int* 34, pp. 167-72.

1981

'The Childs Proposal: A Symposium with Ralph W. Klein, Gary Stansell, and Walter Brueg-
        gemann', *WW* 1, pp. 105-15.
'The Message of P', in J. Jeremias and L. Perlitt (eds.), *Die Botschaft und die Boten: Fest-
        schrift für Hans Walter Wolff zum 70. Geburtstag* (Neukirchen–Vluyn: Neukirchener
        Verlag), pp. 57-66.
'Twelve Cheers for the Risen Christ; Second Sunday of Easter, Psalm 148', in *Augsburg Ser-
        mons: Sermons on the Old Testament Lessons from the New Lectionary and Calendar:
        Old Testament Lessons, Series B* (Minneapolis: Augsburg), pp. 116-22.

1982

'Liberated Leadership: Masters and "Lords" in Biblical Perspective', *CurTM* 9, pp. 282-90.
'A Liberated Lifestyle: Slaves and Servants in Biblical Perspective', *CurTM* 9, pp. 212-21.

1983

'Abijah's Campaign Against the North (II Chr. 13): What Were the Chronicler's Sources?',
        ZAW 95, pp. 210-17.
I Samuel (WBC, 10; Waco, TX: Word Books).
'The Origin and Nature of Our Estrangement', in *The Significance of Judaism for the Life and
        Mission of the Church: The Report of the Fourth International Consultation held under
        the Auspices of the Lutheran World Federation, Department of Studies, Bossey, near
        Geneva, August 1982* (LWF Studies; Geneva: Lutheran World Federation), pp. 19-39.

1984

'Anti-Semitism as Christian Legacy: The Origin and Nature of Our Estrangement from the
        Jews', *CurTM* 11, pp. 285-301.
'The Hebrew Roots of Christian Symbols', *Modern Liturgy* 11.9, pp. 10-11.
'So You Want to Buy an Old Testament Commentary', *CurTM* 11, pp. 237-42.

1985

'Speaking of Prophets Today', *Forum Letter* 14.10, pp. 7-8.

1986

Beginning of the Covenant People (Augsburg Adult Bible Studies, 19.4; Columbus, OH:
        Augsburg).

'Dialog with Gay and Lesbian Lutherans: A Response', *CurTM* 13, pp. 304-306.
'A Valentine for Those Who Fear Yahweh: The Book of Malachi', *CurTM* 13, pp. 143-52.

1987
'Response to "Are We Lovers Anymore?"', *Theological Education* 24.1, pp. 37-39.

1988
'Call, Covenant, and Community: The Story of Abraham and Sarah', *CurTM* 15, pp. 120-27.
Ezekiel: The Prophet and his Message (Studies on Personalities of the Old Testament; Columbia: University of South Carolina Press).
'Ezra', in *HBC*, pp. 372-78.
'Nehemiah', in *HBC*, pp. 379-86.
'Old Testament Studies Today and Tomorrow', *Entree* 5.2, pp. 19-21.
'1 Esdras', in *HBC*, pp. 769-75.
'Samuel', in *ISBE*, IV, pp. 311-12.
'Samuel, Books of', in *ISBE*, IV, pp. 312-20.
'WORDsearch: State of the Art Concordance', *CurTM* 15, pp. 194-96.

1989
'Faith and Sight in Exodus 32–34', *Lutheran Forum* 23.2, pp. 25-26, 31-33.
'I Esdras', in B.W. Anderson (ed.), *The Books of the Bible. II. The Apocrypha and the New Testament* (New York: Charles Scribner's Sons), pp. 13-19.

1990
'The God of the Bible Confronts the Politics of Hunger', *CurTM* 17, pp. 110-17.
'With his Wounds…', *The Lutheran* 3.6, pp. 10-11.

1991
'Celebrating and Sharing the Gift: Reflections on Jacob, Israel's Ancestor', *CurTM* 18, pp. 263-72.
'Christology and Incarnation: Fulfillment and Radical Reinterpretation of the Old Testament Prophets', *Ex Auditu* 7, pp. 9-17.
'Prophet-Mystic and Social Justice: A Response', *BibRes* 36, pp. 69-73.

1992
'Chronicles, Book of 1–2', in *ABD*, I, pp. 992-1002.
'Ezra–Nehemiah, Books of', in *ABD*, II, pp. 731-42.
'First Lesson: Advent-Easter', in T.S. Hanson and R. Gordon (eds.), *Exploring the Yearly Lectionary: Studies in the Series A; Bible Texts* (Minneapolis: Augsburg/Fortress Press), *passim*.

1993
'1 Chronicles', in *HCSB*, pp. 605-607 (Introduction); pp. 607-46 (Annotations).
'2 Chronicles', in *HCSB*, pp. 647-98 (Annotations).
'Commentary Recommendations for the Old Testament', *CurTM* 20, pp. 45-48.
'The Tower of Babel and Pentecost: In Search of a New World Order', *Lutheran Woman Today* 6.5, pp. 10-11.

1994
'Where Christians Must Stand', *Lutheran Women Today* 7.7, pp. 17-19.

1995
'Reflections on Historiography in the Account of Jehoshaphat', in D.P. Wright, D.N. Freedman and A. Hurvitz (eds.), *Pomegranates and Golden Bells: Studies in Biblical, Jewish,
and Near Eastern Ritual, Law, and Literature in Honor of Jacob Milgrom* (Winona
Lake, IN: Eisenbrauns), pp. 643-57.

1996
'Back to the Future: The Tabernacle in the Book of Exodus', *Int* 50, pp. 264-76.

1997
'How Many in a Thousand?', in M.P. Graham, K.G. Hoglund and S.L. McKenzie (eds.),
The Chronicler as Historian (JSOTSup, 238; Sheffield: Sheffield Academic Press),
pp. 270-82.
'Israel/Today's Believers and the Nations: Three Test Cases', *CurTM* 24, pp. 232-37.
'Something New under the Sun: Computer Concordances and Biblical Study', *Christian
Century* 114, pp. 1034-37.

1998
'Prophets and Prophecy in the Books of Chronicles', *The Bible Today* 36, pp. 227-32.

1999
'1 Esdras', in G.R. O'Day and D.L. Peterson (eds.), *The Access Bible: New Revised Standard
Version; with the Apocryphal/Deuterocanonical Books* (Oxford: Oxford University
Press), pp. (Apocrypha) 247-67 (Introduction, footnotes, and commentary).
'The Books of Ezra and Nehemiah: Introduction, Commentary, and Reflections', in *NIB*, III,
pp. 661-851.
'David: Sinner and Saint in Samuel and Chronicles', *CurTM* 26, pp. 104-16.
'Eighteenth Sunday after Pentecost—Last Sunday after Pentecost', in *New Proclamation:
Series A; Easter through Pentecost* (Minneapolis: Fortress Press), pp. 227-311.
'Samuel, Books of', in J.H. Hayes (ed.), *Dictionary of Biblical Interpretation* (2 vols.; Nash-
ville: Abingdon Press), II, pp. 431-35.

2000
'Ezekiel at the Dawn of the Twenty-First Century', in M.S. Odell and J.T. Strong (eds.), *The
Book of Ezekiel: Theological and Anthropological Perspectives* (Symposium Series, 9;
Atlanta: SBL), pp. 1-11.
'Ezekiel, Book of', in D.N. Freedman,(ed.), *Eerdmans Dictionary of the Bible* (Grand Rapids:
Eerdmans), pp. 446-48.
'Ezra', in *HCBC*, pp. 338-44.
'The Ironic End of Joash in Chronicles', in R.A. Argall, B.A. Bow and R.A. Werline (eds.),
*For a Later Generation: The Transformation of Tradition in Israel, Early Judaism, and
Early Christianity* (Festschrift George W.E. Nickelsburg; Harrisburg, PA: Trinity Press
International), pp. 116-27.
'Let Me Not Sing the Story of Your Love Off Key', *CurTM* 27, pp. 253-62.

'I Esdras', in *HCBC*, pp. 698-704.
'Nehemiah', in *HCBC*, pp. 345-52.

2001
'Narrative Texts: Chronicles, Ezra, and Nehemiah', in L.G. Purdue (ed.), *The Blackwell Companion to the Hebrew Bible* (Blackwell Companions to Religion, 1; Oxford: Basil Blackwell), pp. 385-401.

Part II

TEXTS

Shem, Ham and Japheth: The Universal and the Particular in the Genealogy of Nations[*]

Gary N. Knoppers

Considering that the narrative portions of the Chronicler's work focus on Judah and Jerusalem, the genealogical introduction (1 Chron. 1–9) begins in a very curious way. The genealogies of 1 Chronicles 1 switch back and forth from the particular to the universal, from linear genealogies to segmented genealogies. The first verse of the book begins with the primal human 'Adam' and continues in list form to the tenth generation 'Noah' (1 Chron. 1.1-4a). The tabulation of ten names is a miracle of condensation, having been extracted from the much longer and more detailed narrative lineage of Adam in Gen. 5.1-32: 'these are the lineages (תולדת) of Adam'.[1] As a unilineal genealogy, the material in vv. 1-4a features an unbroken line of descent from the first person to Noah. If this lineage stresses depth within one family, the following lineage stresses breadth by tracing in segmented form the descendants of Noah's three sons— Shem, Ham and Japhet (1 Chron. 1.5-23). This material, drawn from Gen. 10.1-29, the so-called Table of Nations, enumerates approximately 70 or 72 descendants of Noah's three sons,[2] symbolizing the totality of the

---

* It is a pleasure to dedicate this essay to Ralph W. Klein, a longtime supporter of Chronicles, Ezra and Nehemiah studies in North America and a past chair of the Chronicles–Ezra–Nehemiah Section of the Society of Biblical Literature. One of his contributions to the study of the Chronicler's work that I continue to use with great profit is his dissertation, 'Studies in the Greek Texts of the Chronicler' (ThD dissertation, Harvard Divinity School, 1966). This research into the additions to LXX Chronicles (clustered near its end) and the textual witnesses to 1 Esdras is an essential study of the textual criticism of Chronicles, Ezra and Nehemiah.

1. Usually attributed to the Priestly source (hereafter, P). The author of Chronicles does not explain the relationships between the persons he lists. One has to follow the context and his source to grasp the sense of this highly condensed lineage.

2. Text-critical variants in Genesis and Chronicles make it impossible to be precise about the exact number.

world's known peoples. The complex genealogical tree relates all of the world's nations to each other through a common ancestor—Noah.

Having branched out to the universal, the genealogies return to the particular. The ensuing ten-name list extending from 'Shem' to 'Abram' (1 Chron. 1.24-27) is extracted from the much longer narrative lineage of Shem in Gen. 11.10-26: these are the lineages (תולדת) of Shem' (P). There is no more discussion of the seed of Ham and Japhet. Hence, the text returns to a particular focus on a single line. Isaac the son of 'Abram, that is Abraham' (1 Chron. 1.27) is the father of Israel (Jacob), the eponymous ancestor of the Israelite people. If the author was concerned simply with the roots of the people of Israel, one might expect him to fashion a descending linear genealogy from Abraham to Jacob. But an exclusive switch from a universal focus to a provincial focus does not occur. Quite the contrary, one finds the genealogist drawing from Gen. 25.12-18: 'these are the lineages (תולדת) of Ishmael' (P) to relate the twelve sons of Ishmael, Abraham's son through Hagar (1 Chron. 1.29-31).[3] He then deals with the various offspring of Qeturah, here declared to be Abraham's concubine (1 Chron. 1.32-33).[4]

Isaac, the father of Israel, briefly makes another appearance (1.34), but the author does not seize the opportunity to address, at least immediately, Isaac's grandchildren through Israel. Rather, he chooses to focus his attention on Isaac's grandchildren through Esau (1 Chron. 1.35-37). If Judah was the author's only interest, he would seem to be avoiding the issue. He abridges and adapts the material in Genesis 36 to deal with the progeny of Isaac's firstborn, the twin brother of Jacob.[5] The interest in

3. E.A. Knauf, *Ismael: Untersuchungen zur Geschichte Palästinas und Nordarabiens im 1. Jahrtausend v.Chr* (ADPV; Wiesbaden: Otto Harrassowitz, 2nd edn, 1989).

4. The segmented genealogy is largely abridged and adapted from Gen. 25.1-3. The description of Qeturah as Abraham's concubine, not found in the author's biblical source, is likely to be the author's own contribution (cf. 1 Chron. 1.4, 28). Qeturah appears in Genesis as Abraham's second wife, taken sometime after the death of Sarah (Gen. 25.1-2). The reference to her as a concubine may be based on a reading of Gen. 25.1-2 in light of Gen. 25.5-6. The latter mentions that Abraham 'gave all that he had to Isaac', but to his sons by his concubines 'Abraham gave gifts...and sent them away from Isaac toward the east'. In other words, 1 Chron. 1.32 is an instance of *semukin*, an exegetical technique made famous by the rabbis in which one text is read in the light of another in close proximity.

5. 1 Chron. 1.35-37. The heading for this segmented genealogy is taken from either Gen. 36.5 or 36.10. The compositional history of the Edomite material in

Judah's southeastern neighbors does not end with the lineage of Esau's heirs. Another segmented genealogy appears in 1 Chron. 1.38-42, abridged and adapted from Gen. 36.20-28, dealing with the 'sons of Seir'.[6] Neither the author nor his biblical sources directly claim that Seir is part of Esau's genealogy. But the writer, following his sources, makes indirect links between the two. The author of the material in Genesis associates Seir with Esau by presenting the genealogy of Seir (Gen. 36.20-28) in the context of the genealogies and lists of Edom (36.1-19, 31-43). The author of Chronicles follows this pattern in his own work. Detailed lists of Edomite monarchs (1.43-51a) and Edomite chieftains (1.51b-54) follow the coverage devoted to the Seirites.[7] The lists of Edomite kings and chieftains are adapted and slightly abridged from Gen. 36.31-39 and 36.40-43, respectively.[8] The attention paid to Edom (1.35-54) is thus extraordinary.

Gen. 36 is complex and much-debated; see R.R. Wilson, *Genealogy and History in the Biblical World* (YNER, 7; New Haven: Yale University Press, 1977), pp. 167-83; E.A. Knauf, 'Alter und Herkunft der edomitischen Königsliste Gen 36.31-39', *ZAW* 97 (1985), pp. 245-53.

6.   The name of Seir (שֵׂעִיר) is associated with hair (שֵׂעָר) and the Genesis narratives repeatedly play on Esau's hairiness (עֵשָׂו, Gen. 25.25; 27.11, 23). The Seirites and Edomites are presented as co-inhabitants of the land in Gen. 36.20 (cf. Josh. 24.4). Most scholars interpret the biblical references to Seir as designating a mountainous part of Edom or as a synonym for Edom itself; see e.g. E.A. Knauf, *Midian: Untersuchungen zur Geschichte Palästinas und Nordarabiens am Ende des 2. Jahrtausends v. Chr.* (ADPV; Wiesbaden: Otto Harrassowitz, 1988), pp. 50-60. It is entirely plausible that the designation of Seir changed over time, as the Chronicler's own narratives seem to attest (2 Chron. 25.11-20; cf. 2 Kgs 14.7-14). See further, P. Bienkowski, 'The Edomites: Archaeological Evidence from Transjordan', in D.V. Edelman (ed.), *You Shall Not Abhor an Edomite For He is Your Brother: Edom and Seir in History and Tradition* (ABS, 3; Atlanta: Scholars Press, 1995), pp. 41-92; B. Dicou, *Edom, Israel's Brother and Antagonist: The Role of Edom in Biblical Prophecy and Story* (JSOTSup, 169; Sheffield: JSOT Press, 1994).

7.   The author's editing of his sources involves changing headings and transitions, and some abbreviation. My concern in this context is with the Chronicler's reuse of his *Vorlage*. A. Lemaire contends that the original list incorporated into Genesis pertained to Aramaean, rather than to Edomite, kings ('Hadad l'Édomite ou Hadad l'Araméen?', *BN* 43 [1988], pp. 14-18.). While accepting the plausibility of this line of argumentation, one must acknowledge that the transformation of 'Aram' (אֲרָם) to 'Edom' (אֱדֹם) was already part of the Chronicler's *Vorlage*.

8.   The reuse of the Edomite King List and the chieftain list is telling. The structure of the lists in Genesis differs from that of Chronicles. In Genesis the transition between Edomite monarchs is: 'RN died and RN2 reigned', whereas in Chronicles the formula is better translated as 'when RN died, RN2 reigned' (RN = Royal Name);

Only after treating the groups associated with Esau does the text turn to
the 'sons of Israel' (2.1-2). The list of Jacob's twelve male progeny both
concludes the section begun in 1 Chron. 1.34, which deals with the progeny of Isaac, and introduces the next section, detailing the lineages associated with each of the Israelite tribes (1 Chron. 2.3–9.1).

A Text in Literary and Theological Disarray?

The genealogy of nations in Chronicles raises a variety of questions. Why
does the text alternate between pursuing matters of depth (linear genealogies) and matters of breadth (segmented genealogies)? Why does the
writer display such a concern with other peoples? What is the nature of the
authorial interest in the origins of the nations populating the larger
Mediterranean world? Why would the writer magnify the position of
Edom at a time when Yehud was struggling to establish itself in the late
Persian period? If Israel is the focal point of the Chronicler's interests,
why mention the descendants of Esau at all? Is this truly a unified presentation or an assemblage of literary layers, the product of many Chron-
iclers? It will be useful to deal with the question of literary disunity and
theological incongruity before tackling larger thematic issues. At issue are
textual problems, repetitions, inconsistencies, discrepancies in style, the
presence of digressions and the claim that the content of much of 1 Chronicles 1 conflicts with the Chronicler's theological interests.

Rudolph has contended for literary and theological disunity, asserting
that most of the text stems from a series of anonymous editors. His work
may be considered as a case-study, albeit a radical one, of the argument
for disunity.[9] In his view, many additions have been made to an original,
largely unilineal descending lineage that extends from Adam to Israel.
Noting that the material in MT 1 Chron. 1.11-16 and 1.17b-24 is absent
from the LXX[B], Rudolph argues that the entire list of Noah's descendants

---

see S. Japhet, *I and II Chronicles: A Commentary* (OTL; Louisville, KY: Westminster/
John Knox Press, 1993), p. 52. In 1 Chron. 1.51, the transition to the chieftain list
reads, 'When Hadad died, the chieftains of Edom were...' In contrast, Gen. 36.40
reads, 'These are the names of the chieftains of Esau by their families (מִשְׁפְּחֹתָם), by
their places according to their names'. In Chronicles the list of Edomite chieftains is
dated generally to the time of Hadad's death. The two lists, paratactically ordered in
Genesis, are largely consecutive in Chronicles.

   9.   W. Rudolph, *Chronikbücher* (HAT, 21; Tübingen: J.C.B. Mohr [Paul Siebeck],
1955).

(vv. 4b-23) is secondary, a later addition that interrupts the flow of the presentation (from vv. 1-4 to vv. 24-27).[10] He also thinks that this material is incongruent with the Chronicler's theology. For similar reasons, Rudolph excises the genealogy of Qeturah's descendants (vv. 32-34a) and views the material about the Edomite kings and chieftains (vv. 43b-54) as later supplements.[11] Considering that Rudolph expunges most of the text dealing with other peoples as later additions, this leaves him with a short, relatively uncomplicated lineage as original to the Chronicler's work (1 Chron. 1.1-4a, 24-27, 28-31, 35-42; 2.1-2). The focus in this reconstruction is on the particular, the line of continuity extending from Adam to Israel. The only attention paid to any other group is that accorded to the children of Esau (1 Chron. 1.35-42).

Serious doubts may be raised, however, whether Rudolph's truncated version of the universal genealogies passes critical muster.[12] To be sure, there are some genuine text-critical issues in the formation of 1 Chronicles 1. Verses 11-16 (from 'and Mizraim' through to 'the Hamathites') are lacking in the LXX[B] and cursives ghc$_2$ and are *sub asteriscus* in the Syro-Hexaplar. In cursive i only vv. 13-16 are missing. All of vv. 11-23 are *sub asteriscus* in cursives cn, although the text-critical significance of these variations is disputed.[13] Verses 11-16 do appear in the MT, the LXX[AN] and the Armenian. The LXX[B] has the *lectio brevior* but, by the same token, the want of this material in LXX[B] is puzzling, given (1) the heading in v. 4 ('The sons of Noah: Shem, Ham and Japheth'); (2) the heading in v. 8 ('the

---

10. Rudolph, *Chronikbücher*, pp. 6-7.

11. In viewing the material pertaining to Qeturah as a later addition, Rudolph (*Chronikbücher*, p. 7) was not stating a new opinion. See E. Podechard, 'Le premier chapitre des Paralipomènes', *RB* 13 (1916), p. 372, and more recently, H.G.M. Williamson, *1 and 2 Chronicles* (NCB; Grand Rapids: Eerdmans, 1982), p. 43. Also viewing the material pertaining to the Edomites and the Seirites as later additions (Rudolph, *Chronikbücher*, p. 9) is R.L. Braun, *1 Chronicles* (WBC, 14; Waco, TX: Word Books, 1986), p. 21.

12. In this context, the arguments for unity raised by scholars, such as M. Kartveit (*Motive und Schichten der Landtheologie in I Chronik 1-9* [ConBOT, 28; Stockholm: Almqvist & Wiksell, 1989], pp. 19-23), M. Oeming (*Das wahre Israel: Die 'genealogische Vorhalle' 1 Chronik 1-9* [BWANT, 128; Stuttgart: W. Kohlhammer, 1990], pp. 73-97), T. Willi (*Chronik* [BK, 24/1; Neukirchen–Vluyn: Neukirchener Verlag, 1991], pp. 15-47), and Japhet (*I and II Chronicles*, pp. 55-56) are substantial.

13. L.C. Allen, *The Greek Chronicles: The Relation of the Septuagint of I and II Chronicles to the Masoretic Text. I. The Translator's Craft*; II. *Textual Criticism* (VTSup, 25, 27; Leiden: E.J. Brill, 1974), I, pp. 98-99; II, p. 159.

sons of Ham: Cush, Mizraim, Put and Canaan'); and (3) the inclusion of Ham's other descendants (vv. 9-10). I am inclined to think that the material in question has been lost from the tradition underlying the LXX[B], although there is no obvious mechanism for haplography. There is another text-critical issue: MT 1 Chron. 1.17b-24a (from 'Arpachshad, Lud...' through to 'Shem, Arpachshad' in v. 24) appears neither in LXX[B] nor in cursives ghc₂ (they, as in vv. 11-16, are *sub asteriscus* in the Syro-Hexaplar). Again, the LXX[B] has the *lectio brevior*. Nevertheless a clear mechanism for haplography is evident (homoioteleuton from ארפכשד to ארפכשד).[14] Given that this material was probably lost from the LXX, the MT represents the more original text.

Turning to larger literary issues, Rudolph's highly abridged version of the material in 1 Chron. 1.1–2.2 presents a coherent linear progression from the first human to Israel with only one interruption, the lineage of the sons of Esau (1.35-42). But to sustain his case, Rudolph has to posit a hypothetical earlier form of the Chronicler's work that has been obscured, if not over-written, by later editors. One should note that the type of horizontal lineages appearing in vv. 4b-27 are not at all unusual within 1 Chronicles 1–9.[15] Segmentation—the formulation of different branches within a larger genealogical tree—can serve many purposes: to posit links among a variety of individuals, families and groups; to draw social, political and geographic connections between ethnic groups and places; and to introduce a hierarchy of kinship relationships within a larger group. Moreover, the segmented lineages of 1 Chron. 1.1–2.2 are not chaotic. Although these materials have been drawn from different contexts in Genesis, they have been organized in a coherent way. Precisely because earlier lines are picked up in later contexts, the phenomenon of segmentation is not a problem from a literary point of view.

The Case for Unity

To these arguments, based largely on comparative and contextual considerations, others may be added. From a literary vantage point, one can

---

14. J. Goettsberger, *Die Bücher der Chronik oder Paralipomenon* (Die Heilige Schrift, 4; Bonn: Peter Hanstein, 1939), pp. 30-31.

15. The genealogies of Judah (1 Chron. 2.3–4.23) are a good example. G.N. Knoppers, '"Great Among His Brothers", But Who Is He? Heterogeneity in the Composition of Judah', *Journal of Hebrew Scriptures* 3/4 (2000) <http://www.purl.org/jhs>; *idem*, 'Intermarriage, Social Complexity, and Ethnic Diversity in the Genealogy of Judah', *JBL* 120 (2001), pp. 15-30.

argue that the genealogy of nations in 1 Chron. 1.1–2.2 is more than a jumble of materials extracted from various contexts in Genesis. The placement of names reflects a larger sense of organization and stylization. The chapter begins with a linear genealogy composed of ten members, extending from primordial time to Noah (vv. 1-4a). Having provided a heading for the next section, 'the sons of Noah: Shem, Ham and Japheth' (v. 4b), the author sets out their respective descendants: approximately 70 (or 72) nations in segmented genealogies (vv. 5-23). There are seven sons of Japheth, seven descendants of Cush and seven descendants of Mizraim. Canaan together with his offspring number 12. The element of stylization extends into the later material. Both Seir and Eliphaz have seven sons. There are twelve sons of Ishmael and twelve sons of Israel.

The enumeration of some 70 (or 72) offspring from Noah's sons is followed by another linear genealogy composed of ten members, beginning with Shem and culminating in Abram (vv. 24-27). Hence, what some scholars describe as an intrusive interpolation does not appear so to others. Whereas Rudolph views vv. 4b-23 as one of a series of disruptive interpolations, Japhet views the same verses as an integral part of the Chronicler's original composition.[16] In her presentation (well-defended in my judgment) vv. 1-4 together with vv. 24-27 comprise an *inclusio* around vv. 5-23. The first ten generations (vv. 1-4) are antediluvian, while the latter ten (vv. 24-27) are postdiluvian. In between lie the 70 (or 72) nations that emerge in the postdiluvian world.

It is true that duplications (e.g. vv. 9, 22-23, 32), inconsistencies (e.g. vv. 17-23, 24-27), discrepancies in style (vv. 11-12, 14-16) and digressions (e.g. vv. 10, 32-33, 51-54) may be found in 1 Chron. 1.1–2.2. Nevertheless, these also occur in the author's *Vorlage* of Genesis. The author abridges much of the material he cites—omitting various formulas, territorial remarks, anecdotal references and chronological notes—but the material he does include is often followed punctiliously. This means that tensions in the text of Genesis are largely reproduced in the text of Chronicles. Indeed, the Table of Nations itself has been called a 'heterogeneous collection of material'.[17] Names such as Meshech, Sheba, Dedan, Uz and Havilah appear two or even three times. Such duplication (or triplication) cannot be explained by the Documentary Hypothesis, because there are variations in style and content within the sources (J and P)

16. Japhet, *I and II Chronicles*, pp. 52-54.

17. D.B. Redford, *Egypt, Canaan, and Israel in Ancient Times* (Princeton: Princeton University Press, 1992), p. 402.

themselves. Gentilics in plural form appear, for instance, in vv. 11-12 in accordance with Gen. 10.13-14 (J), while gentilics in singular form appear in vv. 14-16 in accordance with Gen. 10.16-18 (J). Meshech appears both among the descendants of Japheth in v. 5 (P) and among the descendants of Shem in v. 17 (P). Sheba appears among the descendants of Ham in v. 9 (P), among the descendants of Shem in v. 22 (J) and among the descendants of Qeturah in v. 32 (J).[18] The author's light editing—his adherence to his sources—has its costs, inevitably resulting in repetition and inconsistency. But this situation does not differ substantially from the situation in the Chronicler's treatment of the united and divided monarchies. A conservative reproduction of texts selected from his *Vorlagen* of Samuel and Kings is part, albeit not the whole(!), of the Chronicler's compositional technique.[19] In both cases, the replication of disparate sources unavoidably generates some unevenness in the Chronicler's own presentation.

One can discern another regular pattern in 1 Chron. 1.1–2.2. The text consistently provides information on subsidiary lines first.[20] In this, the Chronicler's compositional technique is indebted to the work of the Priestly writers. For example, 1 Chron. 1.4 lists the sons of Noah as Shem, Ham and Japheth. In the following verses, the descendants of Noah's sons appear beginning with Japheth (1.5-7), continuing with Ham (1.8-16) and concluding with Shem (1.17-23). Similarly, after introducing Abraham's children as Isaac and Ishmael (1.28), the text first lists the offspring of Ishmael (1.29-31). In some cases, the order of the genealogies contained in Genesis—Jacob (Gen. 35.23-26) and Esau (Gen. 36)—is reversed to comply with this preferred arrangement—Esau (1.35-37) and Jacob/Israel (2.1-2). Hence, the text consistently lists peoples whose independent

---

18. In assigning these verses to the Yahwist and the Priestly source, I am simply following convention. Legitimate doubts have been raised about whether the documentary hypothesis is best suited to explain the literary diversity one finds in the Table of Nations. See, e.g., R. Rendtorff, *The Old Testament: An Introduction* (Philadelphia: Fortress Press, 1986), pp. 132-34; Redford, *Egypt, Canaan, and Israel*, pp. 400-408; J. Van Seters, *Prologue to History: The Yahwist as Historian in Genesis* (Louisville, KY: Westminster/John Knox Press, 1992), pp. 174-87.

19. S.L. McKenzie, *The Chronicler's Use of the Deuteronomistic History* (HSM, 33; Atlanta: Scholars Press, 1985); T. Sugimoto, 'The Chronicler's Techniques in Quoting Samuel–Kings', *AJBI* 16 (1990), pp. 30-70; *idem*, 'Chronicles as Independent Literature', *JSOT* 55 (1992), pp. 61-74.

20. P.R. Ackroyd, *I and II Chronicles, Ezra, Nehemiah* (Torch Bible Commentaries; London: SCM Press, 1973), p. 31.

histories will not be recounted prior to the listing of peoples whose development will be recounted (1 Chron. 1.4, 17, 34; 2.1).

In speaking of regular patterns within the genealogies, I do not mean to suggest that the author simply imposed paradigms upon his sources. Quite the contrary, he found some patterns already present within the sources. I am suggesting, however, that the Chronicler continued and elaborated tendencies toward schematization already present within the sources.[21] This he did by reworking and repositioning materials from his *Vorlage* of Genesis and by supplying new rubrics when they were needed.[22] In the case of 1 Chron. 1.1–2.2, headings, summaries and numerical patterns serve a larger purpose—unifying collections of disparate names.

As for the arguments for disunity based on content, the exclusion of the Table of Nations and the lists of Edomite kings and chieftains from the Chronicler's original work presumes that he pursues the narrowest of ideological interests. Two comments from slightly different vantage points may be made about this supposition. First, one can concede, for the sake of argument, much of Rudolph's point about the Chronicler's theological orientation and still view this material as original. By far and away the bulk of the genealogical prologue relates to Israel (1 Chron. 2.1–9.1) and not to other peoples. In its scale, the genealogical prologue presents an unprecedented kinship-based introduction to the people of Israel: their identity, filiations and land. This extensive section is concluded with the summary 'and all Israel was enrolled by genealogies' (וכל ישראל התיחשו, 1 Chron. 9.1). Even in dealing with Israel, the author allocates the bulk of his coverage to the three major groups of his own time: Judah (1 Chron. 2.3–4.23), Levi (1 Chron. 5.27–6.66 [EVV 6.1-81]) and Benjamin (1 Chron. 7.6-12; 8.1-40; 9.35-44). When compared with the coverage allocated to the Israelite tribes, the coverage afforded the rest of the world is relatively brief.

21. See the Excursus on the genealogies in my commentary, *I Chronicles* (AB, 12; New York: Doubleday, forthcoming).

22. Schematization in genealogies and lists, including the use of favorite numbers, is paralleled in ancient Mesopotamia and Greece; see A. Malamat, 'King Lists of the Old Babylonian Period and Biblical Genealogies', *JAOS* 88 (1968), pp. 168-73; M.L. West, *The Hesiodic Catalogue of Women: Its Nature, Structure, and Origins* (Oxford: Clarendon Press, 1985); M.D. Johnson, *The Purpose of the Biblical Genealogies* (SNTSMS, 8; Cambridge: Cambridge University Press, 2nd edn, 1988). Similarly, in early Christian tradition, Matthew's genealogy of Jesus (Mt. 1.1-17) is a highly structured work, consisting of three groups of 14 generations; see G. Mussies, 'Parallels to Matthew's Version of the Pedigree of Jesus', *NovT* 28 (1986), pp. 32-47.

Second, the decision to excise 1 Chron. 1.4b-23, 32-33 and 43-54 because they do not comport with the Chronicler's theology, ironically is based on the premise that the Chronicler cares exclusively about Judah. Perhaps, however, the material about other cultures is not extraneous. Rather than removing entire sections of the text, because they do not accord with one's understanding of an author's purpose, it might be better to re-evaluate one's conception of the author. The Chronicler's ideological interests may not be as narrow and parochial as they are purported to be.[23] Given the literary evidence presented above, one is drawn to the conclusion that almost all of the genealogy of nations stems from the Chronicler's own hand.[24]

The Genealogy of Nations and Map Making

With the exception of some headings and summaries, virtually all of the material in 1 Chron. 1.1–2.2 has been taken from Genesis. The extent to which the Chronicler is indebted to the lists, narratives and genealogies of Genesis can be seen by comparing his text with that of his source:

Chronicles	Genesis
1.1	5.1, 6
1.2	5.9, 12, 15
1.3	4.17; 5.21, 25
1.4	10.1
1.5-7	10.2-4
1.8-9	10.6-7
1.10	10.8
1.11-16	10.13-18a
1.17	10.22-23
1.18	10.24
1.19-23	10.25-29
1.24-27	11.10-26
1.28	16.11; 17.18-19; 25.19

23. Rudolph's assessment of the Chronicler's purpose was undoubtedly affected by his supposition that Chronicles, Ezra and Nehemiah derive from a single author. Many contemporary scholars do not share this presupposition. S. Japhet provides a helpful discussion and overview, 'The Relationship between Chronicles and Ezra–Nehemiah', in J.A. Emerton (ed.), *Congress Volume, Leuven 1989* (VTSup, 43; Leiden: E.J. Brill, 1991), pp. 298-313.

24. There may be some scattered additions to the text, but most of 1 Chron. 1.1–2.2 seems to be original to the Chronicler's work. See further my forthcoming commentary, *I Chronicles*.

1.29-31	25.12-16
1.32-33	25.1-4
1.34a	25.19
1.34b	25.21-26a
1.35a	36.10 or 36.5
1.35b	36.4-5
1.36-37	36.11-13a
1.38-42	36.20-28
1.43-50	36.31-39
1.51-54	36.40-43a
2.1-2	35.22b-26 etc.[25]

In some cases (e.g. vv. 1-4, 24-27), the author extracts names from long narratives; in others, he rearranges blocks of material from Genesis to suit his own purposes (e.g. 1 Chron. 1.29-31, 32-33, 35-54; 2.1-2). As the list indicates, the author is selective in his citations. The paring down of Genesis involves changing headings, omitting some geographical, anecdotal and chronological details, and creating new transitions. The choice of certain genealogies (and not others), the editing and repositioning of those genealogies and the Chronicler's own minor additions produce a distinctively new presentation. Drawing from a variety of passages in Genesis, the Chronicler is able to make these older texts speak with a new voice.

The reuse, culling, selection, rearrangement and supplementation of materials from Genesis raises an additional issue. The writer's approach is fairly comprehensive; he draws from the main genealogical blocks in Genesis—chs. 5, 10–11, 25 and 35–36.[26] The inclusion of these disparate lines manifests broad literary and antiquarian interests, leading one scholar to assert that the unit 1 Chron. 1.1–2.1 'represents the book of Genesis, from which all of its material is taken'.[27] However valid this observation may be, it should be pointed out that in condensing Genesis the Chronicler's interests are not all-encompassing. He bypasses or ignores

25. The citation is only approximate. There are a number of tribal lists in the Hebrew Bible, but the precise order of Israel's sons in 1 Chron. 2.1-2 is unique; see M. Noth, *Das System der zwölf Stämme Israels* (BWANT, 4/1; Stuttgart: W. Kohlhammer, 1930), pp. 3-86; Wilson, *Genealogy and History*, pp. 183-95, 224-30; Z. Kallai, 'The Twelve-Tribe Systems of Israel', *VT* 47 (1997), pp. 80-81; *idem*, 'A Note on the Twelve-Tribe Systems of Israel', *VT* 49 (1999), pp. 125-27. Most of the catalogue is implicitly organized by mother, but unlike some earlier authors (Gen. 29.31–30.24; 35.16-20 [J], 23-26 [P]) the writer omits any direct mention of the mothers and the one daughter (Dinah).

26. Podechard, 'Le premier chapitre', pp. 363-86.

27. Japhet, *I and II Chronicles*, p. 52.

some substantial genealogical materials in Genesis: the Cainite and Sethite lines (Gen. 4.17-26), the lineage of Terah (11.27-32), the lineage of Lot (19.30-38), the line of Nahor (22.20-24) and the descendants of Dedan and Midian (25.3-4).

In my judgment, the genealogy of nations may be compared to one of the genres developed in the Classical and post-Classical worlds—the epitome (ἐπιτομή), a short abridgment or compendium of an older work.[28] The first-known Classical writer to compose such an epitome was Theopompus of Chios, who lived at about the same time or slightly before the Chronicler (c. 378–320 BCE) and wrote an epitome of Herodotus in two books.[29] In Classical antiquity such epitomes generally tended to be schematic summaries, rather than stylish short histories.[30] In the Roman era, when epitome writing became quite popular, authors sometimes used the epitome to introduce much longer accounts of contemporary events. Why does the author include many, but not all, of the genealogies from Genesis? Epitomes by their very nature were selective. Rather than seeing the writer's approach as completely encyclopedic, it might be more helpful to say that the Chronicler's epitome includes more and more genealogical material from Genesis as he nears his chief interest: the genealogies of Israel (1 Chron. 2.3–9.1). The detailed attention given to the descendants of Ishmael, Qeturah, Seir and Esau (1 Chron. 1.28-54) anticipates the very detailed treatment given to the descendants of Israel.

In the Chronicler's genealogy of nations, the lineage principle is employed to organize and classify diverse ethnic data. The spatial dimensions and depth of the coverage are remarkable. The various ethnic groups of the world are traced to a common progenitor. The Chronicler's universal lineages may be compared with works such as the Table of Nations in Genesis, which preceded it, and the reworking of the same in *Jubilees*, which succeeded it. Such biblical and early Jewish genealogies, lists and narrative texts are exercises in 'cognitive mapping', attempts 'to impose order on the chaos of spatial perception'.[31] The resulting statement of relationships may at best only partially comport with external reality.

28. R.A. Kaster, 'Epitome', in S. Hornblower and A. Spawforth (eds.), *The Oxford Classical Dictionary* (Oxford: Oxford University Press, 3rd edn, 1996), p. 549.

29. F. Jacoby, *Die Fragmente der griechischen Historiker* (2 vols.; Berlin: Weidmann, 1923), I, fragments 1-4, 115; G.S. Shrimpton, *Theopompus the Historian* (Montreal: McGill-Queen's University Press, 1991), pp. 183-95.

30. S. Hornblower, 'Introduction', in *idem* (ed.), *Greek Historiography* (Oxford: Clarendon Press, 1994), p. 21.

31. P.S. Alexander, 'Geography and the Bible (Early Jewish)', in *ABD*, II, p. 978.

The beginning and end of the section in Chronicles are of considerable import. The line the Chronicler traces begins with the first human and culminates in the eponymous ancestor of the twelve tribes (1 Chron. 2.1-2). In tracing the origins of a panorama of nations to a common ancestor, the author devotes special attention to the descendants of one of Noah's sons: Shem. Even among these descendants, there is a narrowing of focus. Among Shem's offspring, the writer privileges the descendants of Abraham and Isaac. In calling attention to Abraham's seed, the Chronicler's extensive supplementation of the Table of Nations provides it with a new significance.[32] Whereas the Table of Nations actually gives very little attention to the ancestors of Israel, the Chronicler's genealogy of nations does. Inserting much of the Table of the Nations (Gen. 10.1-32//1 Chron. 1.4-23) into the midst of other genealogies extending from the first person—Adam (1.1)—to the progenitor of the twelve tribes—Israel (2.1)—the Chronicler takes the earlier classification a series of steps further. The narrowing of focus from the 70 descendants of Noah to the descendants of Isaac demonstrates that the writer's purpose was not to compile an exhaustive enumeration of all human cultures, but rather to create a certain picture of humanity—an *imago mundi* (image of the world), reflecting the circumstances of his own time. Selectively employing the information available to him from Genesis, the Chronicler concentrates on those nations to whom he believed his people were most closely related.

The Genealogy of Nations as Theology

In his genealogy of humanity, the author posits a direct connection between the first person and the progenitor of the Israelite tribes. But by the same token, this continuity occurs in the context of segmented genealogies that underscore the blood relations among various peoples of the world. Indeed, if a major purpose of genealogies is to configure or rewrite kinship ties, the unit 1 Chron. 1.1–2.2 establishes such ties between Israel and a host of other nations, most notably Seir and Edom. The opening to the Chronicler's work may be best understood in the context of other relevant works from the ancient Mediterranean world. When one compares the opening chapter in Chronicles with other historical writings from ancient Mesopotamia and Greece, one is struck by a number of features. First, the author begins his genealogies with the primal human, thus providing a universal context for his work. Such a global perspective is, of

32. Kartveit, *Motive und Schichten*, p. 112; Willi, *Chronik*, pp. 17-18.

course, not unique to the Chronicler's writing. It is also characteristic of the Yahwistic (Gen. 2.4b-25) and Priestly (Gen. 1.1–2.4a) creation stories. A universal concern may also be found in other late compositions such as the prayer of Nehemiah 9, which begins with creation (v. 6), the historical litany of Psalm 136 (vv. 1-9) and the beginning of Josephus's *Jewish Antiquities*.[33] In Chronicles, the line of continuity extending from the primal human to Israel confers a certain dignity upon all of Israel's descendants. Living in the Persian period, the residents of Yehud can claim a direct line all the way back to the time of creation. Their ancient ancestor Israel himself stood in a direct line, genealogically speaking, to the first person.

Second, the author does not confer any special title upon the first human. Adam is not described as 'the image of God' (אלהים צלם, Gen. 1.27). The origins of Adam go unexplained.[34] Nor is Adam a liminal figure, as was Adapa in second-millennium BCE Mesopotamian lore, the figure who reappears transformed as Oannes in the *Babyloniaca* of Berossus.[35] There is no indication that the primal human was of any special descent, bridged the divine and human spheres, functioned as either a royal priest or a prophet, enjoyed any special divine favors, or experienced any intimate relations with the gods.[36] In fact, neither Yhwh nor any momentous theological term, such as election, appears in the universal lineages. The first reference to Yhwh occurs appropriately in the context of the genealogies devoted to Israel, specifically the lineage of Judah (1 Chron. 2.3). In Chronicles, Adam is no more and no less than the first human in a series. The omission of titles seems to be part of a larger compositional strategy on the author's part. With the exceptions of Nimrod, the Edomite kings and chieftains, the text does not ascribe any special offices to the figures listed. The Chronicler traces certain lines of descent

33. R. Rendtorff discusses the first two, 'Some Reflections on Creation as a Topic of Old Testament Theology', in E.C. Ulrich Jr, J.W. Wright, R.P. Carroll and P.R. Davies (eds.), *Priests, Prophets, and Scribes: Essays on the Formation and Heritage of Second Temple Judaism in Honour of Joseph Blenkinsopp* (JSOTSup, 149; Sheffield: JSOT Press, 1992), pp. 204-12.

34. Willi, *Chronik*, p. 47.

35. D.B. Redford, *Pharaonic King-Lists, Anals and Day-Books* (SSEA, 4; Mississauga, ON: Benben, 1986); G.P. Verbrugghe and J.M. Wickersham, *Berossos and Manetho: Introduced and Translated* (Ann Arbor, MI: University of Michigan Press, 1996).

36. On such signs of privilege, see D.E. Callendar, *Adam in Myth and History* (HSS, 48; Winona Lake, IN: Eisenbrauns, 2000), pp. 206-207.

among the figures he lists, but he neither establishes nor defends a hierarchy among individuals. Significant achievements or shortcomings are not listed. In exhibiting or not exhibiting certain features, the universal genealogy differs markedly from works such as the Sumerian King List and the Assyrian King List, which mention titles, select military or political achievements, and chronological details.[37]

Third, the genealogies evince a spatial dimension. Names found in the Table of Nations (e.g. Cush [Sudan or Ethiopia], Mizraim [Egypt] and Canaan) in Gen. 10.6 (//1.8) are inherently territorial. The overlap between eponyms, tribal names and place-names is also known from other ancient lands (e.g. Babylon).[38] Although the geographical relevance of the list in Genesis has been stressed by many, some commentators on Chronicles are skeptical that these names have any geographical importance.[39] It is true that the Chronicler omits most of the geographic digressions and explanations in the Table of Nations from his own presentation (e.g. Gen. 10.5, 10-12, 19-20, 30). But this pattern of exclusion is consistent with his compositional technique throughout much of the first part of 1 Chron. 1.1–2.2. Concentrating on the lists themselves, the writer excises many of the headings, anecdotes and conclusions found in his sources (e.g. Gen. 5.2-5, 7-8, 10-11, 13-14, 16-17, 19-20; 10.1, 31-32). Exceptions are to be found, of course, in the lists of the Edomite kings and chieftains (1 Chron. 1.43-54). In any case, the distinction between ethnicity and land suggests, if not promotes, a false dichotomy. Peoples are not free-floating entities unsullied by connections to the material world, but are inevitably tied to certain places and territories. For readers familiar with the various regions of the ancient world, names such as 'Elishah and Tarshish, Kittim and Rodanim' (v. 7) have territorial referents. This is true not only of names gleaned from the Table of Nations, but for other names as well (e.g. Teman, Qenaz, Timna and Amaleq in v. 36).

To put the matter somewhat differently, no one contends that the genealogies of Israel in 1 Chron. 2.1–9.1 lack any spatial dimensions. For the

---

37. T. Jacobsen, *The Sumerian King List* (Assyriological Studies, 11; Chicago: University of Chicago Press, 1939); A.L. Oppenheim, 'Babylonian and Assyrian Historical Texts', in *ANET*, pp. 564-66; Wilson, *Genealogy and History*, pp. 86-101.

38. J.A. Brinkman, *A Political History of Post-Kassite Babylonia 1158–722 B.C.* (AnOr, 43; Rome: Pontifical Biblical Institute, 1968), pp. 270-71; R. Zadok, 'Geographical and Onomastic Notes', *JANESCU* 8 (1976), pp. 117-18.

39. E.g. Rudolph, *Chronikbücher*, p. 7; E. Lipiński, 'Les Japhétites selon Gen 10,2-4 et 1 Chr 1,5-7', *ZAH* 3 (1990), pp. 40-53; Japhet, *I and II Chronicles*, pp. 57-58.

sake of consistency, it would be strange to contend that the genealogies of
1.1–2.2 do. Again, no one contends that the Chronicler's genealogy of
nations lacks a chronological dimension, even though he systematically
excises the chronological information from his sources (esp. in vv. 1-4,
24-27). For the sake of consistency, it would be odd to affirm a temporal
dimension but deny a spatial dimension. One does not need to insist that
all of the eponyms and ethnic names are somehow also place names. This
seems highly unlikely. Nevertheless, many of the names included from the
Chronicler's sources do have geographical associations. The spatial range
of names found in the Chronicler's genealogy of nations far exceeds, in
fact, that found in the Hesiodic *Catalogue of Women*, a work which has
been compared with the Table of Nations.[40] The *Catalogue of Women* contains a series of segmented genealogies that are largely limited to detailing
the names of Greek-speaking peoples, groups and places.[41]

Fourth, the Chronicler admits, much like earlier biblical writers before
him, that Israel was a relative latecomer to the stage of world history.
Eber, the eponymous ancestor of the Hebrews, does not appear until well
into the genealogy of nations (1 Chron. 1.18). Israel (Jacob) appears many
generations later (2.1). Unlike the authors of the Babylonian creation story
Enūma eliš, who correlate the establishment of Babylon with the culmination of the divine creative process, the author does not view the rise of
Israel as coterminous with cosmogony. Israel emerges as part of a longer
historical process. If Israel is to have a privileged place among the nations,
the author tacitly acknowledges that the other nations have some legitimacy as well.[42] After all, in both preliterate and literate societies, having a
history is itself a mark of status and authority.[43]

Fifth, the author follows the Yahwist and Priestly writers in locating the
eponymous ancestor of the Hebrews, Eber, among the descendants of

---

40. R.S. Hess, 'The Genealogies of Genesis 1–11 and Comparative Literature',
Bib 70 (1990), p. 252; Van Seters, *Prologue to History*, pp. 176-77.

41. West, *Hesiodic Catalogue*, pp. 36-124.

42. In this respect the Chronicler seems to be faithful to the force of the materials in
Genesis from which he quotes. On the latter, see F. Crüsemann, 'Human Solidarity and
Ethnic Identity: Israel's Self Definition in the Genealogical System of Genesis',
in M.G. Brett (ed.), *Ethnicity and The Bible* (BibInt, 19; Leiden: E.J. Brill, 1996),
pp. 57-76; M.G. Brett, *Genesis: Procreation and the Politics of Identity* (Old Testament Readings; London: Routledge, 2000).

43. M. Sahlins, *Islands of History* (Chicago: University of Chicago Press, 1985),
p. 49.

Shem. This means that he does not see Israel as indigenous to its land.[44]
Canaan, the figure associated with the land that bears his name, is presented as one of the sons of Ham. If one of Shem's descendants were to
occupy the land of Canaan at some later point, he would have to do so as
an outsider. To this it may be objected that the Chronicler is merely
reproducing older materials bequeathed to him. This he does. But if the
Chronicler wished to depart from the script written by earlier authors (e.g.
the Yahwist and the Priestly writers), he could have modified their
presentations. Comparison with the presentation of *Jubilees* is apt. In his
rewriting of the Genesis narrative, the author of *Jubilees* has Noah
explicitly promise the land of Palestine to Shem (8.12-21). While Shem is
awarded most of Asia, Ham is awarded Africa (8.22-24).[45] In this highly
developed *imago mundi*, Zion becomes the *omphalos* of the earth and the
three Ionian continents—Europe, Asia and Libya (Africa)—are correlated
with Noah's three sons—Japheth, Shem and Ham (8.12–9.15). The author
of *Jubilees* situates Israel in the middle of all peoples and in the middle of
all lands. If Ham to the south is hot and Japheth to the north is cold, Shem
is just right (8.30).[46] As for Canaan, his lot falls very far to the west (9.1).
It is only Canaan's envy of the allotment given to Shem and his rebellion
against his father's wishes that leads him to occupy a territory, 'the land of
Lebanon', that was not his to inherit (10.27-34). When *Jubilees* finally
describes this land as 'Canaan' (e.g. 10.34), the term takes on a whole new
meaning—the land that was stolen by Canaan.

The implications of *Jubilees* are clear. Should one of the descendants of
Arpachshad (the son of Shem) come to occupy the land of Canaan, he
would inherit what was originally and properly his (9.4). By presenting
Canaan as a usurper, the author of *Jubilees* completely revises the force of
Genesis 9–10, even as he faithfully reproduces many individual details.
The Chronicler, by contrast, lets the force of the Table of Nations go

44. *Pace* S. Japhet, 'Conquest and Settlement in Chronicles', *JBL* 98 (1979),
pp. 205-18; *idem*, 'People and Land in the Restoration Period', in G. Strecker (ed.),
Das Land Israel in biblischer Zeit (GTA, 25; Göttingen: Vandenhoeck & Ruprecht,
1983), pp. 103-25; *idem*, *The Ideology of the Book of Chronicles and its Place in Biblical Thought* (BEATAJ, 9; Frankfurt: Peter Lang, 1989), pp. 363-86.

45. P.S. Alexander, 'The Toponymy of the Targumim' (PhD dissertation, University of Oxford, 1974); *idem*, 'Omphalos of the World', *Judaism* 46 (1997), pp. 147-58.

46. J.C. VanderKam, 'Putting Them in their Place: Geography as an Evaluative
Tool', in J.C. Reeves and J. Kampen (eds.), *Pursuing the Text: Studies in Honor of Ben
Zion Wacholder on the Occasion of his Seventieth Birthday* (JSOTSup, 184; Sheffield:
Sheffield Academic Press, 1994), pp. 46-69.

uncontested. His summary (1 Chron. 1.24-27) presents Abram as the tenth generation after Shem, both chronologically and ethnically differentiated from the descendants of Japheth (vv. 5-7) and Ham (vv. 8-16). As in Genesis, Canaan's offspring are Heth, the Jebusites, the Amorites, the Girgashites, the Hivites and so forth (vv. 13-16). This is not to say that the Chronicler's reuse of Genesis lacks its own individual perspective. Rather, as we have seen, this distinctive perspective must be sought in how the Chronicler recontextualizes and extends the Table of Nations within his own presentation.

To do justice to the force of 1 Chron. 1.1–2.2, one has to reckon with the continuity from Adam to Esau and Israel, the common humanity of all peoples and the diversity of the various nations inhabiting the world. Two overlapping dimensions—the linear and the spatial—are present in the universal lineage. On one level, the presentation moves diachronically from Adam and the primeval age to the descendants of Noah, Abraham, Isaac, Esau and Israel in the postdiluvian age. Israel (Jacob) is the focus of the remaining genealogical material in 1 Chronicles 2–9. On this dia-chronic level, the lineages achieve greater elaboration and greater focus as they progress toward the descendants of Israel. Seen in this context, the Chronicler's presentation promotes an *imago mundi* in which the tribes of Israel emerge at the end of a long development. Israel may be the focus of the larger presentation, but the *imago mundi* also presents Israel as very much related to the other nations, which preceded Israel or developed alongside it. All are members of a larger human family. The posterity of Israel will be singled out for exclusive attention, but these descendants live within a community of nations of which they are but one part. If on one level the presentation moves diachronically, situating the appearance of Israel against the background of other peoples, on a second level, the presentation moves laterally, situating Israel spatially within the world it inhabits. The segmented genealogies of Japheth, Ham, Shem, Ishmael, Qeturah, Esau and Seir illustrate the author's acknowledgment that a great diversity of peoples in a great diversity of places inhabit his world. The nations may be linguistically, geographically and ethnically dispersed, but they share a common humanity and a common progenitor.

The ethnographic horizons of the Chronicler's genealogical outline gen-erate a map of the world (*mappa mundi*) in verbal form. The descendants of Abraham and Isaac are situated within a larger international context. The Chronicler's ethnographic perspective displays a variety of contours, but it is basically centered on southern Canaan.[47] Given the setting of the author in Yehud, it is important that the ethnographic ties to those nations traditionally situated to the south and southeast of Judah are particularly strong. The spatial interest, sustained beyond the material extracted from the Table of Nations, extends into the material about Ishmael, Qeturah, Esau, Seir and the Edomite kings and chieftains. In this respect, the Chronicler's vision is less grandiose than that of the author of *Jubilees*. The genealogies of Judah (1 Chron. 2.3–4.23) and Simeon (4.24-43) develop many of the ties hinted at in vv. 29-33 and 35-54 of ch. 1 between the southern tribes and their southern neighbors (2.25-26, 32, 50-53; 4.25, 39-43). The stories about the United Monarchy (1 Chron. 18.11-13; 27.30; 2 Chron. 8.17; 9.1-12) and Judah (2 Chron. 17.11; 20.1-23; 21.8-10, 16-17; 22.1; 25.11-12, 14, 20; 26.7-8; 28.17) continue and elaborate this interest.

By situating the emergence of Israel in the context of the emergence of other peoples in other lands, the Chronicler's work anticipates an important feature of early Jewish historiography. The *imago mundi* becomes a consistent feature of medieval Jewish and Christian literature.[48] Like earlier biblical authors, the Chronicler is most interested in stories about Israel, but he also recognizes that Israel did not emerge out of a vacuum. The universal is very much tied to the particular. Indeed, one can only appreciate the experience of Israel within its land if one has some understanding of other relevant lands and peoples to which Israel is related.

47. Cf. Ezek. 5.5; 38.12. See Kartveit, *Motive und Schichten*, pp. 114-17; Oeming, *Das wahre Israel*, pp. 89-91.

48. P.S. Alexander, 'Notes on the *Imago Mundi* in the Book of Jubilees', *JJS* 33 (1982), pp. 201-203.

A POSSIBLE WORLD OF TEXT PRODUCTION
FOR THE GENEALOGY IN 1 CHRONICLES 2.3–4.23[*]

Gerrie Snyman

Introduction

The genealogies of the Bible, especially those in the first nine chapters of Chronicles, provide ordinary readers with lists of names of persons they have no hope of ever getting to know more closely. Even informed or critical readers have difficulties in constructing *personae* for these names. Although one accepts that they were real people, the historicity of their appearance in a particular list at that particular place in the text and in a specific order is difficult to determine. Readers would know Caleb from the story of the two spies in Canaan (Num. 13). Caleb's courage and faith in Yahweh to bring Israel into the Promised Land prevailed over the cowardice of his comrades who feared the Canaanites. Evidently, Caleb's trust paid off, as he represented Judah on Moses' land commission (Num. 34.19). However, there is doubt about Caleb's biological descent from the tribe of Judah.[1]

It is doubtful that these ancient genealogies provide readers with any reliable representations of history, but this does not mean that they are unsuitable for the reconstruction of history. Genealogies can be quite

---

*   This article explores some issues already treated in an article published in Afrikaans—G. Snyman, 'Wanneer die appels ver van die boom val—Juda se geslags-registerxin 1 Kronieke 2.3–4.23' (= 'When the Apples are Falling Far from the Tree: The genealogy of Judah in 1 Chronicles 2.3–4.23'), *In die Skriflig* 31 (1997), pp. 347-74. In this (English) version there is an emphasis on some theoretical concerns, a lesser focus on the South African context and a definite effort to present an integrated discussion on the material and information found.
    1.   T. Willi, 'Late Persian Judaism and Its Conception of an Integral Israel According to Chronicles: Some Observations on Form and Function of the Genealogy of Judah in 1 Chronicles 2.3–4.23', in T.C. Eskenazi and K.H. Richards (eds.), *Second Temple Studies 2: Temple Community in the Persian Period* (JSOTSup, 175, Sheffield: JSOT Press, 1994), pp. 146-62.

useful in the construction of historical realities.[2] For a historian looking for brute facts, a text that cannot be relied upon to correspond with facts, may be discarded as mere fictionalizing. However, it could very well have served as a presentation of past reality to communities that do not share the philosophical bias with which a critical reader or a modern historian would approach a text.[3] It is of no use to denigrate the genealogies in Chronicles as unhistorical.[4] It does not matter that the genealogies make no sense for us today. What is important is that they made sense for the community for whom the Chronicler compiled them.

Japhet[5] argues that they indeed had a valid social and juridical basis. The aim of the present study is not to validate them on a historical basis but to construct a social environment in which a genealogy once had a function. It is called the *world of text production*. Grasping that world is no easy task, given the paucity of information at one's disposal. This article approaches the world of text production from a socio-historical perspective of the formation of elites (understood in this study to be groups of people that have the power to rule and exert power by way of bureaucracies).[6] After a brief explanation of the theoretical model, and as a result of the particular approach used, the argument starts with an analysis of genealogies in (Southern) Africa in order to see the appeal that genealogies have for elite groups. These genealogies are the point of departure for an initial grasp of Judah's genealogy in Chronicles, since they reflect the role of past and present ruling elites in the social system and collective memory. In this way, readers of this article will be introduced to the world of a real reader situated in Africa, reading Chronicles.

2.   R.R. Wilson, *Genealogy and History in the Biblical World* (YNER, 7; New Haven: Yale University Press, 1977), pp. 54-55.

3.   K.G. Hoglund, 'The Chronicler as Historian: A Comparativist Perspective', in M.P. Graham, K.G. Hoglund and S.L. McKenzie (eds.), *The Chronicler as Historian* (JSOTSup, 238; Sheffield: Sheffield Academic Press, 1997), pp. 19-29 (27).

4.   G.A. Rendsburg, 'The Internal Consistency and Historical Reliability of the Biblical Genealogies', *VT* 40 (1990), pp. 185-206.

5.   S. Japhet, 'The Israelite Legal and Social Reality as Reflected in Chronicles: A Case Study', in M. Fishbane and E. Tov (eds.), *'Sha'arei Talmon': Studies in the Bible, Qumran, and the Ancient Near East Presented to Shemaryahu Talmon* (Winona Lake, IN: Eisenbrauns, 1992), pp. 79-91 (83).

6.   E.C. Hansen and T.C. Parrish, 'Elite Versus State: Toward an Anthropological Contribution to the Study of Hegemonic Power in Capitalist Society', in G.E. Marcus (ed.), *Elites: Ethnographic Issues* (School of American Research Advanced Seminar Series; Albuquerque, NM: University of New Mexico Press, 1983), pp. 257-77 (263).

The presence of elite groups in a genealogy introduces two more worlds with which a reader must reckon: the *story world* and the *historical world to which the text refers*. Elites and social formation constitute the third building block of the argument in this study. People who are remembered in a genealogy are those who had power and exerted influence on other people. Before answering the question of the formation of an elite in the genealogy of Judah, the role of a genealogy in general is put on the table. Judah's genealogy is then analyzed in terms of geographical references and the presence of outsiders. On the basis of this analysis, the question as to who would have benefited from such a genealogy is raised and discussed. Two possibilities are suggested: an implied audience along the lines of Joel Weinberg's model of the citizen-temple community and a real audience in terms of power and the ability to read or write. In the process, a possible *world of initial text reception* is suggested, which is closely linked to the world of text production, as the author(s) and the readers of the book came from the same social sphere in the early Second Temple Period.

Some Theoretical Aspects

Having already alluded to the theoretical concerns with which the genealogy of Judah in Chronicles is approached, I turn now to the text and so the matter of how one does justice to it. The text is far removed from the reader's own life world. The danger is always to let the text serve the reader's own needs or ideologies, so that the reader entrenches his or her own position (unconsciously, of course) by not recognizing his or her own subjectivity during the reading process.[7] The consequence is servility in the face of an uncritical reception, enabling anyone to enforce a particular value system with relative ease. A refusal to take one's subjectivity seriously results in untruths and turns God into a product of one's own ideologies. The result is an ideological manipulation of the biblical message to serve certain political goals, as was the case in South Africa's apartheid past.

7.   B. Krondorfer, 'Abschied von (Familien) Biographischer Unschuld Im Land der Täter. Zur Positionierung Theologisher Diskurse Nach der Shoah', in K. Von Kellenbach, B. Krondorfer and N. Reck (eds.), *Von Gott Reden im Land der Täter. Theologische Stimmen der Dritten Generation seit der Shoa* (Darmstadt: Wissenschaftliche Buchgesellschaft, 2001), pp. 11-29; also N. Reck, 'Der Gott der Täter. Subjektverbergung, Objektivismus und die Un-/Schuldsdiskurse in der Theologie', pp. 29-45, of the same volume.

A reading that does justice to the text is one that takes seriously the historical location of the reader, the author, the story and the event to which the story refers. The text in relation to its author becomes the center of attention. This interest is best served by looking at the ancient text through the filter of its historical context of production in order to assess its value and authority claims in relation to the world in which it originated. It is only after the completion of the filtering process that the values and norms embedded in the text can be relativized and evaluated against those embedded in the readers' context. The hope is that one's own ideologies are constrained, yet not ignored completely.

The point of departure is that the understanding of the biblical text involves five different worlds or contexts that any informed reader should take into consideration. They are as follows:

1. *The world of text, or the story world, textual world.* This is the location where the story takes place, a world that is limited by the boundaries of the text. It is comparable to a stage on which decor is placed in order to create the illusion of a certain place. This place may be real or imaginary.

2. *The world to which the text refers or the historical world.* When the stage setting of the story world is created to reflect a period in history, the historical reality referred to in the story is called the world to which the text refers. The boundaries of the text are now crossed, because knowledge of this world is needed to understand the world of the text.

3. *The world in which the text that tells the story is produced or the world of text production.* This is that time in history when an author wrote down the story. It is not the time when the story is thought to have taken place, nor the stage on which the story takes place, but it is the location in which it is produced (study, library, public square, court).

4. *The world of the author's intended/real audience or world of initial text reception.* A theater with a stage includes many seats. Any production has an audience. Just as someone produces a play on stage to amuse, beguile or stimulate an audience, an author will write a story to attract a whole array of readers, some real, some intended. A text is not conceived in a vacuum, but always with someone in mind.

5. *The world of the real reader or the world of subsequent text receptions.* When a story outlives its author, the world of text production and the world of initial text reception, the text is

transported into a world quite different from that of its origins. It is transported to worlds where there may not be any language connection, as is the case with the Hebrew Bible and with the Greek New Testament. They need to be translated in order to be understood. Moreover, even when translated, the story may not be understood, because the story world refers to aspects that are strange to the worlds of later readers. Only the authors in their world of production and the initial recipients with their world of reception are able to understand these context-specific aspects.

Readers usually follow certain cues when they read the biblical text. Some use an aspect in their own life to open up a text. Others simply follow the storyline or a moral in the story world. Still others follow the historical event to which the story refers, whereas some may try to enter the text by way of the first audience's reaction (as intended by the author). In elucidating at least five possible worlds or contexts related to the text and its reading, it is possible to consider reasons for reading or understanding a text in a particular way. It is a recognition that biblical interpretation as a communicative practice involves interests, values and visions. As Schüssler Fiorenza so aptly illustrates,[8] interpretation not only involves authorial aims and strategies, but also audience perceptions and constructions. Just as texts are loaded with perspectives, so are the readers of those texts.

To Schüssler Fiorenza, social location and political context are central. What one sees depends on where one stands on the social continuum of power. The reading of the biblical text does not occur outside of one's experience of the common circumstances of collective life. Readers read the texts with different symbolic universes in mind. The latter constitute different ways of reading and of constructing historical meaning. In the end, they also constitute different interpretations based on peculiar ethical criteria, theoretical frameworks and religious presuppositions.

Although the focus of this article is less on the interests of the current reader of Judah's genealogy in 1 Chron. 2.3–4.23 than on what Schüssler Fiorenza calls an 'ethics of historical reading'.[9] My own socio-political context prompted me (as author of this essay) in the direction of genealogies. In apartheid South Africa genealogies were important to prove one's purity of race. In the post-apartheid period, it has become quite customary

8.   E. Schüssler Fiorenza, 'The Ethics of Biblical Interpretation: Decentering Biblical Scholarship', *JBL* 107 (1988), pp. 3-17.
9.   Schüssler Fiorenza, 'Ethics', p. 14.

to prove the opposite, in order to indicate some kind of link to Africa so as to claim African citizenship. It is a process of affirming the dignity of South Africans of mixed racial ancestry.[10]

The aim of this essay is to construct a socio-historical context that does justice to an understanding of a genealogy in its historical context. But to do that properly, a brief look at the current reader's own socio-political context is necessary. Not only will the current role of genealogies be illustrated, but (and this is important for the next point) in illustrating the role of a genealogy in current society, readers will grasp the role of an elite in such a genealogy for exerting moral as well as real political power.

Reading a Genealogy in Southern Africa

The subject of genealogy in South Africa highlights one of the ironies of African existence. During apartheid, genealogical research focused on the purity of European origins. There was an uproar in the 1970s, when it was revealed that some great Afrikaner families could indeed be linked to a non-European (that is, African) ancestry.[11] After apartheid, these facts are salutary, as they integrate a group of people with (partly) European roots into African society. On the 2001 web site for '*Stamouers* of South Africa'[12] it is remarked that the inhabitants of South Africa have a common genetic pool, making them one big family with close family ties, since the ancestors came from Africa, Europe, Asia and other places.

But why would one examine a genealogy and use it? In a negative way it constitutes boundary maintenance.[13] On the basis of a genealogy one can say who can become members of a group and who cannot. Creating parameters for a group of people on the basis of descent preserves group solidarity and cultural identity. If someone can claim descent from a particular extraordinary ancestor, then that claim furnishes the 'claimant' with some special features, since he or she at least partakes in the line of this remarkable person. Obviously history must have judged that person

10. I. Rappetti, 'Re-Evaluating Connotations of Race', *Sunday Independent* (27 January 2002), p. 10.

11. J.A. Heese, 'Genealogie of die Studie Van Ons Afstamming', in J.A. Heese, G.S. Nienaber and C. Pama (eds.), *Families, Familiename en Familiewapens* (Die Afrikaner en sy Kultuur, 4; Cape Town: Tafelberg, 1975), pp. 117-44.

12. Go to <http://www.stamouers.com>.

13. D.L. Smith, 'The Politics of Ezra: Sociological Indicators of Postexilic Judaean Society', in P.R. Davies (ed.), *Second Temple Studies 1: Persian Period* (JSOTSup, 117; Sheffield: JSOT Press, 1991), pp. 73-97 (83).

favorably. It would work in one's favor to claim some familial relation to Nelson Mandela, whereas a familial relation to one of the apartheid masters would not count in one's favor, unless it has some opportunistic value. For example, the African National Congress (ANC) capitalized on the fact that one of its members was married to a grandson of H.F. Verwoerd, a former Prime Minister to whom the final institution of apartheid as official state policy is attributed.

On a more personal level, a claim to direct relationship to a well known and respected historical figure may be decisive in a conflict. The association with a respected figure gives the claimant the moral high ground to settle a dispute. Hammond-Tooke[14] calls it the 'basic moral injunction' to respect genealogical seniors or run the risk of being sanctioned by the displeasure of the ancestor. In some religious societies or faith communities, blood relationship and respect for ancestors linked to a religious affinity can clinch a conflict in biblical interpretation.[15] In such a case, a correct interpretation is claimed among a group of people sharing the same faith or belief commitments, as well as some blood affinity to a shared ancestor who commanded respect and had a considerable influence on the institution of that faith community. A claim to membership in the aristocracy of a particular church 'then' constitutes a claim on reading the Bible 'correctly'. In these instances descent plays an important role, as if the qualities, thoughts, philosophy and faith of the ancestors rubbed off on the descendants in equal measures.

In the African communities of South African society descent plays an important role. It structures traditional African society, determining who can become king or chief of a tribe. Nelson Mandela's autobiography[16] starts with a story that takes his descent back to King Zwide in the Drakensberg, 20 generations in the past! By linking himself to a king of 20 generations ago, he creates the appearance of a clan with a common ancestor. This is reminiscent of the Chronicler's reference to Adam as the common ancestor for those who returned from exile. In Mandela's case the emphasis falls on the commonality many diverse groups in southern Africa share. Quite a few groups can trace their origins to the figure of Zwide. Given the time of the publication of Mandela's autobiography—at

---

14. W.D. Hammond-Tooke, 'In Search of the Lineage: The Cape Nguni Case', *Man* NS 19 (1984), pp. 77-93 (85).

15. Snyman, 'Wanneer die Appels Ver Van die Boom Val', pp. 348-51.

16. N.R. Mandela, *Long Walk to Freedom: The Autobiography of Nelson Mandela* (Randburg: Macdonald Purnell, 1994).

the time when a democratic South Africa was emerging after 350 years of colonial rule and apartheid—the aim was to create a sense of unity among the majority of citizens. But Zwide was also king. By relating to him, Mandela created an image of being part of the ruling elite, even 20 generations later.

The naming of the ancestors creates group solidarity, because each can be the other's brother or sister.[17] Members of a group can then act in a more sympathetic way toward other members than toward those who cannot be linked. Group solidarity is cultivated for the functioning of *Ubuntu* (a Zulu understanding of humanity as being-with-others), which, unfortunately, only covers members of a tribe or clan. Clan members are expected to provide other (struggling) members with moral and (especially) financial support. People outside the lineage of a clan or tribe cannot lay claim to these privileges.

An appeal to a genealogy serves to order a society. Mandela's genealogy in his autobiography alludes to the order of Xhosa society in which everyone knows his or her place.[18] Mandela describes how he came from a balanced and harmonious social order that was divided into several houses. His house, in relation to that of the king, was the 'lesser' house, called the Left House or Ixhaba, and its purpose was to solve any royal conflict. Mandela was part of the household of the Xhosa king, but he was never groomed to become a king. He was trained to give advice to the king.

Mandela wants to refute the myth that he is directly descended from a royal line. The royal line in his genealogy only serves to unite a diverse group of people of Nguni descent. But the irony cannot be escaped. While socially ordained to be an advisor of a Xhosa king, the political struggle in South Africa catapulted him into the highest position in terms of government at the time. He was the first president of the first democratically elected government of South Africa. Although not of direct royal blood, his association with the royal lineage links him to a ruling elite.

At Mandela's inauguration, a praise singer created another genealogy. Here the point of departure was effective kinship or affinity and not blood relationships. Two groups of people who exercised a decisive influence on Mandela were named. The first group constituted all the deceased leaders

---

17. D.M. Mzolo, 'Social Function of Clan Praises', in A.C. Nkabinde (ed.), *Anthology of Articles on African Linguistics and Literature: A Festschrift to C.L.S. Nyembezi* (Johannesburg: Lexicon Publishers, 1988), pp. 133-40 (134).

18. Mandela, *Long Walk*, p. 4.

of the ANC (John Dube, Ntondana, Albert Luthuli, Oliver Tambo and Chris Hani). They resembled those *political* ancestors who paved the way for Mandela's assumption of the presidency. By being explicitly named they became involved in the inauguration of the heir of their political legacy.[19]

The second group resembled the people of the immediate Temba clan to which Mandela belonged: Ngubengcuka, the chief who united the tribe in the nineteenth century; Dalinyebo who was chief when Mandela was born; and the grandfather of Jongintaba who had the most influence on Mandela later in his life, especially during the struggle up to his arrest in 1963. The genealogy does not indicate linear descent, but patrilineal agnatic relationships with one reference to Mandela's mother, Nosekeni. The genealogy presented at Mandela's inauguration served to honor all those who had a significant influence on his life. They were the political elite.

In contrast to the downplaying of biological origins in Mandela's praise song at his inauguration, biological descent in earlier Southern African contexts played a decisive role. In Swaziland it was used to win support for the king's house and to rebuild his stature. At the beginning of the twentieth century, Sobhuza II assumed the Swazi throne after an unfortunate regime by Mbandzeni and his son Bhunu, who allowed the loss of several huge pieces of land. Sobhuza's mother, Queen Labotsibeni, consciously started to build a certain mystique around her son's regime, basing her approach on the pattern of the British monarchy.[20] She deliberately linked their descent to Umatalatala of 1550, thereby manipulating descent for political aims. Unfortunately, this kind of manipulation resulted in a one-sided, 'traditional' means of propaganda in the service of the state that espoused a tradition in support of the monarchy in Swaziland.[21]

What is significant in Mandela's genealogy at his inauguration, as well as the mythic genealogy created for Sobhuza II, is the naming of elite groups of people on whose shoulders the wealth and health of the respective communities rested. All the people are portrayed as related to one another in some way, even when biological kinship cannot be shown. In this manner a wide variety of people can be brought together under a

19. G. Fortune, 'Some Recurrent Structures in Shona Praise Poetry', in R.H. Kaschula (ed.), *Foundations in Southern African Oral Literature* (African Studies Reprint Series, 2; Johannesburg: Witwatersrand University Press, 1993), pp. 177-86 (177).

20. L. Vail and L. White, *Power and the Praise Poem: Southern African Voices in History* (Charlottesville: University Press of Virginia, 1991), pp. 159-61.

21. Vail and White, *Power*, p. 192.

single mythic ancestor in order to achieve solidarity. The genealogy is used to give credence to the social position of the one who invokes it. But what is of interest here is the appeal to the past elite of society (former kings, political leaders and chiefs). It resembles an invocation fairly similar to the genealogies in Chronicles.

Elites and Social Formation

One of the features of an elite group is its ability to exert influence on other people.[22] It is significant that the ancestors recalled in Mandela's autobiography and at his inauguration were those individuals who had had a tremendous influence on him. Their summons created a positive picture. But such is not always the case when a reference to an elite group is made. Sometimes the summons of the members of an elite group is experienced in a negative way, as when they are experienced as a faceless group of people conspiring to manipulate events to their own advantage. In this case, an elite is regarded as a group of elected people having privileges withheld from others. In a negative way, it discriminates against those deemed unfit to belong to the elite.

As already noted (n. 6, above), in the present study the word 'elite' is understood in terms of a group of people that has the power to rule and exert power by way of a bureaucracy. An elite constitutes a group of people able to exert power as well as influence over other people within a socio-cultural context. The composition of this group is determined by origins, talents or cultures, and in some cases, race.[23] It is usually a small group within a community with the ability to determine (and control) tastes, fashion, customs, policies and privileges. Its members come and go, but their unstable presence is surpassed by their influence. They are part of a continuous process of rise, flourishing and fall. When they disappear, their influence lingers on, a case of doctrines outliving their creators.[24]

The status of an elite is determined within its socio-cultural context. A ruling elite will be tolerated when the society considers its presence necessary.[25] The formation of elite groups is inherent to human existence,

22. R. Cohen, 'Elite Theory and the Formation of Elites Among the Bura Intellectuals of Nigeria', in Marcus (ed.), *Elites*, pp. 63-91 (66).

23. G.E. Marcus, 'Introduction', in *idem* (ed.), *Elites*, pp. 3-58 (22).

24. Marcus, 'Introduction', p. 42.

25. C.J. Greenhouse, 'Being and Doing: Competing Concepts of Elite Status in an American Suburb', in Marcus (ed.), *Elites*, pp. 113-40 (136).

says Cohen.[26] Because the elite is regarded as superior to the rest of society, the recognition of an elite goes hand in hand with a separation from those who are not part of the elite group. The elite is driven to exclusivity and keeps a distance from ordinary folk.

Family groups, especially family businesses, are known for forming elite groups. The elite identity of an individual is related to the social position or status his or her family holds in society. That position is a direct indication of the social force the person will have on the geopolitical field.[27] The descendants inherit the favorable social position of the ancestors, so that family members receive priority vis-à-vis non-members. For example, in the nineteenth century in the strict caste system of India, birth in the appropriate social structure was a prerequisite for becoming a member of the ruling elite serving the regent.[28] Birth within a particular family bestowed the right to inherit the social standing of that family. The family, in turn, was judged in terms of the existence of generations of loyalty that emanated from them and their ancestors. Loyalty was linked to blood kinship. A similar process can be observed in the book of Esther. The moment Haman fell out of favor with the king, not only he but all his sons were killed.

The task of an elite group, apart from determining fashions, tastes, policies, customs and privileges of society, is to maintain its position as an elite group. An elite group is in constant need of legitimizing its privileged position. One of the techniques by which the group maintains its position of power is keeping the power to prescribe what James Scott[29] calls the 'public transcript'. The public transcript describes the open interaction between subordinates and those who keep them in submission. It is public and comprises not only what is said, but also what is done with the body during this open interaction. In other words, it seems quite comparable to a role one plays according to a particular script. That script is more or less written for a subordinate by the ruling elite.[30]

---

26. Cohen, 'Elite Theory', p. 69.

27. Marcus, 'Introduction', p. 44.

28. L.I. Rudolph and S.H. Rudolph, 'Oligopolistic Competition Among State Elites in Princely India', in Marcus (ed.), *Elites*, pp. 193-220 (193, 212).

29. J.C. Scott, *Domination and the Arts of Resistance: Hidden Transcripts* (New Haven: Yale University Press, 1990).

30. G.F. Snyman, 'Carnival in Jerusalem: Power and Subversiveness in the Early Second Temple Period', *Old Testament Essays* NS 9 (1996), pp. 88-110 (91-93); G.F. Snyman, 'Race in South Africa: A Hidden Transcript Turned Public? The Prob-

Central to the maintenance of the public transcript and the ruling elite's continuous affirmation of power is a visible and/or physical manifestation of that affirmation. In a powerful hierarchical relationship[31] such a manifestation is orchestrated via military displays, parades and public executions. A major instrument with which to maintain power is the prohibition of the free publication of writings. Control over the media allows a ruling elite to decide what may be said and what should be ignored. Writing is important, and one will always see a powerful group trying to secure and enforce writings as the only legitimate ones. For a ruling elite, freedom of the press will always be a thorn in the side. Part of the public transcript is the existence of texts that aim to persuade a subordinate to assume a subordinate position. These texts reflect the values, ideologies and policies of the ruling elite, while portraying the subordinates as willing participants and even enthusiastic supporters of their own subordination.[32]

Power, text and the public transcript are important issues to take into account when one starts to construct a possible world of production for the text of Chronicles. The ability to write and the issue of power are closely related in a time when writing was tedious, difficult and only known to a few. Davies[33] contends that one has to reckon with a general lack of literacy in Palestine, as only about one per cent of the population could read or write. Writing meant power. Davies[34] argues that one should think in terms of a few literate men, who practiced their profession as scribes in a school.

It is possible to construct a school of scribes who authored the books of Chronicles, but the question would be: What kind of elite were they? If Chronicles was issued from such a school, writing would not have been their hobby but their vocation. They would have been in the service of a group of people for whom their writings were valuable and useful. They would have written what their superiors wanted to hear.

lem of Identifying with Esther, Mordecai or Haman in the Book of Esther' (paper delivered at the Annual Meeting of the SBL and AAR, Denver, USA, 17-20 November 2001).

31. Scott, *Domination*, p. 46

32. Scott, *Domination*, p. 4.

33. P.R. Davies, *In Search of 'Ancient Israel'* (JSOTSup, 148; Sheffield: JSOT Press, 1992).

34. Davies, *In Search of 'Ancient Israel'*, p. 106.

With regard to the eighth and seventh centuries, Jamieson-Drake[35] argues on the basis of archaeological evidence that it was unlikely that literacy was passed on without some form of involvement by the administrative powers of Jerusalem. He says that legal, religious and economic aspects would have had an ongoing indigenous stake in the mastering of the skill of written communication. He does not find any evidence that institutions for formal training in writing existed in every village. Villages had writing in so far as they were linked to the ruling elite in Jerusalem, who used this to their advantage in the subordination of these villages. However, in the sixth century when Babylon removed the administrative control systems and the ruling elite managing them, the fall of Jerusalem resulted in a full-scale societal collapse of Judah.[36] Jamieson-Drake argues that the administrative professionals (as part of the ruling elite, I would add) were relatively easy targets for removal. The latter ensured the decimation of the local population in Judah after the fall of Jerusalem.[37]

If Jamieson-Drake's arguments are valid, the world of text production for the books of Chronicles should be pursued in the context of the exiles and the former ruling elite who were removed. Those left behind would not have had the capability of producing texts. Add to this possibility Davies'[38] argument about the lack of general literacy in Palestine. The question is: For whom did the ruling elite write if nobody else could read what they wrote? Given the role of the public transcript as self-maintenance by an elite ruling group, one can argue that they wrote for themselves. In other words, it could be that the text they constructed was meant for self-consumption and self-maintenance. The real audience was not the wider population of the postexilic period or the assembly, although the latter could have been the intended audience. The late Robert Carroll's ideas on the ideology of a text are important here.

> The Hebrew Bible is the ideological literature of an imagined community produced in the Achaemenid or Graeco-Roman period. The 'imagined community' of this categorization is the construction of 'ancient Israel' and the 'first temple' nation which is the subject of the (meta)narrative Genesis–Chronicles. The producers of this ideological literature must be imagined to

---

35. D.W. Jamieson-Drake, *Scribes and Schools in Monarchic Judah: A Socio-Archeological Approach* (The Social World of Biblical Antiquity Series, 9; JSOTSup, 109; Sheffield: Sheffield Academic Press, 1991), pp. 148-49.

36. Cf. Jamieson-Drake, *Scribes*, p. 80.

37. Jamieson-Drake, *Scribes*, p. 145.

38. Davies, *In Search of 'Ancient Israel'*.

be an intellectual elite (whether priests or sages) constructing such literature in relation to their control of the temple community (I am guessing
here!)... The 'original' Hebrew Bible served its own creators' purpose of
maintaining power in their world by constructing an imagined community
occupying an imagined past of which they were the inheritors. So later
communities took over that ideological role of transporting the text into a
charter for their own situation.[39]

Carroll argues that the text was written to maintain the power of the ruling
elite that was established within the Jewish community during and after
the exile. From their ideologies they created an Israel in a story world
that was able to address the needs of the group that produced the text. The
result was an interpretation of Israel's history shaped in such a way
that advanced their positions of power.

The next question is: In what way was the genealogy of Judah in the
books of Chronicles used to legitimize and maintain the power of a particular ruling elite?

Judah's Genealogy in Chronicles

Traditionally, scholars distinguish between segmented and linear genealogies.[40] A segmented genealogy, which takes several segments into account,
reflects more than one line of descent of an ancestor. A linear genealogy
only takes one line into account. Wilson[41] argues that the value of a genealogy lies in the domestic, political and religious perspectives of the society
that produced it. A genealogy says less about the persons it incorporates
than about the people who construct and use it.

Wilson distinguished between three functions of a genealogy. A genealogy that presents a manifesto for descent has a *domestic* function.[42] It
determines the social position of a person. Mandela's position as advisor
to the king was determined by his descent. In this way a genealogy determines the privileges and obligations of a person born into a particular
family. When a genealogy is used to regulate relationships and to control

39. R.P. Carroll, 'The Hebrew Bible as Literature—A Misprision?', *ST* 47 (1993),
pp. 77-90 (81).
40. R.L. Braun, '1 Chronicles 1–9 and the Reconstruction of the History of Israel:
Thoughts on the Use of Genealogical Data in Chronicles in the Reconstruction of the
History of Israel', in Graham, Hoglund and McKenzie (eds.), *The Chronicler as
Historian*, pp. 92-105; Wilson, *Genealogy*, p. 9.
41. Wilson, *Genealogy*, p. 54.
42. Wilson, *Genealogy*, pp. 38-40.

land, it functions as *juridical power* that can be enforced.[43] When someone exerts a claim to a particular position in society or on a piece of land on the basis of the inheritance law, a genealogy submitted as proof of the claim exercises a juridical function. In tribal cultures the position of a chief will go to a certain son of a particular wife of the chief in power. In British aristocracy, a title will fall on the firstborn of the male aristocrat. Mandela would never have become Xhosa king, because he is not from the lineage from which Xhosa kings were crowned. Wilson[44] also refers to the *religious function* of a genealogy, especially in the cult of the ancestor. The ancestors are thought to have real influence on their living offspring. In Mandela's praise song at his inauguration, the appeal to the ancestors of the liberation struggle alludes to a recognition of the role of the ancestors among the living.

The genealogy of 1 Chron. 2.3–4.23 is mainly linear. A direct line is drawn from Judah to David, although there is a limited amount of segmentation in the indication of sidelines. However, these sidelines, which are not taken as far as the time of David, function to link people such as Caleb to the genealogy of Judah.

The geopolitical references in the genealogy of Judah indicate a political function. In fact, it starts already with the introduction in 1 Chronicles 1, which takes the origins back to Adam and Noah. Kartveit[45] calls the introductory genealogy a *mappa mundi* with Israel as the center of the world. 1 Chronicles 1.1–2.2 focuses on Palestinian territory that was kept for Israel as the descendants of Jacob, with the rest of the land around it linked to the descendants of Noah. Japhet received the northern and the western part of the ancient Near East; Ham was settled in the south and southwest; and Shem resided in the east and southeast. Ishmael was connected to the Sinai peninsula; Keturah was associated with the east; and Esau was linked to the territory of Edom and Moab.

The geographical view is strengthened by a focus on a particular genealogy from which Israel originated. In this sense the genealogies serve a clear domestic function. The first two genealogies follow the same structural pattern.[46] Of all the generations of Noah, Shem was elected. From all

43. Wilson, *Genealogy*, pp. 40-44.

44. Wilson, *Genealogy*, pp. 44-45.

45. M. Kartveit, *Motive und Schichten der Landtheologie in 1 Chronik 1–9* (ConBOT, 38; Stockholm: Almqvist & Wiksell, 1989), pp. 114-15.

46. S.J. De Vries, *1 and 2 Chronicles* (FOTL, 11; Grand Rapids: Eerdmans, 1989), p. 37.

the Semitic generations, Abraham was elected. He received, as the first-born of Noah, a birthright to Palestine. That right then went to the youngest son of Isaac, passing Ishmael and Esau. Of Jacob's sons, the birthright was passed on to Judah, and not to Reuben, the eldest son. Even Judah's eldest son was passed. Er, born from a Canaanite woman, died (1 Chron. 2.3). Perez received the birthright and passed it on to Hezron (1 Chron. 2.5, 9-15), and from this lineage David was eventually born.

The genealogy refers to a few strange men and women (1 Chron. 2.3, 17, 34; 4.18, 22). According to Oeming,[47] the Chronicler recognized that strange elements entered the history of Israel through marriage, but the way in which that material was treated is meaningful. He says it is significant that the line of descent stops with the death of Er, the son that a Canaanite woman bore to Judah. Oeming suspects that he had to die, because the union reflected an unholy relationship. No one was supposed to marry a Canaanite woman. In Ezra and Nehemiah they were sent away. It is as if the offspring conceived in these relationships had no real claim to anything. They were nobodies. The genealogy gives Shelah no descendant. The children of Amasa, the son of Abigail (David's sister) and Jether, of Ishmael, are ignored. Absalom's son with Maacah of Geshur dies.

Among the exceptions are Ephrath, a non-Israelite and the widow of Hezron, who became Caleb's wife and gave birth to Hur, the father of a few founders of cities. Sheshan's descendants could be followed through his daughter and his Egyptian servant. According to Sara Japhet,[48] the children of the slave belonged to the master of the slave. Sheshan's line continued through his daughter and slave. Oeming[49] sees a negative aspect in the Chronicler's reference to the Egyptian as a 'servant', who is kept separate from the rest of Israel. Solomon's Egyptian wife (2 Chron. 8.11) is also kept in a separate place.

Japhet is of a different opinion.[50] She is more positive about the addition of strangers to the genealogies of Israel, since their attachment indicates inclusiveness and not exclusivity. People were brought in from outside to form an organic part of the generations. She thinks that the Chronicler wanted to emphasize geographical unity and not ethnic unity. The genealogies should be read as a sociological code that structured society on the

---

47. M. Oeming, *Das Wahre Israel. Die 'Genealogische Vorhalle' 1 Chronik 1–9* (BWANT, 128; Stuttgart: W. Kohlhammer, 1990), p. 121.

48. S. Japhet, *I and II Chronicles* (OTL; London: SCM Press, 1993), p. 84.

49. Oeming, *Das Wahre*, p. 122.

50. Japhet, *I and II Chronicles*, p. 74.

basis of geographical territories and not on the basis of biological relationships.

For her argument she finds justification in the reference to Kiriath-jearim in 1 Chron. 2.53, where Kiriath-jearim is described as the 'son of Shobal'. Reference to the families of Kiriath-jearim (the Ithrites, the Puthites, the Shumathites and the Mishraites) is for Japhet an indication that biological affinity does not play a central role in the genealogies of Israel in Chronicles. These names represent families that became absorbed into the tribe of Judah during Israel's sojourn in Palestine. They brought with them extra territory. Regarding Caleb, who is not biologically related to Judah, Willi[51] argues that he and his descendants played a central role in the history of Israel. They could not be ignored, and the Chronicler incorporated them via Judah into Israel.

The addition of outsiders to the genealogy of Judah increased the territorial boundaries of Judah. The territory east of the Jordan River, which was supposed to be part of Manasseh, came into Judah's possession through Machir (1 Chron. 2.21), who married Hezron. The same goes for the territory under Caleb and Jerahmeel's control, namely, Hebron and the Negev. But these territories were only relevant after the exile. They are incorporated into the story world of Israel so as to lay a claim to that land, as if it really happened.[52] In other words, people were incorporated in the genealogy in order to lay claim to a larger parcel of land for the collective unit that came into being under the name 'Yehud'. For the readers this was a major advantage: with these genealogies as a basis, they could become part of an elite group with certain privileges unavailable to others. Who were they?

The Beneficiaries: The Audience

Two kinds of audiences can be presupposed, a real audience and an implied audience. From an ideological-critical point of view, given the lack of literacy and the role of power in keeping up the public transcript, the real audience would be the ruling elite itself. They were the people who would have read Chronicles or listened to readings of the books. However, even when writing for themselves, the question remains whether they had another audience in mind, a fictional conversation partner for whom the arguments were intended.

---

51. Willi, 'Late Persian', p. 159.
52. Karveit, *Motive*, p. 152.

An Implied Audience

When one takes into consideration the presence of geographical borders as well as the formula 'X, the father of Y' (when Y is a toponym), the impression is created that the intended audience is a group of people who looked for a place to lay their heads in a time of a renewed movement or shifting of population groups. Within the story world, that time would have been after the exile, when people were returning to their original homes. Membership in a community was determined by an indication of descent, location within a particular genealogical line and the claim of an ancestor who played an important role in the history of a genealogy (hence the several anecdotes of some tribal leaders).

Joel Weinberg[53] has suggested that a citizen-temple community was created and based on the concept 'house of the fathers' or *bêt 'abôt*. The citizen-temple community, clearly distinguished from the control exerted by city officials and the management in the temple, was based on a pre-exilic tribal structure. Weinberg defines it as

> an agnatic association, which united real or fictitious families, a large number of members and a complicated inner structure. It necessarily included genealogies and internal solidarity. The *bêt 'abôt* was the result of a consciously intended convergence of the former agnatic units which were dissolved during the exile and the early postexilic times such as the *mišpahâ*. The *bêt 'abôt*, whose main function was social, was a form of organization which included not only laymen in the community, but the priests and Levites as well.[54]

Accordingly, Weinberg sees the genealogies in Chronicles as lists of the returning exiles who sought legitimation of their claims and rights within a newly constructed community.[55] He links these genealogies with the lists in Nehemiah 7 and Ezra 2. He builds his claim around the discovery of at least four toponyms in Judah's genealogy.[56] He regards their presence in Judah's genealogy as an indication that the citizen-temple community contained members who were able to trace their origins to the ancient tribe of Judah. Such a descent enabled people to stake a claim for membership

---

53. J.P. Weinberg, 'Das Wesen und die Funktionelle Bestimmung der Listen in 1 Chr 1–9', *ZAW* 93 (1981), pp. 91-114; *idem, The Citizen-Temple Community* (JSOTSup, 151; Sheffield: JSOT Press, 1992); *idem, Der Chronist in seiner Mitwelt* (BZAW, 239; Berlin: W. de Gruyter, 1996).

54. Weinberg, *Citizen-Temple*, p. 134.

55. Weinberg, *Citizen-Temple*, p. 110.

56. Weinberg, *Chronist*, pp. 280-81.

in the postexilic community, which emerged in the form of a citizen-temple community.

According to Weinberg, the citizen-temple community is the synthesis of a process that came into being in the unique situation of the exile and the return.[57] It was a process of consolidation in which exiles and the returnees were forced into a new social construction with elements of pre-exilic institutions. His distinction between those who returned (and who were responsible for the books of Ezra and Nehemiah) and those who were postexilic (and who were responsible for the books of Chronicles) is curious, as one expects a distinction between those who returned and those they encountered on their return. Instead, his distinction is a differentiation in time. For Ezra and Nehemiah the people with legitimate claims to Yehud were those who returned. They were embodied in the lists in Nehemiah 7 and Ezra 2.[58] They were the sons of Judah and Benjamin. In Chronicles, the list of legitimate heirs of Yehud is enlarged to include more than the sons of Judah and Benjamin. Chronicles seems to have been written much later than Ezra and Nehemiah.

In this postexilic community several related families were united with a conscious solidarity based on the communal ownership of lands. In Weinberg's view, the genealogy functioned within the context of those who took over the reins in Jerusalem. The inclusion of territories that were not part of the territory of the ancient tribe of Judah leads one to infer that the genealogy was constructed in order to include a larger group of people, possibly larger than what originally constituted the territory of the ancient tribe of Judah. What is unclear is whether this group was partly constituted by people who settled in the land during the exile due to the forced removals from other conquered territories. What is clear is that there was a significant group with legitimate claims to be part of Yehud after the exile. Weinberg links their roots to the pre-exilic scribal schools but remains vague about what happened to these schools after the destruction of Jerusalem as an administrative center. Carter thinks that Weinberg is off the mark in his tendency to take texts with ideological interests as self-evident indications of social make-up.[59]

57. Weinberg, *Citizen-Temple*, p. 61.

58. Weinberg, *Chronist*, p. 283.

59. C.E. Carter, *The Emergence of Yehud in the Persian Period: A Social and Demographic Study* (JSOTSup, 294; Sheffield: Sheffield Academic Press, 1999), p. 307.

It seems to me that the implied audience of the books of Chronicles, based on the presence of the genealogies, is likely to have been people who were affected by claims to land based on a claim of descent. They could have been people who were never deported from Judah, or they could have been people moved to Judah by the superpower's policy of mass deportation. In both cases, they would have been excluded from the developing community, if they could not trace their descent to the ancient tribe of Judah. Although the inclusion of a territory larger than the ancient tribe indicates a willingness (or was it political expediency?) to widen the community, it is questionable whether that action was sufficient to open up the society for all in the territory. Add to this the possibility of the text originating within the structures of power and the role of the public transcript to maintain subordination. It is possible that the intended audience, or the audience implied by the text, were people with whom this ruling elite had to legitimize their claims to power and land.

In other words, the following construction of the implied or intended audience is presumed. The author of Chronicles set up an argument to legitimize a new social order. One of the entry requirements was proof of membership in the ancient tribe of Judah. To get as many as possible on board, non-deportees were included. But to get them into the system, they had to have some kind of claim via the pre-exilic order on land or be related to persons or individuals with icon status in Israel's history. It is possible that the genealogies set out the parameters of membership of the new social order in the province of Yehud. Those successful in claiming membership would then have been privileged by the Persian administration.

A Real Audience

Weinberg acknowledges that literacy is a *sine qua non* for the books of Chronicles. However, his construction of an audience for the postexilic texts (as far as he sees one) fits the arguments for an implied or intended audience. Nevertheless, he presupposes a real audience that is much larger than the one constructed when Davies' limitations on literacy in that time are taken seriously. Relatively high production costs made it unlikely that private and subordinated groups would have possessed texts. It is more likely that the readers and authors came from the ranks of a powerful elite. If this is true, the question is: On which side of the fence should the real audience be placed? Would they be on the side of those who were (and remained) inside Yehud, or with those who were outside (in exile) and decided to return with the blessing of the Persian court? It seems to me that the real audience comprised people who came from outside into Yehud, but whether they were descendants of those who were initially deported is open to question.

The impression left by the books of Chronicles is that of continuity between the pre-exilic period and the return from exile, as if the people who were carried away assumed their places in society when they returned. It was as if nothing had happened. Horsley argues that the returnees were members of the families of those who were part of the ruling elite in pre-exilic Judah.[60] Upon their return, they tried to re-establish the previous aristocracy, albeit subordinated to the Persian regime.

Davies is skeptical about such a smooth continuity. In the light of the ideological nature of the biblical texts[61] as well as the interest of the ruling elite in maintaining the appearance of domination through the public transcript, an important motive for the text of Chronicles could be what Davies calls 'the establishment of a national identity in which the status of the existing rulers, of recent immigration, as the indigenous elite, was secured, for their own satisfaction as much as anyone else's'.[62] Davies assumes a socio-historical context in which a group of people from outside forced themselves on the inhabitants of Yehud. They justified their assertion of power and privilege by making the history and the customs of the local people their own. In this regard, Davies refers to an act of ideological imperialism.

Most of the arguments regarding the authorship of Chronicles draw a line of continuity between the postexilic leadership in Jerusalem and the returning exiles. But the return was not as voluntary as is assumed in other postexilic texts (Ezra and Nehemiah). The return originated under pressure from the Persian court, which wanted to fortify the province of Yehud to counter the troubles it faced in Egypt. Nehemiah's erection of the walls of Jerusalem was regarded as part of the fortification of Yehud against a possible Egyptian attack. It is possible to argue—against the books of Nehemiah and Ezra—that Nehemiah did not operate independently.[63]

---

60. R.A. Horsley, 'Empire, Temple and Community—But No Bourgeoisie! A Response to Blenkinsopp and Petersen', in Davies (ed.), *Second Temple Studies 1*, pp. 163-74 (170).

61. Carroll, 'Hebrew Bible'.

62. Davies, *In Search of 'Ancient Israel'*, p. 114.

63. K.G. Hoglund, *Achaemenid Imperial Administration in Syria-Palestine and the Missions of Ezra and Nehemiah* (SBLDS, 125; Atlanta: Scholars Press, 1992), p. 234.

Jerusalem became an important link in the Persian court's policy on the borders of the kingdom. The city's new status led to a heightened military presence, which, in turn, put an additional tax burden on the region. The soldiers had to be sustained and for this reason Jerusalem needed a proper system of government, which would have required additional tax revenue.

The idea that the leaders of Jerusalem collaborated with the Persian administration does not exclude the possibility that they could have been descendants of the Judean exiles. Blenkinsopp argues that the people who settled in Jerusalem originated from the upper echelons of the 'Babylonian immigrants'.[64] They were of Israelite origin, but learned the tools of the trade in a different social order, which they then enforced in Jerusalem. They were loyal to the imperial household and refused to integrate with the local people. They had their own assembly which was organized around ancestral houses under the leadership of tribal elders, with an imperial representative keeping an eye on them. They were a cohesive social entity, preserving jealously their status and privileges. Although they could claim pre-exilic origins, their absence from Jerusalem estranged them from Judah's culture and politics.

Alluding to the Japanese survivors of the atom bomb of the Second World War, Smith calls these returning deportees a 'hibakusha community'.[65] The latter resembled those people who survived the deportation, the military campaign and eventually the exile. Although the exile constituted a negative experience, it served to unify the deportees wherever they turned up in the kingdom. According to Smith, it was logical that conflict would be generated upon their return, as those who remained behind had a different experience.

What appears to have happened is that different experiences brought about a conflict between several interest groups. A heuristic key for resolving the conflict was found in the motif of the exile. The exile was called upon to maintain the boundaries. People who had not gone into exile had to prove their descent on the basis of the genealogies. The problem of the 'strange women' in Nehemiah 13 and Ezra 9–10 could have been caused by a process that included women in the citizen-temple community who had not 'proved' their origins. Different constructions for

64. J. Blenkinsopp, 'Temple and Society in Achaemenid Judah', in Davies (ed.), *Second Temple Studies 1*, pp. 22-53 (53).
65. Smith, 'Politics of Ezra', p. 80.

their origins have been proposed,[66] but whatever their origins, they were considered subversive to the frail order that was being established.[67]

There are other arguments, however, against relating the governing structures in Jerusalem too closely to the returning exiles and their roots in pre-exilic Judah. With the exile, local community structures were destroyed and the leadership core was removed. The leaders and their families were re-established in distant places, making it virtually impossible for these people to return to their homes. The distance from the new settlements to their original homes was too far. Additionally, there was no real need to return, since the entire family was kept together.[68] The people carried away functioned as hostages for those who remained. Rebellion among those left behind greatly diminished, because those taken away could be killed.

The gap resulting from the removal of the leaders in the communities was filled by introducing new leaders from other conquered territories.[69] These imported elements were loyal to the Assyrian rulers, as their well-being was directly linked to the favor of the Assyrian monarch. The same could be said of the ruling elite removed from Judah. They simply plied their trade in another community. Ever since Palestine had been overrun by the Assyrian superpower, there had been conflict between the imported leaders and those who remained behind. The Persians did not break with the Assyrian practice of moving groups of people around and so created new waves of imported rulers in the conquered territories during their regime.

Archaeological evidence in Palestine indicates that renewed settlement activities occurred during the Persian rule of Palestine. Carter estimates an increase of 25 per cent.[70] Hoglund sees the increase as a result of Persian policy to settle people in the rural areas in order to strengthen an

66. R.P. Carroll, 'Textual Strategies and Ideology in the Second Temple Period', in Davies (ed.), *Second Temple Studies 1*, pp. 108-24; T.C. Eskenazi and E.P. Judd, 'Marriage to a Stranger in Ezra 9–10', in Eskenazi and Richards (eds.), *Second Temple Studies 2*, pp. 266-85.

67. Snyman, 'Carninval', p. 98.

68. B. Oded, *Mass Deportations and Deportees in the Neo-Assyrian Empire* (Wiesbaden: Otto Harrassowitz, 1979), p. 22.

69. Oded, *Mass Deportations*, p. 47.

70. C.E. Carter, 'The Province of Yehud in the Post-Exilic Period: Soundings in Site Distribution and Demography', in Eskenazi and Richards (eds.), *Second Temple Studies 2*, pp. 106-45.

agrarian economy and to enlarge the tax base in order to pay for other Persian excursions.[71] The people who settled in these territories formed collective units quite separate from the local inhabitants. They worked land in imperial possession, and no local inhabitant could lay claim to that land, either on the basis of inheritance or occupation rights. Hoglund argues that the local inhabitants could not resist in this matter.[72] There would have been a land problem, if those who returned came back voluntarily and claimed their inheritance. Instead, the people inhabiting the land were under the coercion of the Persian court. Their presence was based on economic reasons.

Although it is possible that they could have come from these territories a century earlier, Davies is more skeptical.[73] His contention that the biblical texts in general (and the postexilic texts in particular) are ideological in nature undermines a link between the new leaders in Yehud and the issue of the returning exiles. What he sees is a group of strange people forcing themselves on local inhabitants, while they, as the new ruling elite, appropriate the local inhabitants' culture and history. I am not sure what advantage there would have been for them to absorb the local culture and history if they did not originate in that territory. Davies thinks there are enough biblical texts creating doubt that these newcomers to Yehud indeed possessed the land as original inhabitants. The genealogy of Judah may be such a text, given the proportion of people excluded. But still, why would people outside be pulled inside? Is it because they are now important and powerful people, and the subordinates would like to associate with them? Then the genealogy would function in the context of those without power, portraying the powerful as one of their own. I doubt this was the case.

From the point of view of the powerful elite, the ruling elite's construction of the history of the kings of Judah would afford more credibility. These kings made a mess, and it is now up to Cyrus and his administration—as Yahweh's favorites—to establish a new social order. They assumed the position of the former royal house. To justify their position, they utilized traditions that left the impression that the only legitimate claimants to the real Israel were those who once lived in or near

---

71. K.G. Hoglund, 'The Achaemenid Context', in Davies (ed.), *Second Temple Studies 1*, pp. 54-72 (70).

72. Hoglund, 'Achaemenid Context', p. 59.

73. Davies, *In Search of 'Ancient Israel'*, p. 82.

Jerusalem,[74] and, one can add, having 'historical claims' on this territory. Naturally, being in power ensured that their claims would never be questioned.

Does it really matter whether the new ruling elite, who took responsibility for the administration of Yehud in Jerusalem, originally came from the ranks of the leadership core taken away from Judah and Benjamin? The fall of Jerusalem and the subsequent exile of people left no one untouched. Those taken away were uprooted and their descendants went through a process of acculturation. They would have been loyal Assyrian or Persian citizens and could even have accepted the super powers' ideologies. Even when one could prove a genealogical line with ancestors who lived in and around Jerusalem, would they not have been more Persian than Jewish in any case?

Carter says that one must allow for a significant level of crisis and upheaval in the lives of those deported and those who remained in the land.[75] Both were without the social and religious institutions that once determined their identity. I think that intellectual life ceased. The deportation cut off people from the archives in Jerusalem. Those who were carried away could no longer maintain the archives, and those who remained behind no longer had a group of people who could access the archives on their behalf. However, economically, life went on for those who stayed behind. They still paid their taxes, only to a different ruling elite. The socio-economic system was, in many respects, similar to the one before Jerusalem's destruction. When the Persians conquered the Neo-Babylonians, the final destinations of the taxes changed yet again.

Briant argues that one should not underestimate the influence of Persian central government on local administration.[76] The extent of the Persian imperial kingdom required the Persian court to use local government as an extension of its power.[77] On the local level, the Persians did not replace the administrators but supplemented them with administrators from other

74. G. Garbini, 'Hebrew Literature in the Persian Period', in Eskenazi and Richards (eds.), *Second Temple Studies 2*, pp. 180-88 (184).

75. Carter, *Emergence of Yehud*, p. 309.

76. P. Briant, 'Pouvoir Central et Polycentrisme Culturel dans l'Empire Achemenide. Quelques Réflexions et Suggestions', in H. Sancisi-Weerdenburg (ed.), *Sources, Structures and Synthesis: Proceedings of the Groningen 1983 Achaemenid History Workshop* (Achaemenid History, 1; Leiden: Nederlands Instituut voor het Nabije Oosten, 1987), pp. 1-31.

77. Briant, 'Pouvoir', p. 13.

territories. The Persians incorporated the local leadership into their own ranks and bought their loyalty by giving them certain privileges.[78]

Acceptance within the Persian structures meant that they became part of the ruling elite, which Briant calls an 'ethno-classe dominante'.[79] They were an aristocracy gathered around the emperor or king. They enjoyed ideological, political and economic privileges that they would, of course, defend at all cost. They did not mix with people in the rest of the kingdom but kept themselves separate. Although Sancisi-Weerdenburg agrees with Briant on the issue of a particular ruling class, she suggests a certain openness to the local rulers.[80] She argues that they could not have been a closed group of people but had to open up toward the local ruling elite because the kingdom extended rapidly. She argues that the cohesion within the kingdom would only have succeeded when the local ruling elite (with power on the grassroots level) was given the opportunity of moving upward within the political hierarchy.[81]

On the question of the identity of the real readers of the book of Chronicles, I would suggest the circle of the author who produced it. That circle was part of the ruling elite, and the work functioned to maintain the public transcript in the face of stiff opposition to its presence. Carter suggests that a new regime with new power brokers and a new ruling elite are rarely welcomed without opposition.[82] The nature of the opposition is open to conjecture. I think the following should be borne in mind. First, in the genealogy of Judah there is a calculated effort to include people who did not form part of the pre-exilic tribe of Judah. Second, since the genealogy refers to nonmembers of the pre-exilic tribe of Judah, one should leave room for a postexilic situation where many people settled in a

78. M.W. Stolper, 'The KASR-Archive', in H. Sancisi-Weerdenburg and A. Kuhrt (eds.), *Centre and Periphery: Proceedings of the Groningen 1986 Achaemenid History Workshop* (Achaemenid History, 4; Leiden: Nederlands Instituut voor het Nabije Oosten, 1990), pp. 195-205 (200).

79. P. Briant 'Ethno-Classe Dominante et Populations Soumises dans l'Empire Achemenide: Le Cas de l'Egypte', in A. Kuhrt and H. Sancisi-Weerdenburg (eds.), *Method and Theory: Proceedings of the London 1985 Achaemenid History Workshop* (Achaemenid History, 3; Leiden: Nederlands Instituut voor het Nabije Oosten, 1988), pp. 137-73 (137).

80. H. Sancisi-Weerdenburg, 'The Quest for the Elusive Empire', in Sancisi-Weerdenburg and Kuhrt (eds.), *Centre and Periphery*, pp. 263-74 (265).

81. H. Sancisi-Weerdenburg, 'Was There Ever a Median Empire?', in Kuhrt and Sancisi-Weerdenburg (eds.), *Method and Theory*, pp. 197-212.

82. Carter, *Emergence of Yehud*, p. 311.

territory in one collective, taxpaying unit. Third, these people were administered by a ruling elite with ties to the Persian imperial government and
with privileges they would exercise.

In the ensuing conflict of interests, and in the interest of maintaining
order in the collective unit they had to administer, the ruling elite portrayed themselves as a group with a legitimate claim to their position of
power. I do not think it really mattered whether they were originally from
Jerusalem and its surroundings or not. What mattered was the ideological
construction with which they justified a presence in Yehud. The inclusiveness of the genealogy suggests that they relaxed the boundaries. Those
who remained in the land and those who were later added (because of the
various population movements that took place) had the opportunity to
become part of the new postexilic community.

Conclusion

Who would have used an ideological construct of Israel and an inclusive
genealogy for Judah in the early days of Persian Yehud? Who would have
benefited from the use of the story of Israel, or at least, from a new look at
the story of the kings of Judah? Would it have been deportees who
returned, as is the impression left by Ezra and Nehemiah? This would be
Weinberg's suggestion. However, if one attributes to an ideological construct a direct, corresponding referent in the historical world (as in common sense realism), the story world become equated with the historical
world. The possibility of interpretation and the ideological use of a genealogy in terms of a symbolic construction are then ignored. In Klein's
terms,[83] the texture and impact to the presentation of Israel's story are lost.

People who would have benefited most from a new construction of the
history of the kings would have been those in power. Briant refers to a
possibility that a local ruling elite would acknowledge Persian control if
their privileges were not taken away.[84] They would serve the Persian
administration according to their local customs and the Persian king, in
turn, would restore their privileges. In this way a solidarity would have
been created between the local elite and the Persian representative.

---

83. R.W. Klein, 'How Many in a Thousand?', in Graham, Hoglund and McKenzie
(eds.), *The Chronicler as Historian*, pp. 270-82 (282).
84. Briant, 'Pouvoir', p. 14.

Carter draws a direct link between an urban elite and literary production.[85] In an urban area people were able to specialize in specific crafts, as
they could extract surplus from the surrounding agrarian economy. In
terms of the world of text production, it would be safe to assume a context
in which there were adequate human skills and financial resources to produce texts. What is less clear is the nature of this world of text production.
Should it be seen as filled with people who came from outside Yehud,
total strangers to its development and subsequent histories? Or had they an
inkling of the previous inhabitants? Or were they part of the local elite
who received certain privileges from the Persian Empire? Even if they
were locals, did they not also arrive at a later stage due to the forced
removals?

Questions like these make Davies' construction a real possibility. People
arrived from everywhere in Yehud, and the new ruling elite created rules
for the membership and based those rules on the geopolitical history of
the territory. The use of a genealogy is ideological in nature and is used
to regulate a new social order established in an economic collective unit
under Persian imperial control. The movement of people by the super-
powers makes it impossible to connect the prehistory of groups to a certain
territory. It does not really matter whether the ruling elite were returning
exiles or not. They were more Persian in orientation than Jewish. Given
the reference to Cyrus at the end of Chronicles, it is likely that the book
originated within the sphere of Persian influence. Then Chronicles became
a text regulating—in a Persian way—membership of a community. This
community was focused on keeping its identity, and its focus on ethnicity
would strengthen National Socialism in Germany more than two millennia
later.[86]

The genealogy links membership to the pre-deportation history of the
territory. The way in which it was done, leaves the impression of groups
wanting to become members of the new economic collective units that
came into being under Persian rule in Yehud. They had to prove descent.

---

85. Carter, *Emergence of Yehud*, p. 287.

86. J. Wiesehöfer, 'Das Bild der Achaimeniden in der Zeit Des Nationalsozialis-
mus', in Kuhrt and Sancisi-Weerdenburg (eds.), *Method and Theory*, pp. 1-14; *idem*,
'Zur Geschichte der Begriff "Arier" und "Arisch" in der deutschen Sprachwissenschaft
und Althistorie des 19. und der erste Hälfte des 20. Jahrhunderts', in H. Sancisi-
Weerdenburg and J.W. Drijvers (eds.), *The Roots of the European Tradition: Proceedings of the 1987 Groningen Achaemenid History Workshop* (Achaemenid History,
5; Leiden: Nederlands Instituut voor het Nabije Oosten, 1990), pp. 149-66.

The Chronicler as Theologian

The Chronicler, on the basis of geographical presence, painted a picture of descent that would have accommodated a larger group of people. It is a process not very different from the one seen in southern Africa, as manifested in Nelson Mandela's biography and inauguration as President of South Africa, or in King Sobhuza II's myth-creating genealogy to unite the Swazi nation under his rule.

THE SECESSION OF THE NORTHERN KINGDOM IN CHRONICLES: ACCEPTED 'FACTS' AND NEW MEANINGS

Ehud Ben Zvi

The shared historical memory of the author and first readers of Chronicles[1] included many 'facts' about which there was no dispute. The meaning of these facts, however, was shaped in different ways,[2] and not all these 'accepted facts' were of equal value. Some were central to the construction of Israel's past, but certainly others were not. The more prominent an agreed 'fact'[3] was within this memory, the stronger was the persuasive power of a convincing interpretation of that fact, and above all, of the

---

1.   Given that the book was read, studied, copied and maintained by the community, the assumption is that the intended readership was relatively similar to the primary readership. It bears note that this readership was actually a rereadership, since the book was meant to be read and reread. From a social perspective, it is obvious that the primary target and actual readership of the book consisted of the relatively few bearers of high literacy in Yehud, that is, its literati.

2.   On these matters see my previous studies, 'Shifting the Gaze: Looking at the Lack of Change in Chronicles. Historiographic Constraints and Their Implications', in M.P. Graham and J.A. Dearman (eds.), *The Land that I Will Show You: Essays on the History and Archaeology of the Ancient Near East in Honor of J. Maxwell Miller* (JSOTSup, 343; Sheffield: Sheffield Academic Press, 2001), pp. 38-60, and 'Malleability and its Limits: Sennacherib's Campaign Against Judah', in L.L. Grabbe (ed.), *'Shut Up Like a Bird in a Cage': The Invasion of Sennacherib in 701 BCE* (JSOTSup, 363; ESHM, 4; Sheffield: Sheffield Academic Press, 2003), pp. 73-105.

3.   It is to be stressed that facts agreed upon within a particular community (e.g. Achaemenid Yehud) do not have to be 'historical facts' in the contemporary sense of the term. For the present discussion the question of whether there was a secession of the North that in any manner resembled the memory of the past upheld in Achaemenid Yehud—or in Roman times, for that matter—is immaterial. What is important for the present study is how the later generations construed the memory of the past, the story they told themselves about their own past, whether it is historical in our terms or not at all.

relevant theological or ideological implications that such interpretation carried.[4]

To explore these matters as they relate to Chronicles, I will focus on several aspects of the explanation given in the book for a central fact in the memory of the Chronicler[5] and the first readers of Chronicles: the division of the Davidic–Solomonic kingdom and the establishment of the Northern Kingdom, which not only lasted for centuries but fixed in place a separation that continued until the days of the provinces of Yehud and Samaria. In other words, the heightened significance of the event was due to its lasting influence on the (hi)story of Israel.[6]

It was inevitable that the question would be raised of when and why this foundational event happened or was allowed to happen in the divine economy. The relationship between the Davidic–Solomonic kingdom and the Davidic kingdom of Judah[7] was complex and involved an intertwining of identity and difference. Moreover, there were tensions between the idea of 'all Israel', which included the Northern Kingdom, and the determination that the populace of the Northern Kingdom was unfaithful to YHWH, because of their separate existence and their rejection of the theology and ritual of the Jerusalem temple.

There is no doubt that the existence of the former Northern Kingdom of Israel, separate from but contemporary with the Davidic kingdom of Judah for most of the monarchic period, was a historical fact accepted by the literati of Yehud, which included the author and first readers of Chron-

---

4.   As far as it concerns Chronicles, there is no difference between the terms 'theological' and 'ideological'. Hereafter, the two terms will be used interchangeably.

5.   By 'Chronicler' I mean the implied author of the book of Chronicles, as construed by its intended and most likely primary rereaders. These rereaders were asked to read the (hi)story narrated in the book. The voice of this implied author carried for them a single narrative that included what *we* would call the parallel and non-parallel accounts. To be sure, the rereaders of the book read and reread it within a world of information that included the stories of the book of Kings—or a very close forerunner of the work as it has survived—but they certainly were asked to read and study the book of Chronicles as it was. It is to be stressed that 'Chronicler' so defined speaks with the voice of the book as whole, and *not* with the voice of the non-parallel accounts alone. It bears note that the non-parallel accounts never existed as a literary unit or as a 'book' in their own right, and as such never advanced a request to be read as such.

6.   Cf. A.C. Danto, *Narration and Knowledge* (New York: Columbia University Press, 1985), esp. pp. 11-14.

7.   Rehoboam is the first individual explicitly called 'king of Judah' in Chronicles, and he is called such by YHWH and at a crucial moment in the narrative (2 Chron. 11.3; cf. את מלכות יהודה in 11.17). On this matter see section 2, below.

icles. The Chronicler could not deny the existence of the Northern Kingdom and the corresponding decrease in the area under the direct, political
rule of the Davidic kings. Moreover, it is not only the existence of the
northern polity that was an agreed-upon fact, but many core elements of
its history[8] and the basic story about its birth.

Thus the Chronicler could not have assigned the secession to a period
other than the end of Solomon's reign and the beginning of Rehoboam's.
Nor could he have associated the story with any northern king other than
Jeroboam (I) or altered the main spatial elements of the story (e.g. the
references to Shechem). In fact, the basic plot of the story of the secession
in Chronicles, most of its details and its outcome—the birth of a separate
polity—are almost identical to those in Kings. The Chronicler's behavior
in this regard is expected and probably unavoidable.

All this taken into account, the seemingly close retelling of the story of
the secession of kings in Chronicles masks the communication of new
meanings, a change of emphases, and historiographical and theological
implications that are certainly unique to Chronicles. Thus whereas the
main facts may remain the same, what the readers learn from them changes
substantially. In this and similar instances, the retelling of known facts
serves to enhance the rhetorical appeal and the possibility of acceptance
for a new story of secession, and above all for the new meanings that it
would carry. Accepted historical facts become necessary components for
the successful communication of the theological messages of Chronicles to
the literati.[9] The shaping of these messages in the present case involved
significant changes in the context in which the facts are set. In Chronicles,
as in most—if not all—historiographical works, the narrative context gives
meaning to the facts, rather than *vice versa*.[10]

---

8. For agreed-upon core facts of the history of the Northern Kingdom other than
the story of its birth, see my previous work, 'Shifting the Gaze', as well as 'The House
of Omri/Ahab in Chronicles', a paper presented at the European Seminar for Historical
Methodology, European Association for Biblical Studies, Rome, August 2001.

9. By the time of the composition of Chronicles there were cultural and social
norms that favored the literary use of imitation. The imitation of writings considered
to be 'classical' works by the community served to provide a sense of worth and legitimacy to the new work. On the use of imitation in the Hebrew Bible—including
examples from Chronicles—see J. Van Seters, 'Creative Imitation in the Hebrew
Bible', *SR* 29 (2000), pp. 395-409.

10. See, for instance, L. Hölscher, 'The New Annalistic: A Sketch of a Theory of
History', *History and Theory* 36 (1997), pp. 317-35 (318-21), as well as the works
mentioned above in n. 2, along with the bibliography cited in them.

1. *The Prominence of the Seemingly Unexplainable in the (Hi)story of the Secession in Chronicles*

Gary Knoppers has noted that the account in Chronicles (unlike Kings) 'depicts Solomon's reign as uniformly illustrious', and 'there are no adumbrations whatsoever of the...division' in this account. Consequently, the Chronicler 'has rendered the secession incomprehensible'.[11] Although I agree with the gist of his explanation to this point, the expression 'incomprehensible' is too vague. The following statement—though wordy—is more precise and helpful: the Chronicler has drawn the attention of the readers of the narrative to a formative event or historical process in which the actions of the main characters seem to defy common expectations.

The readers of the book would have expected the transfer of power to Rehoboam to follow the basic lines of that to Solomon when he became king, except, of course, for changes required by the new circumstances (namely, the temple was already built, and the prior king was already dead). In other words, they expected to be told that the prince became king (1 Chron. 23.1; cf. 2 Chron. 9.31) and then of great festivities, involving numerous sacrifices, in which the assembly (קהל)[12] crowned the new king and anointed him as a divinely appointed ruler (וימשחו ליהוה לנגיד, 1 Chron. 29.22). Moreover, the readers might have expected some reference to the (high) priest in these sacral festivities (1 Chron. 29.20-25, esp. v. 22).[13] Finally they could have anticipated a concluding statement that the new king sat on YHWH's throne and all Israel obeyed him (v. 23).

With these expectations in mind, the readers would immediately notice that in the case of Rehoboam's ascent to the throne something had gone astray from the very outset. According to 2 Chron. 10.1, the coronation was not to occur in Jerusalem but in Shechem. Within the ideological world of Chronicles, this was no mere geographic shift but precluded the possibility of legitimate sacrifices and so left no (ritual) space for YHWH in

---

11. See G.N. Knoppers, 'Rehoboam in Chronicles: Villain or Victim?', *JBL* 109 (1990), pp. 423-40 (429 and 430). The article deals also with the meaning of the event within the book of Kings.

12. The term carries sacral or ritual connotations in Chronicles.

13. For analyses of these verses, see, e.g., H.G.M. Williamson, *1 and 2 Chronicles* (NCB; Grand Rapids: Eerdmans, 1982), pp. 186-88.

the ceremony. Not surprisingly, the term קָהָל ('assembly'), which carries sacral or ritual connotations in Chronicles, does not occur here, but rather the text refers to 'all Israel'.[14] Whereas the reference in Kings to Shechem instead of Jerusalem is comprehensible against the background of 1 Kings 11 (and the so-called DtrH), the same reference in Chronicles calls attention to what seems to be a choice involving either a rejection of the unique status of Jerusalem and its temple or the sacral aspects of the coronation, if not both.

One might argue that the actions of Rehoboam and Israel could have reminded some readers of the events described in 1 Chron. 11.3, in which all the elders of Israel came to Hebron to anoint David. But these readers would also have recalled that the elders came to the king rather than *vice versa*. Far more important, they would have recognized that a claim that Shechem could function as well as Hebron as the legitimate place for crowning a Davidide before YHWH, would have implied that the conquest of Jerusalem and the establishment of the Jerusalemite temple had no lasting impact on Israelite coronations.[15]

Why would Rehoboam (or Israel for that matter) go to Shechem for a coronation rather than to Jerusalem?[16] Why would Rehoboam (or 'all Israel') implicitly reject Jerusalem and its temple? In Chronicles it is not only the secession of the North, but already the first detail in the story that leads up to the secession—the choice of Shechem for the coronation of the Davidide—that seems inexplicable. The matter involves nothing less than the centrality of Jerusalem, its temple and the relationship between YHWH and the Davidide king.

The choice of Shechem over Jerusalem is merely one of several extremely odd events that stand at the core of the narrative of the secession

---

14. The parallel text in 1 Kgs 12.3 reads וכל קהל ישראל. Cf. W. Johnstone, *1 and 2 Chronicles. II. 2 Chronicles 10–36: Guilt and Atonement* (JSOTSup, 254; 2 vols.; Sheffield: Sheffield Academic Press, 1997), p. 24.

15. Certainly, this is not the position of Chronicles, in which the first thing that David, as king of all Israel, did was to conquer Jerusalem and the main accomplishment of the Davidic–Solomonic period was the establishment of the temple.

16. Shechem is mentioned elsewhere in the book only in 1 Chron. 6.52 and 7.28, and in neither case does the reference appear as particularly important. The readers of Chronicles, however, were most likely aware of the city, its importance in their religious traditions and its association with the province of Samaria. Yet, all these connections make the choice of Shechem even more conspicuous. On Shechem and Jerusalem, see also section 3.e below.

in Chronicles. For instance, within the Chronicler's world, there is no clear
reason either for 'all Israel' to call Jeroboam or for the complaint about the
yoke of heavy taxation, and accordingly, for the 'counsel of the youths
that seems to accept that the existence of a clearly non-existing heavy
yoke during Solomonic times. These two examples are worthy of further
exploration.

Turning to the first, within Chronicles the first and only reference to
Jeroboam before the narrative of the secession is 2 Chron. 9.29.[17] Among
the purported sources for the study of the Solomonic Period, the text
explicitly refers to written texts that contained the prophecy of Ahijah the
Shilonite and the visions of the seer Jeddi or Jeddo (יעדי or יעדו) concerning (or, against) Jeroboam.[18] Not only are the readers of Chronicles not
told that Jeroboam is an Ephraimite, but his role over all Ephraimite forced
labor could not have existed in the world described in Chronicles (see
below).[19] Nor is there any place in that world for the narrative in 1 Kgs
11.29-40 or anything similar to it. Thus, while the readers of Chronicles
are told of divine communications concerning Jeroboam that took place in
the days of Solomon, nothing more is said about these communications or
about Jeroboam. Given this narrative world of Chronicles, the question for
which the readers of Chronicles seem to have no answer is, 'Why would
all Israel decide to call Jeroboam?'[20] The question is even more poignant
for these readers, since they are told—implicitly but unequivocally—that

17. King Jeroboam in 1 Chron. 5.17 is King Jeroboam II.
18. Here Chronicles deviates from Kings. There is no reference to these works in
the 'parallel' verse, 1 Kgs 11.41. The question of whether the Chronicler identifies
Jeddi with Iddo (עדו), mentioned in 2 Chron. 12.15 and 13.22, has no bearing on the
matters discussed here. The same holds true for the question of whether the sources
mentioned in 2 Chron. 9.29 (and similar sources mentioned in Chronicles) ever existed,
and if so, whether they were available to the Chronicler and the first readers. On these
matters, see, among many others, M. Noth, *The Chronicler's History* (JSOTSup, 50;
Sheffield: JSOT Press, 1987), esp. pp. 53-54; S.J. De Vries, *1 and 2 Chronicles*
(FOTL, 11; Grand Rapids: Eerdmans, 1989), p. 273; and contrast with A.F. Rainey,
'The Chronicler and his Sources—Historical and Geographical', in M.P. Graham,
K.G. Hoglund and S.L. McKenzie (eds.), *The Chronicler as Historian* (JSOTSup, 238;
Sheffield: Sheffield Academic Press, 1997), pp. 30-72 (39-40). See also Williamson,
1 and 2 Chronicles, pp. 236-37, cf. pp. 17-21.
19. Contrast with 1 Kgs 11.26-28.
20. To be sure, it was easy to answer this question from the perspective of the
book of Kings, but although the readers of Chronicles were probably aware of that
work, they are not asked to consult it but rather the book of Chronicles.

Jeroboam must have been a wrongdoer and that under normal circumstances 'all Israel' should have been well aware of that.[21]

We turn now to Rehoboam's response to the complaints over heavy taxation. Whereas Kings directly associates Jeroboam with taxation and the forced labor of Ephraim, and the reign of Solomon in general with Israelite forced labor, the same does not hold true in Chronicles. In the latter, forced labor was imposed on non-Israelites who lived in the land (2 Chron. 2.1, 16-17 [contrast with 1 Kgs 5.27-32 (EVV vv. 13-18)] and 2 Chron. 8.7-10).[22] Israelites were explicitly exempted from forced labor.[23] Against this background, the demand by Jeroboam and 'all Israel' that Rehoboam lighten the heavy yoke (עול) and workload (עבודה) that Solomon had placed upon them (2 Chron. 10.4) seems not only baseless but also extremely odd. The response of 'the youths' who had grown up with Rehoboam is even more bizarre, for it acknowledges the existence of a heavy yoke and workload that never existed (see 2 Chron. 10.10). The

21. The narrative characterizes Jeroboam as an individual who fled from the pious Solomon to Egypt (2 Chron. 10.2). Within the world of Chronicles, to have rebelled against Solomon is tantamount to being characterized as a wrongdoer.

22. The book of Kings presents two contradictory images of the reign of Solomon regarding forced labor. See 1 Kgs 5.27-32 (EVV vv. 13-18); 11.28 and contrast with 1 Kgs 9.20-22. Chronicles takes up the reconstruction of the past suggested by the latter pericope and rejects that advanced by all the other references and the main narrative in the book. On the relationship between the two accounts, see, for instance, I. Kalimi, ספר דברי הימים כתיבה היסטורית ואמצעים ספרותיים (= *The Book of Chronicles: Historical Writing and Literary Devices*) (The Biblical Encyclopaedia Library, 18; Jerusalem: Mossad Harev Kook/Bialik Institute, 2000), pp. 42-43, 71, 354; A. Siedlecki, 'Foreigners, Warfare and Judahite Identity in Chronicles', in M.P. Graham and S.L. Mckenzie (eds.), *The Chronicler as Author: Studies in Text and Texture* (JSOTSup, 263; Sheffield: Sheffield Academic Press, 1999), pp. 229-66 (252-53); cf. Williamson, *1 and 2 Chronicles*, pp. 201-202.

23. See ומן בני ישראל אשר לא נתן שלמה לעבדים למלאכתו (2 Chron. 8.9). In other words, the Chronicler does not have Solomon force Israelites to become laborers. Of course, he still needed the labor, but for that purpose he drew from the 153,600 non-Israelites who were sojourning (notice the language of 2 Chron. 2.16a) in the land. Although such policies may be comparable to those of the oppressive pharaoh of Exodus (excluding the killing of the males), it is self-evident that Chronicles did not evaluate Solomon's policies in negative terms. The exact opposite is true. This case is particularly interesting given the general tendency of Chronicles on the matter of non-Israelites (e.g. God may convey divine messages through them; they may serve as quasi-prophets; cases of intermarriage between them and Israelites tend to be reported as a matter of fact and the offspring accepted within Israel). The matter, however, is beyond the scope of this contribution and deserves a separate study.

proposed answer moves even further into the absurd, as it states that the up-to-now unheard of forced work of Israel should dramatically increase. The concluding advice of the youth to Rehoboam—to proclaim that his little finger is thicker than the loins of his recently deceased and beloved father—serves as a fitting literary ending to utterly unreasonable and seemingly unexplainable advice (2 Chron. 10.10; contrast with Exod. 20.12; Deut. 5.16 and the logic implied in Mal. 1.6).

According to the story, Rehoboam actually followed the youths' advice and rejected the 'counsel of the elders'.[24] The latter action alone would characterize him as a rebellious and foolish person, since the instruction of priests and counsel of the elders was to be honored (Ezek. 7.26).[25] Rehoboam's acceptance of the absurd advice of the youths and his implied acceptance of their misunderstanding of their immediate past indicate his inability to think rationally and even remember correctly the most recent past. One must add to all this that Rehoboam decided to go to Shechem to be crowned, rather than performing the relevant ceremonies in Jerusalem, and his implicit acceptance of the youths' comments shamed his father Solomon.[26] To complete the picture, there is the report of Rehoboam's first action after the rebellion, to send Hadoram (הדרם) to the northern Israelites (2 Chron. 10.18). Whereas the reference to Adoram's mission in 1 Kgs

24. The response attributed to the elders in v. 7 follows the common motif of a king who deals with his subjects kindly and thus secures their support. The wording of the response is obviously based on but significantly deviates from that of its source, 1 Kgs 12.7 (on the folkloristic feature of the latter, see B.O. Long, *1 Kings* [FOTL, 9; Grand Rapids: Eerdmans, 1984], p. 135).

25. Of course, there might be here a faint echo of the theme of the counsel of elders as opposed to the counsel of able-bodied men in *Gilgamesh and Aga*. But Rehoboam is no Gilgamesh; the youths around him are not the able-bodied men of Gilgamesh; rejecting the advice of the elders does not lead to victory here; and the advice of the youths is plainly unreasonable, for reasons outlined above. If anything, there is here a reversal of the theme that is echoed, and this serves to re-emphasize the wisdom of following the counsel of the elders.

26. To be sure, it is not reported that he repeated these comments in public, as was suggested to him, but he did accept the advice of those who so referred to his father, and it is not reported that he distanced himself from the comment that shamed his father. In fact, the context seems to suggest that he identified with the gist of that comment. 'Loins' (מתנים) here signifies strength (cf. Isa. 45.1; Nah. 2.2). Claims of kings that their fathers who preceded them on the throne have been powerless or ineffectual are not unheard of in the ancient Near East (see Kilamuwa), but they require a supporting context. Within the context of Chronicles such a claim borders on the absurd.

12.18 serves to highlight the king's decision to reinstate forced labor in Israel by the symbolic act of sending the person who was over this institution (אֲדֹרָם אֲשֶׁר עַל הַמַּס; see 2 Sam. 20.24 and cf. 1 Kgs 4.6; 5.28 [EVV v. 14]—אֲדֹרָם is a short form of אֲדֹנִירָם),[27] the note in 2 Chron. 10.19 makes a different point. Since forced labor here was only required from non-Israelites, already the youths' counsel and Rehoboam's acceptance of it point to the court's tendency to de-Israelitize northern Israel.[28] Against this background, the sending of Hadoram, who was in charge of the forced labor, is clearly an attempt to consolidate and publicly legitimize that tendency. The Chronicler reinforced this message by the allusive role of the word מַס here (it appears elsewhere in Chronicles only in 2 Chron. 8.8, which points to the forced labor of the non-Israelites) and above all by the renaming of the main character. Whereas אֲדֹרָם and אֲדֹנִירָם point at 'my (divine) master is exalted',[29] הֲדוֹרָם suggests 'Hadad is exalted'. The two other persons named Hadoram in Chronicles are non-Israelites (1 Chron. 1.21; 18.10), and in one of these cases, Chronicles substitutes יוֹרָם (2 Sam. 8.10) for הֲדוֹרָם (1 Chron. 18.10), precisely to emphasize that the man is not an Israelite.[30] In other words, the Chronicler suggests to his readers that Rehoboam sent a non-Israelite taskmaster to the now de-Israelitized North to enforce symbolically and (eventually) practically their new status as non-Israelites. Of course, within the world of Chronicles such an endeavor can only fail, but it certainly contributes to the characterization of Rehoboam as a king who departs from YHWH. Note

27. The king's action may also have been intended to humiliate Jeroboam by confronting him with his former superior (1 Kgs 11.28) and an elder statesman. Social connotations of shame and honor are deeply intertwined, of course, in this literary report.

28. It is theoretically possible to read the complaint of 'all Israel' about their forced labor, as an expression of their identification with the oppressed non-Israelite *gerîm* upon whom heavy labor was forced. But it is unlikely that the first readers of Chronicles read the book in this way and accordingly lionized 'all Israel' (cf. Exod. 22.20; 23.9; Lev. 19.34; Deut. 10.19) and condemned Solomon. Certainly, the Chronicler did not support such a reading, and it is likely that the readers associated forced labor and foreignness in the land, and perhaps even linked the latter with the rejection of Jerusalem, temple and David.

29. On the meaning of the name אֲדֹנִירָם/אֲדֹרָם, see J.D. Fowler, *Theophoric Personal Names in Ancient Hebrew* (JSOTSup, 49; Sheffield: JSOT Press, 1988), pp. 29, 53, 80.

30. On these matters, see, for instance, *HALOT*, s.v., הֲדוֹרָם; Johnstone, *1 and 2 Chronicles*, II, p. 29.

70	*The Chronicler as Theologian*

also the divine reference to the northern Israelites as Judah's kindred
(אחיכם) immediately following this report (2 Chron. 11.4).

There can be no doubt that all these considerations were intended to
advance a negative characterization of the king, yet the Chronicler asked
these same readers to evaluate Rehoboam in unequivocally positive terms
for this period (i.e. until about the fifth year of his reign; see 2 Chron.
12.1).[31] Most significantly, whereas the campaign of Shishak is presented
as divine punishment, nowhere is the secession of the Northern Kingdom
explained in these terms.[32] To be sure, these observations raise serious

31. In addition, 2 Chron. 11.17 strongly contributes to the characterization of
Rehoboam as a pious king in his first years, and the same holds true for his acceptance
of YHWH's word soon after his succession (2 Chron. 11.2-4). M. Cogan maintains that
the reference to three years in 2 Chron. 11.17 is typological and points to a short period
of time ('The Chronicler's Use of Chronology as Illuminated by Neo-Assyrian Royal
Inscriptions', in J.H. Tigay [ed.], *Empirical Models for Biblical Criticism* [Philadel-
phia: University of Pennsylvania Press, 1985], pp. 197-209 [207-209]). Even if this
were so (which is doubtful), Rehoboam would have been evaluated as a good monarch
in the first period of his reign. For the positive characterization of Rehoboam at this
time (despite 2 Chron. 12.14), see Knoppers, 'Rehoboam in Chronicles', and cf.
P. Welten, *Geschichte und Geschichtsdarstellung in den Chronikbüchern* (WMANT,
42; Neukirchen–Vluyn: Neukircherner Verlag, 1973), p. 127. It is worth stressing that
in sharp contrast with Kings, the first four kings of Judah are characterized in a
generally positive manner, or at the very least in a far more positive manner in Chronicles. All of them—except Abijah—are characterized as having negative periods, but
for most of their reigns they are characterized in positive terms. (D.G. Deboys ['History and Theology in the Chronicler's Portrayal of Abijah', *Bib* 71 (1990), pp. 48-62]
maintains that the Chronicler's portrayal of Abijah is generally positive, but somewhat
reserved.)

32. This observation further undermines any explanation of the secession in terms
of Rehoboam's wrongdoing from the time of Solomon's death to the assembly in
Shechem. Moreover, the shift from a period of unfaithfulness to one of faithfulness
tends to be explicitly marked in Chronicles by appropriate references (e.g. 2 Chron.
12.5-7), none of which occur until well after the assembly met at Shechem. Hence,
there is no reason to assume that the Chronicler exempted this early period from the
positive evaluation of Rehoboam. For an alternative view, see S. Japhet, *The Ideology
of the Book of Chronicles and its Place in Biblical Thought* (BEATAJ, 9; Frankfurt:
Peter Lang, 2nd edn, 1997), p. 162 n. 477, where the author writes, 'only Rehoboam's
actions are responsible for the division [of the kingdom]'. Chronicles, however, does
not state that anywhere. On the contrary, 2 Chron. 10.15 (cf. 9.29) makes her position
untenable. Japhet supports her viewpoint by suggesting that one should dismiss
2 Chron. 10.15 as 'an inconsistent holdover of 1 Kings 12.15' (p. 162 n. 477). But even
if for the sake of argument one were to consider the possibility that the actual—to be

questions for the so-called chronistic reward and punishment theology, an outlook usually connected with the speech of Shemaiah in 2 Chron. 12.5. While this matter will be addressed below,[33] it is sufficient at this stage to

distinguished from the implied—author of the book of Chronicles was suddenly—though momentarily—inattentive and simply copied this verse from Kings without noticing its meaning, the text surely does not invite its readers to dismiss this verse. Japhet's position on this matter seems derivative of her claim 'the book's [Chronicles] outlook may be defined in Ezekiel's words: "the righteousness of the righteous shall be upon himself, and the wickedness of the wicked shall be upon himself"... Each generation is responsible for its deeds and for its own fate' (p. 162). Although Chronicles shows many accounts in which these principles apply, it also shows those in which they do not. A few obvious examples may suffice: YHWH's choice of Solomon cannot be the result of any pious deeds of the king (1 Chron. 22.9-10; cf. 28.5-7; 29.1); numerous people died because of the sin of David (1 Chron. 21.4); prophets were punished (sometimes executed), because they faithfully proclaimed divine messages (2 Chron. 16.10; 24.20-22); the principle that each generation is responsible for its own fate certainly contradicts the reported situation of the generations that were born and died during the 70 years announced by Jeremiah (2 Chron. 36.20-21; and for inter-generational punishment, see also 2 Chron. 29.6-9). I have argued elsewhere that one cannot safely conclude from texts in Chronicles, in which a certain theological principle seems to be governing the narrative, that such a principle applies universally in the work. The book advances a balanced approach in which implicit statements about YHWH's way of governing history in one section are set in 'proportion' by those implicitly advanced elsewhere. See E. Ben Zvi, 'A Sense of Proportion: An Aspect of the Theology of the Chronicler', *SJOT* 9 (1995), pp. 37-51, and *idem*, 'The Book of Chronicles: Another Look', *SR* (forthcoming, 2003). (It should be noted that in a more recent work Japhet approached the issue of the reasons for the secession in a different manner, but still mainly on the basis of 2 Chron. 13. See S. Japhet, *I and II Chronicles* [OTL; London: SCM Press, 1993], esp. p. 657.) Welch advances the claim that 'in his [the Chronicler's] judgment there were good reasons for Israel having refused to endure the rule of the Judean king [Rehoboam], but when the breach was final...he went on to describe in his own terms a war which broke out between Abijah and Jeroboam (II. Chron. c. xiii)...' In other words, the secession was justifiable during the reign of a king such as Rehoboam. See A.C. Welch, *Post-Exilic Judaism* (The Baird Lecture, 1934; Edinburgh: W. Blackwood & Sons, 1935), p. 190. Williamson (*1 and 2 Chronicles*, esp. pp. 238, 251) also seems to echo this approach. It is worth noting, however, that even if one were to argue that the purported weakness of Rehoboam that is mentioned in 2 Chron. 13.7 (or his sinful character at the time of the secession) could have been considered a *reason* for Israel's rebellion, then such a 'reason' certainly disappeared well before the battle of Zemarim, according to Chronicles. On 2 Chron. 13 see section 3.c, below.

    33. For a different approach, according to which the 'the reworking of the material [in Chronicles] preserves...the firm belief in divine recompense on an individual

emphasize that the positive characterization of Rehoboam is another—and perhaps among the most salient—of a series of seemingly unexplainable features in the Chronicler's account of the secession. It is, however, probably not the most salient of all, since according to the text the divine decision to divide the kingdom was announced during the days of Solomon—the best possible period.[34]

Thus, the story of the secession in Chronicles abounds with instances in which common expectations of rational or normal behavior or evaluation are thwarted. All the main characters, including God, are directly implicated in seemingly unreasonable conduct, as is the Chronicler, too. Such an all-pervasive feature of the narrative cannot be dismissed as meaningless in any analysis, nor is there any reason to assume that the intended or primary readers of the Chronicler's version of the secession were asked to do so, or actually did so. This ubiquitous and emphatic characterization of the events and characters provides, in fact, strong textually inscribed indications about the particular construction of the secession story in Chronicles and the meaning(s) that this story may have communicated to its intended and primary rereaderships.[35] In addition, these salient

basis', see A. Frisch, 'Jeroboam and the Division of the Kingdom: Mapping Contrasting Biblical Accounts', *JANESCU* 27 (2000), pp. 15-29 (21).

34. See 2 Chron. 10.15. Not only is it that Ahijah, the Shilonite, is associated with the reign of Solomon in Chronicles (2 Chron. 9.29 and contrast with 12.15), but the word of YHWH had to be proclaimed before the secession itself, that is, during the reign of Solomon. Chronicles was bound to maintain the basic facts agreed upon within the community, which included the fact that Ahijah announced the relevant divine decision. The text shows also the degree of freedom permitted to an author with regard to the transmission of accepted traditions: while the basic meaning of the words of YHWH to Ahijah had to be maintained and so its temporal setting (i.e. during Solomon's reign), the reasons for the event and the attendant circumstances were historiographically malleable. On the differentiation between 'core' facts that are not malleable and malleable facts, see my previous work, 'Malleability and its Limits'.

35. To be sure, this feature could be eliminated from Chronicles if one were to bring into Chronicles all the material in Kings that the Chronicler decided *not* to include. But from the fact that Chronicles was read within a world of knowledge that included Kings, it does *not* follow that Chronicles was not to have been read as work on its own. Although the first readers of Chronicles were surely aware of the contents of the book of Kings, they were never asked *not* to read (and so to reject) the (hi)story narrated in Chronicles. The very opposite is true: the readers of Chronicles were obviously asked to read, reread and accept the value of the narrative in the book of Chronicles, even if—and perhaps more emphatically when—it stood in tension with other narratives that existed within the community. Cf. R. Mosis, *Untersuchungen zur*

instances of seemingly logical incongruence served to call attention to particular issues and narrative or ideological tensions and to their possible resolutions (or lack thereof) within the ideological and narrative world of the book.

Chronicles includes all the main historical facts about the secession that were agreed upon by the community within which and for which it was written. But these facts, even if taken from Kings, are now legitimizing elements in a new story, where they are repeatedly presented as seemingly unexplainable. When incomprehensible behavior is brought to the readers' attention, the importance of explanation becomes a central point in the narrative. Within Chronicles—and particularly given the importance of the reported event in the memory of Israel—it becomes also a central point for theological reflection and historiographical considerations.

2. *Explaining the Seemingly Unexplainable and Imagining the Deity*

The proleptic reference to prophecies or visions concerning Jeroboam, the son of Nebat, when his name is first mentioned (2 Chron. 9.29), already indicates that Jeroboam had a role in the divine plan. The seemingly unexplainable call of 'all Israel' to him serves to involve him in the narrative plot and in the fulfillment of that plan. Significantly, there is no reason to assume that within the world of the book those who called him were aware of his future role in YHWH's plan. Thus, the seemingly unexplainable actions of 'all Israel' were necessary steps in the implementation of a divinely ordained design for Israel's polities in a way unbeknown to them.

The matter becomes explicit in 2 Chron. 10.15-16, where Rehoboam's (illogical) acceptance of the words of the youths about him is explained as a turn of affairs dictated by YHWH. The explicit repetition of לֹא שָׁמַע הַמֶּלֶךְ ('the king did not listen') in vv. 15-16 emphasizes the narrator's contention that such a divinely motivated action was the immediate reason

---

Theologie des chronistischen Geschichtswerkes (FTS, 92; Freiburg: Herder, 1973), p. 169 n. 2. Further, one should take into account the typical way that Chronicles advances positions contrary to those in Kings (or in the so-called DtrH): to omit details from the source texts and then to create a new story either by including information that is not mentioned in them in Kings or by setting the details in different contexts. There are good rhetorical reasons for the preference of this way of creating alternative images of the past over simple denials of the historicity of events reported in Kings.

for the North's rejection of the Davidic dynasty.[36] Within this context the explicit reference to the fulfillment of the divine decision revealed to Ahijah (v. 15) about Jeroboam suggests that from the Chronicler's point of view, such a decision was already made in the days of Solomon.[37] This determination by God involved not only a rebellion and rejection of the 'house of David' (both as a dynasty and as polity) but also the establishment of an additional Israelite polity and the active role of Jeroboam in the formative events of the latter.

The divinely ordained character of the events is finally communicated to the main characters in 2 Chron. 11.4. Within the world of the narrative, the Solomonic kingdom was powerful militarily and should have been able to suppress the rebellion. At this point in the text, Rehoboam sets out to do what one would expect of such a monarch: he plans to attack the rebels. It is at this point in the narrative that he and those who remain loyal to him[38] are explicitly told that the events were caused by YHWH and accordingly that they should not resort to force to change them.[39] Significantly, now that they have learned about the divine plan and its fulfillment, they are given the choice of accepting it and obeying YHWH or of resisting YHWH and attempting to reunite the kingdom. They chose the former route, and this decision is central to the positive evaluation of Rehoboam, a point to which I will return.

To recapitulate, divine causation is presented as the explanation for a turn of events that would have been unlikely had the characters behaved in a reasonable manner. The timing of the events, the selection of the main characters and the actions they take (contrary to what the first readers would expect from them) are all now explained in terms of YHWH's control over the events.[40] Instances of irrational behavior in the narrative

36. See 2 Chron. 21.7 and 2 Kgs 8.19.

37. See also section 3, below.

38. The narrator now refers to 'Rehoboam, king of Judah' and to 'all Israel in Judah and Benjamin'. The expression 'king of Judah' appears here for *the first time* in the historical narrative (it appeared in the genealogical section of the book, in 1 Chron. 4.41 and 5.17, but there it pointed to kings who reigned later than Rehoboam; the same holds true for 1 Chron. 9.1). As for 'Israel', it is now often an ideological term encompassing those who lived in both the northern and the southern polities.

39. There is, of course, the reference to the northern populace as אחיכם ('your kindred'), but the prohibition of attacking them was not based on kinship, but on the fact that 'this matter was brought about by me [YHWH]' (מאתי נהיה הדבר הזה).

40. These include: Israel and Rehoboam's preference of Shechem over Jerusalem; Israel's call to Jeroboam; the manner in which a patently false (according to Chron-

serve to characterize a process through which YHWH's plan for Israel's polities became a 'historical fact'.

A few observations are in order at this point. The explanation of the events in terms of YHWH's action probably seemed the most likely for this concentration of seemingly unexplainable human choices. It implies a theological understanding of YHWH as a deity who may cause people to behave irrationally. Such an understanding is attested elsewhere in the discourse(s) of the period.[41] This explanation is also consistent with Chronicles' demonstration of divine causation in history, namely, as manifested or mediated by human deeds that achieve results that cannot be explained in 'wordly terms' (e.g. Asa's victory over the million man army of Zerah, the Cushite; see 2 Chron. 14.7-14). Still, it is worth stressing that of many memories of Israel's past, Chronicles particularly and emphatically shapes the one about the secession as one in which the unexplainable in human terms is so pervasive, at all levels. For Chronicles, the secession was a most unlikely political and religious event, and at the same time, one of the utmost consequence.

Chronicles' explanation of the secession shows YHWH as one who made crucial decisions concerning Israel that were essentially beyond the expounding power of the Yehudite literati. It is worth underscoring that within this narrative it was during the golden age of Israelite history that YHWH decided that this glorious kingdom should be divided. Not only did the Chronicler depart from the explanation advanced in Kings, but he chose not to justify the divine decision. The Chronicler's decision was intentional and communicated on one level that the historical event of the succession defies human reason. On another level, it revealed YHWH as a deity not bound by the limits of human reason or confined to what humans might predict. Thus, Chronicles reflects, shapes and communicates an understanding of history as a fully unpredictable affair at times, because the deity governing history (and the fate of Israel) may act unpredictably.

icles, but not according to Kings) claim about Solomon's hard yoke on Israel is immediately and widely accepted by both sides; and, above all, Rehoboam's rejection of the advice of the elders in favor of that of the youths, which immediately leads to Israel's rejection of the house of David.

41. Cf. Exod. 8.11, 28; 9.34-35; 10.1; Isa. 6.10; and esp. 2 Chron. 25.19-20 (note the opening phrase in v. 20, ולא שמע).

3. *Other Implications of the Chronicler's Explanation of the Secession*

a. *A Theology of Competing Claims that Inform and Balance Each Other*
Chronicles shapes and communicates a (hi)story of Israel's past to instruct
its intended readers in a number of theological matters, such as the meaning of history, YHWH's requirements of human beings, individual responsibility, divine retribution and the like. The claim of the book to speak
about these matters is grounded on the common assumption that YHWH
governs the world according to principles (cf. Prov. 8.22) that may be
learned from the results of divine activity, that is, from human history—as
reconstructed by the Chronicler.[42] I stressed elsewhere that reported
attestations of events that are coherent with a particular theological principle were *not* meant to be understood as proofs that such a principle had
absolute or universal validity. Quite to the contrary, the Chronicler most
often qualified these principles by pointing to instances in which competing principles were at work. Thus, the intended and primary rereaderships of the book were asked to imagine the world as a place in which a
plethora of divine principles—sometimes at tension with each other—
are at work, and accordingly to construct a theological image of a deity
in whose 'mind' different principles qualify each other. From a historiographical perspective, the result is a narrative in which similar human
actions may lead to a variety of divinely ordained historical results.[43] This
multiplicity of possible historical results allowed relative flexibility in the
articulation of explanations of events in Israel's past, and in the lives of
the audience as well.[44] Such flexibility, however, serves to undermine the
predictability of any event, since the same human 'input' may lead to
drastically different historical results.[45] The narrative fact that the secession of the Northern Kingdom was decided by YHWH during a highpoint
in Israelite history (Solomon's reign) dramatically balances or sets in

42. See my previous work, 'A Gateway to the Chronicler's Teaching: The Account
of the Reign of Ahaz in 2 Chr 28,1-27', *SJOT* 7 (1993), pp. 216-49 (216-17).

43. These results include some that would be clearly inconsistent with divine
principles, *had* they been understood as separate and universally valid. These results
serve as proof positive that these principles were *not* understood in that manner.

44. On these matters, see my 'A Sense of Proportion', and the bibliography cited
there, as well as my forthcoming article 'The Book of Chronicles: Another Look'.

45. Similar concerns appear elsewhere in the HB. See E. Ben Zvi, *Signs of Jonah:
Reading and Rereading in Ancient Yehud* (JSOTSup, 367; Sheffield: Sheffield Academic Press, 2003), *passim*.

proportion theological claims about a firm coherence between human actions and divinely ordained results.[46]

The story of the secession suggests that historical events may be unpredictable and people may behave in incomprehensible ways, and that incomprehensibility may extend to YHWH too. The reason for YHWH dictating this turn of events in Chronicles is not explained in Chronicles, though it is explainable within the usual theological world of Chronicles. There are important implications to this observation. The readers of Chronicles are told that they may learn much about YHWH's governing rules, desires and motives in governing history through their reading of the book. This is the reason for which they are asked to read the book to begin with. But they are also told that crucial aspects of their history should be simply accepted as YHWH's will, even if these aspects seem to defy accepted theological reasoning. In other words, the story of the secession in Chronicles serves to inform and balance the main underlying epistemology on which the entire book is grounded, and surely, this removes any possible claim that it may have to categorical or universal validity.

b. *Rehoboam's Evaluation and its Implications*

Despite his actions during the events that led to the secession of northern Israel, the Chronicler advances a positive evaluation of Rehoboam during the first years of his reign (2 Chron. 12.1-5; cf. 11.17). Such an evaluation serves to highlight the unreasonable character of the rebellion of the North, but there is more than that to this evaluation. To be sure, the first time Rehoboam is given a chance to act with proper knowledge and volition (2 Chron. 11.2-4), he obeys YHWH and is blessed (11.5-23), but what about the time before Shemaiah's speech? The book of Chronicles suggests that Rehoboam could not be held personally responsible for his actions at that time in the narrative, since YHWH caused him to behave in such a way (10.15). This is, in fact, an expected theological stance. The importance of the theological concept of 'warning' in Chronicles—and other texts that eventually were included in the Hebrew Bible—hints at a perspective according to which people must be knowledgeable of YHWH's

---

46. For a discussion of other texts serving the same theological purpose, see my 'Sense of Proportion'. For examples of texts that advance a direct coherence between human action and divine reward, see 2 Chron. 12.2, 5; 14.6; 28.6. The Chronicler's theological position is one in which these claims are intertwined, informed and balanced by reports of instances in which this principle of coherence is not maintained at all by YHWH.

will (or commandment) and be able to make a decision in order for them to be considered responsible for their actions, and judged accordingly.[47]

This being so, and if Rehoboam is not held personally responsible for his actions at the time, then what about the northern Israelites? When, in the world of the narrative, are they able to make informed choices and, therefore, to be held responsible for their actions? Although the exact turning-point in the story is somewhat unclear, the text evidently characterizes the period immediately following Jeroboam's religious innovations (from the Chronicler's perspective, at least) as one in which northern Israelites are described as being able to make a choice. Those who are pious leave Jeroboam's polity and join Judah (2 Chron. 11.13-17).

Thus, the text constructs a kind of negative boundary test, that is, a unambiguous expression of what a pious Israelite should consider to be clearly inconsistent with obedience to YHWH and, therefore, absolutely unacceptable. The text indicates that no Israelite should reject the exclusivity of the Jerusalem temple, its personnel and associated elite,[48] to do so is to reject the legitimate worship of YHWH, and so, to reject YHWH (2 Chron. 13.9-12). To be sure, the Chronicler's message on these matters was directly relevant to the historical situation of the author and the first readers of the book in Achaemenid Yehud. I will return to this matter later.

c. *Implications for How to Read History*
The secession of northern Israel is described in different terms in King Abijah's war speech to the enemy forces (2 Chron. 13.3-12). The latter are identified again as Jeroboam and all Israel (13.4; cf. 10.3; 13.15; the expression ירבעם וכל ישראל appears only in these three verses), and within the world of the text, it is obvious that the speech is intended to dissuade the addressees from fighting Judah. The main persuasive appeal of the speech is based on two propositions. First, kingship was given by YHWH to David and his descendants and, conversely, YHWH's kingdom is the Davidic polity, certainly not that headed by Jeroboam (13.5, 8). Thus, the enemy is fighting no less than YHWH's own kingdom. Second, Jeroboam (and northern Israel) rejected the exclusive claims and traditions of the Jerusalemite temple, as well as its personnel and worship (11.13-17).

---

47. See the excellent discussion in Japhet, *Ideology of the Book of Chronicles*, pp. 183-90.

48. Significantly, this theological construct, which includes temple and the elite, is directly associated with the 'path of David and Solomon' (2 Chron. 11.17).

Such actions are tantamount to forsaking YHWH (13.11, cf. v. 10).[49] These two propositions lead to a logical conclusion: Jeroboam and all Israel are actually waging war against YHWH, and as such they cannot succeed (13.12).

A retelling of the story of the secession is included in the speech to provide a kind of historical background to the situation and to support the main rhetorical claim of the speech. To be sure, such a retelling must be consistent with the facts of the events as known to the characters in the book—and as known to the first readers of the book—to be effective, and this strengthens the persuasive appeal of the speech.

Thus, whereas the secession is associated, as expected, with Jeroboam and Rehoboam, for obvious rhetorical reasons Abijah does not tell Jeroboam and the northern Israelites, who outnumber him and are just about to battle him, that their rebellion against the house of David, the establishment of their own kingdom and even the choice of Jeroboam were all from YHWH. Had Abijah advanced such a claim, he would have seriously weakened the basic argument of his speech. In fact, within its narrative setting, such a claim would have been almost ludicrous, and the more so since this would have been the basic theological claim of his enemies: that Jeroboam's coronation and the establishment of the Northern Kingdom were supported by Israel's deity,[50] and accordingly, those who fight against Jeroboam and Israel are actually waging war against YHWH.

In Chronicles, pious kings who deliver important speeches are characterized as good, powerful rhetors (cf. 2 Chron. 20.5-13). As such, Abijah has skillfully to sidestep the obvious fact that Jeroboam and Israel actually succeeded in the past, by either denying any lasting meaning to that success or by associating negative meanings with it, or both. So Abijah emphasizes first the totally contingent character of such a success: it just happened that at the time of the rebellion Rehoboam was 'young and soft-hearted' (נער ורך לבב). By doing so, not only does he take away any claim for lasting significance of their earlier success, but strengthens the negative characterization of Jeroboam. He is presented now as a seditious servant who, only appropriately, paired with worthless scoundrels (אנשים רקים בני בליעל), set resolutely (יתאמצו) to take (unfair) advantage of a

---

49. Although the second argument is given more narrative space than the first, the two are clearly interwoven. See the reference to 'the path of David and Solomon' in 2 Chron. 11.17.

50. 'Usurpers' surely claimed divine legitimacy for their rule, their polities and their cultic innovations (or reforms) in the ancient Near East.

youth unfit for battle (cf. Deut. 20.8). Thus, in his retelling of the story, Abijah: (1) makes use of a common ancient Near Eastern understanding that slaves or servants who rebel and leave their masters are asocial characters that should be subdued, lest the fabric of society be weakened;[51] (2) assigns shame rather than honor to Jeroboam's success; (3) through his emphasis on Jeroboam and his scoundrels rhetorically disassociates 'all Israel' (that is, those who stand before him ready for battle) from the shameful reported actions and from their leader; and (4) connotes that Jeroboam's success was due only to a temporary set of circumstances that no longer exist (2 Chron. 13.6-7), so as to implicitly state that his success should not be construed as a sign of YHWH's support of him. The rest of the speech makes the case that those who stand against the Davidic king wage war against (not for) YHWH.

The Chronicler, however, does more than just pen an excellent rhetorical speech. The attention of the primary readership is drawn to understand speeches within their setting in the history of Israel. Within Chronicles, Abijah's speech does not negate or detract from the permanent value of the word of YHWH, such as that which came to Shemaiah (2 Chron. 11.2-4).[52] Whereas the speech of Abijah serves its narrative purpose and portrays the king as a pious man, it provides neither an explanation for the continued existence of the Northern Kingdom for centuries after the speech, nor accounts for the separate existence of Yehud and Samaria in the Chronicler's own day. It also does not explain Abijah's actions after the defeat of Jeroboam and 'all Israel'. The enduring significance of the divine speech will be discussed in the next section, but it is worth noting that the recounting of the secession in 2 Chronicles 13 and its relation to the earlier point that the secession is from YHWH conveys a meta-narrative claim about how the readers are to receive the claims advanced in separate units within the work.

Even if its theme and rhetoric are clearly contingent on its circumstances within the world of the narrative, the speech remains an integral part of Chronicles as a whole. The process of reading and rereading the book brings to the forefront an allusion created by the choice of words in the description of Rehoboam that goes beyond the immediate purposes of

---

51. See, e.g., R.J. Ratner, 'Jonah, the Runaway Servant', *Maarav* 5-6 (1990), pp. 281-305.

52. The expression ויהי דבר is uncommon in Chronicles, appearing only here and in 1 Chron. 22.8, which contains another central statement.

the speech in the book. Whereas Abijah portrays Rehoboam as an inexpe-
rienced, 'tender' youth, easy to take advantage of, the precise words that
the Chronicler places in Abijah's mouth, namely נער ורך לבב, remind
the readers of the only other personage to whom the precise phrase נער
ורך is associated in Chronicles and in the entire Hebrew Bible, namely
Solomon, and more precisely Solomon in relation to the construction of
the temple (1 Chron. 22.5; 29.1). Of course, Abijah does not attempt to
state in these circumstances that Rehoboam was a second Solomon, but his
words carry in a way unbeknown to the character in the book a significance that becomes apparent to the reader. The comparison between
Solomon and Rehoboam is not meant to emphasize the need for help from
their respective parents (1 Chron. 22.5; 29.2-9), after all, within the world
of Chronicles, Solomon left his son a kingdom ready to be governed, as
one might expect a noble and pious ruler to do. The commonality between
the two cases concerns the seemingly unexplainable behavior of YHWH
and the power of divine decisions irrespective of human actions. The deity
chooses and blesses Solomon with peace and the completion of the temple
before Solomon could have 'earned' such a blessing. The choice of Solomon is YHWH's alone and is neither explainable nor predictable within the
usual patterns of the Chronicler's historiography; it cannot be abstracted
from them (1 Chron. 22.9), nor can it be derived at the time from any
personal attribute of the king. The same may be said for the lasting
division of the kingdom.[53]

53. It should be noted that Rehoboam is described as behaving in an unreasonable
manner in 2 Chron. 10, but not as an irresolute, 'soft-hearted' king. If anything, one
may think that his heart hardened, so as to contribute to the fulfillment of YHWH's
designs. See the discussion above in section 2. Rehoboam's sending of the taskmaster
to confront Israel has nothing to do with being irresolute (see above) nor is the choice
of words in 2 Chron. 10.18bβ consistent with such a characterization. Verbal forms of
אמץ in the hithpael point to resolute action (2 Chron. 10.18; Ruth 1.8). According to
the narrative, facing the outburst of open rebellion, surrounded now by an enemy who
has just killed his representative and will certainly kill him if he is caught (they were
'resolutely' against him; see 2 Chron. 13.7), he mounts the chariot and flees to his
capital to organize his troops and quash the rebellion (2 Chron. 11.1). He is never condemned for this action; in fact, this would have been the expected behavior of a
resolute monarch under these conditions. For a different position, see Japhet, *I and II
Chronicles*, p. 692.

d. *The Word of YHWH to Shemaiah: Resolving Tension with Agreed Historical Facts and Implications for Yehud*
YHWH's word to Shemaiah is brief but has pervasive and enduring impli-
cations. Not only does it state that the establishment of the Northern
Kingdom is due to YHWH, but it also forbids the Judahite king from
attacking the North to reassert control over it.[54] This second aspect of the
divine communication solves a vexing historiographical and ideological
problem in Chronicles. Not only did Rehoboam not attack the North, but
no pious Judean king after him tried to do so in order to re-establish the
Davidic–Solomonic kingdom, even when the narrative implies that such
would have been possible.

The most obvious example of this situation concerns Abijah, who
(according to Chronicles) won a mighty victory over the North. In fact, the
Chronicler notes that the northern Israelites were subdued (2 Chron.
13.18) and that Jeroboam never gained strength in the days of Abijah
(13.20). But if such was the case, then why did Abijah take only three
border cities—which not incidentally were most likely within the territory
of Persian Yehud?[55] Certainly, the Chronicler would have recognized that

54. The expression ויאסר אביה את המלחמה in 2 Chron. 13.3 indicates that once
the two armies met, Abijah took the initiative to begin the battle (cf. 1 Kgs 20.14).
However, in the context of this story his main initiative was to utter his speech to the
enemy troops, so as to avoid the battle altogether (it is unlikely that the Chronicler was
describing him as delivering the speech to them in the midst of the battle). In any case,
one cannot learn from Abijah's initiative in 2 Chron. 13.3 that the Judean king should
be construed as the one who initiated the hostilities. In fact, this campaign resembles
others in which a pious king is tested by an enemy attack (e.g. 2 Chron. 14.8-14; see
Deboys, 'Chronicler's Portrayal of Abijah', pp. 49-50). The speech and the great
disparity between the two forces contribute to the characterization of Jeroboam as the
aggressor. Abijah is, therefore, neither advancing a policy contrary to that of Rehoboam nor rejecting YHWH's word that came to Shemaiah, since self-defense was not
prohibited. Of course, according to Chronicles, despite all military preparations the
enemy will be much larger than Judah's army, and the fate of Judah will depend on
whether the nation turns to YHWH for help. This word of YHWH prohibited Rehoboam
(and any other king) from attacking the North to reunite the parts of the kingdom. Its
lasting importance is never abrogated in Chronicles. For a different perspective, see
Japhet, *I and II Chronicles*, p. 689.

55. See the obvious example of Bethel (cf. Ezra 2.28//Neh. 7.32). It is worth noting
that this is the last time Bethel is mentioned by name in Chronicles. The other two
cities, Jeshanah and Ephron, are mentioned in 2 Chron. 13.19 but then nowhere else in
Chronicles. It is likely that the area was included within the territory of Josianic Judah,

he could have brought the rebellion of Israel against the house of David and YHWH (2 Chron. 10.19; 13.5, 8) to an end at that moment. But the issue extends beyond Abijah. Chronicles reports that no Judahite king ever initiated a war aimed at reconquering Israel.[56] This matter raises serious theological questions, because within the worldview of Chronicles, letting Israelites dwell in the Northern Kingdom is tantamount to letting them to live outside the kingdom of YHWH (1 Chron. 17.14) and follow a sinful religious path. To be sure, the Chronicler could not have told readers that Judah annexed northern Israel and reunited the kingdom, since the corpus of facts about Israel's history that was accepted by the Chronicler's community would have simply pre-empted such a possibility. The word of YHWH to Shemaiah provides the requisite theological explanation.

It is worth noting that the significance of the word of YHWH to Shemaiah does not vanish even after the destruction of the Northern Kingdom. To be sure, there is no possible theological need now to dethrone a non-Davidic king, but still the Judahite kings do not annex the North. The leading Judahite kings of the time, Hezekiah and Josiah, are characterized as rulers who encouraged northern Israelites to worship YHWH properly at Jerusalem, and they were largely successful in this endeavor, purging the North as well as the South from theologically improper cultic objects and installations (2 Chron. 30.1–31.1; 34.6-7).

There is no doubt that within the world of Chronicles, both of these kings could have annexed the North. This is obviously true after such a major political and military success as Hezekiah's defeat of Sennacherib,[57] and elsewhere Chronicles notes their ability to go north and effect with popular support a purge of altars and *bāmôt* (2 Chron. 31.1; cf. 34.4).[58]

whose northern border was probably similar to the eventual border between the provinces of Samaria and Yehud.

56. The Chronicler explicitly describes Jeroboam and Baasha as those who took the initiative in Israelite–Judahite wars. The only Judahite king who precipitates war with the North is Amaziah, who took this 'unreasonable' step only because YHWH caused him to do so (2 Chron. 25.17-20, esp. v. 20). Since Abijah's adversaries are his 'kinsmen', he attempts to avoid the battle.

57. The fact that historically Senacherib defeated Hezekiah has no bearing on the issue advanced here. Within the world of the narrative, not only did Hezekiah defeat Sennacherib, but he was 'exalted in the eyes of all the nations' and many brought him tribute (2 Chron. 32.23). But if so, why did he not annex the North?

58. Compare 2 Chron. 34.4 with 2 Kgs 23.15-20. It is worth noting that 2 Chron. 30.25 and 34.7 refer to the geographical territory that comprises both the North and the South as 'the land of (all) Israel' (ארץ ישראל). This reference conveys an important

The theological gap created by the failure to reconstitute the Davidic–Solomonic kingdom under such circumstances is only underscored by the fact that Hezekiah and to some extent Josiah are portrayed in Chronicles in a way that is reminiscent of David or Solomon.[59]

Yet Chronicles informs its readers in numerous ways that neither Hezekiah nor Josiah became kings of a reconstituted 'United Kingdom'. First, nowhere it is stated that the elders or chiefs of the northern tribes crowned these Davidides as kings over them, or that the kings took such honors for themselves. Moreover, the relevant narratives about these kings in Chronicles consistently refer to them as kings of *Judah* (2 Chron. 30.24; 34.24, 26; cf. 32.8, 9, 23; 35.21). This appellative stands in clear contrast with the use of the term 'king of Israel' for David and Solomon in the same narrative (2 Chron. 29.27; 30.26; 35.3, 4; cf. 35.18—which includes David and Solomon). Further, these narratives clearly imply that the *polity* over which these kings reign is the kingdom of Judah. For instance, they consult שׂרים who are clearly Judahite (see, among others, 2 Chron. 30.2, 6, 12, 24; 31.8; 32.3, 6; 35.8). When Chronicles describes Sennacherib's attack against Hezekiah and Judah, there is no reference to any campaign against Northern Israel. When he dies, it is 'all Judah and the inhabitants of Jerusalem' who mourn him (2 Chron. 32.33; cf. 35.24 for Josiah). In addition, had there been a new Davidic kingdom in the historical narrative, when would it have narrowed to 'Judah and Jerusalem' alone? There is no account of a second loss of the North anywhere in Chronicles.

Again the Chronicler could not have told the readers of the book that Hezekiah or Josiah annexed northern Israel and reconstituted the 'United Kingdom'. The corpus of facts about Israel's history that were accepted by the community for which Chronicles was written would have simply pre-empted such a possibility from even being raised.[60] The theological

ideological message regarding the land, as it goes beyond the actual extent of the territory of the Judahite polity. The text also alludes to 1 Chron. 13.2 (and to David) and may be seen as a veiled critique of David's treatment of the *gerîm* (1 Chron. 22.2). Cf. H.G.M. Williamson, *Israel in the Books of Chronicles* (Cambridge: Cambridge University Press, 1977), pp. 123-24.

59. E.g. 2 Chron. 29.2, 25, 26; 30.1, 5 (cf. 1 Chron. 21.2), 26. For a summary of the scholarly debate on whether the Chronicler portrays Hezekiah in terms of David or Solomon or both, see M.A. Throntveit, *When Kings Speak: Royal Speech and Royal Prayer in Chronicles* (SBLDS, 93; Atlanta: Scholars Press, 1987), pp. 121-25, and his contribution to the present volume.

60. Kings does not claim that either Hezekiah or Josiah annexed the former Northern Kingdom. In this regard, its claim is consistent with historical facts as we

explanation—that the existence of a divided polity is from YHWH, and so it cannot be overcome by human hands—shapes the stories about two mighty, pious kings, who could have annexed the North but did not do so. Although these two kings did not annex the North, it is not the case that they did nothing for their northern kinsmen.[61] As mentioned above, these pious rulers of Judah attempted to bring northern Israelites to worship YHWH properly at Jerusalem. They were at least partially successful in reuniting Israel as *a correct worshiping community around the Jerusalemite temple, its ritual, claims, traditions and leadership.*

These historical narratives and the theological significance they assign to these events in the monarchic past carried substantial ideological implications for Achaemenid Yehud and particularly for its relations with Samaria and the Yahwistic traditions of the latter. If the ideological proposition that northern Israel is to Samaria as monarchic Judah is to Yehud is accepted,[62] then two observations follow: (1) the Samarians are Israel, and (2) their polity is separate from Yehud and should remain that way, because it is YHWH's will. Yehud should not attempt to conquer and incorporate the North or any portion thereof,[63] even if this were possible,[64] and Yehud should also not attempt to build any alliances with the North.[65] Discourses about inviting the northern Israelites/Samarians to follow the LORD and, accordingly, to accept the exclusive role of the Jerusalemite

know them. For a likely reconstruction of Josianic Judah, see N. Na'aman, 'The Kingdom of Judah Under Josiah', *TA* 18 (1991), pp. 3-71, and the forthcoming volume in the European Seminar in Historical Methodology on this matter.

61. On the literary and ideological transformation of Israel when this kingdom ceased to exist, see my 'Gateway to the Chronicler's Teaching', esp. pp. 237-39.

62. It holds true in almost all cases, but there are a few instances of 'boundary trangressions'. In 2 Chron. 28.9-15, for example, the Yehudite readers of Chronicles are asked to identify themselves with pious Israelites rather than Judahites. See my 'Gateway to the Chronicler's Teaching', esp. pp. 237-46.

63. The northern Israelite territories that pious Judahite kings were allowed to conquer and rule were within the borders of Achaemenid Yehud (e.g. Bethel). Cities outside these territories (e.g. Samaria and Shechem) were never conquered by a Judahite king.

64. Historical circumstances in Yehud pre-empted such a possibility, but the existence of an Israelite non-Yehud (i.e. Samaria) and above all that of an ideologically construed anti-Jerusalem (i.e. Shechem, see section 3.e.) demanded a theological explanation in Chronicles.

65. On the undesirability of alliances with the North, see G.N. Knoppers, '"YHWH is not with Israel": Alliances as a *Topos* in Chronicles', *CBQ* 58 (1996), pp. 601-26 (612-22, 624).

temple are not only possible, but also commendable. But to be sure, these discourses carried a strong geo-political dimension. If the northerners dwelling outside the province of Yehud lived in a polity that allowed their full acceptance of the Jerusalemite temple ideology and ritual, then they may remain in their own towns (2 Chron. 31.1),[66] but if this is not the case, just as during the time of the secession and for all the independent existence of northern Israel, then pious Israelites must move to Yehud and fortify it (2 Chron. 13.13-17).[67] To remain in the North under these conditions is tantamount to forsaking YHWH and so makes them liable to divine punishment (cf. 2 Chron. 30.6-9).

Therefore, the concept of 'all Israel' here leads to a theological demand that the Samarians Yehuditize themselves and to a threat of divine punishment if they fail to do so. In the actual world of the primary readership of Chronicles, neither the Samarian center of power nor most Samarians would Yehuditize themselves or agree with the exclusive, Jerusalem-centered position advanced here. Within the worldview of Chronicles, the Samarian positions and actions would bring the wrath of YHWH against them. But even so, the political secession of northern Israel, along with all its implications, was due to YHWH, and it was not supposed to be overcome by human hands or words.[68]

e. *Shechem, Jerusalem, and Persian Period Yehud*

The first unexplainable decision in the story of the secession was the selection of Shechem over Jerusalem as the place for coronation. To be sure, the reference to Shechem was also among the core facts from which the Chronicler could not deviate. References that are a discursive neces-

---

66. Notice the key ideological demand that Hezekiah advances in 2 Chron. 30.8: 'Yield yourselves to the LORD and *come to his sanctuary* [i.e. Jerusalem], *which he has sanctified forever*, and serve the LORD your God' (NRSV, my emphasis). Northern Israel must acknowledge that it is impossible to serve YHWH by worshipping at any sanctuary other than the Jerusalemite temple. Thus, the Chronicler erects the boundaries within which a Jerusalemite-centered diaspora may exist. The issue is of a central theological importance and deserves a separate study, which I plan to carry out in the future.

67. Chronicles allows for exceptional cases such as Elijah, who remains in the North but is attentive to the Davidic kings and notes how they have gone astray by imitating and even surpassing his own kings in evildoing. The Elijah of Chronicles does not interact with the dynasty of Ahab but with the Davidic kings of Jerusalem (2 Chron. 21.12-15).

68. At a later period, the Hasmoneans clearly rejected this theological stance.

sity, however, do not lose meaning. Instead, they gain meaning within the narrative.

Although in Chronicles Shechem is mentioned only here and in 1 Chron. 6.51 (EVV v. 67) and 7.28, it is likely that the literati in Achaemenid Yehud would have been aware of the traditional and religious significance of Shechem and the associated Mt Gerizim. To be sure, for Jerusalemite readers in the Hellenistic Period—and for Roman Period Samaritans and Jews—the symbolic polarity of Shechem/Mt Gerizim and Jerusalem/ Mt Zion was an important theological component of some of their discourses,[69] and sometimes it deeply affected politics as well.[70] Even if Chronicles was written before the Hellenistic period and so before the building of the Samarian/Samaritan temple,[71] as is possible, the building of the temple strongly indicates pre-existing Samarian traditions associated with the city.[72] The Yehudite literati who lived in the Achaemenid period were well aware of these traditions. In fact, some traditions about the sacral role of Shechem were included in their own literature (e.g. Gen. 12.6-7; 33.18-20; Josh. 24.1, 25).[73]

69. See, for instance, I. Kalimi, 'Zion or Gerizim? The Association of Abraham and the Aqeda with Zion/Gerizim in Jewish and Samaritan Sources', in M. Lubetski, C. Gottlieb and S. Keller (eds.), *Boundaries of the Ancient Near Eastern World: A Tribute to Cyrus H. Gordon* (JSOTSup, 273; Sheffield: Sheffield Academic Press, 1998), pp. 442-57. Strongly worded, negative comments about the people of Shechem (or Samarians/Samaritans) abound in Jerusalemite literature from the Hellenistic period (e.g. Sir. 50.25-26).

70. The most obvious and dramatic case is the destruction of the Samarian/Samaritan temple by John Hyrcanus I (Josephus, *Ant.* 13.254-65; *War* 1.62-63).

71. The date of the building of the Samarian/Samaritan temple is a matter of debate. The usually proposed dates span from late fourth century to early second century BCE. For a summary of positions and reference to the main studies on the matter, see Kalimi, 'Zion or Gerizim?', pp. 455-57. The process of rebuilding the city of Shechem began by the late fourth century (Stratum IV). The city had become a major urban center in the Ptolemaic period (Stratum III). For a summary of the archaeological evidence and the main works on the matter, see E.F. Campbell, 'Shechem', in *NEAEHL*, IV, pp. 1345-54, and J.E. Seger, 'Shechem', in E.M. Meyers (ed.), *The Oxford Encyclopaedia of Archaeology in the Near East* (5 vols.; New York: Oxford University Press, 1997), V, pp. 19-23.

72. See also Sh. Talmon, 'מסורות במקרא על ראשית תולדות שומרונים' (= 'Biblical Traditions on the Early History of the Samaritans'), *Eretz Shomron* (Jerusalem: Israel Exploration Society, 1973), pp. 9-33.

73. The matter raises the issue of whether we might here too encounter a case of 'facts' upon which the community agrees, whose significance may be revisited but not

Chronicles could not have advanced spatial settings of the secession different from those agreed upon by the community any more than it could have changed the temporal settings. Lack of malleability regarding these facts necessarily led to the reference to Shechem in 2 Chron. 10.1. But whereas the choice of Shechem as the meeting place for the assembly is clearly understandable within the (hi)story narrated in Kings—and there it is due at least in the main to political considerations—the situation in Chronicles is vastly different. In the latter, a cultic connotation and above all an unexplainable dimension to the selection of the city come to the forefront. The readers of Chronicles are left to deal not only with the question of why YHWH caused the secession, but also of why YHWH made an anti-Jerusalem possible, an institution that could only lead Israel astray. The book's response is that the answer to this question is with YHWH, but beyond the reach of the Yehudite literati, including, of course, the author of Chronicles and its first readers.

---

their 'factuality'. But other alternative or complementary explanations can be advanced, and the whole issue is, of course, beyond the scope of this contribution. It is worth noting, however, that there are also several negative traditions associated with Shechem in the literature accepted as authoritative by the Jerusalemite literati that undermine the others. For instance, according to Gen. 35.4, it is a fitting burial place for representations of 'foreign gods'. One may note also the spatial setting of the stories of Dinah's rape (Gen. 34) and of the failed kingship of Abimelech (Judg. 9). Cf. Y. Amit, 'עריכה מובלעת ופולמוס סמוי פרשת אונס דינה' (= 'Implicit Redaction and Latent Polemic in the Story of the Rape of Dinah'), in M.V. Fox *et al.* (eds.), *Texts, Temples and Traditions: A Tribute to Menahem Haran* (Winona Lake, IN: Eisenbrauns, 1996), pp. 11*-28* (21*-22*).

FROM THE IMPIOUS MANASSEH (2 KINGS 21)
TO THE CONVERT MANASSEH (2 CHRONICLES 33):
THEOLOGICAL REWRITING BY THE CHRONICLER

Philippe Abadie

While wondering about the epistemology of historical work applied to the Bible, Damien Noel noted that this task is confronted by a double challenge: the patient research of past facts and the biblical representation of this same past through a theologically oriented discourse, which one also is obliged to treat as a fact of history. Before concluding, he writes, '…the study of Israel's history is not simply a historical operation, it is equally concerned with the theology of revelation, ecclesiology and the historicity of salvation'.[1]

In an obvious way, although by nature and by law strongly different, history and theology get tangled in this quest, where it is necessary to respect the specificity of both disciplines. The entire work of the Chronicler fits into the scheme of this direction as has been amply shown (among other works too numerous to be cited)[2] in the two preceding volumes of this series, *The Chronicler as Historian*[3] and *The Chronicler as Author*.[4] For the present study, my concern will be less with scrutinizing the connection of the Chronicler to history or to literature than of examining

1. D. Noël, 'L'histoire d'Israël en faculté de théologie?', in J. Doré and F. Bousquet (eds.), *La Théologie dans l'Histoire. Faculté de Théologie et de Sciences religieuses, Institut Catholique de Paris* (Paris: Beauchesne, 1997), pp. 59-71 (70): '…l'étude de l'histoire d'Israël n'est pas une simple opération historienne, elle concerne également la théologie de la Révélation, l'ecclésiologie et l'historicité du salut'.

2. But see the majesterial work of S. Japhet, *The Ideology of the Books of Chronicles and its Place in Biblical Thought* (BEATAJ, 9; Frankfurt: Peter Lang, 2nd edn, 1997).

3. M.P. Graham, K.G. Hoglund and S.L. McKenzie (eds.), *The Chronicler as Historian* (JSOTSup, 238; Sheffield: Sheffield Academic Press, 1997).

4. M.P. Graham and S.L. McKenzie (eds.), *The Chronicler as Author: Studies in Text and Texture* (JSOTSup, 263; Sheffield: Sheffield Academic Press, 1999).

certain features of his/her theological rewriting. In order to do this, I will focus my attention on the history of King Manasseh, who cannot fail to leave the reader perplexed, since the treatment of his reign differs from one tradition (the book of Kings) to the other (the book of Chronicles).[5]

The Type-Figure of the Impious Person: Interpretation of the Narrative of 2 Kings 21.1-18

According to the narrative of 2 Kings 21, Manasseh is the type-figure of the impious king. The deuteronomistic theological schema that underlies the exilic edition of the book of Kings in fact makes Manasseh directly responsible for the Judean deportation on the basis of the verdict announced in vv. 11-12: 'Because Manasseh, King of Judah, has committed these detestable sins... I am going to bring such a disaster on Jerusalem and Judah that both ears of everyone who hears of it will tingle.' The reforming work of Josiah can only delay this inexorable sanction, according to the speech of the prophetess Huldah to the king's messengers (2 Kgs 22.16-20). This point is made even more strongly in 2 Kgs 23.26-27: 'Nevertheless, the LORD did not turn away from the heat of his fierce anger which burned against Judah, because of all the sins Manasseh had committed against him'. The main point here is that the judgment has already been pronounced. This laconic nature undoubtedly explains the laconism of chs. 24–25 in dealing with the faults committed by the last kings of Israel,[6] as well as the final reference to the 'sins of Manasseh' in 2 Kgs 24.3-4, where the text cites the atrocities of the bands of Chaldeans, Moabites, and other Ammonites sent against Judah:

> Surely, at the command of the LORD all this happened to Judah in order to remove them far from his presence. It was because of the sins of Manasseh, all that he had done, and also because of the innocent blood that he had shed and by which he filled Jerusalem, that the LORD was not willing to forgive.[7]

5.   To say nothing of the other reports, such as the Prayer of Manasseh, texts discovered at Qumran, the *Ascension of Isaiah* 2.1–5.14 (trans. A. Caquot, in *La Bible. Écrits intertestamentaires* [Bibliothèque de la Pléiade; Paris: Gallimard, 1987], pp. 1019-33), or the image of the king produced by rabbinic tradition much later.

6.   The theological judgment is essentially placed in the deuteronomist's frame of the introductory notices of Jehoahaz (2 Kgs 23.32), Jehoiakim (23.37), Jehoiachin (24.9) and Zedekiah (24.19-20). The case is very different in Jer. 21–22.

7.   There we see a direct reference to 2 Kgs 21.16, in spite of what is written by P. Buis, *Le livre des Rois* (SB; Paris: J. Gabalda, 1997), p. 295. Moreover, we read this

Beyond these theological reprises in the interior of the book, the narrative structure of 2 Kings 21 manifests the inexorability of judgment at the same time that it constructs the portrait of the 'impious person'.[8] The affirmation of v. 9, which alone links the disobedience of Israel and the evil acts of Manasseh towards his people, appears central here. Around this, the narrative is organized in a chiasm:

A   Introduction (v. 1)
 B   General theological judgment against Manasseh:
                        'He did evil in the eyes of God' (v. 2)
   C   Detail of the sins of Manasseh (vv. 3-8)
      D   'But they did not obey, and Manasseh led them astray' (v. 9)
   C'   The 'judgment' against King Manasseh (vv. 10-15)
 B'   The worst of the faults of Manasseh:
                        'in doing evil in the eyes of God' (v. 16)
 A'   Conclusion (vv. 17-18)

Following the brief, typical introduction to the story of each reign (2 Kgs 21.1), v. 2 pronounces in a general manner the theological judgment delivered by the redactor with reference to election. One observes especially the contrast between the action of God on behalf of Israel and the evil actions of Manasseh that place him on the side of the 'nations'.

The pronouncement of the misdeeds committed by the king in vv. 3-8 was similarly a judgment, and of a sort more strongly developed than for any other Judean king. Manasseh finds himself reduced to the level of the rulers of Northern Israel, who had already been pronounced unqualified to rule the people of God. The narrative upholds essentially two counts of indictment that render him another Baasha of Israel:[9] the Judean king 'did

on p. 279: 'With Manasseh one has reached the point of no return, where individual reforms and conversions are no longer able to justify the existence of the Davidic kingdom. This is the logic of the covenant according to Deuteronomy (Deut. 7.4; 8.20; 11.17; 28.45; 29.21-27)' ('Avec Manassé on a atteint le point de non-retour où réformes et conversions individuelles ne pourraient plus rendre au royaume de David le droit à l'existence. C'est la logique de l'alliance selon le Deutéronome: Dt 7,4; 8,20; 11,17; 28,45; 29,21-27'). See also, P. Buis, 'Rois (livre des)', in *DBSup*, X, col. 703, where 2 Kgs 23.26-27 is identified as the key to unlock the door to this entire period.

8.   For what follows, see the very insightful study of K. Smelik, 'The Portrayal of King Manasseh: A Literary Analysis of II Kings XXI and II Chronicles XXIII [*sic*]', *OTS* 28 (1992), pp. 129-89.

9.   Smelik's Figure 9 ('Portrayal of King Manasseh', p. 141) attempts to highlight an apparent correspondence by noting that three of the expressions used for Manasseh

what was evil in the eyes of the LORD' (יעש הרע בעיני יהוה, vv. 2a, 6b; taken up again in v. 16b) and 'provoked his anger' (להכעיסו, 2 Chron. 33.6-7) by magical practices. To this the narrative will add further that he 'committed these abominations' (עשה...התעבות האלה, 2 Kgs 21.11a) and 'sinned' (hiphil חטא, 2 Kgs 21.17). In imitation of the nations that God had driven out from before Israel, Manasseh built high places and idolatrous altars, even though Jerusalem was where the LORD had inscribed his name forever (vv. 2-4). The height of Manasseh's sin is reached in the immolation of his own son by fire (v. 6), human sacrifice that returned to the practices of his grandfather, Ahaz of Judah (2 Kgs 16.3), and beyond, to the times of Ahab, king of Israel (1 Kgs 16.34). In the context of the larger narrative, the period of Hezekiah's reforms (2 Kgs 18–20) is totally overshadowed by a time when the king of Israel had offended the Lord 'more than all the kings who had preceded' (1 Kgs 16.33). Along the same lines, one finds the notice in v. 3: 'He rebuilt the high places that Hezekiah, his father, has destroyed, and he also erected altars to Baal and made a sacred pole (*asherah*), as Ahab, king of Israel, had done'.

Once again, the Judean king is compared to the 'impious' kings of Israel (Jeroboam, Basha and Ahab), which disqualifies his affiliation with the Davidic line. In contrast, it is said of 'pious' Josiah that 'he did what was right in the eyes of the LORD and walked exactly in the way of David his father, without deviating to the right or the left' (2 Kgs 22.2).[10] The erection of the graven idol in the temple itself (again, *asherah* of v. 7a) seals this tragic corruption of the double election, Jerusalemite and Davidic (vv. 7b-8).

This play on comparisons is a product of a 'flash-back'[11] that was intended to contrast the figures of Manasseh and Hezekiah on the one hand, and to link those of Manasseh and Ahab on the other hand. The two divine speeches in vv. 4[12] and 7-8 provide other dimensions to the play. They also

are also found in the report of 1 Kgs 15.34–16.13—only lacking the mention of 'abominations' (תעבות), which one finds associated solely with Ahaz (2 Kgs 16.3).

10. On several occasions, the book underscores this 'rectitude' of David (1 Kgs 11.33, 38; 14.8; 15.5), and with some variations, this same positive judgment is passed on various kings of Judah: Asa (1 Kgs 15.11), Jehoshaphat (1 Kgs 22.43), Joash (2 Kgs 12.3 [EVV v. 2]), Amaziah (2 Kgs 14.3), Azariah (2 Kgs 15.3), Jotham (2 Kgs 15.34) and finally Hezekiah (2 Kgs 18.3). The formulation of judgment is typically deuteronomic (see Deut. 6.18; 12.25; 13.19 [EVV v. 18]; 21.9).

11. See Smelik, 'Portrayal of King Manasseh', pp. 153-59.

12. One would note the interplay between this verse and 1 Kgs 14.21, which in the context of schism, introduces the reign of Rehoboam 'to Jerusalem, the city that the

give to the sequence its theological structure in setting the impiety of Manasseh directly before 'all the law that was prescribed for my servant Moses' (v. 8b). In this theological reminder, the saving acts of God appear in the past tense[13]—unlike the acts 'to come', which all signify judgment.[14] The reference to the Law introduces the place of the 'people' who, much more than the king and his descendants, will have to suffer the fatal consequences (exile and deportation) of the acts practiced by the impious monarch.[15]

This last remark helps to shed light on the assertion in v. 9: 'They didn't obey, and Manasseh led them astray'. Just like the impious king (כתועבת הגוים אשר הוריש יהוה מפני בני ישראל, 2 Kgs 21.2), the people of Judah are reduced to the level of the nations that God had destroyed before them (לעשות את־הרע מן־הגוים אשר השמיד יהוה מפני בני ישראל, 21.9). Beyond the parallelism of expression, the similar structure that links the personal faults of the king to the disobedience of the people prepares for the divine speech that follows. In it the focus moves from the 'impious' king to the whole of the 'guilty' inheritance, Israel.

In fact, the speech of the Lord is mediated by 'his servants the prophets' (2 Kgs 21.10-15) to respond to the faults of the king (vv. 3-8), without excluding the sins committed by 'Jerusalem and Judah'. One finds here similar literary proceedings, such as the reference to the nations represented in v. 11b by 'the Amorites', and the recourse to the 'flash-back' that alludes to the destruction of 'Samaria' (in v. 13a). In the same verse, one should call attention to the mention of Ahab, which forms a new response to v. 13: 'I will stretch out over Jerusalem the measuring line used against Samaria, the same level used for the house of Ahab'. From then on, the reader of the book is invited to read in this personal destiny (the death of Ahab, 1 Kgs 22) the fate reserved for all (the end of Samaria [2 Kgs 17], the first fruits of the destiny reserved for Jerusalem and Judah). Once again, the figure of the impious Manasseh appears to include Israel as a whole. In this connection, one can recall the verdict pronounced by the prophet Elijah against Ahab in 1 Kgs 21.21:[16] 'I am going to bring disaster

LORD has chosen among the tribes of Israel to put his name there'. See also Deut. 12.5, 11; 14.24; 1 Kgs 8.16; 11.36 and Jer. 3.17.

13. The nations exterminated before Israel (vv. 2 and 9); the election of Jerusalem (vv. 4 and 7); the gift of the law (v. 8).

14. The destruction of Jerusalem and Judah (vv. 12-14). See Smelik, 'Portrayal of King Manasseh', p. 138.

15. Smelik ('Portrayal of King Manasseh', pp. 160-63) develops this last point.

16. We also recall that in 2 Kgs 21 the context is clearly prophetic (see v. 10).

on you; I will consume you, I will cut off from Ahab the males, slaves and free men in Israel'. This last connection seems all the more pertinent, as in a prophetic context, the punishment is postponed (1 Kgs 21.29 brings to mind even 2 Kgs 22.16-17).

One will not be surprised henceforth that the judgment concerning the 'abominations' committed by Manasseh embraces the whole of Israelite history, 'since the day when your fathers left Egypt all the way up to today' (v. 15), without being limited to the personal destiny of the Judean king.

How does v. 16 fit into the logic of this theological narrative? Undoubtedly, it demonstrates that beyond the divine verdict, a point of no return has been reached. The mention of 'blood of the innocent' (דם נקי) by which Manasseh bathes 'Jerusalem from one end to the other' (פה לפה) makes the land lose its sacredness. It finds itself irreversibly defiled, profaned, reduced to the level of the nations. Everything in this pronouncement tells of the surplus of evil, the abundance attained in the horror, beginning with the opening of the pronouncement itself: 'and also' (וגם).[17] Saturated with non-sacrificial blood, the land can do nothing but vomit up its inhabitants, as Deut. 18.9-12 proclaims:

> When you enter the country the Lord your God gives you, you will not learn to act *in the abominable ways of the nations there*; let there not be found among you anyone who sacrifices his son or daughter to the fire, consults oracles, practices sorcery, divination, spells, charms, consults ghosts or spirits, or consults the dead. Because every man who does this is an abomination to the LORD, and *it is because of such abominations that the LORD your God is about to drive out the nations before you.*

Once again, Israel in its sin is assimilated into the nations.

The narrative conclusion of vv. 17-18 adds nothing more, except that it illustrates the judgment by a double stroke, in recalling (1) the abominations committed by Manasseh (v. 17), which have the value of (2) preventing him from being buried 'in the City of David'. The result is his burial 'in the garden of his palace, the garden of Uzza' (v. 18), a kind of

---

17. Saying this, we situate ourselves at a *single new narrative*, without ignoring the fact that the report is the fruit of a literary-historical complex. D. Noël ('La critique du pouvoir dans les livres des Rois' [thesis under the direction of J. Briend, Institut Catholique de Paris, 1985], pp. 202-10) distinguishes a double deuteronomistic redaction: Redactor 1: vv. 2-3, 5, 7a, 10-15, 15a; Redactor 2: vv. 7b-9. To this is added a redaction in *weqatal* in vv. 4 and 6. The author attributes, finally, v. 16 to a pre-chronistic redaction (present elsewhere in the book). From a very different perspective, Smelik ('Portrayal of King Manasseh', pp. 163-66, with n. 137) holds that 'the division of the text into different literary strands remains highly problematic'.

damnation of the memory that will also extend to his son Amon (see 2 Kgs 21.26).

As brief as it is, my reading of 2 Kgs 21.1-18 has illumined its theological choices, highlighted in the narrative as much as in reference to the whole of Kings. This reading will enliven the comparative interpretation of 2 Chronicles 33 and permit us to define more precisely its theological choices.

The Type-Figure of the Convert: Interpretation of the Narrative of 2 Chronicles 33.1-20

A simple look at a synopsis[18] shows that the Chronicler largely takes up the narrative of the book of Kings but makes an appropriate inflection: the reign of Manasseh is described in a double movement of sin (vv. 2-8) and repentance (vv. 12-13). This binary construction is not unique to this narrative alone, it is a consistent feature of the book, since one finds it in the reigns of Rehoboam (2 Chron. 10–12),[19] Asa (2 Chron. 14–16),[20] Joash (2 Chron. 23–24), Amaziah (2 Chron. 25) and Uzziah (2 Chron. 26). Yet one will note a significant reversal in the five cases cited, the 'faithfulness' precedes 'the sin'. That the opposite occurs in 2 Chronicles 33 gives the Manasseh narrative a particular tonality.[21]

From a literary point of view, the Chronicler takes over almost verbatim the deuteronomistic materials in vv. 1-9 (= 2 Kgs 21.1-9) and develops them according to the theological criteria in its conclusion (vv. 18-20 = 2 Kgs 21.17-18).[22] This dependence does not prevent a treatment quite

18. P. Vannutelli, *Libri synoptici Veteris Testamenti seu Librorum Regum et Chronicorum loci parallelli* (Rome: Pontifical Biblical Institute, 1931–34), remains the great classic. A. Bendavid, *Parallels in the Bible* (Jerusalem: Carta, 1972), pp. 151-52, indicates the differences between the texts by a change in color (in red). I also cite J. Kegler and M. Augustin, *Synopse zum chronistischen Geschichtswerk* (Bern: Peter Lang, 1984 [2nd edn, 1991]).

19. G.N. Knoppers ('Rehoboam in Chronicles: Villain or Victim?', *JBL* 109 [1990], pp. 423-40) has judiciously brought out the theologically structured character of this narrative.

20. R.B. Dillard, 'The Reign of Asa (2 Chronicles 14–16): An Example of the Chronicler's Theological Method', *JETS* 23 (1980), pp. 207-18, offers another example achieved by this theological formulation written into the narrative.

21. S. Japhet, *I and II Chronicles: A Commentary* (OTL; Louisville, KY: Westminster/John Knox Press, 1993), p. 1001.

22. Without entering into the discussion, I hold that the Chronicler used the book of Kings in a textual state near that of the MT. I distinguish my position from that of

different from the divine verdict (2 Kgs 21.10-15), which is summarized in a single verse (2 Chron. 33.10), nor does it prevent the omission of 2 Kgs 21.16.

More fundamentally, the author inserts material without parallel in 2 Chron. 33.11-17, material that is both historical and theological. Does the Chronicler depend on a source not possessed (or unknown, or even neglected) by the author of Kings? What about the imprisonment of Manasseh in Babylon (v. 11), which is not attested by any other biblical or Assyrian source? Without predicting an answer that will arise from the reading, let us note that an imprisonment of Manasseh in Babylon by an Assyrian ruler is historically very improbable; Nineveh would be a more credible place for such an imprisonment. This leads to the question about the nature of such a narrative: is it theological midrash or a historical document?

To respond to this, let me first attend to the structure of the narrative, which confers a place of central importance to the conversion of the king:[23]

A				Manasseh is king (v. 1)
	B			The religious *infidelities* of Manasseh (vv. 2-9)
		C		In punishment, Manasseh is deported to Babylon (vv. 10-11)
			D	Repentance of the king, following his deliverance (vv. 12-13)
		C'		Manasseh restores Jerusalem (v. 14)
	B'			The religious *reforms* of Manasseh (vv. 15-17)
A'				The end of the reign. Amon is king (vv. 18-20)

Undoubtedly, this structure serves the theological concerns of the author more than it informs the reader about the real history of Manasseh. By placing the repentance of the king in the center, followed by his deliverance, the narrative illustrates a theme dear to the Chronicler and makes of Manasseh an emblematic figure of conversion—in which he again fits into the Davidic paradigm.[24] If such is the case, 2 Chronicles 33 totally reverses the image produced by the narrative of 2 Kings 21. This new problematization of the figure opens up a double theological theme.

A. Graeme Auld, *Kings Without Privilege* (Edinburgh: T. & T. Clark, 1994), for whom both *Chronicles* and *Kings* depended on the same, older source.

23. Smelik ('Portrayal of King Manasseh', p. 170) proposed a slightly different structure (A, v. 1; B, vv. 2-8; C, v. 9; D, vv. 10-13; C', v. 14; B', vv. 15-17; A', vv. 18-20), which makes less of the opposition between Babylon (C) and Jerusalem (C').

24. If it is true, as has been shown by G.N. Knoppers ('Images of David in Early Judaism: David as Repentant Sinner in Chronicles', *Bib* 76 [1995], pp. 449-70), that David also represents in the eyes of the Chronicler the image of the converted sinner.

Personal Sins and Conversion

According to the theology expressed in 2 Kgs 21.10-15, Judah's short-comings have a cumulative value and reaches a threshold with Manasseh, without the possibility of return. No such thing is found in 2 Chronicles 33. There the emphasis is placed first on the personal shortcomings of King Manasseh. This provokes a series of modifications in vv. 2-8 (however with reference again to the author's source).

To produce an even greater effect of generalization, the author uses the plural 'baals' and 'sacred poles' (2 Chron. 33.3), instead of the singular in 2 Kgs 21.3. Similarly, in v. 6a the king makes 'his sons' (plural) go through the fire (compared to the singular 'son' in 2 Kgs 21.6a). The transgression is even more striking, as one contemplates its impact: the near-complete destruction of the royal line. One can read here a discrete allusion to another 'impious king' in Chronicles, namely Saul, who died with his three sons and all his house with him (1 Chron. 10.6). The resemblance is even more pronounced, since Saul (1 Chron. 10.13)[25] and Manasseh (2 Chron. 33.6) are both accused of consulting mediums.

Conversely, in v. 3a alone is the reference to Hezekiah maintained without the mention of Ahab and the parallel with him found in the book of Kings. Certainly, the book of Chronicles grants little place to the history of the Northern Kingdom and only mentions its rulers in connection with the kings of Judah.[26] It is Ahab, however, who plays an important role in 2 Chronicles 18, where he appears as the antithesis of the Judean Jehoshaphat.[27] Undoubtedly, this silence betrays a new theological orientation of the Chronistic narrative.

More than these slight changes in appearances,[28] one should remember the modification of 2 Kgs 21.9 that one finds in 2 Chron. 33.9:

---

25. Also, God turned (סבב) the kingdom over to David (v. 14b).

26. It would be wrong to conclude that the kingdom of Israel was not a real concern in the book. See R.L. Braun, 'Reconsideration of the Chronicler's Attitude toward the North', *JBL* 96 (1977), pp. 59-62; and especially, H.G.M. Williamson, *Israel in the Books of Chronicles* (Cambridge: Cambridge University Press, 1977).

27. G.N. Knoppers, 'Reform and Regression: The Chronicler's Presentation of Jehosaphat', *Bib* 72 (1991), pp. 500-24.

28. The question of the *Vorlage* used by the Chronicler has been under discussion since the discovery of the pre-Masoretic texts at Qumran. See S.L. McKenzie, *The Chronicler's Use of the Deuteronomistic History* (HSM, 33; Atlanta: Scholars Press, 1985), especially the Excursus, 'Chr's K Vorlage', pp. 119-58.

2 Kgs 21.9	2 Chron. 33.9
But they did not obey, *Manasseh led them astray*	But *Manasseh led astray the Judeans and the inhabitants of Jerusalem*
to the point that they did more evil.	to the point that they did more evil.

In this rewriting, Manasseh at first sight appears as the unique corrupter of his people, who are victimized, in turn, by an impious king. The tone of v. 10 is radically transformed: 'The LORD speaks to Manasseh and to his people, but they do not take heart'.

Only the first two words (וידבר יהוה) are common to both narratives. The reference to the prophets, which permits one to assume previous warnings, is not taken up by the Chronicler, nor is the divine speech that follows (2 Kgs 21.10-15) and draws the consequences of a long history of infidelity 'from Egypt up until this day'. The emphasis of the chronistic story bears has much more to do with the immediate context of the impious reign of Manasseh. If Israel—as its king—'does not give ear' to the commandments of the Lord, it is less of the people being rebellious and stiff-necked than a matter of them having been 'led astray' by Manasseh.

Again, the long history of Israel seems overshadowed[29] for the benefit of the immediate context, to the point that the narrative is theologically centered on the single figure of Manasseh. Such a perspective is consistent with the retribution theology that the Chronicler presents:[30] the evil committed by a king is followed by an immediate punishment, just as real-life justice is the immediate cause of numerous blessings. The addition of vv. 11-17 is a product of such logic, and these verses do not come from a 'historical' source unknown to the author of Kings. According to the

---

29.   One may note, moreover, how the exodus has little place in Chronicles (see Y. Amit, 'The Position of the Egypt Exodus Tradition in the Book of Chronicles', *Te'uda* 2 [1982], pp. 139-55). Elsewhere ('Quelle place occupe l'Exode dans le livre des Chroniques?', *Cahiers de l'Atelier* 482 [1998], pp. 90-100), I have attempted to account for the 'autochtonous' milieu of the book of Chronicles in opposition to the milieu of the Babylonian *golah*, which is the origin of the book of Ezra ('Le livre d'Esdras, un midrash de l'exode?', *Trans* 14, Mélanges Jacques Briend 1 [1998], pp. 19-31).

30.   R.B. Dillard, 'Reward and Punishment in Chronicles: The Theology of Immediate Retribution', *WTJ* 46 (1984), pp. 164-72; S. Romerowski, 'La théologie de la rétribution dans les Chroniques', *Hokhma* 35 (1987), pp. 1-34. One may see here an extension of the theme of personal responsibility such as is enunciated in Ezek. 18 and 33.

principle of divine retributive justice, the sin of Manasseh (and of him alone, to read the narrative) is immediately punished by the Assyrian invasion, followed by the exile of the ruler to Babylon (v. 11). The place of the 'people', which is important in the book of Kings, is totally over-shadowed here, regardless of all narrative logic. Distinguishing himself from the model set by his source, the Chronicler establishes an immediate relationship of cause and effect between vv. 10 and 11. In no case could the punishment be postponed to the more or less distant future, which would include (beyond the guilty individual) the community of Israel.

Is it necessary to see here only a mechanical view of retributive theology? Without totally ruling it out, let me note in positive terms that the author carries out a stunning reversal compared with the sequence of events in his source in granting a 'chance of salvation' to each generation, without expecting an accumulation of sins over several generations. Such a model will also work for Jehoiakim (2 Chron. 36.6-7) and Jehoiachin (2 Chron. 36.10), both punished for their sins by the armies of Babylon. Curiously, no such thing is said of Zedekiah.

The rest follows from these beginnings. The grim ordeal provokes in Manasseh a reversal, a true repentance: 'But in his distress, he sought (חלה) the face of the LORD, his God, he humbled himself greatly before the God of his fathers; he prayed to him' (vv. 12-13a).

Consequently God allowed himself to be moved by Manasseh, who then 'knew that it is the LORD who is God' (v. 13b). One finds again in this structure of a conversion, one that the Chronicler used in connection with David, after he sinned by taking a census of a people who belonged only to God (1 Chron. 21).[31] The restoration of Jerusalem (v. 14) and the religious measures that accompany it (vv. 15-16) are the concrete working out of the repentance, on a map that is more theologically constructed than strictly historical. One can compare these actions to similar ones undertaken by Asa (2 Chron. 15.8), among others.[32] In closer narrative

---

31. See Knoppers, 'Images of David in Early Judaism'. As Williamson has written (*I and II Chronicles* [NCB; Grand Rapids: Eerdmans, 1982], p. 389), it remains no less true that 'in terms of the experience of an individual, Manasseh furnishes the most explicit and dramatic example of the efficacy of repentance in the whole of the Chronicler's work'.

32. This repentance is a matter of a theological *topos* of the book, as has been shown by P. Welten, *Geschichte und Geschichtsdarstellung in den Chronikbüchern* (WMANT, 42; Neukirchen–Vluyn: Neukirchener Verlag, 1973).

logic, once Jehosaphat repented of his sin (2 Chron. 18.1b), he appears as the convert (19.4-11). We should note, however, a significant difference between these two texts: in both cases the speech of a 'seer' (15.1-7; 19.2-3) provokes the right act of the king; here the text remains elliptical, establishing a link all the more narrow and immediate between the response of God ('he listened to his plea and brought him back to Jeru-salem and to his kingdom', v. 13b) and the present action of the king (v. 14). The reuse of the verb בנה ('to build') is only appropriate here, since it reverses the previous facts of the narrative: Manasseh the sinner had built 'high places' and altars to all the starry hosts (vv. 3-5); once converted, though, he built an outer defense for the City of David (v. 14) before tearing down the idolatrous altars he had built in the past (v. 15). By means of this phenomenon of verbatim repetition, a reversal of facts is effected: the turn is from impiety to cultural reformation.[33]

The wording of v. 17a—'the people, however (אבל עוד), continued to sacrifice at the high places'—seems to limit the impact of such a collective return to God, curiously reversing what was read in v. 9. Would Manasseh be more skillful in leading his people astray than in leading them in con-version? The strange ending of this same verse does not remove, however, a certain loyalty from the people's sacrifices, which were offered, 'but only to the LORD their God' (v. 17b). It is necessary to separate then the improper place of sacrifices on the 'high places' (במות), which are in-scribed in the theological vision of the unique (deuteronomistic) sanctuary and the worship rendered, which did not involve an idol.

At the end of the narrative, and despite the very partial reprise of the theological judgment of 2 Kgs 21.17-18, the impression of Manasseh's reign left to the reader of the Chronicles narrative is far from being nega-tive. On the contrary, 2 Chron. 33.18-20 establishes a certain equilibrium between the impiety of the king and *his conversion*, the former bearing on the latter by means of repetition: reprise of the source–*conversion*–impiety:

---

33. Table 16 proposed by Smelik ('Portrayal of King Manasseh', p. 177) parallels 'Manasseh's sins with his actions after his conversion'. R. Alter (*The Art of Biblical Narrative* [New York: Basic Books, 1981]) has amply documented the importance of this phenomenon of repetition in biblical writings.

(v. 18) <u>The rest of the acts of Manasseh</u>,
   his prayer to God and the words of the seers who spoke to him in the
  name of the LORD, God of Israel,
    These are [written] in the Acts of the kings of Israel.
(v. 19) *His prayer and [God's] granting him,*
<u>all his sins</u>, his infidelity...and put up sacred poles and idols
   before he humbled himself,
   these are written in the Acts of Hozai.
(v. 20) <u>Manasseh rested with his fathers and was buried in his palace</u>.
<u>Amon, his son, succeeded him as king</u>.

Reading this conclusion to Manasseh's reign carefully, the king is inscribed in the long list of those kings who reformed worship, a list that included such luminaries as Jehoshaphat, Hezekiah and Josiah—a Josiah whose destiny was infinitely more dramatic, since he died in full youth, which could only be a divine penalty in the eyes of the Chronicler (2 Chron. 35.19-25)![34] The contrast between the peaceful end of one and the tragic fate of the other does not call into question the faith rattled by the Babylonian exile (book of Kings) as much as it does the conversion that is always possible for each generation (book of Chronicles). Each narrative furnishes a symbolic theology of the whole, rather than a direct, historical source.[35]

A Recovery of the Narrative Model of 1 Chronicles 10.13-14
My reading aimed to describe the unusual course of the royal figure Manasseh, from his impiety (Kings) to his conversion (Chronicles). In doing this, I have brought to light the appropriate theological accents of the chronistic narrative that fit with the idea of retributive theology. How else does one explain the extreme longevity of Manasseh's reign—55 years—other than by introducing the theme of conversion? Thus, the narrative does not rest on historically informative material, unrecovered by the book of Kings, but it constructs a theological 'fiction' through a

34. This holds true in spite of the attempt by H.G.M. Williamson ('The Death of Josiah and the Continuing Development of the Deuteronomic History', *VT* 32 [1982], pp. 242-48) to show that the report preceded the writing of the Chronicler and was picked up again by a late deuteronomistic redaction.

35. Quite correctly, J.-L. Ska (*Les énigmes du passé. Histoire d'Israël et récit biblique* (Le livre et le rouleau, 14; Brussels: Lessius, 2001) shows that the biblical writing 'formed' the believing conscience of Israel more than it 'infomed' Israel about its past. And that was the case for the book of Kings as it was for Chronicles.

narrative that owes more to the enlightening homily of the scribes of the Second Temple than to the factual accuracy of the events reported. By a curious reversal of elements, the rebuilding of Jerusalem by Manasseh after 'his conversion' fits the scheme of the prophetic announcement of the work undertaken by Nehemiah around 445.[36] This is something that one can also reread in light of Isa. 49.16-17: 'Behold, on my palms I have engraved you, that your walls are constantly before me. They hasten your builders...'[37]

For further support, one can approach the chronistic narrative from another point of view, employing the typological approach of P.R. Ackroyd[38] and R. Mosis.[39] Beyond the theology of immediate retribution, 2 Chron. 33.1-20 thematizes the theological sequence 'exile'–'restoration' on the narrative model of 1 Chron. 10.13-14. Thus, the personal experience of Manasseh can be read beyond an individual level as paradigmatic of the history of Israel, reflecting its own exile to Babylon.[40] In this way all could see themselves in Manasseh's conversion.

One can highlight various signals in favor of this reading. First, the description of the torture endured by Manasseh 'with hooks' echoes the fate reserved for Jehoiachin in Ezek. 19.9 ('in a cage with hooks [חחים]'), and the expression in v. 11: 'they will drive (הלך) him to Babylon (בבלה)' echoed, with a slightly different vocabulary, by 2 Chron. 36.10: 'he brought (בוא) him to Babylon (בבלה)'.

Second, the narrative maintains close connections with the reports of the reigns of Ahaz (2 Chron. 28) and Hezekiah (2 Chron. 29–32), who respectively represent the exile (the closed temple: 2 Chron. 28.24-25) and the restoration (the reopened temple: 2 Chron. 29.3-19). In particular, the description of the repentance of Manasseh in vv. 12-13 corresponds to the exhortation of Hezekiah in 2 Chron. 30.6-9:

36. R. Mason, *Preaching the Tradition: Homily and Hermeneutics after the Exile* (Cambridge: Cambridge University Press, 1990), pp. 169-70.

37. In place of the MT 'your sons' (בניך), one should read—with Qumran, the Targum and a Hebrew manuscript—'your builders' (בוניך), which forms an antithesis with 'your destroyers' in the following line.

38. P.R. Ackroyd, 'The Theology of the Chronicler', *LThQ* 8 (1973), pp. 101-16; reprinted in his *The Chronicler in his Age* (JSOTSup, 101; Sheffield: JSOT Press, 1991), pp. 273-89.

39. R. Mosis, *Untersuchungen zur Theologie des chronistischen Geschichtswerkes* (FTS, 92; Freiburg: Herder, 1973).

40. It is scarcely possible to sustain Smelik's 'historicist' point of view ('Portrayal of King Manasseh', p. 175).

> Sons of Israel, return to the LORD…and he will return to those among you
> who are left, those who have escaped from the grip of the kings of
> Assyria… Because it is by your return to the LORD that your brothers and
> your sons will be able to find compassion from those who deported them.
> And they will able to return to this country, because the LORD, your God, is
> merciful and compassionate and he will not turn his face from you, if you
> return to him.

Third, the attitude of Manasseh (and his people), who neglected the divine
warnings ('The LORD spoke to Manasseh and to his people, but they
did not pay attention [קשב]', v. 10) anticipates the events of 2 Chron.
36.15-16: the LORD dispatched to his people some messengers, who were
turned away in derision;[41] also, in his anger, God sent against them a
hostile army (ויבא יהוה עליהם את שרי הצבא אשר למלך אשור,
2 Chron. 33.11; and ויעל עליהם את מלך כשדיים, 2 Chron. 36.17).

If the reality of the exile is registered in vv. 10-11, the restoration of
Israel is equally suggested in vv. 12-13: at the heart of the ordeal, the king
(the symbol of Israel) turns his heart to the Lord, who responds to him and
delivers him from Babylon (v. 13). The themes and theological vocabulary
of this text immediately call to mind 2 Chron. 7.14: 'If my people who are
called by my name, humble themselves, pray, seek my face and repent of
their wicked ways, I will hear from heaven; I will pardon their sins and
heal their land'.

Along these theological lines, the action undertaken by Manasseh in
v. 14, 'afterward, he built a rampart (הומה) outside the City of David',
corresponds to the restoration undertaken by Nehemiah according to the
narrative of Nehemiah 1–7, as has already been noted.

Without forcing issues, one sees how the theological writing of the
chronistic narrative may be taken in a double manner, individually (through
the experience of conversion of the king) and collectively (the exile of
Israel and her restoration) without one interpretation excluding the other.
By these theological and literary means, the Chronicler reintroduces the
reality of Israel into the narrative, but in a completely different way than
the deuteronomistic author in the book of Kings. It is less about realizing
the reasons for the exile and its consequences, the collapse of the royal
Davidic institution, than about suggesting to Israel that its return to the

---

41. Aside from the reasons already adduced, this play on internal echoes in the
book explains the omission of the phrase in 2 Kgs 21.10, 'by the ministry of his servants the prophets'. The Chronicler reserves this mention for the immediate announcement of the exile.

land depends on its return to God in faithfulness—according to the word-play used on the verb שוב in 2 Chron. 30.7-9 (see above). In this light, Manasseh appears with all his ambiguities as the reflection of Israel, the believing community that must always repent. One understands henceforth the theological choices made by the Chronicler that led him to engage in a complete rewriting of this figure's reign.

THE RELATIONSHIP OF HEZEKIAH TO DAVID AND SOLOMON IN THE BOOKS OF CHRONICLES[*]

Mark A. Throntveit

> The space which the Chronicler has devoted to Hezekiah's story is one way of expressing that Hezekiah is the greatest Judean monarch after David and Solomon.
>
> —Sara Japhet[1]

Given the scholarly consensus expressed above by Japhet, what is the relationship between the Chronicler's three royal luminaries: David, Solomon, and Hezekiah?[2] The portrayal of Hezekiah in 2 Chronicles 29–32 comes at a crucial juncture in the Chronicler's presentation. This is indicated, in part, by the extent to which he diverges from his *Vorlage*, 2 Kings 18–20.[3] Nearly all commentators draw attention to the fact that 2 Kings and Isaiah devote the bulk of their accounts to such political matters as Sennacherib's invasion, Hezekiah's illness, and the Babylonian intrigue to elicit Hezekiah's support against Assyria (2 Kgs 18.9–20.19//

---

[*]   An earlier version of this study was presented in a special session of the 'Chronicles–Ezra–Nehemiah Section' of the SBL (Chicago, 1988) and appeared as 'Hezekiah in the Books of Chronicles', in D.J. Lull (ed.), *Society of Biblical Literature 1988 Seminar Papers* (SBLSP, 27; Atlanta: Scholars Press, 1988), pp. 302-11, at the request of Ralph Klein. It is a pleasure to dedicate this version to Ralph—friend, colleague, fellow Lutheran…and my mother's 'favorite adult forum speaker'.

1.   S. Japhet, *I and II Chronicles* (OTL; Louisville, KY: Westminster/John Knox Press, 1993), p. 912.

2.   In this study, 'the Chronicler' will be used to designate the anonymous author of 1–2 Chronicles, a work composed in Jerusalem sometime during the Persian Period. The book of Ezra–Nehemiah, while sharing some of the concerns of the Chronicler and coming from roughly the same time, is from a different hand. For a concise treatment of these issues, see R.W. Klein, 'Chronicles, Book of 1–2', in *ABD*, I, pp. 992-1002.

3.   See the helpful synoptic comparisons in *Hezekiah in Chronicles and Kings (Isaiah): A Synopsis by Ralph W. Klein*, available online at <http://www.ot-studies. com/Documents/hezekiah.htm>.

Isa. 36.1–39.8), relegating Hezekiah's reforms to a single verse (2 Kgs 18.4). In stark contrast to this, the Chronicler apportions three chapters to the reform (2 Chron. 29–31) and treats the more political concerns that exercised his predecessors in an abbreviated and theologically motivated fashion (2 Chron. 32).[4]

With regard to these more political concerns, the Chronicler's tendency to idealize pious kings by the omission of material deemed to be inconsistent with their characterization is particularly evident.[5] The omission of 2 Kgs 18.14-16 (the deuteronomistic first stage of the invasion that reports Hezekiah's capitulation and attempt to appease Sennacherib with tribute payments), as well as the drastic abridgement of 2 Kgs 18.17-37// Isa. 36.2-22 (Sennacherib's demand for capitulation through his messenger), and 2 Kgs 19.1-34//Isa. 37.1-35 (Hezekiah's appeal), provide the clearest examples of this perspective.[6] Less clear are the reasons for the Chronicler's presentation of Hezekiah's illness and recovery (2 Chron. 32.24-31//2 Kgs 20.1-19).[7] By adding a note stating, 'God left him to himself, in order to try him and to know all that was in his heart' (v. 31b),

---

4.   See, especially, H.G.M. Williamson, *1 and 2 Chronicles* (NCB; London: Marshall, Morgan & Scott, 1982), pp. 350-88; S.L. McKenzie, *The Chronicler's Use of the Deuteronomistlc History* (HSM, 33; Atlanta: Scholars Press, 1985), pp. 159-68; R.B. Dillard, *2 Chronicles* (WBC, 15; Waco, TX: Word Books, 1987), pp. 226-61; Japhet, *I and II Chronicles*, pp. 910-98; L.C. Allen, 'The First and Second Books of Chronicles', in *NIB*, III, pp. 602-32; and S. Tuell, *First and Second Chronicles* (Interpretation; Louisville, KY: John Knox Press, 2001), pp. 211-30.

5.   In his unpublished dissertation, W.F. Lemke has shown that the Chronicler usually idealizes pious kings by omitting derogatory material, 'Synoptic Studies in the Chronicler's History' (ThD dissertation, Harvard Divinity School, 1964), p. 245; see as well his 'The Synoptic Problem in the Chronicler's History', *HTR* 58 (1965), pp. 349-63. The retention of material critical of Solomon (2 Chron. 10.4, 10-11, 14// 1 Kgs 12.4, 10-11, 14), however, suggests that this chronistic characteristic needs to be used with caution. See B.E. Kelly, 'Messianic Elements in the Chronicler's Work', in P.E. Satterthwaite, R.S. Hess and G.J. Wenham (eds.), *The Lord's Anointed: Interpretations of Old Testament Messianic Texts* (Grand Rapids: Baker Book House, 1995), pp. 257-58; and my 'The Idealization of Solomon as the Glorification of God in the Chronicler's Royal Speeches and Royal Prayers', in L.K. Handy (ed.), *The Age of Solomon: Scholarship at the Turn of the Millenium* (Studies in the History and Culture of the Ancient Near East, 11; Leiden: E.J. Brill, 1997), pp. 411-27.

6.   See Dillard, *2 Chronicles*, pp. 255-56.

7.   For helpful suggestions regarding the significance of Babylon for the Chronicler's interpretation, see P.R. Ackroyd, 'The Chronicler as Exegete', *JSOT* 2 (1977), pp. 2-32.

the Chronicler has positively reinterpreted his *Vorlage* to present a blemish as a beauty mark.

As one might expect from this brief sketch, the secondary literature concerned with these chapters (especially ch. 32), their parallels, and the thorny historical and theological problems that grow out of their inter-relationship is immense, certainly too vast to be covered within this limited space. [8] Thus, this article will confine itself to one significant aspect of the Chronicler's distinctive account: the relationship of Hezekiah to David and Solomon.

The debate as to whether the Chronicler seeks to depict Hezekiah as a second David or a second Solomon continues to uncover proposed Davidic and Solomonic allusions in Hezekiah. While many of the comparisons between these kings are valid, there appears to be no means by which these claims may be judged. A modest start in this direction might be made with the proposal of two simple criteria: (1) that the alleged comparison be unique to the Chronicler, and (2) that the alleged comparison only occurs with reference to Hezekiah and David and/or Solomon alone. Justification for the first criterion arises from contemporary scholarship's reluctance to utilize material already present in the Chronicler's *Vorlage* in the construction of a chronistic theological perspective without extensive critical examination.[9] The same may be said for those elements of 'pro-priestly revision'[10] that appear in parts of 1 Chronicles 15–16 and 23–27. It will become evident in the course of this study that this criterion is of relatively little importance for this investigation.

---

8. Dillard (*2 Chronicles*, p. 226) provides a helpful introductory bibliography of materials that present the classic arguments and positions.

9. T. Willi's insistence on the importance of the parallel passages and consequent detailed analysis of the Chronicler's 'exegesis' of the sacred text found in Samuel–Kings serves only as a corrective to wholesale neglect of the *Vorlage*. See his *Die Chronik als Auslegung* (FRLANT, 106; Göttingen: Vandenhoeck & Ruprecht, 1972).

10. The term is Williamson's, who uses it to denote the redactor(s) responsible for the minor expansions in 1 Chron. 15–16 and the more extensive additions to 1 Chron. 23–27, correcting the Chronicler's neglect of the priests in relation to the Levites and providing Davidic legitimation for both. On the whole question, see Williamson, 'The Origins of the Twenty-Four Priestly Courses: A Study of I Chronicles xxiii-xxvii', in J.A. Emerton (ed.), *Studies in the Historical Books of the Old Testament* (VTSup, 30; Leiden: E.J. Brill, 1979), pp. 251-68; and J.W. Wright's counter-proposal in 'The Legacy of David in Chronicles: The Narrative Function of I Chronicles 23–27', *JBL* 110 (1991), pp. 229-42.

Such is not the case, however, for the second criterion. Here, much confusion exists, with the result that characteristic expressions applied to many of the Chronicler's favorites are adduced in support of the contention that Hezekiah is being presented as either a second David or a second Solomon rather than simply one of the pious Davidic kings the Chronicler holds up to his people. On the other hand, Japhet has recently argued that the comparisons drawn between Hezekiah and David and/or Solomon also appear for other kings, suggesting that the figure of Hezekiah

> and that of his reign, are idiosyncratic, with their own specific features and contours, determined by Hezekiah's personality, specific historical position, and the data from which his portrait is structured...a figure who should be seen in the lively particulars of his person, deeds and historical circumstances, rather than in the generals of a stereotypical 'type'.[11]

Both of these misappropriations can be avoided by rigorous adherence to our second criterion: that the alleged comparison only occurs with reference to Hezekiah, David and/or Solomon alone.

I turn now to an examination of the major attempts to see Hezekiah as either a second David or a second Solomon in light of these criteria.

Hezekiah as a Second David

The major attempt to see Hezekiah as a second David is that of R. Mosis.[12] This is a corollary to his suggestion that the Chronicler has adopted the reigns of Saul, David, and Solomon as paradigms of three possible situations in which Israel might be found: Saul's apostasy, David's faithfulness, or Solomon's future blessing.[13] Since Solomon's realization is by definition future-oriented, Hezekiah must be patterned on either Saul or David. Thus, Mosis calls Hezekiah 'a second David'[14] based upon the following evidence. First, 2 Chron. 29.2 claims that Hezekiah 'did what was right in the eyes of the Lord, according to all that David his father had done'. Second, 2 Chron. 32.1-23 describes Jerusalem's deliverance from Sennacherib and so parallels the description in 1 Chronicles 14 of David's deliverance from the Philistines. Both describe a victory over foreign powers as a reward for seeking either Yahweh or the ark, and

---

11. Japhet, *I and II Chronicles*, p. 998.
12. R. Mosis, *Untersuchungen zur Theologie des chronistischen Geschichtswerkes* (FTS, 92; Freiburg: Herder, 1973), pp. 164-69.
13. Mosis, *Untersuchungen*, p. 165.
14. Mosis, *Untersuchungen*, p. 189: '...einen zweiten David'.

Hezekiah's military preparations and the Assyrian invasion itself preclude comparisons with Solomon, 'the man of peace'. Finally, after claiming that the postexilic restoration of the cult in Ezra 1–6 is typologically Davidic, Mosis displays the parallels between this restoration and Hezekiah's cleansing of the temple and Passover (2 Chron. 29.3–31.1).

H.G.M. Williamson[15] has challenged these comparisons by arguing, first, that *Vorlage* considerations considerably weaken the force of 2 Chron. 29.2, which simply reproduces the earlier deuteronomistic judgment of 2 Kgs 18.3, itself a stereotyped formula.[16] Second, Williamson explains that 2 Chron. 32.1-23 has been carefully reworked to omit Hezekiah's initial capitulation (2 Kgs 18.14-16) and the taking of Judah's fortified cities (2 Kgs 18.13//Isa. 36.1), obvious *Vorlage* alterations that tell against Mosis. In addition, in Chronicles the victory was due to Yahweh's intervention, not Hezekiah's military activities ('the Lord saved Hezekiah', 2 Chron. 32.22, no parallel). Furthermore, the omission of 2 Kgs 18.7b-8 ('He rebelled against the king of Assyria, and would not serve him. He smote the Philistines as far as Gaza and its territory, from watchtower to fortified city') suggests that the Chronicler may have intended to portray Hezekiah, at least partially, as a 'man of peace'. Finally on this point, the unparalleled notice that 'Solomon went to Hamath-zobah, and took it' (2 Chron. 8.3) calls into question an unqualified depiction of a peaceful Solomon. Williamson's last observation is that the parallel with Ezra 1–6, of course, depends upon the prior assumption of the common authorship of Chronicles and Ezra–Nehemiah.[17]

Williamson's critique is convincing, but it by no means exhausts the possible allusions to David that have been suggested. In a detailed article discussing the Chronicler's thematic structure, Halpern[18] collects several

15. H.G.M. Williamson, *Israel in the Books of Chronicles* (London: Cambridge University Press, 1977), pp. 124-25.

16. Japhet (*I and II Chronicles*, p. 915) thinks that this is a 'significant element in the Chronicler's portrayal of Hezekiah' and questions Williamson's dismissal of the comparison as a 'stereotyped expression', noting that 'the Chronicler has systematically omitted all comparisons to David found in Kings…except for the stories of Hezekiah here and Josiah in 34.2'.

17. For another review of the persistent question of authorship in Chronicles and Ezra–Nehemiah see M.J.D. Selman, *1 Chronicles: An Introduction and Commentary* (TOTC, 10a; Downers Grove, IL: Inter-Varsity Press, 1994), pp. 65-71, and the bibliography cited there.

18. B. Halpern, 'Sacred History and Ideology: Chronicles' Thematic Structure—Indications of an Earlier Source', in R.E. Friedman (ed.), *The Creation of*

motifs that may be construed as effecting parallels, although it must be acknowledged that this is not Halpern's purpose in presenting these parallels and that he himself is convinced of the Chronicler's intention to portray Hezekiah as a second Solomon.[19] Of these, the motif of prosperity, often marked with the formula 'wealth and honor', is the most pervasive. 1 Chronicles 18.2-11 presents a series of reports depicting David's exaction of tribute. These may be paired with the notice that 'many brought gifts to the Lord to Jerusalem and precious things to Hezekiah king of Judah', (2 Chron. 32.23a, no parallel). It must be questioned, however, if the exacting of tribute is the same thing as receiving gifts. It is also striking that several texts dealing with David's transfer of kingship to Solomon (1 Chron. 22.3-4, 5b, 14-16; 28.1, 14-18; 29.2-5, 6-8, 12, 21) repeat the motif of wealth and parallel similar statements about Hezekiah's wealth (2 Chron. 30.24-26; 31.4-12; both without parallel in Kings). Third, David's regnal summary contains the notice that David 'died in a good old age, full of days, riches, and honor' (1 Chron. 29.28), which is picked up in the summary of Hezekiah's reign (2 Chron. 32.27-30, no parallel) and 2 Chron. 32.23b (no parallel), 'he was exalted in the sight of all nations from that time onward'. 1 Chronicles 14.1, 2, 17, might be cited as a closer parallel.

While all these references to Hezekiah's prosperity are without *Vorlage*, and so may be construed to arise from the Chronicler's intention to portray Hezekiah as a wealthy and highly honored king in the Davidic tradition, the Chronicler has also utilized this motif to enhance the positive portrayal of other pious Judean kings, most notably Solomon (2 Chron. 1.12, 14-17; 2.6-9; 3.4-7, 14; 4.7-8, 18, 19-22; 5.1; 8.17-18; 9.9-28), but also Asa (14.12-15, no parallel), Jehoshaphat (17.5, 9, 11; 20.25, no parallel), Uzziah (26.6-15, no parallel) and Jotham (27.3-5, no parallel).

A similar situation obtains with the motif of victory in war that is depicted as the result of the king's seeking Yahweh. David's victory in 1 Chron. 14.13-17 is paralleled with that of Hezekiah (2 Chron. 32.1-23), but also with those of Asa (14.6, 10-14, no parallel), Jehoshaphat (20.1-30, no parallel), Amaziah (25.7-10, 11-13, no parallel), Uzziah (26.5-6, no parallel) and Jotham (27.5-6, no parallel).

The presence of these motifs in conjunction with other Davidic kings lessens their significance for our purposes. This is not the case with

---

Sacred Literature: Composition and Redaction of the Biblical Text (Berkeley: University of California Press, 1981), pp. 35-54.

19. Halpern, 'Sacred History and Ideology', p. 51.

Halpern's isolation of the motif of Yahweh saving the king. 2 Chronicles 32.22 reports Yahweh saving Hezekiah and the inhabitants of Jerusalem and recalls the same notice with regard to David, who was also saved wherever he went (1 Chron. 18.6, 13//2 Sam. 8.6, 14).[20] The only other relevant occurrence (1 Chron. 11.14) is textually suspect precisely at the word 'save', though it, too, relates to David.[21]

Dillard has suggested other Davidic parallels for Hezekiah (listed in increasing order of probability):

1. 2 Chronicles 32.6 describes Hezekiah's appointment of military officers and 'mirrors the earlier work of David (1 Chr 23–27)'.[22] David's activity, however, is limited to ch. 27, which is to be regarded as secondary.[23]

2. 2 Chronicles 32.21, which mentions the destroying angel, 'recalls events after David's census (2 Sam 24 // 1 Chr 21)'.[24] The differences between these two accounts make the parallel somewhat improbable, even if the parallel satisfies the requirements of our criteria.

3. 2 Chronicles 31.11-14 deals with Hezekiah's provision for storerooms in the temple under the auspices of the Levites. Dillard pairs it with David's similar activities in 1 Chron. 9.26; 23.28; 26.22 and 28.12.[25] As only Hezekiah and David are connected in this way and in the absence of *Vorlage* difficulties, we may accept this judgment in the case of 9.26; 26.22 and 28.12. 1 Chronicles 23.28, however, as part of the pro-priestly revision, must be excluded from consideration.

4. 2 Chronicles 32.5b ('and he strengthened the Millo in the City of David') is the most interesting in this regard, since Dillard claims this activity 'likens Hezekiah once again to David and Solomon (1 Chron. 11.8; 1 Kgs 11.27)'.[26] While the Davidic reference is secure, the reference to Solomon has been omitted by the

---

20. Halpern, 'Sacred History and Ideology', p. 51.

21. Instead of the MT's וַיּוֹשַׁע ('Yahweh saved'), the LXX, Syriac and Arabic read וַיַּעַשׂ ('Yahweh did').

22. Dillard, *2 Chronicles*, p. 257.

23. Dillard, *2 Chronicles*, p. 174.

24. Dillard, *2 Chronicles*, p. 258.

25. Dillard, *2 Chronicles*, p. 251.

26. Dillard, *2 Chronicles*, p. 257.

Chronicler and so is found only in Kings.[27] I find myself in agreement with Coggins, who says that 'Here as elsewhere it appears as if a deliberate comparison is being made between Hezekiah and David'.[28]

5. In 2 Chron. 30.12, the expression 'the people acted with one accord' (literally, 'one heart/mind', לֵב אֶחָד), one of the Chronicler's ways of emphasizing the 'undivided loyalty of the people toward pious *kings*', finds an exact match only in 1 Chron. 12.39 (EVV v. 38), the report of David's accession.[29]

Further examples of the Chronicler's intention to depict Hezekiah as a second David that are not paralleled in his *Vorlage* and that apply only to these two kings are found in Hezekiah's royal speeches (2 Chron. 30.6-9; 32.7-8).[30] 2 Chronicles 30.6 refers to 'the God of Abraham, Isaac and *Israel*', recalling the same epithet in David's prayer (1 Chron. 29.18). The only other instances of this expression in the Hebrew Bible are found on the lips of Moses (Exod. 32.13, without 'the God of') and Elijah (1 Kgs 18.36). The tenor of this speech, which seeks to gather all Israel—particularly those 'brothers' from the North—for cultic reform, echoes David's similar concern at the start of his reign (1 Chron. 13.1-4).

The admonition, 'Be strong and courageous, do not fear or be dismayed', in Hezekiah's second speech (2 Chron. 32.7), parallels exactly David's words of encouragement to Solomon (1 Chron. 22.13), except for David's singular imperatives and Hezekiah's plural imperatives, due to their respective audiences. Furthermore, both pairs of imperatives are

27. See P. Welten, *Geschichte and Geschichtsdarstellung in den Chronikbüchern* (WMANT, 42; Neukirchen–Vluyn: Neukirchener Verlag, 1973), p. 71: 'Amazingly, apart from our place, "Millo" occurs in Chronicles only at 1 Chron. 11.8 in conjunction with David's conquest of the city. "Millo" is completely lacking in the Solomon traditions, where the expression, though occurring at 1 Kgs 9.15, 24; 11.27, is totally ignored by the Chronicler' ('Millo begegnet erstaunlicherweise in der Chronik, abgesehen von unserer Stelle, nur 1 Chr 11,8 im Zusammenhang mit der Eroberung der Stadt durch David. Ganz fehlt Millo in der Salomoüberlieferung, wo der Ausdruck 1Kön 9,15.24; 11,27 noch begegnet, was vom Chronisten völlig übergangen wird').

28. R.J. Coggins, *The First and Second Books of the Chronicles* (CBC; London: Cambridge University Press, 1976), p. 281.

29. Dillard, *2 Chronicles*, p. 245 (my emphasis).

30. On the significance of the royal speeches for the structure and theology of the books of Chronicles, see my *When Kings Speak: Royal Speech and Royal Prayer in Chronicles* (SBLDS, 93; Atlanta: Scholars Press, 1987).

repeated in 1 Chron. 28.20, where David again encourages his son (separated only by 'and do'), which refers to the building of the temple and is not relevant to Hezekiah's audience. Since it too makes use of the second pair of imperatives, Jehoshaphat's salvation oracle (2 Chron. 20.15, 17) might be cited in refutation of this evidence. It is the combination of the two sets of imperatives that is most important, however, and this combination occurs only in the references to David and Hezekiah.

Four items, then, meet our criteria: Hezekiah and David are compared concerning the matters of the storerooms (1 Chron. 9.26; 26.22; 28.12; 2 Chron. 31.11-14); לב אחד (1 Chron. 12.39 [EVV v. 38]; 2 Chron. 30.12); reference to 'the God of Abraham, Isaac, and *Israel*' (1 Chron. 29.18; 2 Chron. 30.6); and the encouragement formulae of 1 Chron. 22.13; 2 Chron. 32.7. We may conclude from this investigation that the Chronicler is concerned to depict Hezekiah as a second David in ways that other pious Judean kings are not.

Hezekiah as a Second Solomon

The most persuasive attempt to argue that the Chronicler regarded Hezekiah as a second Solomon is that of Williamson.[31] This argument is a corollary of his suggestion that 'in Hezekiah's recapitulation of Solomon's achievements it is as though the Chronicler is taking us back prior to the point of division where the one Israel is united around a single temple under the authority of the Davidic king'.[32] Of the evidence he presents in favor of his position, six items are especially cogent.

First, 2 Chron. 30.26 ('So there was great joy in Jerusalem, for since the time of Solomon the son of David king of Israel there had been nothing like this in Jerusalem') is 'certainly the most obvious link between Hezekiah and Solomon and it is one which could not be said of any of the intervening kings'.[33]

Second, 2 Chron. 30.23, in which the whole assembly decides to keep the feast for an additional seven days, strongly recalls the prolongation of the feast at the dedication of the temple by Solomon in 2 Chron. 7.8, 9.[34]

---

31. Williamson, *Israel*, pp. 119-25; *idem*, *1 and 2 Chronicles*, pp. 350-88.
32. Williamson, *1 and 2 Chronicles*, p. 351.
33. Williamson, *1 and 2 Chronicles*, p. 371.
34. Williamson, *1 and 2 Chronicles*, p. 371; cf. Dillard, *2 Chronicles*, p. 229.

Third, 2 Chron. 30.6-19 employs four verbs of repentance that figured prominently in Yahweh's answer to Solomon's prayer at the dedication of the temple (2 Chron. 7.14): 'repent, return' (שוב, vv. 6, 8, 9), 'humble oneself' (כנע niphal, v. 11), 'pray' (התפלל, v. 18; cf. 30.20, 24) and a synonym for 'seek' (דרש, v. 19; בקש in 7.14).[35] In addition, Yahweh promises (7.14) that if his people 'who are called by my name humble themselves, and pray and seek my face, and turn from their wicked ways, then I will hear from heaven, and will forgive their sin and heal their land', terminology that is picked up in 2 Chron. 30.20: 'And the Lord heard Hezekiah and healed the people'. While *some* of these verbs are employed in the descriptions of subsequent kings,[36] which is only to be expected given the paradigmatic nature of both the prayer and the divine response for the Chronicler's presentation, *all* of these references coalesce only in the Chronicler's treatment of Hezekiah.

Fourth, in the midst of 2 Chron. 30.9 ('[they] will find compassion with their captors') is an echo of 1 Kgs 8.50 ('grant them compassion in the sight of those who carried them captive'). The second half of 1 Kgs 8.50 was omitted in the Chronicler's parallel account of Solomon's prayer at the temple dedication, only to appear here in the mouth of Hezekiah, the second Solomon.[37]

Fifth, Hezekiah's immediate concern for the temple is emphasized at the time of his accession (2 Chron. 29.3) as was Solomon's (2 Chron. 1).

Sixth, at the end of their work on the temple (8.16; 29.35b) both kings receive similar summaries of their accomplishments.[38]

Williamson's other arguments for seeing Hezekiah as a second Solomon are less convincing:

First, it is difficult to see how *David's* words of encouragement to Solomon (1 Chron. 22.13; 28.10, 20), when repeated by Hezekiah (2 Chron. 32.7), make Hezekiah a second Solomon.[39]

---

35. Williamson, *1 and 2 Chronicles*, pp. 367-70.

36. Surprisingly, in 2 Chron. 33.12-13 the reign of Manasseh is portrayed in this way. I am indebted to H.G.M. Williamson for bringing this to my attention in personal conversation. His reading of an earlier draft of this paper and subsequent discussion are also much appreciated.

37. Williamson, *Israel*, p. 124 n. 4 (quoting personal conversation with S. Japhet).

38. Williamson, *1 and 2 Chronicles*, p. 351; cf. Dillard, *2 Chronicles*, p. 228.

39. Williamson, *1 and 2 Chronicles*, p. 382. Williamson's point—that Joshua's later use of the phrase to encourage the people (Josh. 10.25) strengthens the Moses–Joshua/David–Solomon typology—remains unchallenged.

Second, similarly, while it is true that the mention of 'Beersheba to Dan' (2 Chron. 30.5) means that now, under Hezekiah, 'the land is regarded as having returned to its full Solomonic extent',[40] the land had already attained that extent in the time of David (as 1 Chron. 21.2 makes clear), and is never so described in the Solomonic materials, even if it is strongly implied.

Third, application of material to Solomon (that has also been seen as Davidic) is found in 2 Chron. 31.2-3, where Hezekiah restores the divisions of the priests and Levites (v. 2)—as well as the prescribed offerings (v. 3)—after the fashion of Solomon (2 Chron. 8.12-15).[41] Ackroyd, for one, has argued that this 'echoes the activities of David, particularly in 1 Chron. 23–26'.[42] Unfortunately, the whole matter is complicated by the differing views these scholars hold on the presence of redaction in 1 Chronicles 23–27. On Williamson's view, which I have basically adopted in this paper, the Davidic material is secondary—part of the pro-priestly revision—and thus does not preclude the parallel.

Fourth, with a slight alteration of the MT in accordance with the LXX, 2 Chron. 32.22b reads, 'and he gave them *rest* on every side' (NRSV),[43] thereby including Hezekiah among those pious kings who received this special blessing for their faithfulness. While it is true that this concept is especially concerned with Solomon,[44] as Williamson notes, both Asa (14.1, 5-7; 15.5, no parallel) and Jehoshaphat (20.30, no parallel) were also beneficiaries.[45]

Fifth, similarly, Hezekiah's exaltation 'in the sight of all nations', (32.23)—while it does recall Solomon (9.23-24)—is also a part of the Chronicler's distinctive portrait of David (1 Chron. 14.17, no parallel), Jehoshaphat (2 Chron. 17.10-11; 20.29, no parallel) and Uzziah (26.8, no parallel).[46]

---

40. Williamson, *1 and 2 Chronicles*, p. 366; *idem, Israel*, p. 123.

41. Williamson, *1 and 2 Chronicles*, p. 373; *idem, Israel*, p. 122.

42. P.R. Ackroyd, *I and II Chronicles, Ezra, Nehemiah* (TBC; London: SCM Press, 1973), p. 187.

43. MT: וינהלם, 'he guided/cared for them'; LXX: κατεπαυσεν αυτους/וינח להם. See the discussion in Japhet, *I and II Chronicles*, pp. 975, 991-92.

44. See R.L. Braun, 'Solomon the Chosen Temple Builder: The Significance of I Chronicles 22, 28, and 29 for the Theology of Chronicles', *JBL* 95 (1976), pp. 581-90.

45. Williamson, *1 and 2 Chronicles*, p. 385.

46. Williamson, *1 and 2 Chronicles*, p. 385.

Sixth, the same may be said regarding the application of the motif of 'wealth and fame' (32.27-29) to Hezekiah.[47] As my preceding analysis has indicated, this important concept is regularly applied to the Chronicler's favorites.

Along these same lines, however, Dillard has discovered another possible Solomonic allusion in the detail of the reference to 'shields' (מגנים) at 2 Chron. 32.27, the section describing Hezekiah's wealth. Though some recent translations (NAB, JB, NJB) have emended the text at this point along the lines of the proposal in *BHS*, to 'jewels/gems' (מגדנים), Dillard appropriately remarks, 'Shields were kept in treasuries; this emendation would be at the expense of the author's effort to parallel Hezekiah with Solomon (9.16; 12.9)'.[48]

Halpern repeats many of Williamson's observations and adds one of his own, 'The notion of the priests' self-sanctification occurs only in the accounts of Solomon's and Hezekiah's reigns (2 Chron 5.11; 29.15, 34)'.[49] This is correct, as the Davidic reference in 1 Chron. 15.14—which would make this applicable to David, Solomon, and Hezekiah, not Solomon and Hezekiah alone—is part of the 'pro-priestly' expansion related to 1 Chronicles 23–27.

Eight items, then, meet our criteria: (1) the explicit statement in 2 Chron. 30.26; (2) the community's decision to extend the temple celebrations for an additional seven days (7.14 and 30.23); (3) the utilization of all four of the thematic verbs found in God's answer to Solomon's dedicatory prayer (7.14 and 30.6-19); (4) the echo of omitted material in Solomon's dedicatory prayer (1 Kgs 8.50) on Hezekiah's lips (2 Chron. 30.9); (5) concern for the temple at the time of accession (1.3-8 and 29.3); (6) similar summaries regarding their work on the temple (8.16 and 29.35b); (7) the use of 'shields' as a token of wealth (9.16; 12.9 and 32.27); and (8) the self-sanctification of the priests (5.11 and 29.15, 34). As was the case with the Davidic parallels to Hezekiah above, we may conclude on the basis of this investigation that the Chronicler was also concerned to depict Hezekiah as a second Solomon in ways that other pious Judean kings are not.

47. Williamson, *1 and 2 Chronicles*, pp. 386-87; *idem, Israel*, p. 122.
48. Dillard, *2 Chronicles*, p. 254.
49. Halpern, 'Sacred History and Ideology', p. 50.

Hezekiah as a Second David and a Second Solomon

The previous two sections have examined the major attempts to depict Hezekiah as either a second David or a second Solomon. On the basis of the two criteria developed at the start of this study (genuine chronistic material and application of the comparison with David or Solomon to Hezekiah alone), it appears that neither position can be sustained to the exclusion of the other. This suggests that a mediating position, in which Hezekiah is seen as both a second David and a second Solomon, would more fully account for the evidence. Dillard has collected a number of indications that this is precisely the case. It remains for me now to investigate those parallels and determine which are free of *Vorlage* dependence and which apply the comparison with David *and* Solomon to Hezekiah alone.

First, 2 Chron. 31.3, which records Hezekiah's provision for the regular offerings, echoes similar statements about David (1 Chron. 16.37-40) and Solomon (2 Chron. 2.4; 8.12-13).[50]

Second, 'Just as David and Solomon provided from their own wealth for the temple (1 Chr 29.1-5; 2 Chr 9.10-11), so also, Hezekiah provides from his property' (2 Chron. 31.3).[51] The force of this argument is somewhat weakened by the occurrence of this same motif in the reign of Josiah (2 Chron. 35.7-9). The fact that Josiah comes after Hezekiah adds an interesting wrinkle to the discussion in that this later appearance would not prevent the allusion from depicting Hezekiah as a second David and Solomon.

Third, 2 Chron. 31.8, which speaks of Hezekiah blessing the people, recalls the blessing administered by David (1 Chron. 16.2, cf. v. 43). The parallel with Solomon (2 Chron. 6.3) may be questioned on the grounds that 'blessed' (בֵּרַךְ) may function here with the meaning 'greeted' (cf. NAB), though that seems overly scrupulous. As these references are not applied to other kings (with the exception of 31.3) and since they are not present in the Chronicler's *Vorlage*, we may retain them as evidence for the Chronicler's patterning of Hezekiah upon both David and Solomon.

Fourth, a more qualified assessment is required in the matter of the appointment of the priests and Levites (2 Chron. 29.11-14; 31.2, 11-20).

---

50. Dillard, *2 Chronicles*, p. 249.
51. Dillard, *2 Chronicles*, p. 249.

While both David (1 Chron. 15.3-24; 23–26) and Solomon (2 Chron. 8.14-15) are involved in this activity,[52] and no other kings are so described, the Davidic references are found in sections regarded as secondary, and the Chronicler has been careful to present Jehoiada, the priest, in this way as well (2 Chron. 23).

Fifth, 2 Chron. 29.31-33, in which the people respond to Hezekiah's appeal with offerings and contributions for the temple, 'mirrors events at the time of David, Solomon, and Moses (Exod 36.6-7; 1 Chr 29.6-9; 2 Chr 7.7)'.[53] This characteristic motif also occurs in the Chronicler's description of Joash's reign (2 Chron. 24.8-14) and appears to be different from the *Vorlage* of 2 Kgs 12.9-16.[54]

Sixth, a similar judgment may be rendered with regard to the motif of 'success' (2 Chron. 31.21; 32.30). In addition to the important occurrences of this term in the reigns of David (1 Chron. 22.11, 13; 29.23) and Solomon (2 Chron. 7.11), Asa's reign is also characterized in this way at 14.6 (EVV v. 7) (no parallel).

A final theme supportive of this position actually arises out of an observation made by Williamson, who notices that the Chronicler is fond of adding a note concerning the assembling of all the people for major occasions.[55] This is especially true with regard to David (1 Chron. 11.3, 4; 23.1; 28.1), Solomon (2 Chron. 1.2; 5.2), and Hezekiah (30.1, 5).

Thus, while not every alleged comparison can be accepted without reservation, three items suggest that there is sufficient warrant for claiming the Chronicler is concerned to present Hezekiah as both a second David and a second Solomon: provision for regular offerings (1 Chron. 16.37-40; 2 Chron. 2.4; 8.12-13; 31.3); the blessing of the people (1 Chron. 16.2; 2 Chron. 6.3; 31.8); and the assembly of all the people (1 Chron. 11.3-4; 23.1; 28.1; 2 Chron. 1.2; 5.2; 30.1, 5).

Conclusions

If, as the evidence presented above would seem to indicate, the Chronicler has made an effort to portray Hezekiah as both a second David and a second Solomon, the question arises as to why he has done so. Two observations may be made by way of conclusion.

---

52. Dillard, *2 Chronicles*, p. 229.
53. Dillard, *2 Chronicles*, p. 237.
54. Williamson, *1 and 2 Chronicles*, p. 318; *contra* Rudolph.
55. Williamson, *1 and 2 Chronicles*, pp. 113, 366.

First, while this analysis has challenged Williamson's contention that the Chronicler sought to portray Hezekiah as a second Solomon, his major point, that the Chronicler's reason for this portrayal was to typify the restoration of the situation prevailing under Solomon—that is, the reunification of the old Northern and Southern Kingdoms under Hezekiah[56]—is strongly supported. If the reigns of David and Solomon are seen to be one, the parallels adduced between Hezekiah and Solomon are strengthened by the addition of those between Hezekiah and David, not weakened. Furthermore, once we have rigorously applied our initial criteria to make certain the case that it is the combined reigns of David and Solomon that the Chronicler seeks to reproduce in his portrayal of Hezekiah, many of the alleged parallels that were dispensed with can be cited as secondary evidence for the Chronicler's overall intention to provide a solution to the problem of the divided monarchy.

Further support for this interpretation is to be found in Halpern's interesting observation that there is a decided break in the narrative of Chronicles following the reign of Hezekiah: 'From Manasseh onward, the whole rest/prosperity/salvation complex disappears';[57] 'Hezekiah is the last king of whom it is said that Yhwh was with him, saved him, rescued him, gave him any sort of rest, brought foreigners to pay tribute to him, and so forth'.[58] In addition to the cessation of these common motifs, even such previously regular features as burial and accession formulae undergo observable change following the reign of Hezekiah. In the accession formulae the name of the queen mother disappears after Hezekiah, as does the stipulation of interment 'in the city of David' in the burial notices.[59] All of which leads Halpern to conclude, 'there is an inclusio formed there between Hezekiah and the "United Monarchy"'.[60]

Second, we are led then to ask the question: Are the reigns of David and Solomon best understood as a unity? Recent years have witnessed a growing consensus that they are. Otto Plöger was among the first to propose that David's preparation for and Solomon's construction of the temple formed 'a single, coherent act'.[61] This proposal was substantiated in a

56. See Williamson, *Israel*, pp. 119-31; *idem*, *1 and 2 Chronicles*, pp. 25-26, 350-51; Throntveit, *When Kings Speak*, pp. 110-13.
57. Halpern, 'Sacred History and Ideology', p. 41.
58. Halpern, 'Sacred History and Ideology', p. 49.
59. Halpern, 'Sacred History and Ideology', p. 48.
60. Halpern, 'Sacred History and Ideology', p. 50.
61. Otto Plöger, 'Reden und Gebete in deuteronomistischen and chronistischen Geschichtswerk', in *idem*, *Aus der Spätzeit des Alten Testaments: Studien: Zu seinem*

series of works that denied the separation of the David History and the Solomon History into two distinct periods and argued that both kings are treated comparably, since: both were selected by divine choice (1 Chron. 17.11; 22.7-10); both ascended to the throne with the full support of 'all Israel' (11.1-3; 29.22b-25a); and both were equally devoted to the temple cult.[62] Williamson's summary may be taken as illustrative of the current situation that sees the Chronicler concerned 'to present the reign of David and Solomon as a single, unified event within the divine economy for the life of the nation, in which the complementary nature of the two kings' functions plays an important role...'[63] But if the crucial point with regard to the interpretation of these two kings is the complementary nature of their function within a single, unified event, and if the Chronicler is in fact interested in presenting Hezekiah as a return to that golden age of the United Monarchy, his presentation of Hezekiah as a second David *and* a second Solomon is precisely what we should expect.

Furthermore, such an understanding of the Chronicler's purpose has ramifications for the overall structure of the books of Chronicles. The unity of David and Solomon's reigns, along with the theological re-establishment of that unity in the reign of Hezekiah, argues against subdividing the reigns of Saul (1 Chron. 10), David (1 Chron. 11–29), and Solomon (2 Chron. 1–9), and suggests that the following four-part division is most appropriate:

1. 1 Chronicles 1–9 offers a genealogical introduction focusing on the tribes of Judah and Benjamin (who comprised the Chronicler's postexilic audience), Levi (that is, the priests), and the family of David.

2. 1 Chronicles 10–2 Chronicles 9 deals with the United Monarchy of (Saul), David and Solomon. In addition to the material above, this section is framed by two crucial events in the history of the nation, first noticed by Ackroyd and subsequently employed by

60. *Geburtstag am 27.11.1970* (Göttingen: Vandenhoeck & Ruprecht, 1971), pp. 50-66 (56): '...einen zusammenhängenden Akt'.

62. R.L. Braun, 'Solomonic Apologetic in Chronicles', *JBL* 92 (1973), pp. 503-16; *idem*, 'Chosen Temple Builder'; H.G.M. Williamson, 'The Accession of Solomon in the Books of Chronicles', *VT* 26 (1976), pp. 351-61. For a convenient summary of the evidence see W. Riley, *King and Cultus in Chronicles: Worship and the Reinterpretation of History* (JSOTSup, 160; Sheffield: JSOT Press, 1993), pp. 85-86.

63. Williamson, 'Eschatology in Chronicles', *TynBul* 28 (1977), pp. 115-54 (140).

Williamson, Allen, and Throntveit.[64] The end of Saul's reign is marked by the statement that God '*turned* the kingdom *over* to David' (1 Chron. 10.14 NRSV). This is echoed at the beginning of Rehoboam's reign with the statement that the division of the kingdom following Solomon's death 'was a *turn of affairs* brought about by God' (2 Chron. 10.15 NRSV) where 'turned over' and 'turn of affairs' are both based on the Hebrew root סבב.

3.   2 Chronicles 10–28 treats the Divided Monarchy. Here the fortunes of Judah following the separation of the Northern Kingdom are measured against the yardstick of the united reigns of David and Solomon.

4.   2 Chronicles 29–36 is concerned with the Re-United Monarchy from Hezekiah to the Babylonian Exile. The Assyrian defeat of the Northern Kingdom (2 Chron. 30.6) and Ahaz's apostasy (28.6, 24-25) had dramatically reversed the situation at the start of the Divided Monarchy. Through his repair of the temple, reinstitution of worship, and invitation to the North to join in Passover, Hezekiah restores the ideal situation of David *and* Solomon that had been lost.

---

64.   See P.R. Ackroyd, 'The Chronicler as Exegete', *JSOT* 2 (1977), pp. 2-32 (9); Allen, *1 and 2 Chronicles*, p. 365; M.A. Throntveit, '1 Chronicles', in *HCBC*, p. 319; Williamson, *1 and 2 Chronicles*, p. 96.

Part III

THEMES

ASPECTS OF GENERATIONAL COMMITMENT
AND CHALLENGE IN CHRONICLES*

Leslie C. Allen

In Chronicles, Israel's mandate is to 'remember' God's 'covenant...for a thousand generations', according to the adapted quotation of Ps. 105.8 in 1 Chron. 16.15. Each generation has a responsibility to appropriate the faith handed down by its predecessors. The Chronicler calls on his own generation to pursue the path that leads to spiritual restoration. This policy by God's grace would make possible a break with the oppressive past that otherwise haunted each postexilic generation. A prime clue to the importance of each generation in Chronicles is the use of the phrases 'the God of their/your/our/his fathers' and 'the God of your/our/his father', generally employed in apposition to the divine name and occurring 32 times. Although no direct parallels with Samuel–Kings appear, most of these phrases had separate origins in older literature. Chronicles drew together different literary threads and wove them into a comprehensive fabric to promote its own theological agenda. My task in this study is to trace the traditions and texts on which the Chronicler drew as the basis of his recurrent phraseology and to see how he used it in particular contexts in order to shed light on an important aspect of his thought.[1]

*   I am happy to dedicate this essay to Ralph Klein in celebration of his scholarship. Our common fascination with Chronicles goes back a long way, to our respective doctoral studies on either side of the Atlantic and to a spirited exchange in *HTR* 61 (1968). In more recent years we have been fellow members of the congenial Chronicles–Ezra–Nehemiah Section at SBL Annual Meetings, ever learning.
    1.   Cf. the brief, helpful review by S. Japhet in *The Ideology of the Book of Chronicles and Its Place in Biblical Thought* (BEATAJ, 9; Frankfurt: Peter Lang, 2nd edn, 1997), pp. 14-19; also T. Römer's Excursus, 'Der "Gott der Väter" im "chronistischen Schrifttum" (und in Ex 3f.)', in *idem, Israels Väter. Untersuchungen zur Väterthematik im Deuteronomium und in der deuteronomischen Tradition* (OBO, 99; Freiburg: Universitätsverlag; Göttingen: Vandenhoeck & Ruprecht, 1990), pp. 344-52. Neither study makes a distinction between pronominal variants within the overall formula.

1. *'God of [David] your/his Father'*

In one of the Isaiah narratives used by the Deuteronomist, a messenger formula that introduces a speech the prophet made to Hezekiah is supported by a dynastic formula: 'Thus says Yahweh, the God of David your father' (2 Kgs 20.5 = Isa. 38.5). The appositional phrase refers to the continuity of worship within the dynasty[2] and in particular alludes to the blessings that potentially accrue to the contemporary heir of the dynastic founder. It corresponds in an *inclusio* to the phrase 'for my servant David's sake' at the end of the speech. Chronicles at times transfers material found in Samuel–Kings to a new context. In this case the complete initial clause reappears at the head of Elijah's letter to King Jehoram of Judah in 2 Chron. 21.12. The borrowed formula now has a negative function. It reinforces accusations that the king has not lived up to the dynastic traditions fostered by his royal predecessors, Asa and Jehoshaphat. In Chronicles David is a role model for Israel's worship thereafter, but Jehoram, married to the daughter of Ahab and Jezebel (v. 6), had failed to maintain such orthodoxy. In contrast, at 2 Chron. 34.3 Josiah, 'while still a boy, began to seek the God of David his father', by correcting the religious deviations perpetrated by his predecessors toward a pristine standard. Seeking Yahweh is the sum of spirituality in Chronicles. It is characteristically predicated of David and Solomon, who function not only historically as dynastic founders but theologically as spiritual archetypes. Kings who take David as their model become, in turn, role models for their successors and also for the postexilic community of faith. Thus in 2 Chron. 17.4 Jehoshaphat 'sought the God of his father[3] and walked in his commandments'. And, with a retention of the formula's original reference to David, in 1 Chron. 28.9 the founder king himself exhorts Solomon to 'know the God of your father and serve him with a single heart and a willing soul'. Dynastic succession becomes a window to spiritual commitment that each believing generation should emulate.

2. *'God of our Father(s)'*

This version of our basic phrase was evidently used in apposition to the divine name in postexilic worship, tracing continuity with past religious

2.   E. Jenni, 'אב *'āb* father', in *TLOT*, I, pp. 1-13 (8).

3.   The reference is to Asa rather than to David (MT, v. 3), which for good reasons commentators generally follow the LXX in deleting as an ill-fitting expansion.

tradition. Thus in Ezra 7.27 Ezra's testimony of thanksgiving begins, 'Blessed be Yahweh, the God of our fathers'. Similarly in 1 Chron. 29.10 David prays, 'Blessed be Yahweh, the God of our father Israel'. Here we may find room for v. 20, 'Then David said to all the assembly, "Bless Yahweh your God". And the assembly blessed Yahweh, the God of their fathers.' In this case the narrative formulation ('their') has been influenced by oral worship practices (cf. 'Yahweh, God of...our fathers' in the prayer of v. 18, to be considered below).

Returning to Ezra 7.27, it is significant that Ezra concludes his testimony by saying, 'The hand of the Lord my God was upon me' (v. 28). The progression from the general 'God of our fathers' to the personal affirmation 'my God' has many parallels in Chronicles, as we will be noticing later; we have just encountered it in reverse at 1 Chron. 29.20. In Ezra's case divine empowerment is in view, but usually in Chronicles human commitment, that of a new generation, is the focus when 'God of our fathers' is employed. In principle, both themes find parallels in the Psalms, though the precise formula does not appear. For the theme of (potential) empowerment we may compare the beginning of a communal lament, Ps. 44.2 (EVV v. 1):

> God, with our ears we have heard,
> our fathers have told us,
> the deeds you did in their days.

Chronicles is generally closer to Ps. 78.5-8 in its expression of an obligation to pass on the old, old story to each new generation in order to inculcate spiritual commitment. Verse 7 reads:

> so that they should put their trust in God
> and not forget God's deeds
> but keep his commandments.

Yet Chronicles can use the specific phrase 'God of our fathers' in prayers for empowerment. There are two instances. First, in 2 Chron. 20.6-7 King Jehoshaphat leads a communal lament: 'Yahweh, God of our fathers, are you not God in heaven? Did you not, God, drive out the inhabitants of the land before Israel and give it to the progeny of Abraham your friend forever?' Significantly, there follow in vv. 7 and 12 vocatives of personal commitment, 'our God'. Second, in 1 Chron. 12.18 (EVV v. 17) David, uneasily suspecting the activity of spies, expresses the prayerful wish, 'May the God of our fathers see and intervene in judgment'. One of his officers gives an inspired response to David's lamenting plea: 'Your God is the one who will help you' (v. 19 [EVV v. 18]). Once again there is a personal sequel to the formula in the phrase 'your God'; the tradition is ratified for the member of a new generation who espouses God's cause.

In 1 Chron. 29.18 the 'fathers' explicitly refer to the patriarchs in the course of David's passionate outpouring of praise and prayer: 'Yahweh, God of Abraham, Isaac and Israel, our fathers, keep these purposes and thoughts forever in the minds of your people'. Similarly, at the beginning of David's speech there appears, 'Blessed be you, Yahweh, God of our father Israel, forever and ever' (v. 10), as was noted above. The patriarchs are mentioned as implicit recipients of wealth from God. David's horizontal prayer, intended by the Chronicler for God's people across the centuries to hear, is that whenever the people are so materially empowered they may use their wealth in the interests of the sanctuary. Here too the self-committing vocatives 'our God' (vv. 13, 16) and 'my God' (v. 17) accompany the formula 'God of our fathers'.

3. *'God of your Fathers'*

The explicit patriarchal references I have just noticed in 1 Chronicles 29 are associated in earlier Old Testament literary traditions with this variant of the formula, 'the God of your fathers'. It refers in speeches to the fulfillment, realized or potential, of divine promises to the patriarchs, once in relation to progeny (Deut. 1.11) but generally concerning the land (Exod. 3.13, 15-16; Deut. 1.21; 4.1; 6.3; 12.1; 26.7; 27.3;[4] Josh. 18.3). When we compare these references with the evidence of Chronicles, apart from the patriarchal allusions in 1 Chronicles 29, two further parallels emerge. First, we can now appreciate that Jehoshaphat's prayer at 2 Chron. 20.6, in using the formula 'God of our fathers' as a petitionary variant of the formula used to address humans, was implicitly paving the way for the promise of land associated with Abraham in v. 7. The second parallel is of a general nature. It is noticeable that some of the Deuteronomic references to fulfillment of the promise of land already employ not only the patriarchal formula associated with it but its contemporary counterpart: 'the land that Yahweh *your God* gives you' (Deut. 1.21; 6.1-2; 27.3). Here is a relatively extensive literary source for the twinning feature that Chronicles puts to fresh and plentiful use.

---

4.   Here only the pronominal suffix is singular, referring to Israel.

The cases of 'the God of your fathers' in Chronicles are used in authoritative speeches and fall into two categories. The first category occurs only once. King Hezekiah, as part of his cultic reforms, makes a speech to the priests and Levites in 2 Chron. 29.5: 'Sanctify yourselves and sanctify the temple of Yahweh, the God of your fathers, and remove the filth from the sanctuary'. There is a parallel with a speech Ezra made to returning priests and Levites, to whose safekeeping valuables were entrusted during the journey to Jerusalem: 'and the silver and gold are a freewill offering to Yahweh, the God of your fathers. Guard them and keep them…' (Ezra 8.28-29). Comparison of these two cult-oriented texts shows that they relate to a new opportunity for religious personnel and bring a challenge for them to venture to play out their traditional roles in service of the temple. Their religious heritage is used as a lever to commit them to a new task from which they might otherwise be inclined to shrink.

The other usage of 'the God of your fathers' also relates to a challenge, but now to the people, and here again an Ezra text supplies a comparable postexilic setting. Ezra addresses the assembly that was guilty of breaking the Torah by intermarriage and exhorts them as follows: 'Make confession to Yahweh, the God of your fathers, and do his will' (Ezra 10.11). They drifted away from the God of the covenant nation, and they are urged to embrace their spiritual tradition afresh. In Chronicles the formula—in one case a counterpart to the formula—creates the same sense of blameworthy distance in contexts of warning and challenge. In three separate episodes speeches are addressed to members of the Northern Kingdom. The episodes comprise a series in which there is movement from a negative tone to a positive one. First, in 2 Chron. 13.12 King Abijah of Judah categorically warns the northerners against warfare with Judah: 'Do not fight against Yahweh, the God of your fathers, because you cannot succeed'. A complementary phrase 'your God' is noticeably absent from the speech; it is pointedly replaced by a dissonant 'Yahweh *our* God', with reference to Judah (vv. 10-11). Second, in 2 Chron. 28.9-10 the prophet Oded tells the northern army: 'Because Yahweh, the God of your fathers, was angry with Judah he handed them over to you, but you have committed killing among them with a rage that has reached up to heaven… Are you not guilty of sins against Yahweh your God?' There is dire warning here, but it is mitigated by the closing 'your God', which opens a door to restoration of their relationship to God. Third, in 2 Chronicles 30 King Hezekiah sends a message to Israelites in the North, tribespeople who had not been deported:

> People of Israel, return to Yahweh, the God of Abraham, Isaac and Israel…
> Do not be like your fathers and your brothers who were unfaithful to the
> God of their fathers. Do not dig in your heels like your fathers, but surren-
> der to Yahweh and come to his sanctuary…and serve Yahweh your God.
> (vv. 6-8)

There follows a positive motivation in v. 9: 'For Yahweh your God is gracious and merciful'. In this case the formula 'God of your fathers' is
replaced by one that lists the patriarchs; we recall that 1 Chron. 29.18 used
a combined version. Here the intention is to recall a great heritage shared
by northern and southern tribes. The doubled 'your God' winsomely offers
a new potential, in the second instance in a setting of positive divine
characterization. These three episodes poignantly present the nuanced
perspective of Chronicles toward the northerners. For observant readers
the formula 'Yahweh, the God of your fathers' recalls not only the three
patriarchs and the everlasting covenant associated with them (1 Chron.
16.16-17), but also the twelve sons of Israel, whose genealogies in terms
of twelve tribes that make up the people of God are painstakingly set out
in 1 Chronicles 2–9. By way of a fitting conclusion one may anticipate the
next section of the essay by referring to 2 Chron. 30.22, which depicts the
wonderful ideal of southerners and northerners worshiping together and
'giving thanks to Yahweh, the God of their fathers'.

4. *'God of their/his Fathers'*

These two varieties of the formula, referring to people and king respectively, may be taken together. The latter occurs in narrative contexts, the
former also in speeches. They fall into two categories, negative and positive. Let us look first at nine statements with a negative significance.[5] A
good starting point is 2 Chron. 28.6: 'Pekah ben Remaliah killed 120,000
Judeans in one day…because they had abandoned Yahweh, the God of
their fathers'. This providential reason seems to have an intertextual link
with Judg. 2.12, where the Israelites 'abandoned Yahweh, the God of their
fathers', who are identified as the exodus generation. Both texts use the
short form of the Hebrew third masculine plural pronominal suffix; elsewhere in Chronicles the long form is used in this version of the formula.
The texts speak of an ominous rift that had taken place. A generation of

---

5.   There is a tenth, already included in the third section, that occurs in a speech at
2 Chron. 30.7.

prodigals had left the spiritual home of their predecessors. There is also a close rapport between Judg. 2.12 and the divine explanation of the exile in 2 Chron. 7.22, in that the exodus generation is explicitly in view in the latter text: 'It was because they abandoned Yahweh, the God of their fathers, whom he had brought out of Egypt... Therefore he brought all this calamity upon them.' The parallel passage in 1 Kgs 9.9 has 'Yahweh their God, who brought out their fathers'. In this striking polarization of the exodus and the Judean exile the Chronicler preferred to use his distinctive generational idiom, thus accentuating the break with a positive past. He was doubtless influenced by Deut. 29.24 (EVV v. 25), which uses the same question and answer format as the Kings passage, but puts the answer in the form, 'It was because they abandoned the covenant of Yahweh, the God of their fathers, whom he had brought...' In 1 Chron. 5.25 a corresponding statement is made about the eastern half of the tribe of Manasseh, as representatives of the exiled Northern Kingdom, 'They were unfaithful to the God of their fathers', and so warranted divine expulsion from the land.

Other negative statements are on a less momentous scale and refer to the ever-present danger of a fresh generation dropping the torch of faith. According to 2 Chron. 21.10, King Jehoram of Judah 'abandoned Yahweh, the God of his fathers' and therefore Libnah seceded from the realm. This very statement of a break with spiritual tradition is made in 2 Kgs 21.22 concerning King Amon. The Chronicler has switched it to refer to an earlier evil king. In 2 Chron. 24.18, during the second, apostate part of Jehoram's reign, Judah 'abandoned the temple of Yahweh, the God of their fathers'. In providential reprisal they suffered defeat at the hands of the Arameans, 'because they had abandoned Yahweh, the God of their fathers', v. 24 repeats. According to 2 Chron. 28.25 Ahaz engaged in pagan worship, thus 'angering Yahweh, the God of his fathers'.

In Jehoshaphat's reign a shadow rests over the people, who refused to follow his spiritual leadership: 'Yet the high places were not removed; the people still failed to set their hearts upon the God of their fathers' (2 Chron. 20.33; cf. 1 Kgs 22.43). A literary arc extends between this text and 2 Chron. 33.17, where the reformed Manasseh has a better, if imperfect, effect on the people's spirituality: 'However, the people were still sacrificing at the high places, but only to Yahweh their God'.[6] The

---

6. The arc runs via the negative statement about the people in the reign of the good King Jotham: 'But the people were still acting corruptly' (2 Chron. 27.2; cf. 2 Kgs 15.35).

complementarity of the appositional divine phrases in these related texts accentuates the shift.

The last negative reference is poignant and tragic: 'Yahweh, the God of their fathers, sent word persistently to them through his messengers, because he had compassion on his people and on his residence' (2 Chron. 36.15). The divine overtures were rejected and there is now no room for a corresponding 'their God'. The absence is made blatant by the one-sidedness of 'his people', a regular complement of 'their God' in the common covenant formulation used in the Old Testament (cf. 1 Chron. 17.21// 2 Sam. 7.24). Yet, characteristically for the Chronicler, destruction and exile do not spell the end. The closing verse of Chronicles is full of reassuring hope, derived from Ezra 1.1-3, which supplies what was lacking earlier. Cyrus, in his divinely instigated edict to the Persian empire proclaims, 'Whoever of all *his people* is among you, may Yahweh *his God* be with him' (2 Chron. 36.23). Divine provision is made for positive actualization, with restoration of the two-sidedness of the covenant relationship.

I turn now to positive narrative statements that use these varieties of the formula. They are ten in number. In the second section of this study I have already had occasion to deal with two of them, in 1 Chron. 29.20 and 2 Chron. 30.22. Two new ones relate to the Northern Kingdom, as part of the Chronicler's agenda to convince his Judean constituency of the traditional inclusivity and spiritual potential of the people of the North. In 2 Chron. 11.16, just after the division of the kingdom, 'Those who set their hearts to seek Yahweh, the God of Israel, came...from all the tribes of Israel to Jerusalem to sacrifice to Yahweh, the God of their fathers'. And in 2 Chron. 30.18-19, when the Northern Kingdom had fallen and only one kingdom remained, Hezekiah prays with similar language for ritually unclean northerners who wanted to celebrate Passover at the temple: 'May Yahweh, who is good, make atonement on behalf of anyone who sets his heart to seek Yahweh, the God of his fathers'.

The rest of the occurrences lay out ideals of traditional spirituality that were embraced by Judah, though in some cases northerners too are included. Thus in 2 Chron. 13.18, after open conflict with the Northern Kingdom, 'the Judeans prevailed because they relied on Yahweh, the God of their fathers'. In 2 Chron. 14.3 (EVV v. 4) 'Asa commanded Judah to seek Yahweh, the God of their fathers, and to practice the Torah and the body of commandments'. Subsequent success is attributed to the reason that 'we have sought Yahweh our God' (v. 6 [EVV v. 7]), with repetition of the verb to seek and capping of the divine formula by its contemporary counterpart.

In 2 Chron. 15.12, still in Asa's reign, Judah, along with northern refugees, 'entered into a covenant to seek Yahweh, the God of their fathers, with all their hearts and souls'. In 2 Chron. 19.4 Jehoshaphat, after Asa's subsequent apostasy, 'brought them'—namely, 'the people from Beersheba to the mountainous region of Ephraim'—'back to Yahweh, the God of their fathers'. In 2 Chron. 33.12 Manasseh is used as a model for all such repentant restoration: 'He entreated Yahweh his God and humbled himself intensely before the God of his fathers'. Again the complementarity of the divine formulas attests the appropriation of spiritual traditions. Finally, in 2 Chronicles 34, in the course of Josiah's response to the finding of the Torah scroll, the residents of Jerusalem, threatened by Huldah's prediction of their coming involvement in Jerusalem's fall (vv. 24-28), 'acted according to the covenant of God, the God of their fathers' (v. 32). Northerners too were caught up in Josiah's reforming zeal: 'He made all that were found in Israel to worship Yahweh their God. As long as he lived, they did not stop following Yahweh, the God of their fathers' (v. 33). This northern experience is graced with the complementary formula of appropriation.

Conclusions

With or without that complementary formula, the comprehensive phrase 'the God of...father(s)' in all its varieties is a powerful indicator of actualization or its absence in Chronicles. The Chronicler employed older literary traditions, direct intertextuality with earlier material, and current liturgical and cultic usage in order to disseminate the overall formula throughout his work as a rhetorical device for spiritual challenge and commitment. The purpose of his creative borrowing was that his own and later generations might firmly grasp the baton of traditional faith, while they each ran their laps as living representatives of the faith community.

Throughout this investigation the second noun of the formula has been consistently rendered as 'father(s)', in order to capture the comprehensive, repetitive uniformity of the Hebrew. If one asks who precisely are included, a limited range of equivalents present themselves. Sometimes it is the patriarchs who are in view. Once it is the exodus generation. At times it is the immediately preceding generation. Most often the reference is a general one, to preceding generations, with or without a temporal distance from the present generation. Modern versions have tackled this issue in different ways. The NIV and NJPS have followed the traditional English rendering 'father(s)' throughout. Other versions, aware of the archaism and/or preferring inclusive language, have avoided 'father(s)' when it does not refer to male parentage. Thus the GNB, NJB, and NRSV use 'ancestors' (and 'ancestor' in 1 Chron. 29.10). The REB has two policies, reflecting an evident fact that Chronicles had two (sets of) translators for the two books. In 1 Chronicles the traditional 'fathers' is retained. In 2 Chronicles, however, 'forefathers' occurs, but with exegetical nicety 'fathers' appears in 2 Chron. 11.16; 15.12; 30.7, as references to immediately preceding generations.[7] The option 'ancestors' is often too limiting a rendering in Chronicles. 'Predecessors' or 'forebears' would be a better inclusive choice in most cases.

---

7.   I am surprised by the inconsistent renderings 'the God of his fathers' in 2 Chron. 21.10 and 'the God of David your father' in v. 12, which appear to be carelessly taken over from the NEB.

THE ARK IN CHRONICLES

Christopher T. Begg

In Jer. 3.16 one meets the striking announcement: 'in those days, says the Lord, they shall no more say, "the ark of the covenant of the Lord (ארון ברית יהוה)". It shall not come to mind, or be remembered or missed; it shall not be made again.'[1] The concluding part of this announcement was, in fact, historically verified. Jewish tradition (see *b. Yom.* 21b, 54b) attests that an ark was not part of the fabric of the Second Temple. Matters are, however, more complicated regarding the fulfillment of the prophet's prediction about the ark's not 'coming to mind, being remembered or missed' in the future. On the one hand, in a series of exilic/ postexilic writings (i.e. Ezra–Nehemiah, Second/Third Isaiah, Ezekiel, Haggai, Zechariah, and Malachi)—their (greater or lesser) cultic interests notwithstanding—there is indeed no mention of the ark. On the other hand, in another key postexilic document (Chronicles), one meets no less than 46 occurrences of the term ארון (often with some further specification) in reference to the 'ark' of the First Temple[2]—to say nothing of the ark's prominent place in two other complexes that received their final form in

---

1.   On this text see H. Cazelles, 'Israël du nord et arche d'alliance, Jér 3.16', *VT* 18 (1968), pp. 147-58; M. Weinfeld, 'Jeremiah and the Spiritual Metamorphosis of Israel', *ZAW* 88 (1976), pp. 17-56 (19-26); C. Schäfer-Lichtenberger, '"Sie wird nicht wieder hergestellt werden." Anmerkungen zum Verlust der Lade', in E. Blum (ed.), *Mincha. Festgabe für Rolf Rendtorff zum 75. Geburtstag* (Neukirchen–Vluyn: Neukirchener Verlag, 2000), pp. 229-41. Throughout this article the RSV translation is followed.

2.   The term ארון occurs an additional four times in Chronicles (2 Chron. 24.8, 10, 11 [twice]); here, however, the reference is to the wooden 'chest' used for collecting monies for the repair of the temple. On the Chronicler's various specifying designations for the ark, see G. von Rad, *Das Geschichtsbild des chronistischen Werkes* (BWANT, 54; Stuttgart: W. Kohlhammer, 1930), pp. 46-47 and n. 36; S. Japhet, *The Ideology of the Book of Chronicles and its Place in Biblical Thought* (BEATAJ, 9; New York: Peter Lang, 2nd edn, 1989), pp. 96-100.

the exilic/postexilic period (i.e. DtrH and P).[3] The Chronicler's obvious interest in an object that was not a component of the temple of his time and that had presumably disappeared from the scene already centuries before[4] has long been noted as something remarkable, and various suggestions have been proposed to account for that interest. In this study, I wish to review such proposals and to offer some reflections of my own on the matter. First, however, it is necessary to consider in more detail what the Chronicler reports about the history of the ark, particularly in relation to the account given of it in his source, Samuel–Kings.[5]

The Ark's Progress

It is striking that of the 46 references to the ark in Chronicles, the overwhelming majority (39) occurs in just two central contexts: David's transfer of the ark to Jerusalem (1 Chron. 13–16) and Solomon's installation of the ark in the temple (2 Chron. 5–6). Of the remaining, 'peripheral' references to the term, the first appears as part of the 'genealogical prologue', 1 Chronicles 1–9.[6] To his listing of the three family lines descended from Levi in 1 Chron. 6.1-15 (EVV 6.16-30), the Chronicler appends the following statement:

> These are the men whom David put in charge of the service of song in the house of the Lord after the ark rested there (ממנוח הארון). They ministered with song before the tabernacle of the tent of meeting, until Solomon had built the house of the Lord in Jerusalem; and they performed their service in due order. (6.16-17 [EVV 6.31-32])

With this first mention the Chronicler presumes 'the ark' to be an entity familiar to his audience. He likewise establishes a whole series of key

---

3. On the conceptions of the ark in these two documents, see Schäfer-Lichtenberger, 'Verlust', pp. 235-39.

4. Of course, we do not know when and in what circumstances the ark actually 'disappeared'; for a discussion of the subject, see M. Haran, 'The Disappearance of the Ark', *IEJ* 13 (1963), pp. 46-58 (he holds that the ark disappeared under the impious King Manasseh).

5. For the purposes of this investigation, I shall be working with the following, widely-shared presuppositions about Chronicles: (1) Chronicles and Ezra–Nehemiah are two separate works; (2) Chronicles dates from the later postexilic (middle-late Persian/early Hellenistic) period; and (3) the Chronicler is literarily dependent on some form of the books of Samuel–Kings.

6. On this segment, see M. Oeming, *Das wahre Israel: Die 'genealogische Vorhalle' 1 Chronik 1–9* (BWANT, 128; Stuttgart: W. Kohlhammer, 1990).

associations for the ark that will be developed in his subsequent references to it: 'rest', the Levites, their musical activities, the two great patrons of the ark, Kings David and Solomon, and its temporary (the 'tent') and permanent (the temple) residences.

The ark makes a much more prominent appearance early on in the Chronicler's story of King David (1 Chron. 10–29), that is, in 1 Chronicles 13–16,[7] where it is brought by him from Kiriath-jearim to Jerusalem and where the term 'ark' occurs no less than 29 times. The Chronicler's source for this narrative is 2 Samuel 6, the conclusion of the so-called Ark Narrative (1 Sam. 4–6; 2 Sam. 6).[8] David's fetching of the ark, as described in 2 Samuel 6, transpires in two stages, the first abortive (vv. 1-11) and the second successful (vv. 12-23). The Chronicler reproduces this double movement of the source story in 1 Chron. 13.5-14 and 15.25–16.3, 43.[9] At the same time he also amplifies his version of these source segments at the beginning (1 Chron. 13.1-4, David's proposal that all Israel now attend to the ark [no *Vorlage*]), the middle (1 Chron. 14.1-17//2 Sam. 5.11-25, Hiram's assistance in David's building projects, the confirmation of David's kingship, his Jerusalem-born children, and double victory over the Philistines; and 15.1-24, David's instructions to the Levites in view of his second, upcoming attempt at moving the ark [no *Vorlage*]), and end (16.4-42, David's additional instructions to the Levites following the

7. On this segment, see R. Mosis, *Untersuchungen zur Theologie des chronistischen Geschichtswerkes* (FTS, 92; Freiburg: Herder, 1973), pp. 44-81; P. Welten, 'Lade-Tempel-Jerusalem: zur Theologie der Chronikbücher', in A.J.H. Gunneweg and O. Kaiser (eds.), *Textgemäss. Aufsätze und Beiträge zur Hermeneutik des Alten Testaments. Festschrift E. Würthwein* (Göttingen: Vandenhoeck & Ruprecht, 1979), pp. 169-83 (173-77); T.C. Eskenazi, 'A Literary Approach to Chronicles' Ark Narrative in 1 Chronicles 13–16', in A.B. Beck *et al.* (eds.), *Fortunate the Eyes that See: Essays in Honor of David Noel Freedman in Celebration of his Seventieth Birthday* (Grand Rapids: Eerdmans, 1995), pp. 258-74; N. Dennerlein, *Die Bedeutung Jerusalems in den Chronikbüchern* (BEATAJ, 46; New York: Peter Lang, 1999), pp. 38-67.

8. The Chronicler, who begins his continuous narrative only with the death of Saul (1 Chron. 10) leaves aside the earlier portion of the Ark Narrative (1 Sam. 4–6) that concerns the period before Saul's kingship. In 2 Sam. 6 the term 'ark' appears a total of 15 times.

9. From 2 Sam. 6.12-23 the Chronicler completely omits the content of vv. 20-23, which relate the unseemly, anti-climatic wrangle between David and his wife Michal about the former's self-exposure before the ark. On the other hand, he reproduces the source's introduction to this episode, that is, Michal's witnessing David's display and 'despising' him for this (2 Sam. 6.16//1 Chron. 15.29), which in his own presentation is thus left curiously hanging in the air.

ark's arrival in Jerusalem and their execution of these [no *Vorlage*]). The massive scale of these expansions already bespeaks the importance the Chronicler attaches to the ark's coming to Jerusalem.

1 Chronicles 13–16 opens with a brief *Sondergut* segment (13.1-4) in which David asks for and receives all Israel's endorsement of his plans for the ark. The core of this segment is v. 3: 'Then let us bring again the ark of our God to us; for we neglected it (לא דרשנהו, literally "did not seek")[10] in the days of Saul'.[11] David's statement here intimates several important points: the whole people ('we'), not just the king or the cultic officials (cf. the priests and Levites mentioned in v. 2), have responsibility for the ark. Saul's reign was marked by a universal neglect of that responsibility, the implication being that the reign's all-encompassingly disastrous outcome (see 1 Chron. 10) was God's punishment for this.[12] If then things are ever to improve for Israel, all must now (re-)assume responsibility for the long-neglected ark.

The Chronicler tells of David's first, abortive attempt at moving the ark in 13.5-14 in close dependence on 2 Sam. 6.1-11. In particular, he takes over the source's indeterminacy about the identity of those who 'carry' the ark to the cart on which it is then transported (13.7//6.3) as well as its mention of God's smiting Uzzah for touching the ark (13.9-10//6.6-7). Unlike Samuel, however, the Chronicler will pick up on these items subsequently, making them the starting point for the instructions David issues prior to his second attempt at moving the ark.

In both versions the first attempt to move the ark ends with the ark being deposited in the house of Obed-edom for three months (13.14//6.11). Unlike Samuel, the Chronicler fills this interlude by way of two extended insertions: 14.1-17 and 15.1-24. The first of these units, drawn from

---

10. On דרש as a *Leitwort* of the Chronicler, see C.T. Begg, '"Seeking Yahweh" and the Purpose of Chronicles', *LS* 9 (1982), pp. 128-41. It is not clear whether the referent of the suffix of the above form is the ark ('it') or rather God himself ('him'). Given the intimate connection between ark and Deity in Chronicles, both are likely to be in view.

11. The wording of 1 Chron. 13.3 echoes that of the Chronicler's indictment of Saul in 1 Chron. 10.13-14: '…Saul also consulted a medium seeking guidance (לדרוש) and did not seek guidance from the Lord (ולא דרש ביהוה)…' At the same time, its formulation also extends and specifies that earlier charge: it was not Saul alone who had failed to 'seek the Lord', but the entire people, that failure being concretized precisely in their neglect of God's ark.

12. The Chronicler's depiction of the end of Saul's reign seems to be composed with the catastrophe of the Exile in view. See Mosis, *Untersuchungen*, pp. 17-43.

2 Sam. 5.11-25 (see above), makes no mention of the ark.[13] By contrast, the second (a creation of the Chronicler) revolves around the measures taken by David regarding the ark in view of the new attempt that will be made to move it. These measures involve pitching a tent for it in Jerusalem (15.1)[14] and David's reassembling 'all Israel' there for the transfer (15.3; cf. 13.1-4). In particular, however, David's intervening measures focus on the cultic officials and their responsibilities vis-à-vis the ark. Under this head, it is above all the question of who is now to 'carry' the ark that the unit highlights. Already in v. 2a David clarifies the matter with his directive that 'no one but the Levites may carry the ark'. In issuing this directive, the king (v. 2a) relies on a previous divine decision: '*for* the Lord chose them [the Levites] to carry the ark of the Lord (לשאת את ארון יהוה) and to minister to him (לשרתו) forever'. Here the Chronicler clearly draws on Deut. 10.8, 'At that time the Lord set apart the tribe of Levi to carry the ark of the covenant of the Lord (לשאת את ארון ברית יהוה), to stand before the Lord to minister to him (לשרתו) and to bless in his name, to this day'.[15] David returns to the subject in 15.12, where he instructs the chiefs of the Levitical families (see vv. 5-11) to 'consecrate' themselves for their task of 'bringing up' the ark to the place he has had prepared for it (see v. 1). In 15.13 he then proceeds to allude to the previous attempt at moving the ark and its disastrous outcome (13.5-14) as further motivation for the Levites' assigned role: 'Because you did not (carry it) the first time, the Lord broke forth upon us [see 13.11], because we did not care for it in the way that is ordained (לא דרשנהו כמשפט)'.[16]

13. For suggestions as to what prompted the Chronicler to reposition the material of 2 Sam. 5.11-25 to the point where he does, see the studies cited in n. 7.

14. This notice serves to prepare 2 Sam. 6.17 (///1 Chron. 16.1), which says that David placed the ark in the tent 'which he had pitched for it'.

15. The literary dependence of 1 Chron. 15.2 on Deut. 10.8 notwithstanding, the Chronicler implicitly diverges from his source in that whereas for Deuteronomy the Levites who carry of the ark are themselves priests (see Deut. 31.9, '*the priests* the sons of Levi who carried the ark of the covenant of the Lord'), the Chronicler—in accordance with P—assigns the priests and Levites to two separate clerical categories. On the Levites in Chronicles, see U. Glessmer, 'Leviten in spät-nachexilischer Zeit. Darstellungsinteresse in den Chronikbüchern und bei Josephus', in M. Albani and T. Arndt (eds.), *Gottes Ehre erzählen: Festschrift für Hans Seidel zum 65. Geburtstag* (Leipzig: Thomas Verlag, 1994), pp. 125-51.

16. David's concluding phrase here echoes his statement in 13.3, 'we neglected him/it (לא דרשנהו) in the days of Saul'. At the same time, it also adds an important precision: care for the ark needs to be 'in accordance with the ordinance', that is, the divine choice of the Levites as the sole porters of the ark (Deut. 10.8, as evoked by

The Levites' duties as the primary custodians of the ark (as assigned them at this point by David) are not, however, limited to carrying it. Rather, in 15.16-24 David proceeds to entrust them with two further, ark-related (and more on-going) responsibilities: music-making (a task they share with seven priests who blow trumpets [15.24a]) and serving as 'gatekeepers' before the ark (15.18b, 23, 24b).

The Chronicler generally follows his source (2 Sam. 6.12-19) closely about David's successful transfer of the ark to Jerusalem (1 Chron. 15.29–16.3). In place, however, of the former's indeterminate reference to 'the bearers of the ark of the Lord' (2 Sam. 6.13), he identifies the Levites as its porters (1 Chron. 15.26), in accordance with David's injunction (15.2). He likewise refers to the ark itself four times (15.25, 28, 29; 16.1) with the formula, 'the ark of the covenant of the Lord (ארון ברית יהוה)', a phrase not used in 2 Sam. 6.12-19 (nor by himself in what precedes). In so doing he is probably drawing once again on the passage Deut. 10.8 (see above), where this same designation occurs.[17]

Prior to his report about the people's departure to their homes after the festivities before the ark that had just come to Jerusalem (1 Chron. 16.43// 2 Sam. 6.19), the Chronicler interjects another long *Sondergut* segment (1 Chron. 16.4-42) featuring additional directives by David. These instructions, picking up on those of 15.1-24, include the king's provisions for the ark's care in its permanent Jerusalem home by both the Levites (16.4, they are to thank and praise YHWH 'before the ark'; 16.37, Asaph and his kin are to minister daily before the ark) and the priests (16.6, two of these are to blow their trumpets continuously before the ark; cf. 15.24a).

The second, culminating moment in the Chronicler's 'Ark Narrative' comes when Solomon installs the ark in a requisite residence, namely, in the temple (2 Chron. 5–7//1 Kgs 8). In between the ark's arrival in Jerusalem (1 Chron. 13–16) and its installation in the temple there, the Chronicler, however, keeps redirecting attention to the ark (and the question of its eventual definitive 'place') in the long transitional segment (1 Chron. 17–2 Chron. 4) dealing with the later reign of David, the arrangements made by him for Solomon's accession, and the latter's early kingship. In

David in 15.2). Otherwise, attempts at 'caring for/seeking' the ark—as well-meaning as these may be—will only lead to renewed expressions of divine wrath.

17. On the above designation of the ark (which occurs a total of twelve times in Chronicles, only two of which [2 Chron. 5.2//1 Kgs 8.1; 2 Chron. 5.7//1 Kgs 8.6] have a *Vorlage* in Samuel–Kings), see Japhet, *Ideology*, pp. 96-100. On the significance of its introduction precisely at this point in the Chronicler's account, see Eskenazi, 'Approach', pp. 270-71.

this segment the ark is mentioned five times, only one of which has a *Vorlage* in DtrH. First, in 1 Chron. 17.1 (//2 Sam. 7.2) David expresses concern about the ark's having accommodations inferior to his own 'house of cedar', that is, the tent he had previously erected for it (1 Chron. 15.1; 16.1//2 Sam. 6.17). Thereafter, at the end of a lengthy address to Solomon, his designated heir (1 Chron. 22.7-19), David urges him to build YHWH a house and to install both the ark and the sacred vessels there (v. 19). The aged David returns to the subject in an address (1 Chron. 28.2-8) to the assembled Israelites, where he begins by alluding (28.2) to his earlier intention (see 17.1) to provide the ark—here qualified as 'the footstool of our God (אלהינו רגלי להדם)'[18]—with 'a house of rest (מנוחה בית)'. In this same context, David proceeds (28.11-12) to entrust to Solomon a 'plan (תבנית)', written by the Lord's own hand (28.19), for everything associated with the temple he is to build, of which the last component to be mentioned is the golden cherubim whose wings cover 'the ark of the covenant of the Lord' (28.18). Finally, in his *Sondergut* introduction to his version (2 Chron. 1.7-13) of the story of the new King Solomon's dream at the high place of Gibeon (1 Kgs 3.3-15), the Chronicler makes a parenthetical allusion (1.4) to the fact of David's earlier transfer of the ark to Jerusalem and pitching a tent for it (see 1 Chron. 15.1; 16.1).[19]

As noted above, the climax to the Chronicler's story of the ark comes in 2 Chronicles 5–7, when on the occasion of the dedication of the temple, the ark is installed within it. As does its deuteronomistic counterpart, 1 Kings 8, the Chronicler's account consists of three main segments: (1) the installation itself (2 Chron. 5.2-14//1 Kgs 8.1-11), (2) Solomon's prayer (2 Chron. 6.1-42//1 Kgs 8.12-53) and (3) closing observances (2 Chron. 7.1-10//1 Kgs 8.54-66).[20] In both versions references to the ark are naturally concentrated in their respective opening segments with the

18. On this phrase, which she views as an 'innovation' by the Chronicler in its application specifically to the ark—as opposed to the temple (thus Pss. 99.5; 132.7; Lam. 2.1)—see Japhet, *Ideology*, pp. 76-79.

19. Conversely, the Chronicler omits the concluding notice of the source story (1 Kgs 3.15) about Solomon's offering sacrifices 'before the ark of the covenant of the Lord' following his return from Gibeon to Jerusalem. For the Chronicler there is no need for Solomon to 'counterbalance' his previous 'illegitimate' sacrifices at the Gibeon high place (1 Kgs 3.4) in this way, since for him Gibeon itself is—at this moment—still a legitimate sanctuary, given the presence there of the Mosaic tent of meeting and bronze altar (see 2 Chron. 1.3, 5).

20. For further comparison of the two versions, see Dennerlein, *Bedeutung*, pp. 180-95.

term appearing nine times in 2 Chronicles 5 and eight in 1 Kgs 8.1-11. Otherwise, the Chronicler's notices concerning the ark here largely coincide with those of DtrH. For example, both use the phrase 'ark of the covenant of YHWH' twice (5.2//8.1; 5.7//8.6), have the tent of the meeting and the sacred vessels being 'brought along' with the ark (5.5//8.4), identify 'the priests' as the ones who bring the ark into the inner sanctuary (5.7//8.6), speak of the cherubim's wings covering the ark (5.8//8.7), and refer to the ark's poles (5.9//8.8) and the 'tablets' placed in the ark at Horeb by Moses (5.10//8.9). In this instance, then, the Chronicler did not see fit to amplify significantly or modify DtrH's Solomonic ark story as he did in the case of David's bringing the ark to Jerusalem. The one noteworthy divergence between the two presentations of the ark's installation in the temple concerns the identification of those who carry it prior to its being brought into the inner sanctuary (both accounts agree that this was done by 'the priests' [5.7//8.6; see above]). In 1 Kgs 8.3 the ark is (initially) 'lifted up' by 'the priests', while in 2 Chron. 5.4 the same action is attributed to 'the Levites'. Here then, the Chronicler takes care to adjust the source notice to his own earlier depiction (see 1 Chron. 15.2, 15, 25) of the Levites carrying the ark to Jerusalem under David.

After being featured in 2 Chronicles 5//1 Kgs 8.1-11, the ark recedes in the two following sections of the Chronicler's and DtrH's temple dedication accounts (see above), being completely absent in fact, from the third of these (the closing observances). The middle section, which the accounts have in common—Solomon's prayer (2 Chron. 6//1 Kgs 8.12-53)—contains one joint, passing reference to the ark (in 6.11//8.21 Solomon recalls his having placed 'the ark in which is the covenant of the Lord' [i.e. the tablets inscribed with the terms of that covenant; see 2 Chron. 5.10//1 Kgs 8.9] in the house for the Lord's name built by him [see 6.10//8.20]). Significantly, however, the Chronicler rewrites the ending of Solomon's prayer (1 Kgs 8.50-53) so as to introduce an additional, concluding reference to the ark (2 Chron. 6.41-42). In so doing, he places on the lips of Solomon the words of Psalm 132 (vv. 8-10 and then v. 1), the only psalm to mention the ark explicitly. Specifically, he has Solomon recite (6.41a) a close approximation to the acclamatory words of Ps. 132.8: 'And now arise, O Lord (קומה יהוה) God, and go to thy resting place (לנוחך),[21] thou

---

21. This term echoes the 'rest language' used earlier by the Chronicler in connection with the Lord, the temple and the ark; David put the Levites in charge of the service of song in the temple, 'after the ark rested there (הארון ממנוח)' (1 Chron.

and the ark of thy might (עֻזֶּ וַאֲרוֹן)'.[22] In context, this quotation of the psalm verse serves to underscore Solomon's achievement: the transfer of the Lord's ark to its resting place, for which the psalmist prays, comes about when Solomon sets the ark in the house he has built (see 2 Chron. 6.10-11).

As with the pre-Davidic period of his history (1 Chron. 1–9), the Chronicler's account of the post-Solomonic epoch (2 Chron. 10–36) mentions the ark only once—and that quite *en passant*. It occurs in the context of Chronicles' expansive narration of Josiah's Passover celebration (2 Chron. 35.1-19; compare 2 Kgs 23.21-23), where the king first enjoins the Levites (35.3): 'put the holy ark (תְּנוּ אֶת אֲרוֹן הַקֹּדֶשׁ)[23] in the house which Solomon...built; you need no longer carry it upon your shoulders'. Commentators differ as to the correct reading and precise meaning of the MT form rendered 'put' by RSV here. There seems to be general agreement, on the other hand, about the overall meaning of Josiah's injunction in its immediate context, that is, he is telling the Levites that they are no longer to engage in the task of carrying the ark assigned them by David (see 1 Chron. 15.1, 12, 15; 16.1; 2 Chron. 5.4) but are rather to devote themselves (according to the continuation of Josiah's address to the Levites in 35.4b-6) to prepare for the Passover observance. As far as I can determine, however, scholars have not raised several further relevant questions about how the Chronicler intends Josiah's injunction to be taken. Why, for example, does this injunction come so late in his history, that is, just prior to the series of catastrophes that commence with Josiah's own untimely death (2 Chron. 35.20-27) and culminate in the Exile itself (2 Chron. 36.17-21)? Why, in fact, could not the same order have already been issued by Solomon once the ark had been duly installed by him in the temple?[24] Furthermore, is the significance of the fact that the Chronicler

6.31), and announced 'I had it in my heart to build a house of rest (בֵּית מְנוּחָה) for the ark of the covenant of the Lord and for the footstool of our God...' (1 Chron. 28.2).

22. In both Ps. 132.8 and 2 Chron. 6.41a, there is further an echo of the opening words of the 'ark song' of Num. 10.35, recited by Moses when the ark set out: 'arise, O Lord (קוּמָה יהוה)...'

23. The expression 'holy ark' occurs only here in the Old Testament; see von Rad, *Geschichtsbild*, p. 47.

24. In this connection compare 1 Chron. 23.26—a text often associated with 2 Chron. 35.3—where David, already prior to the temple dedication in which these items will be carried by them (see 2 Chron. 5.5), states regarding the Levites, 'They no longer need to carry the tabernacle or any of the things of the service', and then goes on (23.28-32) to assign them new duties as assistants to the priests.

attributes the above injunction precisely to Josiah, a king whom he—in this going beyond his deuteronomistic *Vorlage* (2 Kgs 23.29-30)—will shortly charge with a failure to heed a divine directive, that is, not listening to the words of Neco 'from the mouth of God' (2 Chron. 35.22)? Finally, how does Josiah's instruction that the Levites henceforth desist from their task of carrying the ark relate to David's confession in 1 Chron. 13.3 that Israel had 'neglected' the ark 'in the days of Saul'? Could it be then that the Chronicler is intimating that with his directive of 35.3 Josiah is in effect (wrongly) telling the Levites to resume that 'neglect' of the ark that characterized the reign of Saul and thereby set in motion a set of events that eventuated in Israel's being reduced to a state like that into which it fell at the end of Saul's reign?[25]

Conclusion

After this review of the Chronicler's story of the ark from Saul to Josiah, I now return to the question with which I began: What is the significance of the ark for the Chronicler, writing as he is at a time when that object had long since disappeared from the scene? The standard scholarly response to this question is that the ark, as a venerable relic deriving from the time of Moses himself, had an essential role in legitimating (1) the temple where it came to rest and/or (2) the claims of the Levites for a role in the temple cult. Having fulfilled that role, though, the ark itself became 'dispensable', so dispensable that the Chronicler gave no thought to the possibility of or need for a new ark in Israel's postexilic cult.[26]

---

25. On Mosis's view of the end of Saul's reign as a foreshadowing of what happened to Israel at the Exile, see n. 12.

26. See, for example, the following representative statements on the matter: 'The Chronicler is interested in the ark as the embryo and core of the Jerusalem sanctuary' (Mosis, *Untersuchungen*, p. 54 [my translation]); 'the ark and the king are only of significance as enablers of the Jerusalem cult' (Welten, 'Lade', p. 183 [my translation]); '...so too can Israel leave some its earlier milestones behind—David and the ark—yet retain what is central to tradition... The prominence of the lost ark, and the prominence of the lost monarchy, do not imply an expectation that either will be restored' (Eskenazi, 'Approach', p. 273); '...with its transfer into the Temple the cultic significance of the Ark shifts to the Temple. Thereby the ark becomes dispensible' (Dennerlein, *Bedeutung*, p. 44 [my translation]). That the ark in Chronicles serves above all to legitimate the Levites' claim to a role in the temple cult—rather than the temple itself—is the view of von Rad, who states (*Geschichtsbild*, p. 100 [my translation]): 'Now we understand the surprising interest with which the Chronist follows

While naturally acknowledging such a past-legitimating function for the ark in Chronicles, I do wish to question here whether, in fact, the Chronicler excludes any present or future significance for the ark—as scholars simply seem to assume. I raise the question in light of a series of interrelated considerations.

(1) If the ark has only a past-legitimating function, why does not the Chronicler confine himself to the—already quite abundant—references to the ark found in Samuel–Kings? Why instead does he introduce a whole series of additional references to the ark (e.g. his citation of Ps. 132.8 with its acclamation of the ark in 2 Chron. 6.41 at the conclusion and climax of Solomon's prayer of dedication, in place of the ending of the king's deuteronomistic prayer [1 Kgs 8.51-53], which he otherwise takes over largely unchanged)? Why too does he go to the trouble of devising various new, non-deuteronomistic names for the ark ('footstool of our God', 1 Chron. 28.2; 'the holy ark', 2 Chron. 35.3), which serve to accentuate its status?

(2) The ark was one of many 'goods' (these including national independence, the Davidic monarchy, wealth, international prestige, a unified people comprising twelve tribes) that, in the Chronicler's presentation, characterized the time of David and Solomon—the time precisely when the ark was the object of Israel's respectful attention—but that were conspicuously absent from the people's life in the Chronicler's own time. Is it plausible, however, in a strongly parenetic work as such Chronicles, with its insistence that right behavior is richly rewarded, that all these 'goods' are presented by him only as a reminder of what Israel has irrevocably lost? Is not the Chronicler's portrayal of them more likely intended to evoke the hope that all of them—as the already restored temple—might be recovered through further efforts by Israel to please God?

(3) Extending the foregoing consideration, I recall that in the case of one of the above 'goods', that is, the Davidic monarchy, Hugh Williamson has argued in detail and convincingly that the Chronicler is indeed looking to its eventual revival.[27] But if the Chronicler did hold such a hope concerning the long-defunct monarchy, might he not also have entertained a similar one concerning the long-gone ark—especially given that he so intimately associates the fortunes of the ark with the two kings of Israel's best days?

the history of the ark's transfer. With its bringing into the Temple, cultic rights for the Levites were, at the same time, legitimated.'

27. H.G.M. Williamson, 'Eschatology in Chronicles', *TynBul* 28 (1977), pp. 115-54.

(4) One must also consider here the Chronicler's relation to the P strand. Christa Schäfer-Lichtenberger has recently argued that the exilic/postexilic P-document regards the ark as an object, which, given the precise divine specifications concerning its construction (Exod. 25.10-22), is one capable of being remade for use in Israel's future cult.[28] Chronicles, however, is a work that evidences the influence of P—alongside and in opposition to that of the Deuteronomi(sti)c tradition—above all in cultic matters (see, e.g., the differentiation between priests and Levites, or the reminiscence of Lev. 9.24 [P], which the Chronicler inserts into his rewriting of 1 Kgs 8 in 2 Chron. 7.1, where a fire from heaven consumes the sacrifices on the altar). But if P, the Chronicler's chief authority and inspiration for cultic matters, envisaged a postexilic future for the ark, might not the latter, under the influence of P, have done so as well?

(5) Though most acknowledge that the ark functioned to legitimate the First Temple by its presence there, this raises a further question: If the First Temple required the presence of the ark to be legitimated, would not the Second Temple have needed the same? Could the latter structure be fully legitimate as long as it lacked an ark?

(6) Finally, I recall my proposed interpretation of 2 Chron. 35.3 in light of 1 Chron. 13.3. In that interpretation, these two texts would refer to a 'neglect' of the ark in two epochs of Israel's history that ended in total disaster: the reign of Saul and post-Solomonic Judah. Conversely, the intervening period—the reigns of David and Solomon when the ark did receive due attention from king, Levites, and people—was Israel's golden age. The Chronicler's own time was, it would seem, another period in which there was little thought of the ark (witness Jer. 3.16 and the non-mention of the ark by Ezekiel, Haggai–Zechariah, Second and Third Isaiah, Malachi, and Ezra–Nehemiah), with all the attendant losses for and limitations to the nation's life this entailed—as was only to be expected, given the experience of the Saulide and post-Solomonic periods. Against this background, is it not possible then that in his portrayal of David assembling all Israel to fetch the ark (1 Chron. 13.1-4, *Sondergut*), the Chronicler is calling all Israel of his own time to turn its attention to the ark once again, in hopes that by so doing it might secure the same salutary effects that David and Solomon's care for the ark secured for them and their people?

---

28. Schäfer-Lichtenberger, 'Verlust', pp. 238-39 and n. 48.

I am aware that the foregoing considerations do not add up to a conclusive case that the Chronicler in fact entertained hopes for a new (or recovered)[29] ark that would eventually find its way into the Second Temple, thereby conferring definitive legitimacy on that structure. They are offered rather with a view to stimulating further discussion about the self-evidency of the opposite proposition, namely, that the Chronicler certainly had no such hopes regarding the ark. Beyond that modest scholarly intention, this study also offers me the opportunity of expressing my esteem for the work of Ralph Klein and my best wishes for his future studies.

29. The letter to the priest Aristobulus cited in 2 Macc. 1.10–2.18 (2.4-8) attests the existence of a tradition that, at the time of the Exile, the prophet Jeremiah hid the ark (along with other objects associated with the temple) in a cave and that God would someday make the site known. Note the comment of Mosis, *Untersuchungen*, p. 121, concerning the *Tendenz* of this passage: 'It is intended to highlight the provisional character of the Second Temple in that the holy furnishings of the canonical Mosaic period, the tent, the ark, and the altar, were, according to the will of God, denied to this Temple and its time' (my translation). Mosis further argues that the tradition behind 2 Macc. 2.4-8 originated at a time fairly close to the Chronicler's own. Conceivably, then, the Chronicler was familiar with some variant of the Maccabean tradition. If so, he would have found in that tradition a basis for denying full legitimacy to the current temple, as well as for the hope that that temple could someday come into possession of the missing ark, which would confer on the temple a status equal to that of its prede-cessor.

CYRUS IN SECOND AND THIRD ISAIAH, CHRONICLES, EZRA AND NEHEMIAH*

Roddy L. Braun

At the SBL's annual meeting in Washington, DC, in 1993, I was invited to present a paper in connection with a program marking the fiftieth anniversary of Martin Noth's *Überlieferungsgeschichtliche Studien*. I suggested that future studies should direct some attention to Cyrus: 'Is it possible that the author of Chronicles or that of Ezra viewed the Persian Cyrus in any sense as the fulfillment of the messianic hope? If Second Isaiah could do this, why not Chr.?'[1]

Literature on Cyrus in Second Isaiah seems to have blossomed in the last decade.[2] In Chronicles too, books and articles have appeared that point

* I am very pleased to be asked to offer this paper as a tribute to my colleague, mentor, and friend, Dr Ralph Klein. Dr Klein and I were first colleagues in the Hebrew Department of Concordia Senior College, Fort Wayne, Indiana. Ralph later served as the advisor for my doctoral dissertation at Concordia Seminary, St Louis, Missouri. The dissertation was of course on Chronicles ('The Significance of 1 Chronicles 22, 28, and 29 for the Structure and Theology of the Work of the Chronicler'), and under Dr Klein's gentle but persistent prodding I was able to produce a work in 1971 of which I remain proud, and which I believe has been instrumental to the work of numerous other researchers over the years. We remained friends during the 1970s, when doctrinal dissention wrecked the educational structure of the Lutheran Church-Missouri Synod, and both of us lost our positions as a result. It is with deep gratitude and appreciation that I dedicate this paper to Dr Ralph Klein.

1. R.L. Braun, 'Martin Noth and the Chronicler's History', in S.L. McKenzie and M.P. Graham (eds.) *The History of Israel's Traditions: The Heritage of Martin Noth* (JSOTSup, 182; Sheffield: Sheffield Academic Press, 1994), pp. 63-80.

2. Among the most extensive studies are those of R.G. Kratz, *Kyros im Deutero-jesaja-Buch: Redaktionsgeschichtliche Untersuchungen zu Entstehung und Theologie von Jes 40–55* (FAT, 1; Tübingen: J.C.B. Mohr, 1991); A. Laato, *The Servant of YHWH and Cyrus: A Reinterpretation of the Exilic Messianic Programme in Isaiah 40–55* (ConBOT, 35; Stockholm: Almqvist & Wiksell, 1992); and the commentary by J.D.W. Watts, *Isaiah 34–66* (WBC, 25; Waco, TX: Word Books, 1987).

to a significantly different and more important role for Cyrus than has been recognized in the past.[3] This article looks at those passages of the Old Testament that refer to Cyrus and seeks to assess his place in Old Testament thought. What was the nature of the Chronicler's hope? Could Cyrus be 'the messiah' who embodied God's promises for Israel and who was responsible for the building of the Second Temple? The relevant sections are found in Second Isaiah, at the end of 2 Chronicles and the beginning of Ezra.

Cyrus in Second Isaiah

Cyrus is mentioned twice in Isaiah (many commentators consider these texts as parts of one larger section). The first is Isa. 44.23-28, which is introduced by a doxology (v. 23). The messenger formula, 'Thus says the LORD...' (44.24 and 45.1), set apart 44.25-28, which is hymnic or even creedal in form, with participles modifying 'Yahweh' positioned at the beginning of each line, as well as frequently elsewhere. The climax for this section occurs in v. 28, where the final line seems to express purpose:

> Who says to Cyrus, 'My shepherd',
>   and he will fulfill all my desire,
> by saying to Jerusalem, 'You shall be built',
>   And (to) the temple, 'You shall be constructed'.

In vv. 24-27, which do not mention Cyrus by name, Yahweh is pictured as the God who does everything, the creator God (v. 24) and the God of all wisdom, who frustrates the false prophets in their lies but confirms the words of his servant[4] by doing them (vv. 25-26). It is this Yahweh who now commands Cyrus to carry out his order that Jerusalem be rebuilt and inhabited. The commands to the ocean and rivers (v. 27) to dry up point to a new exodus, and are in anticipation of the coming of Cyrus, who will be in fact the one who gives command that Jerusalem and the temple are to be rebuilt.

---

3.   R. Mason, *Preaching the Tradition: Homily and Hermeneutics after the Exile* (Cambridge: Cambridge University Press, 1990); W. Riley, *King and Cultus in Chronicles: Worship and the Reinterpretation of History* (JSOTSup, 160; Sheffield: Sheffield Academic Press, 1993); S. Japhet, *The Ideology of the Book of Chronicles and Its Place in Biblical Thought* (Jerusalem: Bialik Institute, 1977).

4.   MT reads the singular, 'his servant', despite the parallel with 'his messengers'. 1QIsa and LXX also read the plural.

In v. 28, Cyrus is named רְעִי, which is pointed in the MT as רֹעִי ('my shepherd').[5] This is striking, and I am not aware that it is used of any other foreign leader.[6] Even when understood as 'shepherd', its specific nuance remains questionable. It is used of all types of leaders, both good and bad, at various levels. Passages such as Isa. 56.11 use the term for evil leaders. In the famous invective in Ezekiel 34, it is used of evil rulers. However, it is frequently used for a king or ruler (see 40.11), including David (34.23-24; cf. 37.24-25), who is termed shepherd, servant, and prince. Even the LORD himself (34.15; see also Ps. 23). The difficulty of the 'shepherd' imagery in Zech. 10.2, 3, and ch. 11 is legendary.

Isaiah 45.1-17 (8-13)

The second occurrence of the name *Cyrus* is found in Isa. 45.1, which is a part of the longer pericope, 45.1-7.[7] It also begins with the messenger formula (v. 1) and concludes (v. 7) with no less than five participles describing God as the One 'who does peace and creates evil'. The climax of this section proclaims, 'I am Yahweh, who does everything!' (v. 7) and so recalls both the first verses of the previous section and the 'I am Yahweh who does everything' of 44.24.

Yahweh stands at the center of this pericope, and it is his hand that is to be seen in the actions of Cyrus' victories. This is emphasized by the emphatic personal pronoun אֲנִי used with a finite verb in v. 2, by the numerous first person verb forms throughout the section, and most obviously by the fourfold repetition of 'I am Yahweh' (vv. 3, 5, 6, 7), which is magnified in turn by the contents of v. 5 ('I am the LORD, and there is no other; besides me there is no god') and v. 6 ('I am the LORD, and there is no other'). It may well be that this monotheistic emphasis is meant to allay possible criticism that support of Cyrus means support of Persian dualism.[8]

Cyrus' victories are significant for Cyrus, for Israel and for the world. They are accomplished: (1) that Cyrus may know that it is Yahweh, the God of Israel, who has called him ('I surname you, although you do not

---

5.   The pointing רֵעִי ('my friend') is also possible. See Zech. 13.7.

6.   Scripture speaks of God leading Israel as a flock in the wilderness by the hand of Moses and Aaron (Ps. 77.21 [EVV v. 20]; Isa. 63.11. See J.W. Vancil, 'Sheep, Shepherd', in *ABD*, V, pp. 1187-90 (1189-90).

7.   C. Westermann (*Isaiah 40–66* [OTL; Philadelphia: Westminster Press, 1969], pp. 152-54) and R.N. Whybray (*Isaiah 40–66* [NCB; Grand Rapids: Eerdmans, 1975], p. 102) see 44.24–45.7 as a single pericope.

8.   Laato, *Servant*, p. 184.

know me', stands in apparent contrast to 2 Chron. 36.23 and Ezra 1.2, in which Cyrus calls Yahweh by name and credits him with having given him [Cyrus] all the kingdoms of the earth); (2) for the sake of Jacob/Israel, who is termed God's 'servant' (עבד) and his 'chosen' (בחיר) [despite the choice of Cyrus, his work is directed toward the good fortune of Israel—he does not replace Israel in God's plan]); and (3) so that all the world may know that Yahweh alone is God (v. 6). Cyrus' work has universal significance, since all the world is encompassed in God's plan, which is to be brought to pass through Cyrus.

The verbs throughout are generally imperfects. This makes the initial verb of the section, which is a perfect ('to Cyrus, whose right hand I *have* grasped'), even more significant, suggesting that Cyrus' work has already begun. This same point is repeated in v. 4b, where the imperfect אקרא is striking, 'I *have* called you by your name'. Cyrus has already been taken by Yahweh's hand, although his work remains to be done.

Most strikingly, Cyrus is identified by Yahweh in v. 1 as being 'his anointed (משיחו)'. I will leave fuller treatment of this word for later. Here I will only note that this is the only occasion in the Old Testament where the name משיח is applied to a foreign king. This is certainly surprising at the least. It becomes even more so when we notice that throughout these sections there is no mention of a Davidic ruler other than in Isa. 55.3.[9] Other significant words and phrases also modify Cyrus in this section. It is Cyrus whom God has taken by the hand (v. 1), who has been called by name by the God of Israel (vv. 3, 4) and who has been surnamed by him (v. 4).

Other Isaianic References to Cyrus

While the two references above are the only ones in Isaiah referring to Cyrus by name, it is commonly understood that other passages in Second Isaiah refer to Cyrus as well, although there is not complete agreement on which passages fit into that category. The most obvious is certainly 45.9-13, which—although separated from vv. 1-7 by the doxology of v. 8—clearly seems to apply to Cyrus, and is sometimes included with the two previous sections in what has been termed 'The Cyrus Song'.[10] The

9.   See K. Seybold, 'משח', in *TDOT*, IX, pp. 43-54 (52-53).

10.   See M. Haller, 'Die Kyrioslieder bei Deuterojesaja', in H. Schmidt (ed.), Εὐχαριστήριον: *Studien zur Religion und Literatur des Alten und Neuen Testaments: Hermann Gunkel zum 60. Geburtstage, dem 23. Mai 1922* (FRLANT, 36; 2 vols.; Göttingen: Vandenhoeck & Ruprecht, 1923), I, pp. 261-77.

NRSV even inserts the word 'Cyrus' directly into its translation in v. 13, adding a footnote to indicate that the Hebrew reads 'him'. If vv. 9-13 (or 9-17) are taken to refer to Cyrus, they concern the aftermath of Cyrus' choice by Yahweh and of Cyrus' subsequent victories. Israel then takes issue with Yahweh and responds negatively because of the unorthodox manner in which he is proceeding by choosing a foreign king as Israel's redeemer and the builder of Jerusalem and the temple. To this attitude Yahweh responds firmly that the clay has no business in asking the potter why he has chosen to work as he does, and reaffirms his choice of Cyrus:

> [13] I have aroused Cyrus [Heb. 'him'] in righteousness,
>   and I will make all his paths straight;
>   he shall build my city
>   and set my exiles free,
>   not for price or reward,
>   says the LORD of hosts. (Isa. 45.9-13 NRSV)

While the annotators of the *New Oxford Annotated Bible* seem to believe that the reference to Cyrus ends in 45.13,[11] they also think that Cyrus is the one whom Yahweh has 'roused from the east' (41.2-4) and stirred up from the north (41.25), whose rise Yahweh and Yahweh alone, has foretold from the beginning (41.26-29). However, it understands *the servant* in 42.1 to be Israel, seemingly guided by 'my chosen' (42.1b and the reading of the LXX in 42.1a). The notes for this edition of the Bible show some ambiguity here, attaching the 'new things' in 48.6 to Cyrus' victories, although 43.18-19, to which it also alludes here, is described as a 'New Exodus' without reference to Cyrus.

Some such understanding of the entire section, as that of the NRSV annotators, is the more traditional and common view. Others, however, have for many years seen Cyrus behind a sizable complex of passages. Both Laato and Kratz, for example, include as 'Cyrus passages' (in addition to 44.24-28; 45.1-7) the following: 41.1-7, 21-29; 45.9-13; 46.8-11; and 48.12-16.[12] They do not include 42.5-9.

If one looks at these passages in detail, it becomes clear that they cover the same general topics as 44.24–45.7. An individual is called, for example, 'a victor from the east' (41.2), and the point is that YHWH has

---

11. V.R. Gold and W.L. Holladay, '45.9-13', in B.M. Metzger and R.E. Murphy (eds.), *The New Oxford Annotated Bible* (Oxford: Oxford University Press, 1994), p. 928. Watts (*Isaiah 34–66*, pp. 158-63), however, sees the entire scene (vv. 14-25) as a dialogue between Yahweh and Cyrus.

12. Laato, *Servant*, p. 3; Kratz, *Kyros*, p. 16.

roused him up and given nations before him (41.2-5). He also is one 'stirred up from the north...from the rising of the sun' (41.25), who will trample on rulers (41.25), and the emphasis now falls upon the fact that YHWH alone has declared this (vv. 26-27). This is the one who will build YHWH's city and set his exiles free (45.13). He is 'a bird of prey from the east, the man for my purpose' 46.11), with the focus again on Yahweh's action and his announcement of the fact beforehand. He has declared the former things (46.9), and now announces a new plan (46.11). Isaiah 48.12-16 appears almost as a summary: the themes again are the absolute uniqueness of YHWH (v. 12), his role in creation (v. 13), and God's declaration of his plan (v. 14). This happens through one whom YHWH loves (v. 14) and includes the destruction of Babylon (v. 14). God has called him, and he will prosper (v. 15). This final verse adds the note also of God's spirit (v. 16; cf. also the first Servant Song, 42.1).

It is worth noting, in fact, that Watts argues that all of chs. 40–48 deal with the time of Cyrus (539–523 BCE) and that the *servant* of 42.1 is Cyrus.[13] In addition, in Isaiah 49–66 each section refers to a reigning Persian king (49.1–52.12, Cambyses/Darius; 52.13–57.21, Darius/Xerxes; chs. 58–61, Artaxerxes; and chs. 62–66, also Artaxerxes). However, only Cyrus is mentioned by name. There is to my knowledge no passage in Third Isaiah that has been linked with Cyrus.[14]

Cyrus in Ezra–Nehemiah and Chronicles

Having considered the portrayal of Cyrus in Isaiah 40–66, we will now turn our attention to what is commonly called the Chronicler's History.[15]

13. It is noteworthy that Watts finds three differing referents of the highly charged term 'servant of the Lord' in Isaiah. These are: (1) the nation Israel; (2) Cyrus, as well as the other Persian leaders; and (3) faithful Israel. However, Watts suggests that the 'Suffering Servant' of Isa. 53 refers to an Israelite ruler of Darius' day, most likely Zerubbabel, whose mysterious absence from the records following Zech. 6.11-13 has often been noted.

14. J.L. Berquist (*Judaism in Persia's Shadow: A Social and Historical Approach* [Minneapolis: Augsburg/Fortress Press, 1995], p. 42) speculates that 'Deutero-Isaiah's prophecies may well have brought together an alliance of the priestly and political factors among the Jewish exiles', which in turn worked to wrest control of their colony.

15. I will not enter here into the debate concerning the precise extent of the Chronicler's History. However, the analysis will be pursued in such a manner as to keep various portions of Chronicles and Ezra–Nehemiah isolated.

Of the two primary occurrences, the first reference to Cyrus in 2 Chronicles 36 is usually considered to be derived from that of Ezra 1.[16] I will accordingly deal first with the text from Ezra 1.

Ezra 1.1-4

> [1] In the first year of King Cyrus of Persia, in order that the word of the LORD by the mouth of Jeremiah might be accomplished, the LORD stirred up the spirit of King Cyrus of Persia so that he sent a herald throughout all his kingdom, and also in a written edict declared: [2] 'Thus says King Cyrus of Persia: The LORD, the God of heaven, has given me all the kingdoms of the earth, and he has charged me to build him a house at Jerusalem in Judah. [3] Any of those among you who are of his people—may their God be with them!—are now permitted to go up to Jerusalem in Judah, and rebuild the house of the LORD, the God of Israel—he is the God who is in Jerusalem; [4] and let all survivors, in whatever place they reside, be assisted by the people of their place with silver and gold, with goods and with animals, besides freewill offerings for the house of God in Jerusalem'.
> (Ezra 1.1-4 NRSV)

These few verses give a very rich understanding of Cyrus' view, and/or the author's view, of Cyrus' position and activity:

1.   Cyrus' actions are in fulfillment of an unspecified prophecy or prophecies of Jeremiah.
2.   It is said that it is Yahweh himself who 'stirred up' the spirit of Cyrus.
3.   Cyrus' message is said to have been delivered orally and in writing throughout 'all his kingdoms'.
4.   Cyrus specifically names 'Yahweh' as 'the God of heavens'.
5.   Cyrus declares that it is Yahweh who has given him all the kingdoms of the earth.
6.   Cyrus has been given a charge to build Yahweh's house in Jerusalem.
7.   Yahweh is the God who is in Jerusalem.
8.   Any of Yahweh's followers in Cyrus' kingdom is permitted to return to Jerusalem, the site of Yahweh's temple, and rebuild it.
9.   Any of Yahweh's followers not returning to Jerusalem is to assist those who do return with offerings of food, money, and equipment.

---

16.   For the arguments, see H.G.M. Williamson, *Ezra, Nehemiah* (WBC, 16; Waco, TX: Word Books, 1985), pp. xxiii-xiv, xxxiii-xxxiv, 6-8.

Some points are identical with those of Second Isaiah, although expressed at times differently. Yahweh is the God of all, who has stirred up Cyrus and given the entire earth into his hands. He has been charged to build Yahweh's house, which is in Jerusalem. These actions have been previously announced.

At the same time, there are several modifications. Isaiah spoke of God's purpose and plan, while that plan is here said to have been spoken through Jeremiah (v. 1). The only epithet applied to Cyrus here is 'King…of Persia'. There is no mention of a messiah or shepherd. Cyrus, however, knows the name of the LORD and that the LORD has given him all the kingdoms of the earth (contrast Isa. 45.4, where Cyrus does not 'know' Yahweh). There is explicit mention of the captives who wish to return to Jerusalem, and 'encouragement' for others to help fund the expedition.

Ezra 1.5-11 is not a part of Cyrus' edict but records the reaction of the Jews in Babylon to that edict. All who were around the exiles aided them with vessels of silver and gold and other items (v. 6). These verses also note that Cyrus handed over the temple vessels that Nebuchadnezzar had removed from Jerusalem, counting them out to Sheshbazzar, who is here called the 'prince' (Hebrew, הנשיא; in 5.14, פחה, 'governor') of Judah. This provision is made in Cyrus' memorandum recorded in Ezra 6.3-5.

Within the Aramaic portion of the book, Ezra 6.2-5 records that Darius later searched the royal archives and found a memorandum of Cyrus' decision that has the appearance of being an official memo and 'action order'.

> [1] Then King Darius made a decree, and they searched the archives where the documents were stored in Babylon. [2] But it was in Ecbatana, the capital in the province of Media, that a scroll was found on which this was written: 'A record. [3] In the first year of his reign, King Cyrus issued a decree: Concerning the house of God at Jerusalem, let the house be rebuilt, the place where sacrifices are offered and burnt offerings are brought; its height shall be sixty cubits and its width sixty cubits, [4] with three courses of hewn stones and one course of timber; let the cost be paid from the royal treasury. [5] Moreover, let the gold and silver vessels of the house of God, which Nebuchadnezzar took out of the temple in Jerusalem and brought to Babylon, be restored and brought back to the temple in Jerusalem, each to its place; you shall put them in the house of God'. (Ezra 6.1-5 NRSV)

As might be expected, this 'in house' note lacks all of the diplomatic 'niceties' of Cyrus' finished edict found in 1.2-5, such as: (1) the use of the name 'Yahweh' and the designation of him as the 'God of heaven' (v. 2), (2) Cyrus' confession that it is Yahweh who has given him all the kingdoms of the earth and (3) the statement that God has commanded him (Cyrus) to build the temple. On the other hand, additional details necessary for the efficient bureaucratic handling of the task of rebuilding the temple are included, such as (1) the size of the temple and the building materials to be used in constructing it, (2) that the cost of the project was to be paid from the royal treasury and (3) that the gold and silver vessels that Nebuchadnezzar brought to Babylon were to be restored to the temple. Darius' command goes on not only to command Tattenai and Shetharbozenai not to hinder the work on the temple, but seems to direct them to supply the cost of the temple from the revenue of the province Beyond the River (vv. 6-9).

The name Cyrus also occurs in Ezra 4.3, 5, where his edict is quoted by Zerubbabel and the other leaders of Israel in response to 'the adversaries of Judah and Benjamin' who wish to assist them in the building of the temple, to the effect that Cyrus has commanded them *alone* to build the temple, and they will do so. The opposition to the building and the resultant stoppage of work then continued 'all the days of Cyrus' (vv. 4-7). These verses are clearly editorial, connecting the time of Cyrus not only with Darius but also with Ahasuerus (v. 5) and Artaxerxes (v. 7) as well. The verses also introduce the Aramaic portion of the book (4.8–6.18).

The remaining cases of the name Cyrus (Ezra 3.7; 4.3, 5; 5.17; Dan. 1.21; 6.28; 10.1) do not add substantially to our knowledge of Cyrus.

2 Chronicles 36.22-23
The final reference to Cyrus that we will consider is at the end of 2 Chronicles 36:

> [22] In the first year of King Cyrus of Persia, in fulfillment of the word of the LORD spoken by Jeremiah, the LORD stirred up the spirit of King Cyrus of Persia so that he sent a herald throughout all his kingdom and also declared in a written edict: [23] 'Thus says King Cyrus of Persia: The LORD, the God of heaven, has given me all the kingdoms of the earth, and he has charged me to build him a house at Jerusalem, which is in Judah. Whoever is among you of all his people, may the LORD his God be with him! Let him go up'. (2 Chron. 36.22-23 NRSV)

This passage, as mentioned above, is commonly considered to be taken from Ezra 1 (although the opposite opinion is also held by some), and so I have delayed its discussion to this point. It is essentially identical with the first part of the edict in Ezra 1.2-4, up to v. 3, 'may his God be with him, and let him go up…' This rather abrupt ending is itself probably the primary reason that the form of the edict found in Chronicles is usually considered secondary.

To understand Chronicles' view of Cyrus, it is necessary also to recall the verses that stand immediately before these in his work:

> [20] He took into exile in Babylon those who had escaped from the sword, and they became servants to him and to his sons until the establishment of the kingdom of Persia, [21] to fulfill the word of the LORD by the mouth of Jeremiah, until the land had made up for its sabbaths. All the days that it lay desolate it kept sabbath, to fulfill seventy years. (2 Chron. 36.20-21 NRSV)[17]

In Chronicles, the 'word' of Jeremiah (v. 21) that is mentioned in both Ezra and 2 Chron. 36.22, but without elaboration, is construed to refer specifically to the 70-year period of punishment noted in Jeremiah (see Jer. 25.11 and 29.10). Furthermore, the reference has been interpreted in terms of the 'sabbath rest' of Leviticus 26, where, however, no time period is found.[18]

While certain bits of historical information about Cyrus are found in Ezra/Chronicles and in Second Isaiah (e.g. Cyrus is identified as the King of Persia, and his proclamation concerning the return of the exiles to Judah and the construction of the temple is in fulfillment of the LORD's will), one does not find in Ezra or Chronicles the bold theological interpretation of his role as 'shepherd', 'friend' or 'messiah' that one meets in Second Isaiah. Nor is there comment in Ezra or Chronicles on the significance of God choosing a *foreign* king to restore his people, land and temple. Apart from matter-of-course, historical references (Ezra 3.7; 4.3, 5; 5.17), Cyrus does not reappear later in the narrative.

2 Chronicles names no Judean king after Zedekiah. The initial return takes place under the control of one Sheshbazzar, who apparently was not a Davidide.[19] Ezra 1.8 has Cyrus and his treasurer, Mithredath, hand over the temple vessels to Sheshbazzar, who is titled 'the prince (הנשיא) of Judah' (cf. 1.11). Ezra 2.1, which is copied from Neh. 7.6, mentions that exiles came up from Babylon with, among others, Zerubbabel, who bears no title. Beginning with Ezra 3, it is Zerubbabel 'the son of Shealtiel' who erected an altar in the seventh month (3.1) and who 'made a beginning' of

17. H.G.M. Williamson (*1 and 2 Chronicles* [NCB; Grand Rapids: Eerdmans, 1982], pp. 417-19) believes that these verses actually conclude the work of the Chronicler and that vv. 22-23 have been added from Ezra 1 by a later writer.

18. See Japhet, *I and II Chronicles: A Commentary* (OTL; Louisville, KY: Westminster/John Knox Press, 1993), pp. 1075-77.

19. Williamson, *Ezra–Nehemiah*, pp. 6, 17.

the temple in the second month of the second year. With the priest Jeshua (cf. also 5.2), Sheshbazzar is mentioned in 5.14, together with the note that Cyrus had made him governor (cf. Ezra 2.63 = Neh. 7.65), and he had 'laid the foundations of the house of God' (5.16). Following Zerubbabel, the scepter of a Davidic messiah, or a messiah of any kind, does not seem to rise again.

Messianism

The word *messiah* has various meanings in the Old Testament. The Hebrew מָשַׁח simply means 'to anoint with oil'. In Israel's history, kings and priests (and perhaps prophets as well) were anointed with oil as a part of their commissioning and were accordingly God's anointed.

With the dynastic promise to David in 2 Samuel 7//1 Chronicles 17, *messiah* seems to receive a new specificity of meaning. While others may be anointed, *the* messiah, *the* anointed one, is now a special ruler, a king in David's line, who will bring military victory, peace, prosperity and justice to Israel. Juel, in an excellent article in *Eerdmans Dictionary of the Bible*, summarizes the general view of the messiah as follows:

> There were Jews whose future hopes were invested in a king from the line of David, 'the Lord's anointed' (Ps. Sol. 17). In their visions, the king would deliver Israel from foreign bondage (Roman) and establish an ideal kingdom in which justice would rule. This 'messianic eschatology' is probably the way most students of the Bible have been taught to think of 'messiah' and 'messianic.[20]

In the Old Testament this Davidic line was pre-eminent. Nevertheless, a broader perspective also remains. While in some cases it was understood to be a Davidic descendant who would appear to root out Israel's enemies and introduce a kind of Davidic–Solomonic golden age for Israel, by others it came to be understood as one whose coming would inaugurate a kind of golden age upon another level. It would in fact introduce the end of time, which would usher in the Kingdom of God itself, not just upon earth, but upon a grander, heavenly plain. It would be like the 'son of man' of Daniel 7, after whose coming the saints of God would receive the kingdom. In a broader sense yet, as Juel notes, the term *messiah*, or at least many of the ideas associated with it, continue to develop:

20. D. Juel, 'Messiah', in D.N. Freedman (ed.), *Eerdmans Dictionary of the Bible* (Grand Rapids: Eerdmans, 2000), p. 889.

Readers of the Old Testament developed a wide variety of alternative expectations, however, in which a royal figure was either completely absent or subordinated to another deliverer... Others whose view of the future was cast in the form of bizarre visions (apocalypticists) often had little room for a messianic figure.[21]

Perhaps the servant passages of Second Isaiah deserve to be included among these other developing ideas. Laato concludes, for example, that the servant passages and the Cyrus passages share an unusually large number of common elements.[22] Many of these elements, Laato believes, have their ultimate roots in ancient Near Eastern concepts of royalty.[23]

There are indications that the idea of the Messiah and of the end time were undergoing significant rethinking and modification in the exilic and postexilic period. It is certainly understandable that in the throes of the exile, and with the virtual disappearance of the Davidic line that followed, questions related to Israel's future, including that of the Messiah, should surface with renewed vigor.

Already in Jeremiah and prior to the exile, emphasis was placed on the LORD's promise to the two houses, that of David and that of the Levitical priests:

> [25] Thus says the LORD: Only if I had not established my covenant with day and night and the ordinances of heaven and earth, [25] would I reject the offspring of Jacob and of my servant David and not choose any of his descendants as rulers over the offspring of Abraham, Isaac, and Jacob. For I will restore their fortunes, and will have mercy upon them. (Jer. 33.25-26 NRSV; cf. 33.17-22)

This idea of king and priest in tandem continued into the postexilic age. A strong case can be made that the question of a twofold 'messiahship' came to a crisis in the time during and shortly after the construction of the Second Temple. In the short book of Haggai, to be dated about 520 BCE, Zerubbabel is regularly paired with the high priest Joshua (1.12, 14; 2.2, 4), except in the final verses, where only Zerubbabel is mentioned (2.20-23). In First Zechariah, however, the situation is more complex. In 3.1-9, both Zerubbabel and Joshua are mentioned, but it is Zerubbabel who is called

21. Juel, 'Messiah', pp. 889-90.
22. Laato, *Servant*, p. 21.
23. Both Laato (*Servant*, pp. 185-86) and Riley (*King*, pp. 33-34) see much of this terminology reflected also in Pss. 89 and 132. It might be noted that these psalms also contain a significant vocabulary present in both Second Isaiah and Chronicles, such as the theology of rest.

'my servant the Branch' (v. 8). These 'two olive trees' are referred to again in 4.1-10a, 10b-14. In the midst of a section assigning great authority and praise on Zerubbabel, perhaps v. 9 is most relevant: 'The hands of Zerubbabel have laid the foundation of this house; his hands shall also complete it'.[24] Here pre-eminence seems to be given to the Davidide, Zerubbabel. While Zerubbabel is absent from 3.8 and Joshua from 4.1-10, matters are even more complex in Zech. 6.9-13:

> [11] Take the silver and gold and make a crown, and set it on the head of the high priest Joshua son of Jehozadak; [12] say to him: Thus says the LORD of hosts: Here is a man whose name is Branch: for he shall branch out in his place, and he shall build the temple of the LORD. [13] It is he that shall build the temple of the LORD; he shall bear royal honor, and shall sit upon his throne and rule. There shall be a priest by his throne, with peaceful understanding between the two of them. (Zech. 6.9-13 NRSV)

In the passage as it now reads, it is Joshua the high priest who is identified as the 'Branch' and designated to build the temple. But especially the words of v. 13 ('and there shall be a priest by his throne') suggest strongly that the text here originally read 'Zerubbabel', beside whose throne would be the priest Joshua. This passage is often cited as indicative of the fact that Zerubbabel suddenly and mysteriously disappeared, and in a sense, the Davidic messianic hope with him. There is no mention in the prophetic literature of any other Davidic survivor. In the minds of some, it is Zerubbabel whose death is interpreted in Isaiah 53 as substitutionary for the sins of Israel.[25]

Questions about the nature of Israel's future hope surely continued. Reference here might be made to the Qumran scrolls, where there are two, if not three, apparent messiahs. It is clear in the New Testament as well, where Jesus' disciples answer his query, 'Who do people say that the Son of Man is?', with the names of John the Baptist, Elijah, and Jeremiah or one of the prophets (Mt. 16.13-16).[26]

---

24. In Ezra, it is in fact Sheshbazzar, whose identity with Zerubbabel is today generally denied, who is credited with laying the foundations of the house of God (Ezra 1.8; 5.16).

25. Cf., e.g., Watts, *Isaiah*, pp. 222-33.

26. See also Jn 1, where the writer seems to gather every name and title referring to the Messiah, and the baptismal statement of the Father in Mt. 1.11 and parallels, which is commonly understood to link the royal messianic Jesus with the Suffering Servant. And of course they abound in both the Old and New Testament Apocrypha. See my *Jesus: His Name and Titles* (San Jose: Writers Club Press, 2000).

Messianism in Second and Third Isaiah

When one reads through these last chapters of Isaiah from the specific perspective of the messianic hope, it is surprising that the idea of a Davidic messiah is of so little prominence. While Second Isaiah is known for its themes of salvation and deliverance, of the new exodus, and the servant of the LORD, anything corresponding to a messianic hope such as is found, for example, in the major prophets such as First Isaiah, Jeremiah and Ezekiel, is absent in Second Isaiah. In this part of the book it is again and again the LORD himself who is coming (40.3, 10-11), who is doing a new thing (43.19), whose reigning is announced and who returns to Zion (52.7-8). David himself is mentioned only in 55.3, and there is no mention of a Davidic descendant.

The only real exception here, as I have indicated earlier, is Cyrus, who is designated as the LORD's messiah in 45.1. In 44.28 it is Cyrus who will rebuild Jerusalem and the temple. Riley concludes:

> In receiving the commission to build the Temple, Cyrus inherits the chief symbol of the legitimacy of the Davidic dynasty... In this way, the conclusion to the Chronicler's work demonstrates that the task entrusted to David's successors has passed outside the Davidic House...[27]

If the servant of 42.1-4 and the following verses is identified with Cyrus, he is here blessed with other typical messianic functions, as the one who will establish justice (42.1, 4), who will be a light to the nations (42.6), and who will release the prisoners from the dungeon (42.7).[28] Other servant songs, such as 49.1-4, 5-7, where the servant is in the MT identified with Israel, also seem to encompass many of the usual messianic functions.[29] The servant here has a mission to Israel as well.

The messianic picture is totally lacking in Third Isaiah, where both the apocalyptic and priestly images are clearly present. Here it is God himself who acts (cf. esp. 59.15b-16), who will be an everlasting light, who creates a new heaven and a new earth, a rejoicing Jerusalem (65.17-18), and the peaceable kingdom (65.25), and who comes in fire and will gather all nations and tongues (66.15, 18).

---

27. Riley, *King*, pp. 154-55.

28. Riley, *King*, pp. 154-55.

29. Laato (*Servant*, pp. 186-87) believes that in these chapters, characteristics previously attributed to the Messiah have been redistributed to Cyrus and to Israel.

160   *The Chronicler as Theologian*

Messianism in Chronicles/Ezra

The question of the Davidic messiah in the Chronicler's work has always been debated. On the one hand, there is an intense interest in the Davidic kings throughout Chronicles, as well as extensive panegyrics such as that surrounding Abijah in 2 Chronicles 13. On the other, there is the surprising absence of any perceived Davidic or messianic expectation at all, either at the end of Chronicles or, for that matter, anywhere in Ezra–Nehemiah.[30]

As a result and to oversimplify a bit, we could say that attitudes toward a coming messiah in Chronicles have in the past varied between one of the following three positions: (1) a messiah from David's line will come (this might be considered the common traditional position); (2) the work of David's line reached its culmination in the establishment of the temple and its cultus; (3) Chronicles is non-messianic and non-eschatological. To these positions, there must be added, on the basis of recent studies, two more: (4) while maintaining the significance of the Davidic dynasty for the postexilic period, some understand that significance as something less than the full and usual understanding of messianic, and more in a programmatic or typological sense; (5) others believe that the messianic hope has been transferred from the Davidic house to Cyrus (or to Cyrus' house).

Somewhat in line with these latter two suggestions, it seems that some of those who have found a messianic hope in Chronicles have been careful to express their positions in a carefully nuanced manner. Japhet, for example, has stated in connection with the fall of Judah:

> It seems as if the Chronicler has reserved his judgment on the issue of the Davidic dynasty, an aspect of Israel's history which has not reached its culminations... Combined with his genealogical list of I Chron. 3.17-21, where the Davidic house is traced to the latest generations, probably his own contemporaries, this reticence may point to one of his most compelling convictions: an expectation of the renewal of the Davidic monarchy.[31]

30. See S. Japhet, *The Ideology of the Book of Chronicles and Its Place in Biblical Thought* (BEATAJ, 9; New York: Peter Lang, 2nd edn, 1997), pp. 493-504. (Note that this is a different edition from the one cited in n. 3).

31. Japhet, *I and II Chronicles*, p. 1072. I continue to maintain that 1 Chron. 1–9, as well as 1 Chron. 23–27, are secondary, despite the fact that an increasing number of scholars, such as Japhet and Williamson, argue for the authenticity of these chapters. This means, in my opinion, that 1 Chron. 3, which extends the line of David several generations past Zerubbabel, is not attributable to the Chronicler. Morever, any number of those who accept the integrity of 1 Chron. 3 nevertheless consider as a later addition at least vv. 18-24.

Or as Williamson states in his discussion of 1 Chronicles 17:

> ...it is evident that at the completion of the period of Davidic-Solomonic rule he [the Chronicler] intends his readers to regard the dynasty as indeed eternally established, and various later references further make this explicit (2 Chron. 13.5; 21.7; 23.3). Although the term 'messianic' is perhaps too strong, it must be concluded that the Chronicler still cherished the hope that one day the Davidic dynasty would be re-established over Israel.[32]

As far as I can determine, neither Williamson nor Japhet deals with the topic of the possible messianic role of Cyrus. Similarly, it appears that the recent work of Riley, whose main point seems to be that Cyrus supplanted the Davidic dynasty, concludes:

> When the Chr's political situation (the continuing absence of a Davidic regent) and liturgical situation (the continued celebration of the Davidic covenant) are taken together, the Chronicler's portrayal of David and his house in cultic terms may be seen as an emphasis on the religious contribution that the dynasty has made and as a disavowal of the necessity for a post-exilic Davidic successor to the throne of Israel.[33]

However, all students of Chronicles are agreed, it would seem, that the temple and its cultus stand at the center the Chronicler's vision of the future, whether it would be attended by a messiah or not. Mason may be quoted most recently:

> It is the election of David and the Davidic dynasty which is central... This 'choice' extends also to Solomon... It is important to stress, however, against those who see a form of messianism in the Chronicler's emphasis on the choice of David and the Davidic line, that the purpose in this choice is the building of the temple.[34]

In view of the fact that the primary goal of the Davidic king is the construction of the temple and the establishment of the temple cult, it is perhaps not going too far to question whether the absence or presence of a messianic king is really of any more than symbolic significance.

Summary and Conclusions

There has been much discussion in recent years about the limits of the Chronicler's work, while the discussion of its *purpose*—which seems to

---

32. Williamson, *1 and 2 Chronicles*, p. 134, with reference to the dynastic oracle of 1 Chron. 17.1-27. See also his 'The Dynastic Oracle', *TynBul* 28 (1977), pp. 115-54.
33. Riley, *King*, p. 35.
34. Mason, *Preaching*, p. 123.

have been laid aside for a while—is being raised again. In many respects the two issues may seem to have little to do with each other. It would seem to make a substantial difference, however, in assessing the purpose of the Chronicler's work to know whether that work ends with the destruction of the temple, with the edict of Cyrus, with the construction of a new temple, with the actual dedication of the new temple, or somewhere else.[35]

It is certainly true, in any case, that the continuation of Ezra–Nehemiah contains little if anything that would speak positively to the question of Davidic messianism. We have seen that the concept of a messiah (especially of a Davidic messiah) was always ambiguous, but it was vigorously discussed at the time of the exile and later. At no time would this have been truer than during the days of the exile and its aftermath. The understanding of Cyrus in Second Isaiah and Chronicles appears to be a part of that 'messianic flux'. Cyrus was no doubt an important person, and according to both texts, he was instrumental in the restoration of the temple. He had been chosen by God himself for that role. But at the time of the writing of these two works it was not yet obvious what the final outcome would be.

Second Isaiah, writing at a time when the Davidic dynasty was under the dominance of the Babylonians, saw Cyrus as the one who would not only overcome Babylon, but who would champion the cause of God's people, release them from their captivity, restore them to their homeland, and be responsible for the reconstruction of Jerusalem and its temple. He named Cyrus as the LORD's shepherd and his messiah. In some sense the promise made to David and what it entailed was being fulfilled by a non-Israelite ruler from another part of the world.

Chronicles has been variously dated, stretching all the way from the time of Josiah's reform until the end of the Persian empire or even later. If 2 Chron. 36.22-23 is included as a part of the original book of Chronicles (either written by the author or borrowed by him from another) it would have to be at least later than 540 BCE; and if the Chronicler's original work included Ezra 1–6, the date for Chronicles would be 516 BCE or beyond. If these verses were borrowed from Ezra–Nehemiah and were written or borrowed by the Chronicler himself, they would, of course have to be later

35. In an earlier study ('Chronicles, Ezra, and Nehemiah: Theology and Literary History', in J.A. Emerton [ed.], *Studies in the Historical Books of the Old Testament* [VTSup, 30; Leiden: E.J. Brill, 1979], pp. 52-64) I argued that the vocabulary, style, and thought patterns of Ezra 1–6 suggest that the original writing of the Chronicler extended at least to some such ending.

than Ezra–Nehemiah—post-400 BCE. If these verses were not attached to Chronicles by the original author, then of course there is no basis for using them to discern the Chronicler's attitude toward Cyrus, unless he understood that his work would be read as a precursor to Ezra–Nehemiah. This leaves many options open, but all of them place the Chronicler later, and some much later, than the most likely dating for Second Isaiah in the late exilic period.

It might be noted that even if 2 Chron. 36.22-23 is not a part of the Chronicler's original writing, vv. 20-21 (if the 70 years be understood in anything like a literal sense) brings the date of Chronicles down to the time of Cyrus or the dedication of the temple. Again, whichever ending is original, it is markedly similar to the ending of 2 Kings, which pictures Israel in Babylon and benefiting from an act by a foreign ruler. While it is tempting to date the 70 years from the same terminus as does Kings (i.e. the accession of Jehoiachin), this would bring us to the time of Cyrus' edict. It seems a remarkable circumstance that the exile in 586 is just 70 years from the dedication of the temple in or about 516 BCE.

The Chronicler, as has been noted, moves rapidly and rather dispassionately through the period from Josiah's death, through the last kings of Judah and to the exile, concluding with a deuteronomic-like explanation of events in 2 Chron. 36.11-21 (see esp. vv. 11-15). It is really only the absence of a Davidic king, and his replacement by Cyrus, which differentiates the endings of DtrH and the Chronicler's work. It might not be too farfetched to find each writer at a point in time where he simply did not know or understand what the future would hold. The writer of Second Isaiah was in much the same situation. So DtrH, writing just before the rise of Cyrus, saw the release of Jehoiachin as at least potentially positive. Beyond that he was non-committal.

Prior to the return from Babylon, Second Isaiah looked upon the rise of Cyrus enthusiastically. This was a new and a glorious thing that the LORD was doing, and he was doing it through Cyrus. For some reason, that possibility seemed to surpass any possibility associated with the house of David. The writer of Second Isaiah seems to have believed that God's promises to Israel of a messianic deliverer were now being fulfilled through a foreign ruler and through the people of Israel itself (Isa. 55.3).

The Chronicler lived somewhat later, and he and his situation must have seemed very different from that of Second Isaiah. The temple had been built (or at least announced) under the aegis of Cyrus and through the instrumentality of Zerubbabel. But now any hope of a Davidic revival seemed far removed at best. Does hope lie with the Persian dynasty? With the rise of a new David? With the temple and its cult? Or in some combination of the above. Perhaps the author just did not know.

In his provocative study, *The Dawn of Apocalyptic*, Paul Hanson has described the history of postexilic Judaism as a conflict between two groups within Judaism, which may be termed 'the visionaries' and 'the hierocrats'. The visionaries represent essentially the prophetic voice; the hierocrats are the priestly party. Hanson believes that apocalyptic literature owed its origins to the victory of the hierocratic party. The visionaries, or prophets, resorted to the language and thought of apocalyptic to express their views.[36]

To use Hanson's terms, Second Isaiah was a visionary, the Chronicler a hierocrat. Second Isaiah thought in terms of deliverance, salvation, and restoration; the Chronicler's focus was directed toward the rebuilt temple. Just as David and Solomon had achieved their primary goal with the construction of the temple, so the dedication of the Second Temple would have accomplished the purpose of the LORD working through Cyrus.

Third Isaiah, it might be noted, stands at a later date than Second Isaiah and reflects a development more closely akin to the Chronicler than does Second Isaiah. Here too there is an increased emphasis upon the temple, and above all upon the Sabbath (in the latter case far surpassing the emphasis of the Chronicler). Prophecy has been institutionalized, even to the point that the Chronicler has included the prophet in the temple service, and even the choir! But in other cases, unlike the situation seen in Zech. 13.2-6, there remain prophetic notes, such as a certain openness to foreigners, which is found in both Second and Third Isaiah as well as Chronicles, and in clear contrast with Ezra–Nehemiah, where complete separation is the ideal.

Second Isaiah resolved the question of the messianic hope by transferring it (or at least a part of its function) to Cyrus, and perhaps another part to the people of Israel (cf. Isa. 55.3). But here too the end result was to be the construction of a new temple. Chronicles solved the same issue by concentrating entirely upon the construction of the temple and letting the issue of 'Cyrus' and Zerubbabel remain silent. With the temple a present reality and the cultus functioning under its high priest, that issue would perhaps be clearer at some later time.

36. P.D. Hanson, 'The Chronicler: The Victorious Hierocratic Party Returns to a More Conciliatory Position', in *idem, The Dawn of Apocalyptic* (Philadelphia: Fortress Press, 1975), pp. 269-79. Hanson does not discuss Second Isaiah.

THEOLOGY OF WORSHIP IN CHRONICLES

John C. Endres

In his 1994 article, 'Recent Research in Chronicles', John Kleinig concluded his review of studies on the temple and its services with the advice that 'further work needs to be done on the arrangement and significance of the services at the temple'.[1] These remarks follow the publication of his own monograph, which filled an important gap in this field of study by demonstrating a significant correlation between choral music and song and the ritual of sacrifice at the Jerusalem temple.[2] Even though considerable progress has been made describing the arrangement of temple services in Chronicles, its significance requires further attention.

A new task faces those interested in the theology of the Chronicler: how to make the transition from worship service to theological predication. A most helpful suggestion comes from Samuel Balentine in his study, *The Torah's Vision of Worship*.[3] Following research by Frank Gorman, he suggests that worship is reported in ritual descriptions and that ritual is 'a *primary means for a community of faith to do theology*, not simply a symbolic act of social construction'.[4] In addition, Balentine identifies worship clues found in numerous Torah passages and demonstrates how these texts speak as much to Israel's worship life as to its awareness of its historical past. In fact, his book makes the claim that—as Israel's basic activity—worship proves more telling than the historical retelling. In this way he interweaves a theology of creation (witnessed in the worship reflected in

1. J.W. Kleinig, 'Recent Research on Chronicles', *CRBS* 2 (1994), pp. 43-76 (61).
2. J.W. Kleinig, *The Lord's Song: The Basis, Function and Significance of Choral Music in Chronicles* (JSOTSup, 156; Sheffield: JSOT Press, 1993).
3. S.E. Balentine, *The Torah's Vision of Worship* (OBT; Minneapolis: Fortress Press, 1999).
4. Balentine, *Worship*, p. 90. Balentine summarizes material in F.H. Gorman Jr, *The Ideology of Ritual: Space, Time, and Status in the Priestly Theology* (JSOTSup, 91; Sheffield: JSOT Press, 1990), esp. pp. 59-60 (emphasis in original).

Gen. 1.1–2.4a) with a theology of covenant, reflected especially in the Sinai texts.

The primary goal of this study, applying Balentine's insights on the Pentateuch to the books of Chronicles, will be to argue that the Chronicler's theological vision is often expressed in a powerfully imaginative fashion in the worship services that he describes as part of his retelling of Israel's history. In fact, I want to suggest that the Chronicler's way of retelling Israel's sacred history in his time, through careful and inspired processes of interpretation, serves many of the same goals as the lifetime's work of Ralph Klein, whom we honor with these essays. I would claim that the proclamation of the Word to the community at worship constitutes the same real goal in both cases. In sum, I suggest that Ralph Klein's contribution to our era and future generations mirrors in an important way the gift and grace of the author of Chronicles.

Worship Services in Chronicles

Chronicles includes numerous worship texts that we could consider. Simon De Vries analyzes a group of them in a helpful article, 'Festival Ideology in Chronicles'.[5] Each of the five ceremonies he analyzes constitutes a worship service, but of a particular type: one of Israel's annual pilgrim festivals that were incumbent on observant Israelites. His study demonstrates how each of these services was conducted under the authorization of the Davidic king and was observed on proper dates according to set rituals. Each description contributed to the Chronicler's portrayal of the way Israel had worshiped in the past (probably similar to the contemporary experience of worship in the Chronicler's day, most likely in the Persian era),[6] and also projected this vision of worship forward into Israel's future. Thus, the rhetorical impact of such festivals in Chronicles was to persuade Judean leaders to preserve and to rectify their worship

---

5.   S.J. De Vries, 'Festival Ideology in Chronicles', in H.T.C. Sun *et al.* (eds.), *Problems in Biblical Theology: Essays in Honor of Rolf Knierim* (Grand Rapids: Eerdmans, 1996), pp. 104-24. In this study he analyzes the following texts with a 'festival schema': (1) 2 Chron. 7, Solomon's dedication of temple (= Tabernacles); (2) 2 Chron. 15, Asa's covenant renewal (= Weeks); (3) 2 Chron. 29, Hezekiah's re-dedication of the temple; (4) 2 Chron. 30, Hezekiah's Passover; (5) 2 Chron. 35, Josiah's Passover.

6.   See, e.g., the discussion in R.W. Klein, 'Chronicles, Book of 1–2', in *ABD*, I, pp. 992-1002.

along lines already well established and confirmed theologically. De Vries helps to capture the Chronicler's view of the three pilgrim festivals, especially as they impressed Jews during the Second Temple era.

There are other narratives in which the Chronicler describes types of public worship that do not fall into the category of 'festival schema', and these stories provide additional information about the way that Israel worshiped at more particular times in its social and religious life as a community. Some of these additional 'services' are the following: David's introduction of the ark into Jerusalem and the song that accompanied it (1 Chron. 15–16); Solomon's ritual introduction of the ark into the newly constructed temple and the service of its dedication (2 Chron. 5.2–7.11);[7] an ad hoc ritual at the temple during the reign of Jehoshaphat, occasioned by the threat of enemy troops marching from the east (2 Chron. 20).[8] Finally, I will comment on the temple rededication and Passover celebration during the time of Hezekiah (2 Chron. 29–30). The goal is to demonstrate the Chronicler's theological approach to various life and social settings in Israel through attention to its worship services.

Coincidentally, each of these latter four narratives also appears in a list of prayer passages in Chronicles that Samuel Balentine treated in an essay dedicated to the memory of Roddy Braun.[9] He treats 17 prayers in Chronicles, but most of them appear in the mouths of four kings: David, Solomon, Jehoshaphat and Hezekiah.[10] In that essay Balentine's goal was to demonstrate how the 'recorded prayers serve Chr's [Chr = the Chronicler]

---

7. I wish to expand De Vries's coverage of this event (2 Chron. 7.1-11, the celebration of Tabernacles) to include the rituals concerned with the ark's entry and the temple dedication and prayer service.

8. I have previously commented on three of these worship services. See my, 'Joyful Worship in Second Temple Judaism', in L.M. Luker *et al.* (ed.), *Passion, Vitality, and Foment: The Dynamics of Second Temple Judaism* (Harrisburg, PA: Trinity Press International, 2001). In this article I will build on this previous study, but the focus will prove decidedly more theological in its final synthesis.

9. S.E. Balentine, '"You Can't Pray a Lie": Truth *and* Fiction in the Prayers of Chronicles', in M.P. Graham, K.G. Hoglund and S.L. McKenzie (eds.), *The Chronicler as Historian* (JSOTSup, 238; Sheffield: Sheffield Academic Press, 1997), pp. 246-67.

10. For David he lists 1 Chron. 14.10; 17.17-29; 21.8, 17; 29.10-29; for Solomon, 2 Chron. 1.8-10; 6.14-42; for Jehoshaphat, 2 Chron. 20.6-12, 21; and for Hezekiah, 2 Chron. 30.18-19. Although this list does not include all his texts, it nevertheless clearly demonstrates the importance of the passages treated in this study for a theology of prayer.

larger compositional goals'.[11] For him, the Chronicler demonstrated how central the temple was in Second Temple Jewish life by his arrangement of prayer texts in his narrations of the reigns of David and Solomon. Since prayer and worship are so closely linked, these prayer texts will also advance our notion of worship in Chronicles.

The Ark Enters Jerusalem (1 Chronicles 15–16)

The Chronicler envisions the procession of the ark from Gibeon to Jerusalem as a well-organized liturgical procession. According to this text, David 'assembled all Israel' (1 Chron. 15.3), using the verbal root קהל, which is used elsewhere of a religious (and thus liturgical) gathering or congregation. He then describes in great detail the groups of Levites and priests participating in the processional ceremony; his listing of names and tasks not only gives a sense of the ceremony's grandeur, but it also allows various priestly and levitical groups to recognize their own predecessors in this story. In vv. 1-24 (no parallel in Samuel) the Chronicler lists approximately 860 Levites, according to their family groupings and also according to their tasks: they consecrated themselves (v. 12) and carried the ark of YHWH in procession to its new place in Jerusalem, where many of them participated by playing musical instruments and also by singing, while some small number fulfilled the role of doorkeepers for the ark (vv. 18b and 24b). This author has recast the scene by identifying many of its participants by name, mostly from levitical families and some small number of priests. With so many involved in the procession, carrying the ark of YHWH and singing and playing musical instruments, we can imagine a type of processional worship of God. Much like pilgrimage groups in other settings, their worship occurred as they moved together toward a sacred location, a holy ground. This particular site was made holy by the weight of a tradition about Ornan's threshing floor as the eventual site for God's house and altar of sacrifice (1 Chron. 21.15–22.1//2 Sam. 21.22–22.1).

For the Chronicler, the major change from the book of Samuel in his description of this worship service was the scope of the music[12] and

11. Balentine, '"You Can't Pray a Lie"', p. 259.
12. In 15.28, the Chronicler mentions musical instruments beyond those in 2 Samuel: trumpets (sounded by priests) and harps, cymbals, and lyres (played by Levites): 'So all Israel were bringing up the ark of the covenant of YHWH with shouting and the sounding of the shophar, *with trumpets and cymbals, making sounds on harps and lyres*' (Chr's additional instruments in italics).

singing, especially by levitical groups. He also emphasized the importance of the Levites as bearers of the ark, since God had chosen them to 'carry the ark of God; for YHWH had chosen them to carry the ark of YHWH and to minister to him forever' (1 Chron. 15.2).[13] This highlighting of the levitical singing led to a change in David's posture in the procession: David's dancing 'with all his strength' before YHWH (עז מכרכר בכל, 2 Sam. 6.14) is transformed into a description of his vesture and that of his levitical companions who were bearing the ark and leading the song (מכרבל במעיל בוץ, 1 Chron. 15.27).[14] Then we hear something unusual: the Levites bearing the ark conducted sacrifices, seven bulls and seven rams (1 Chron. 15.26).[15] David led in procession, 'leaping and dancing before YHWH' (מרקד ומשחק, 1 Chron. 15.29//מפזז ומכרכר, 2 Sam. 6.16)—much to the disgust of Michal—and then performed two more ritual actions: placing the ark within the special tent prepared for it and offering 'burnt offerings and peace offerings before God' (1 Chron. 16.1). This part of the service concluded with David blessing the people in YHWH's name (16.2) and distributing rich, edible gifts to each person present (16.3). Thus far we have witnessed the following ritual activities: procession with song, leaping and dancing, music and song, moving the ark into its new sacred space and the offering of sacrifices (on two occasions), the solemn blessing of the people and the ritual of blessing them with gifts of food.

13. This translation and the others from Samuel, Kings, and Chronicles come from: J.C. Endres, W.R. Millar and J.B. Burns (eds.), *Chronicles and Its Synoptic Parallels in Samuel, Kings, and Related Biblical Texts* (Collegeville, MN: Liturgical Press, 1998).

14. It is not clear, though, that the Chronicler intended a major change in the narrative here: the shift from 'dancing' to vesture does not erase the fact that David is clearly dancing two verses later (15.29) and that he danced earlier (13.8). The effect of his editing seems to be to create a notion of a great procession of official worshipers wearing white linen robes.

15. In the MT of 1 Chron. 15.26//2 Sam. 6.13 there is an interesting textual variation on the number of sacrificial animals: Chronicles reads 'seven bulls and seven rams' (C^MT) instead of an 'ox and a fatling' (S^MT). 4QSam^a offers the same reading as Chronicles, and S.L. McKenzie (*The Chronicler's Use of the Deuteronomistic History* [HSM, 33; Atlanta, GA: Scholars Press, 1984], p. 50) concludes that the reading in Chronicles most likely represents the *Vorlage* of Samuel, which the Chronicler knew and used. Thus the Chronicler's readings ('seven bulls and seven rams') is not a tendentious reading, because it preserves a very early version of the text.

All these ritual actions demonstrate why this entrance liturgy for the ark occurred 'with rejoicing' (15.25). Levites must have experienced joy in their newfound tasks and status, especially the enviable—though fearful—task of carrying the ark in procession, while many others of their group led all Israel in song and dance. Ritual actions, such as sacrifices to God, seemed to occasion more joy as well as the capacity to give away from what they had received (in an important gesture of honoring God's creation), which was reciprocated by a double blessing: in word and in gifts of food. To this point the ceremony bespeaks a God of beneficence, who shares the fruits of creation, whose dignity is not compromised by vigorous music, dance and song.

Another major aspect of this worship service concerns the specification of the Levites' ministry and a remarkable psalm-prayer (1 Chron. 16.7-36) that was sung. But both sections—the directions for the Levites and the psalm-prayer—deserve to be considered together as witnesses to the Chronicler's theology of worship. At the outset he described the levitical ministry: David 'appointed before the ark of YHWH some of the Levites to serve, to invoke, to give thanks and to praise YHWH God of Israel' (1 Chron. 16.4). Elsewhere I have argued for an understanding of this tripartite description of sung prayer as referring to invocation of God's help, and thanksgiving and praise prayer, similar to various kinds of prayer witnessed in the book of Psalms.[16] Some have objected that it is difficult to translate the first of these types (לְהַזְכִּיר) with the verb 'to invoke', but it has been argued that the verb 'remembering' in Chronicles generally constitutes part of a ritual that includes prayer for God's intervention,[17] much like a psalm of lament or supplication.

True, the Chronicler probably was not reporting form-critical categories recognized by modern scholars. But he was writing at a time of significant compositional and editorial work on the Psalms, when sensitivity to psalm types had grown.[18] But these basic voices of prayer recall generations of worshipers, and they also seem to summarize the ways to address God in the particular psalms of thanksgiving that the Chronicler composed and

16. Endres, 'Joyful Worship', pp. 165-69.

17. R.M. Shipp, '"Remember His Covenant Forever": A Study of the Chronicler's Use of the Psalms', *ResQ* 35 (1993), pp. 29-39 (30-32).

18. For example, note the exposition of R.J. Tournay, *Seeing and Hearing God with the Psalms: The Prophetic Liturgy of the Second Temple in Jerusalem* (JSOTSup, 118; Sheffield: JSOT Press, 1991).

inserted into his narration of the ark's procession to the City of David. As Sara Japhet notes, 1 Chron. 16.8-33 can rightly be called 'a hymn of thanksgiving', while vv. 34-36 constitutes a section of 'thanksgiving and supplication'.[19] The descriptors she uses contain the three main categories of song entrusted to the Levites—invocation/supplication, thanksgiving and hymnic praise—and all appear in this song, which the Chronicler viewed as David's charge to the Levites. In a sensitive study of this text, R. Mark Shipp notices the following divisions of levitical song in the content of this song: vv. 8-14 as a 'thanksgiving section', vv. 15-22 as the 'remember section', vv. 23-33 as the 'praise section' and vv. 34-36 as the 'give thanks section'.[20] Although I basically agree with this analysis, I would describe the final section a bit differently, focusing on both petition and thanksgiving. Here the notion of thanksgiving 'surrounds' a clear petition:

> Give thanks to YHWH, for he is good; for his grace is forever. Say also, 'Save us, God of our salvation; gather us and deliver us from the nations; to give thanks to your holy name, to take pride in your praise'. (1 Chron. 16.34-35)

There are alternative ways of interpreting v. 35, and one of the most help-ful is Kleinig's. He views vv. 8-34 as a song of thanksgiving and v. 35a, with its rubric 'say also', as a set of petitions to be addressed to YHWH.[21] As he concludes, 'petitionary prayer is thus associated with the proclama-tion of praise',[22] since the contents of the praise and thanksgiving section serve as encouragement for petitioners, and further praise seems to be presented as motivation for the deity.

In the Chronicler's view of this event, as mentioned earlier, the 'service' or 'ministry' appointed for the Levites was to offer invocation, praise and thanksgiving to God, especially in music and choral song. But he has refashioned the entire narrative to suggest that the worship service of the

19. S. Japhet, *I and II Chronicles* (OTL; Louisville, KY: Westminster/John Knox Press, 1993), p. 316.

20. Shipp, 'Remember His Covenant Forever', pp. 35-37.

21. Kleinig, *Lord's Song*, pp. 142-48. He sees vv. 8-34 as an integral 'song of thanksgiving' because of the *inclusio* in vv. 8 and 34, created by repetition of the imperative הודו (p. 142). Thus, v. 35 stands outside that literary structure as a separate element (p. 148), though the two 'moments' are related to each other liturgically and, I would say, theologically.

22. Kleinig, *Lord's Song*, p. 148.

ark's procession into the city of David had similar goals: to bring praise and thanksgiving to God, but not without petition for divine intervention when the people were in need. Presumably, in the era of the Chronicler the small Jewish community centered in Jerusalem required such assistance from God, and this narrative obliquely proposed a way for them to bring their petitions to God along with their praise and thanksgiving.

The author of Chronicles, of course, knew well that David had offered sacrifices on the spot when the ark entered the city (2 Sam. 6.17), but he changes the verb to a plural in 16.1 ('they presented burnt offerings and peace offerings before God') and then seems to suggest in the next verse that David had authorized this ritual[23] (1 Chron. 16.2, 'when David had finished offering up the burnt offerings and peace offerings...'). The Chronicler envisions sacrifices in Jerusalem at the occasion of the entry of the ark, but the insertion of the psalm of thanksgiving and petitions in the next chapter, as the continuing role of the Levites, suggests that Israel's worship of God should contain two related sections: offering of sacrifices and choral song and music by levitical choirs. Both ritual action and ritual song play an important role in worship of God according to this particular format. For the Chronicler, worship is comprised of vocal (music, sung prayer of praise, thanksgiving, invocation) and ritual (gestures, sacrifices, meals) actions. Rejoicing (15.25) characterizes such worship and includes the great thanksgiving antiphon of the Second Temple era: 'Give thanks to YHWH, for he is good; for his grace is forever' (16.34).

The Ark and the Temple of Solomon (2 Chronicles 5–7)

The following service, directed by King Solomon, combines another entry procession of the ark with the dedication service for the temple. By comparison with the text in 1 Kings 8, this ceremony of worship resembles its 'source' much more closely than the previous one, but the present study will reveal a significant alteration of viewpoint and theological perspective brought about by some apparently minor rewriting of the text. But first I look at the structure of this section:[24]

---

23. Such is the interpretation of Japhet, *I and II Chronicles*, p. 314.

24. For this outline I am indebted to the description of Japhet, *I and II Chronicles*, pp. 573-74.

A   5.2–6.2   Liturgy of introduction of the ark into the newly constructed temple

    A1 (5.2-10)   Transfer of the ark to the temple (by priests and Levites, in a solemn assembly of all Israel), to 'its place, to the shrine of the house, to the Holy of Holies' (v. 7), with descriptions of various cultic objects (vv. 8, 10) and with animal sacrifices (v. 6)

    A2 (5.11–6.2)   A liturgy: when the priests exited from the shrine and were joined east of the altar by many Levites singing along with the 120 priests making music on the clarions; then a cloud filled the temple as a sign of divine presence (v. 14); and finally, Solomon proclaimed that he had built God a house (6.1-2).

B   6.3-11   Solomon addresses the assembly of Israel: he recalls God's proclamation to David to build him a house (2 Sam. 7).

C   6.12-42   Solomon's prayer to God (praise of God; prayer that God accept the temple; prayers of intercession for Israel in its various needs; an entry hymn, a processional).

D   7.1-11   Conclusion of the dedication ceremony (theophanic experience of YHWH in fire descending on burnt offerings; Levites providing ritual song; consecration of the middle court, the place of sacrifices offered by the king and people; dating of the festival, which lasted seven days, in the seventh month).

This outline demonstrates that Solomon's speech and long prayer are both framed by liturgical actions: by introduction of the ark, sacrifice and dedication of the temple. But the prayer (6.12-42), the centerpiece of the section, is considered by some as the focal point of the entire section as the Chronicler has refashioned it.[25]

The Chronicler adapted the account in Kings in several ways. In 5.11–6.2 (A2 above), he added the note that the priests who had not consecrated themselves exited the temple, and he supplies a detailed description about the Levites and their musical instruments. He notes that musicians (both priests and Levites) joined in the song of thanksgiving and praise by the Levites: 'For [he is] good, for his graciousness [is] forever'. In Solomon's prayer (C above), the Chronicler seems to have corrected Kings on the location and posture of Solomon at prayer: he was kneeling on a bronze platform (2 Chron. 6.13), rather than simply standing before the altar (1 Kgs 8.22). At the conclusion of this prayer the Chronicler omitted a verse that described the people of Israel as specially set apart by God, as proclaimed by Moses the prophet (1 Kgs 8.53); instead he introduced a

25. W. Johnstone, *Chronicles and Exodus: An Analogy and Its Application* (JSOTSup, 275; Sheffield: Sheffield Academic Press, 1998), pp. 289-93.

processional song distilled from Psalm 132. Finally, Solomon's prayer of blessing (1 Kgs 8.55-61), with its focus on the deuteronomic notions of 'rest', prophetic word and covenant, is replaced by the theophanic vision of fire descending on the sacrifices (2 Chron. 7.1-3).

The additional information about Levites playing music and singing and about the priests lining up to play clarions seems to indicate liturgical arrangements important for the Chronicler, perhaps reflecting worship in the Jerusalem temple during his own time. The same might be said of the detail about his prayer, kneeling on the bronze platform. But the first of these details may entail a theological precision as well: it focuses attention on the antiphonal that was sung, so characteristic of Chronicles and other postexilic texts: 'For [he is] good, for his graciousness [is] forever' (5.13).[26] This oft-sung verse appeared in the 'psalm of thanksgiving' at the worship ceremony in David's era (16.34), and it praises the on-going goodness and steadfastness of YHWH in language reminiscent of the Mosaic covenant, even though some deuteronomic phrases for covenant relations are omitted (e.g. 1 Kgs 8.56-61). I suggest, then, that the Chronicler connects the placing of the ark in the temple with God's goodness and blessing that are related to the covenantal relationship with Israel.

But which covenant does the Chronicler recall here? Although we recognize deuteronomic/Mosaic rhetoric in the repeated refrain, Chronicles occasionally omits references to Moses and the exodus and the 'election' of Israel. For example, 1 Kgs 8.51-53, with its description of Israel as God's inheritance, is replaced by Ps. 132.8-10, with language that brings David to the fore, as an anointed one and one whose 'faithful deeds' are recalled.[27] As McKenzie notes, the net effect is to advise Israel to place its hope more in God's promise to David (connected with the temple and the city Jerusalem, especially in Ps. 132 and its parallels to 2 Sam. 7) than in the covenant with Moses; for McKenzie the issue is one of emphasis, not of omission of every reference to the mosaic covenant.[28] Here I would agree, since Psalm 132 clearly recalls the triple choice of David, city and resting place for the ark, which the Chronicler has drawn together in

26. Cf. L.C. Allen, '"For He is Good…"': Worship in Ezra–Nehemiah', in M.P. Graham, R.R. Marrs and S.L. McKenzie (eds.), *Worship and the Hebrew Bible: Essays in Honour of John T. Willis* (JSOTSup, 284; Sheffield: Sheffield Academic Press, 1999), pp. 15-34.

27. There is ongoing dispute about the interpretation of David's 'faithful deeds': are they deeds done by David (subjective genitive, Dillard) or done to David (objective genitive, Williamson)? See the discussion in Kleinig, *Lord's Song*, p. 169 n. 2.

28. McKenzie, *Chronicler's Use of the Deuteronomistic History*, pp. 85-86, 89.

his rewriting of the tradition. In the postexilic era this fresh emphasis on Davidides might appear strange, but perhaps the Chronicler meant to suggest that faithful worship at the (rebuilt) temple, using traditional liturgical texts and rituals, could provide some kind of experience of the 'faithful deed' done by David. To suggest an answer to the preliminary question: the Chronicler probably indicates both covenants—Mosaic and Davidic—but wishes to emphasize the Davidic actualization of the earlier covenant with its focal point in the Jerusalem temple.[29] The Chronicler's view of worship here seems to draw on a series of earlier covenantal experiences, to suggest that in worship the people of Israel experience all of them in a somewhat inclusive fashion. Theologically, one should not attempt to divide the people's experience of God with Moses from that with David.

At three points during this worship service the Chronicler mentions choral service/song in places where it is not present in the Kings text: 5.11-14 (esp. v. 13), 7.1-3 and 7.4-6. Kleinig expands on these three additions made to the 'account of the inauguration of worship at the temple in Jerusalem'.[30] The first addition of the thanksgiving refrain followed the exit of the priests from the temple, after they had successfully introduced the ark there: 'they worshiped and gave thanks to YHWH, "For [he is] good, for his graciousness [is] forever"' (7.3). Only after the choral song, joined by the Levites, did the cloud fill the temple (5.14)—a sign of God's presence, which was precipitated by the choral song. As Kleinig puts it, 'the choral service evoked the divine glory'.[31] In 7.1-3, however, the choral song functions quite differently: here it constitutes a response of the entire congregation of Israel to Solomon's lengthy prayer and God's acceptance of the burnt offerings and sacrifices. These details completely refashion the account in 1 Kgs 8.54, and in one important detail it contrasts with the choral song after the ark had been located in the temple: there the priests and Levites sang, while here all Israel joined in the song.

---

29. Another pointer in this direction is the way that the Chronicler repeats the notion that the people went forth from the festival service 'rejoicing and with good hearts' (2 Chron. 7.10//1 Kgs 8.66) and then further applies the notion when he adapts the text of Ps. 132.9, 'let them sing out', which becomes: 'let them rejoice in good[ness]' in 2 Chron. 6.41. In other words, the Dtr rhetoric in 1 Kgs 8.66 has been proleptically introduced in the Chronicler's version, through his editing and addition of Ps. 132 for Solomon's service at the temple, which heightens Davidic connections, though without erasing the Dtr language.

30. Kleinig, *Lord's Song*, p. 161.

31. Kleinig, *Lord's Song*, p. 165.

The third injection of choral song into the narrative follows immediately in 7.4-6. Following the lead in 1 Kgs 8.62-63, the king and all the people sacrificed a huge number of animals as a 'peace offering': 22,000 oxen and 120,000 sheep. Chronicles adds:

> The priests were standing according to their offices and the Levites with the instruments of music for YHWH, that David the king had made *to give thanks to* YHWH, *for his steadfast love lasts forever*, when David was praising with their hands. The priests were sounding the clarions opposite them, and all Israel were standing there. (2 Chron. 7.6 [my emphasis])

Now the Chronicler has made clear that choral song was established by David, who fashioned the musical instruments, and that it was sung by Levites and priests, and presumably all the people. The huge public sacrifices should be accompanied by song, belying suggestions that Israel's sacrifice was always a silent affair. Then the Chronicler returns to his source in Kings, recounting the subsequent consecration of the middle court (v. 7), the seven-day festival and consecration of the altar, and an additional seven days for the observance (vv. 8-9). In both versions they rejoiced 'because of the good that YHWH had done for David'; the net effect of all this liturgical celebration was great benefit ('good') and blessing from God, and Chronicles demonstrates that Israel's proper response to this blessing is not only sacrifice but also song, always expressed with joy (שמח).

Finally, I want to emphasize the inclusion of prayer for Israel's well-being, especially in time of trials and distress, which the Chronicler incorporates from the long prayer of Solomon in 1 Kgs 8.22-53. This later author agrees that the temple is a house of prayer, a place for petition to God for God's people (v. 53), Israel, especially when they suffer distress because of their sins. These petitions also carry the subtle notion that the temple may be a place for confession of sin and its eradication, as argued by Johnstone,[32] but the rhetoric of prayer certainly stands out more strongly for petition to God, as in lamentation psalms. So the king's prayer corresponds well with one of the goals of worship, assigned earlier to the Levites, to 'invoke' God. In this ceremony, Levites take their place at choral song, later giving thanks. The Chronicler presents a variegated theology of worship, in the sense that the rituals differ, but he clearly wants Israel to realize that their God is worthy of praise and thanksgiving, because God appears to them in theophanic experiences and also graces

---

32. Johnstone, *Chronicles and Exodus*, pp. 292-93.

them with 'good' blessings. Here also the worship is joyful and it revolves around the thanksgiving antiphonal.

A Fast and Thanksgiving for a Time of War (2 Chronicles 20)

The third worship service that I discuss differs considerably from the previous two, which focused on the ark and the temple, central symbols of God's presence with Israel. Here, on the other hand, the issue prompting worship is not a religious symbol, but the dangers imposed by an enemy on the march, the fear of attack and battle. Rather than acknowledging God's presence in their established worship symbols, Israel now goes to God to plead for assistance in a time of peril, when no other means of deliverance seems possible.

I prefer to speak of this event as an ad hoc occasion for prayer and worship, rather than as a regular, appointed occasion for celebration. This vignette clearly constitutes one of the prime moments of need that Solomon included in his prayer at the dedication of the temple (2 Chron. 6.19-39). Commentators usually mention this general correspondence to the dangers enumerated in Solomon's prayer,[33] and the Chronicler himself recalls the generic plea to God in time of danger: 'If disaster comes upon us, the sword of judgment or pestilence or famine, we will stand before this house and before you—for your name is in this house—and we will cry to you out of our distress and you will hear and you will deliver' (2 Chron. 20.9).[34] Two more possibilities from the earlier petitions and cases mentioned by Solomon could be specified:

> And if your people Israel is struck down before an enemy, because they sinned against you, if they return and praise your name and pray and make supplication before you in this house, then give heed from the heavens and pardon the sinning of your people Israel and return them to the land which you gave to their ancestors. (2 Chron. 6.24-25)

> If your people goes out to battle against its enemies, in the way by which you send them, and they pray to you [on] the way to this city which you have chosen and the house which I have built for your name, then heed from the heavens to their prayer and the supplication and act for their cause. (2 Chron. 6.34-35)

33. E.g. H.G.M. Williamson, *I and II Chronicles* (NCB; Grand Rapids: Eerdmans, 1982), p. 296; Japhet, *I and II Chronicles*, pp. 790-91.

34. S.S. Tuell, *First and Second Chronicles* (Int; Louisville, KY: John Knox Press, 2001), p. 182, describes this verse as 'a neat, concise summary of 2 Chron. 6.3-42'.

I favor the second, since it refers to a situation of war, even though the Jehoshaphat story in 2 Chronicles speaks more clearly to a defensive posture in battle; still, it does refer to God's initiative as their direction in this encounter, at least regarding 'the way' in which they go. Perhaps the exact identification is not crucial to our understanding of the situation, since it clearly represents a situation in which Israel's king Jehoshaphat and his people, as Solomon of old, had recourse to prayer in the temple to beg God to intervene for them in time of attack by enemies.

In response, the king declares 'a fast' (20.3), a type of ritual that during the Second Temple period seemed to focus both on 'recognition of disaster and prayer to God in time of need'.[35] One key to this ceremony seems to be a type of prayer for divine intervention, which Psalms scholars have described as a 'communal lament' prayer. When found elsewhere, such laments usually respond either to danger or destruction of God's city, typically Jerusalem (e.g. Pss. 44, 74, 79 and 137). They usually include some of the following elements (verses cited for their appearance in 2 Chron. 20): address to God (v. 6, 'YHWH God of our ancestors'); complaints against the enemy (vv. 10-11, Ammonites, Moabites, and people of Mt Seir attack, even though they have no good reason to do so) and implicitly against God (vv. 6-7, in rhetorical questions such as: 'Do you not rule over all the kingdoms of the nations?'); the confession of trust (v. 6d, especially: 'in your hand [are] power and might so that none can withstand you'); petition (v. 12a, 'will you not give judgment against them?'); and motivation to God (v. 12b, 'we do not know what we should do, but our eyes are upon you').[36]

One element seldom found in a lament psalm (but always sought by the language and by the context) is a divine response to the complaint/request. In scholarly debate it was often called the 'oracle of salvation';[37] it was noted in Ps. 12.6 but elsewhere simply hypothesized. In this communal lament it appears that the Levite Jahaziel publicly utters such a salvation oracle in response to the king's complaint and prayer to God in face of danger (20.14-17). After calling for the attention of all the inhabitants of Judah and Jerusalem and of the king in particular, he reports God's opening words, so common in prophetic oracles of salvation: '...thus YHWH

---

35. Endres, 'Joyful Worship', p. 180. On pp. 181-82 several examples of which are noted: Zech. 7.5; Isa. 58.4; Neh. 1.4-10; Jon. 3.5-7; Joel 2.12-27.

36. For a similar analysis, see: R.B. Dillard, *2 Chronicles* (WBC, 15; Waco, TX: Word Books, 1987), pp. 154-57.

37. Cf. Williamson, *1 and 2 Chronicles*, p. 297, for a brief discussion.

says to you, "Do not be afraid, and do not be dismayed before this great horde, for the battle is not yours but God's"' (20.15). These first words from the levitical prophet[38] address Jehoshaphat's mood, reported earlier: he 'was afraid and he set himself to inquire of YHWH' (20.3a). Then the divine speech gives the real reason for the suggested confidence: God will fight the battle (v. 15b). Although v. 16 explains in precise geographical detail the route of the enemy approaching from the Rift Valley (i.e. the Dead Sea region), the Levite's expressed concern is more spiritual than tactical: Judah and its leader are to conduct themselves in utter humility and confidence in God, whose 'deliverance/victory' (את ישועת יהוה) can be expected.[39] Japhet and others note the close literary imitation of Exod. 14.13-14 in 2 Chron. 20.17; in each case Israel is commanded to believe and see God's victory for them: וראו את ישועת יהוה עמכם appears in both texts. Theologically situated in the holy war tradition, the Levite's oracle helps Persian-era Israelites to realize that their God is about to work a new saving-action in their day, much in the tradition of the exodus from the Egyptians: in both cases they are to be 'passive witnesses of his victory over their enemies'.[40]

For the purposes of a theology of worship, the postures and responses of those involved in this ceremony take on a certain importance. After hearing Jahaziel's words, Jehoshaphat 'bowed down with his face to the ground' and all the rest of the inhabitants of Judah and Jerusalem 'fell [down] before YHWH to worship YHWH' (v. 18). Hearing God's reported word leads to a posture of worship, and it seems to respond to the opening questions to God in Jehoshaphat's lament: Do you not rule over all nations? Are not all of Abraham's offspring the recipients and heirs of this land, and now those who have a temple built for your name (20.6-8)? Hearing God's name, YHWH, had previously led to a posture of worship, and here again the Levite's oracle reports that same sacred name in a promise of victory for them; what else could they do but worship? In a dramatic scene the Chronicler demonstrates how worship responds to divine intervention in Israel's daily and extraordinary life-events, far beyond their regular visits to the temple for regular offerings, sacrifices and worship.

The Levites, on the other hand, 'rose up…to praise YHWH the God of Israel with a very loud voice' (20.19). They fulfilled here one of the func-

38. On Levites, cultic figures as prophets, see Dillard, *2 Chronicles*, p. 157.
39. Japhet, *I and II Chronicles*, p. 795.
40. Kleinig, *Lord's Song*, p. 174.

tions to which they were appointed by David: praising YHWH in the presence of the ark (cf. 1 Chron. 16.4).[41] Then, just a bit later, the king appointed singers for YHWH 'to praise [him] in holy array as they went out before the army, saying "Give thanks to YHWH, for his loving-kindness lasts forever!"' (v. 21). These levitical singers again offer the special song of thanksgiving, following the pattern of sung prayer in the services with David (1 Chron. 16.34) and Solomon (2 Chron. 5.13; 7.3, 6). They sing thanksgiving even before God secures the victory and delivers them from their enemies.[42] For Kleinig, the Chronicler has effected a significant innovation here: 'the Levitical choir thus acted as the vanguard of the army. With them the LORD himself stood at the head of his army', secured by 'invocation of his name in sacred song'.[43] The Chronicler describes the effect in battle of the Israelites song: 'At the time when they began singing and praising, YHWH put liers-in-wait against the Ammonites and Moabites and people of Mt Seir who had come against Judah, and they were routed' (2 Chron. 20.22).

This service of fast and thanksgiving in time of war contains several elements that contribute to a theology of worship. First, there is the narrative implication that performance of worship coincides with divine activity for 'Israel', that is, for Judahites in this story of the kingdom just as it was for Hebrews coming out of Egypt. The prayer and ceremonies almost seem to effect God's activity, so much so that worship of the divine name bears a numinous power for those who proclaim it properly, that is, in praise of God. When this occurs, they can almost thank God in advance of the saving acts. This is true not only of narratives reported by the Chronicler but also seems characteristic of the process and theology of lament psalms, where a promise of thanksgiving is often embedded within the very lament psalm itself, pointing toward a saving activity and a song of thanksgiving. Second, the appointed song is again the thanksgiving antiphon (20.21), bringing public lament into the wider scope of Israel's

41. But Kleinig (*Lord's Song*, p. 175) notes that 'this performance of praise by these Levites was an extraordinary occurrence', since they seem to be leading praise but not at a time of sacrifices. However, it seems that the presence of the ark was the central indicator of their giving praise in 1 Chron. 16.4.

42. Dillard (*2 Chronicles*, p. 158) discusses the prominent role of music within Israel's war traditions. Among other texts, he mentions the following: Josh. 6.4-20; Judg. 7.18-20; Job 39.24-25. He also supposes that music accompanied the divine warrior psalms: Pss. 47, 96, 98, etc.

43. Kleinig, *Lord's Song*, p. 177.

worship. Finally, as we come to expect, they returned to Jerusalem 'with joy' because 'YHWH had made them rejoice' (v. 27).

'Return to YHWH': Restoring Worship and Passover Under King Hezekiah (2 Chronicles 29–30)

A fourth worship text further demonstrates the Chronicler's great interest in worship of YHWH. It begins with narration of the rededication of the temple for worship, conducted by 'all Israel', thus implying the necessity of popular participation in genuine worship. Second, it closely ties Hezekiah's concern for worship with that of David and Solomon, so it looks to the past for inspiration.

The report of Hezekiah's restoration of the temple for worship and the celebration of Passover leads to the notion that all Israel purified itself of any elements of foreign worship. This elimination of non-Yahwistic paraphernalia and notions was found in 2 Kgs 18.4, but the deuteronomistic comment differs greatly from the Chronicler's report: the account in 2 Kings credits the cleansing actions to King Hezekiah, and the Chronicler omits any mention of the removal of the bronze serpent made by Moses.[44] Chronicles adds non-synoptic material (29.3–30.27), and it subtly leads to his new interpretation that 'all Israel' participated in the removal of dangerous idols from their midst.

He removed the high places and broke down the pillars and cut down the asherah. He broke up into pieces the bronze serpent that Moses had made because until those days, the Israelites were offering incense to it: it was called Nehustan. (2 Kgs 18.4)	When all this was finished, all Israel who were present went out to the cities of Judah and broke down the pillars, hewed down the asherim, and pulled down the high places and altars from all Judah and Benjamin, and in Ephraim and Manasseh, completely. Then all the Israelites returned each to his holding (and) to their cities. (2 Chron. 31.1)

We can observe here how the activity of a Judean king has been transformed into a renewal program for the entire people, including some from the north. In 2 Chronicles 29–30, the Chronicler expands the account to include: the impact of cleansing the temple of all impurity (brought in by Ahaz), the re-establishment of the proper worship rituals therein and the joyful celebration of Passover and Unleavened Bread. The Chronicler's

---

44. As Japhet notes (*I and II Chronicles*, p. 962), this object—quite important for the Deuteronomists—had apparently become 'an obsolete reference for the Chronicler'.

reworking of these verses in 2 Kings demonstrates the necessity and effectiveness of worship for Israel's common life.

This complicated section consists of four elements: (1) cleansing and rededication of the temple (29.3-30), (2) celebration of the temple restoration (29.31-36), (3) invitation to all Israel to gather in Jerusalem to celebrate Passover at the house of God (30.1-9) and (4) celebration of Passover (30.10-27). The restoration of the temple and its worship recalls the dedication of the temple and its worship under Solomon, showing how Israel must adhere to its grand worship traditions as part of a restoration of its full life in the postexilic era. In the view of the Chronicler, the restoration of the temple is a necessary prerequisite to successful celebration of Israel's most important pilgrim festival, the combined feast of Passover and Unleavened Bread. Worship, then, depends on the cleansing of the pollution of Hezekiah's ancestors, especially those of his father Ahaz. It will lead to resumption of the various kinds of sacrifice appointed for worship in the temple and of the burnt offerings in concert with levitical song. These actions prepare for a successful celebration of the great pilgrim festival that recalls their heritage as a people in covenant with their God, celebrated at the center of their renewed city, its temple. Here the Chronicler interweaves worship in crisis (ch. 29) with an annual festival (ch. 30) that connects Israel with its roots. These events prepare Israel to take further action focused on the worship of YHWH alone by ridding their cities, towns and villages of the vestiges of idolatry (31.1).

Many commentators wrestle with the question of the historicity of these chronistic compositions. They often argue that cultic details in these narratives that contradict normal Jewish practice suggest that the Chronicler has not fabricated these ceremonies.[45] So they reason that the Chronicler probably relied on sources that are no longer extant. Although the historicity of these narratives is not the primary concern, many suggest that for the Chronicler there were actual events and practices, preferably in the time of Hezekiah, that corresponded to his idea of public worship. Since my goal remains the theological focus of these worship stories, it helps to imagine an author reflecting on the meaning of a type and pattern of worship that

---

45. Japhet (*I and II Chronicles*, p. 935), takes note of certain problems in the narrative, such as Passover celebration in the second month, and she raises a pertinent question: 'If the whole thing was…a free creation, why would it be composed along unusual and non-conventional lines instead of accepted, legitimate principles?' See also McKenzie, *Chronicler's Use of the Deuteronomistic History*, pp. 170-73; Williamson, *I and II Chronicles*, pp. 361-64.

has actually been experienced, either at the time of composition or in the memorable past.

The purification and rededication of the temple follow for the Chronicler, directly after he repeats what he found in his source, that Hezekiah 'did what was right in the eyes of YHWH according to all that David his [fore]father had done' (2 Chron. 29.2//2 Kgs 18.3). Attention to the temple, then, put Hezekiah into the tradition of David, who had schematized the plan for temple and personnel and transmitted it to Solomon. His first act, it seems, was to reopen the temple's doors, which had been closed by his father Ahaz's actions (2 Chron. 28.24): 'he opened the doors of the house of YHWH and repaired (piel חזק) them' (29.3b). It may be that the Chronicler's use of חזק here was intended as a play on Hezekiah's name (יחזקיהו), perhaps to underscore his role as the 'repairer' or 'strengthener', in a theological sense. Then he assembled the priests and Levites and addressed them, exhorting them to participate in this purification and consecration of the temple (29.5-11). Because their ancestors acted unfaithfully (מעל) and sinned, the temple suffers from filth or pollution (נדה),[46] which they must take out or expunge from the sanctuary. After listing the Levites who participated (29.12-14), the story recounts their progress: they 'purified' the house of YHWH, especially its innermost part, and brought out everything that was unclean, and then they proceeded with the ceremonies of consecration: eight days for the outer court, and another eight days for the house of YHWH (29.15-17).

Two important points stand out. First, to 'purify' means to cleanse of the impurities, to deliver the temple from a state of pollution, while to 'consecrate' implies the opposite, to make holy, and perhaps even more, 'beyond purity' to bring the temple 'to an elevated state'.[47] Both verbs denote strong action, but one concerns removal while the other involves changing the status of the object or structure. In the Chronicler's view, both Levites and priests engage in two kinds of activity here, both of which lead to a (re)consecration of YHWH's court and house. And then they go to the king and report on their actions and reinstall its sacred vessels and the table for the bread, precisely those things rejected by Ahaz (29.18-19). Second, the two rounds of consecration, two periods of eight

46. A very strong word, used only here in Chronicles (Japhet, *I and II Chronicles*, p. 917), which refers to ritual impurity and is known from priestly literature (Williamson, *I and II Chronicles*, p. 353). See also H.-J. Fabry, 'נדה', in *TDOT*, IX, pp. 232-35 (233).

47. Japhet, *I and II Chronicles*, p. 922.

days, takes them until the sixteenth of the first month. Since Passover usually begins on the fourteenth, it could not begin at that time this year, since the temple itself was not yet consecrated. So the narrative has established a reason for celebrating the pilgrim festival of Passover in the second month. In two distinct ways this author emphasizes the importance of a state of holiness (קדש), for the temple itself but also for worship at a pilgrim festival.

After all these preparations, the ceremony of consecration followed (29.20-30), beginning with the offering of various sacrifices, the sin offering, the sprinkling of blood against the altar (vv. 21-24), to make atonement for all Israel (v. 24).[48] The second element consists of the burnt offerings, during which time the Levites were stationed in the temple and commanded to begin their music and song (and also the priests with their clarions) when the ceremony of burnt offerings began (v. 27). At the same time the assembly bowed down, until the burnt offerings were completed:

> Then Hezekiah ordered the offering of the burnt offering at the altar. At the time the burnt offering began, there began the song of YHWH and the trumpets with the playing of the (musical) instruments of David king of Israel. All the assembly bowed themselves down as songs were sung and trumpets blown, all until the completion of the burnt offering. (2 Chron. 29.27-28)

As Kleinig notes, 'the presentation of the burnt offering was the centre of the whole sacrificial ritual', and it was coordinated with the choral rite, and all of it focused on the praise of YHWH.[49] Apparently, the Levites also bowed down, completing the group of those who worshiped by this dramatic gesture and also completing the ritual of public sacrifices.

In response, all the assembly was now invited by the king to bring forward their own private offerings, both thank offerings and burnt offerings (brought by those 'of generous heart', 29.31). Note that this part of the ceremonies included זבחים, offerings that participants cooked and then shared in the sacrificial banquets at the temple.[50] Although this ceremony seems quite complex, it also seems to have been constructed in a fashion to indicate a pattern of worship (with the basic elements of worship) for people of the Chronicler's era, especially in Jerusalem. The rite includes public sacrifices and music and song, along with physical

48. This section follows closely the analysis of Kleinig, *Lord's Song*, pp. 112-14.

49. Kleinig, *Lord's Song*, p. 103. Here again the duty of Levites to engage in praise of God (הלל) is emphasized.

50. Kleinig, *Lord's Song*, p. 103.

prostration, and would conclude with personal sacrificial offerings, much of it shared in a liturgical meal of some sort. No wonder the Chronicler can conclude this section by speaking of the great rejoicing of the king and all the people over what had been initiated for them: 29.30, 36 (root שׂמח). The Chronicler not only described the ceremonies (both preparatory and actual worship actions) but also indicated the mood of worship: praise, thanksgiving, and especially, great rejoicing.

In ch. 30 the Chronicler moves even closer to prescription of Israel's normal ways of worship by his narration of the great Passover ceremony in the time of Hezekiah. First, since this festival should be an inclusive celebration, Hezekiah sent the message not only to Judah but also to all Israel, with a concerted effort to invite the northern tribes to Jerusalem. Some northerners accepted, humbly. He also mentions explicitly the inclusion of resident aliens from Israel (30.25), reminding his hearers of earlier prescriptions to include the resident aliens (גרים). Second, this Passover celebration clearly acknowledged God's great generosity to Israel in its past, as YHWH had rescued them from destruction and exile. Although the Chronicler does not mention the exodus from Egypt here, its pattern emerges clearly in his references to the possibility of return from their sin as prelude to return to their land in a great experience of God's compassion (30.9).[51] This pattern mirrors language in Solomon's temple prayer (2 Chron. 6.36-39),[52] thus providing another parallel between these two kings and their worship services.

Another similarity between the two kings is found in the word 'heal' (root רפא): 2 Chron. 7.14//30.20.[53] But the most important aspect of Hezekiah's prayer on this occasion of the Passover festival is his plea for those who had eaten the Passover sacrifice in a state of ritual impurity: 'Hezekiah prayed on their behalf saying, "May the good YHWH make atonement for each one who sets his heart to seek the God YHWH God of his ancestors, even though not according to the purity of the sanctuary"' (30.18-19). As many commentators note, the Chronicler here articulates

---

51. This fourth worship service lacks the 'thanksgiving antiphon' found in the other three, but the language in 30.9, of YHWH as 'gracious and merciful' (חנון ורחום) comes close to the notion of YHWH's everlasting *hesed* (חסד).

52. For this reference, see Yehudah Qayil, *Sepher Dibre Hayammim* (2 vols.; Jerusalem: Mossad Harev Kook, 1986), II, p. 843.

53. A notable difference between the two texts is the direct object of God's healing: in this chapter YHWH healed 'the people', while in the earlier text, following repentance, God will heal 'their land'.

the priority of a right heart, a spiritual intention in celebrating the festival sacrifice, as being of more importance than fulfillment of ritual directives. As Graham comments, 'Such intense focus on the heart and internal orientation of the worshipper is a far cry from the hollow legalism and ritualism that so many associate with the books of Chronicles'.[54]

Two recent commentaries witness admiration of this prayer as a victory over ritualism,[55] but this 'victory for the heart' should not cause us to overlook the great emphasis on the joyous character of the celebration: in vv. 21 and 26 the author speaks of 'great joy', while v. 23 also mentions how the people celebrated an additional seven days of Passover 'in joy'. Such joy demonstrates the people's accord with God in the worship service and it also accompanies great celebrations that include the full gamut of ceremonies, including the celebrative banquets or meals after the people's voluntary sacrifices. The Chronicler employs the root שׂמח ('joy') five times in chs. 29–30, so these ceremonies represent a victory over so-called ritualism. Moreover, he suggests that the rituals of worship, exercised with a whole heart, actually lead to great rejoicing and to the experience of unity within the community and with its tradition (2 Chron. 30.26). The correspondences that link Hezekiah's actions with those of David and Solomon serve to pull together a notion of worship that is whole-hearted, joyful, inclusive and responsive both to God's demands and to God's love for compassion and mercy.

A Variegated Theology of Worship

These worship services in Chronicles introduce the audience to various rituals for different 'moments' in Israel's life as a worshiping community. David's procession with the ark to Jerusalem initiates a new location for worship connected to the ark. Solomon enacts a temple dedication ceremony, replete with prayer to God for a people in need. Hezekiah completes a rededication ceremony for Solomon's temple after its pollution by sinful kings. Jehoshaphat's 'fast' and ceremony at the temple in a time of crisis picks up on a major theme of Solomon's great prayer at the dedication of

54. M.P. Graham, 'Setting the Heart to Seek God: Worship in 2 Chronicles 30.1–31.1', in Graham, Marrs and McKenzie (eds.), *Worship and the Hebrew Bible*, pp. 124-41 (138).

55. Cf. Tuell, *First and Second Chronicles*, pp. 220-221; and P.K. Hooker, *First and Second Chronicles* (Westminster Bible Companion; Louisville, KY: Westminster/ John Knox Press, 2001), p. 256.

the temple, and his lament petition connects in subtle ways with similar emphases in the stories of Hezekiah (30.18-19) and David (1 Chron. 16.4). Israel worships not only for praise, not only in time of gratitude, but also in time of invocation and lament over crises.

Although the ceremonies differ considerably, the Chronicler interweaves motifs that bind them together in a rich tapestry of worship. Three of the four ceremonies include the great litany, 'For his mercy endures forever (כל לעולם חסדו)', which expresses deep gratitude to YHWH. In the ceremony from David's time the Chronicler quoted from Ps. 106.1 (1 Chron. 16.34), but in the Solomon narratives he makes the language his own, describing the worship of the temple dedication as using song and music from David's arrangements (2 Chron. 5.13; 7.3, 6). In the holy war from Jehoshaphat's time the singers appointed by the king sang this refrain as they celebrated God's victory over their enemies (20.21). Only in the Hezekiah section is the language completely lacking, though it seems to have been transformed there into language of graciousness and compassion (חנון ורחום) as descriptors for God. In all cases, however, worship includes singing of refrains like these, a new and constitutive element of postexilic worship in Jerusalem.

Finally, we note the mood of worship as the Chronicler reports it. In each of these ceremonies the root שמח appears, signifying joy or rejoicing. In the psalm prayer of David's ceremony the Chronicler has chosen verses with this concept from two different psalms: 1 Chron. 16.10//Ps. 105.3; 1 Chron. 16.31//Ps. 96.11. In directing the Levites and their kindred to raise up joyful song and music, he uses the same word (1 Chron. 15.16). When he describes Solomon's temple dedication, he substitutes this word for another verb in a psalm: 2 Chron. 6.41//Ps. 132.9. Later he uses the same word to describe the mood of the whole people after their celebration of the festival (2 Chron. 7.10). Jehoshaphat's time is marked by the same mood, after YHWH wages battle for them, for they return to Jerusalem with joy (2 Chron. 20.27) and playing their musical instruments. Finally, Hezekiah's ceremonies of rededication and the Passover festival are both characterized by this joy (2 Chron. 29.30, 36; 30.21, 23, 26).

The newly described pattern of worship—burnt offerings, public sacrifices, music and song, thanksgiving sacrifices and the eating of joyful meals together—allows people of the Second Temple era to realize what their God intended for them in their Jerusalem temple: praise, thanksgiving, and petition, offered to God in a ritual complex that can help them realize their identity as the people of God. This invitation of the Chronicler to his people is to engage in worship that is whole-hearted, joyful, inclusive and responsive—both to God's demands of them and also to the implications of worshiping a God characterized by steadfast love, compassion and mercy. These new focal points and symbols in worship make powerful theological assertions about the God to whom they are bound by ritual action and ritual word.

JERUSALEM—THE DIVINE CITY:
THE REPRESENTATION OF JERUSALEM IN CHRONICLES
COMPARED WITH EARLIER AND LATER JEWISH COMPOSITIONS*

Isaac Kalimi

1. *Introduction*

Jerusalem, the nursery of much of Israel's literary and spiritual heritage, is represented in various Jewish writings throughout the generations. The purpose of this study is to review the representation of Jerusalem in Chronicles compared with the earlier and later Jewish compositions. I hope to show the presentation of Jerusalem in the book of Chronicles (micro) within the comprehensive framework of Jewish writings (macro); to observe the issue in the restricted text of Chronicles, while comparing it with early and late biblical historiography as well as with post-biblical (in the widest range of the term) perspectives. Furthermore, the goal is to draw attention to the subject in the setting of the Chronicler's own time, place, religious context and distinct historical circumstances. Only from such broad perspectives may one consider and evaluate properly the uniqueness of the Chronicler's approach towards the topic under review.

2. *The Chronistic View of Jerusalem Compared with the Deuteronomistic View*

a. *The Capital of the 'Kingdom of the Lord', the Site of his Throne and Sanctuary*
Both histories, the chronistic and the deuteronomistic, regard the Davidic dynasty as the only legitimate one for the Southern Kingdom. Thus, Athaliah is considered in both compositions to be an interloper (2 Kgs 11.1-20//

* This study is based on guest lectures that were delivered at Boston University (17 November 1999) and at Bar-Ilan University (7 March 2000). I would like to thank my colleagues Professor Simon B. Parker and Professor Joshua Schwartz for their kind invitations.

2 Chron. 22.10–23.21).[1] There is, however, an important difference between the two histories on this issue. The DtrH saw other legitimate
dynasties elected by God, such as those of Jeroboam (1 Kgs 11.29-39) and
Jehu (2 Kgs 9.1-10; 10.30) in the Northern Kingdom. According to chronistic history, however, all the kings of Israel were illegitimate and rebellious (2 Chron. 13.6-8—an 'addition'). The only lawful and permanently
chosen dynasty in the nation's history is the Davidic dynasty: 'the Lord
God of Israel gave the kingship over Israel [= southern and northern tribes]
to David *forever*, for him and his sons, by a covenant of salt' (2 Chron.
13.5—an 'addition').[2]

Now, since all the kings of the Davidic dynasty were located in and
reigned from Jerusalem,[3] the Chronicler has introduced a unique concept
concerning the city:

1.   The legitimate kings in Jerusalem were descendants of Solomon,
     who sat on *'the throne of the Lord'* (1 Chron. 28.5b; 29.23a—an
     'addition').
2.   The Kingdom of Judah is described as *'the kingdom of the Lord
     in the hand of the sons of David'* (2 Chron. 13.8—an 'addition').

Hence, Jerusalem emerges in Chronicles as the only capital of 'the kingdom of the Lord' and a location of 'the throne of the Lord'. It hosted all
the kings of the Davidic dynasty, the only dynasty chosen to represent God
on earth.

The existence of God in the city is also obvious from his permanent
presence in his sanctuary, which is named by the Chronicler as 'a house of
rest for the ark of covenant of the Lord, and for the footstool of our Lord'
(1 Chron. 28.2; 2 Chron. 6.41a—'additions'). God's name dwells in Jerusalem's temple continuously and his entire being is always involved with
it ('mine eyes and mine heart', 2 Chron. 7.16//1 Kgs 9.3). God had chosen

---

1.   Notice also, 'Now the wicked Athaliah and her associates had broken into the
temple of God' (2 Chron. 24.7—an 'addition').

2.   For the expression, 'covenant of salt', see Lev. 2.13 and especially Num. 18.19.
See also I. Kalimi, *Zur Geschichtsschreibung des Chronisten. Literarisch-historio-
graphische Abweichungen der Chronik von ihren Paralleltexten in den Samuel- und
Königsbüchern* (BZAW, 226; Berlin: W. de Gruyter, 1995), p. 299; *idem, The Book of
Chronicles: Historical Writing and Literary Devices* (The Biblical Encyclopaedia
Library, 18; Jerusalem: Bialik Institute, 2000), p. 337 (Hebrew).

3.   Of course, I am excluding the first seven or seven and a half years of David's
reign, which were spent in Hebron (1 Chron. 3.4//2 Sam. 5.4-5; 1 Chron. 29.26-27//
1 Kgs 2.11).

the place also as 'a house for sacrifices' (2 Chron. 7.12 is an 'addition' to 1 Kgs 9)—a distinctive biblical phrase that appears only in Chronicles.[4]

Jerusalem is depicted by the Chronicler, therefore, as an absolutely theocratic city, 'the city of God/the Lord' in the full sense of the word, more so than in any other biblical work. Indeed the Chronicler changed the burial place of King Amaziah of Judah and wrote that he had been buried 'in the city of Judah (בעיר יהודה)' (2 Chron. 25.28), while his *Vorlage* relates that Amaziah had been buried 'in the city of David (בעיר דוד)' (2 Kgs 14.20).[5] But he never uses 'the city of God/the Lord' in the material he adds or instead of the name 'Jerusalem' in Samuel–Kings. However, since Judah is described as *'the kingdom of the Lord'*, one can deduce that 'the city of Judah' is in fact 'the city of the Lord/God'.

b. *The Chosen City of God*

The Chronicler recognizes Jerusalem as the chosen city of God, the center for his rituals and cults, the home of his only legitimate central temple. Accordingly, the author copied all the related texts concerning Jerusalem as the chosen city that appear in the book of Kings. For instance, in the prayer of Solomon in 2 Chron. 6.5-6 (//1 Kgs 8.16), it is reported that God approved of David:

> Since the day when I brought my people out of the land of Egypt, *I did not choose any city in all the tribes of Israel in which to build a house* for my name to be there. Neither did I choose any man as prince over my people Israel; *but now I have chosen Jerusalem for my name to be there* and I have chosen David to be over my people Israel.[6]

---

4.   For more detail on the role of the temple in the Chronicler's view, see M.J.D. Selman, 'Jerusalem in Chronicles', in R.S. Hess and G.J. Wenham (eds.), *Zion, City of Our God* (Grand Rapids: Eerdmans, 1999), pp. 43-56 (48-52).

5.   Although the name 'city of Judah' does not appear elsewhere in biblical literature, it is not a scribal error in the book of Chronicles, as some scholars claim. See, e.g., E.L. Curtis and A.A. Madsen (eds.), *The Books of Chronicles: A Critical and Exegetical Commentary* (ICC, 11; Edinburgh: T. & T. Clark, 1910), p. 447; M. Rehm, *Textkritische Untersuchungen zu den Parallelstellen der Samuel-Königsbücher und der Chronik* (Alttestamentliche Abhandlungen, 13.3; Münster: Aschendorffsche Verlagsbuchhandlung, 1937), p. 71; W. Rudolph, *Chronikbücher* (HAT, 21; Tübingen: J.C.B. Mohr [Paul Siebeck], 1955), p. 280, and compare his note in *BHS*, p. 1553; H.G.M. Williamson, *1 and 2 Chronicles* (NCB; Grand Rapids: Eerdmans, 1982), p. 331; see also RSV *ad loc.* It is rather a deliberate substitute by the Chronicler. See Kalimi, *Geschichtsschreibung*, p. 93; *idem, Book of Chronicles*, pp. 102-103.

6.   See also 1 Kgs 11.26; cf. Deut. 12.5, 11, 14, 18, 26.

The conclusion of Mordechai Cogan, that the concept of 'the divine choice of the Temple's city [= Jerusalem] is absent from the book of Kings and included in the book of Chronicles',[7] is completely inaccurate. The absence of the words 'Neither did I choose any man as prince over my people Israel; but now I have chosen Jerusalem for my name to be there' (2 Chron. 6.5b-6a) from the MT of 1 Kings 8 (and partly from the Greek version of 3 Kingdoms [the first half] and the Greek version of 2 Chronicles [the second half]), is due to homoioteleuton: 'for my name to be there... for my name to be there (לְהְיוֹת שְׁמִי שָׁם...לְהְיוֹת שְׁמִי שָׁם)'.[8] Indeed, the Qumran version of 1 Kgs 8.16 (4QKgs[a]) contains the words that are missing from the MT.[9] Moreover, Jerusalem as the chosen city of God also appears twice later on in Solomon's prayer—1 Kgs 8.44, 48 (//2 Chron. 6.34, 38), as well as in other places, such as 2 Kgs 21.7 (//2 Chron. 33.7):

> And he [= Manasseh] set the graven image of the idol, which he had made, in the house of God, of which God said to David and Solomon his son: 'In this house, and *in Jerusalem, which I have chosen out of all the tribes of Israel*, will I put My name forever.[10]

These verses indicate that the concept of Jerusalem as a divinely chosen city is not unique to the chronistic history, but rather appears already in the DtrH.

While the omission of the words of 2 Chron. 6.5b-6a from the Hebrew version of 1 Kings 8 (and partially from the above-mentioned Greek versions) should be regarded as the result of textual corruption, the analysis of Mulder and Selman must be rejected as well. Selman claims that the

7. See M. Cogan, '"The City that I Chose"—The Deuteronomistic View of Jerusalem', *Tarbiz* 55 (1986), pp. 301-309 (308) (Hebrew).

8. Compare Rehm, *Textkritische Untersuchungen*, pp. 66, 79-80; Williamson, *1 and 2 Chronicles*, p. 216; R.B. Dillard, *2 Chronicles* (WBC, 15; Waco, TX: Word Books, 1987), p. 46; *contra* B. Stade, *The Books of Kings: Critical Edition of the Hebrew Text* (The Sacred Books of Old Testament, 9; Leipzig: J.C. Hinrichs; Baltimore: The Johns Hopkins University Press, 1904), p. 103; D.W. Staerk, 'Zum alttestamentlichen Erwählungsglauben', *ZAW* 55 (1937), pp. 1-36 (26 n. 1); J.A. Montgomery, *The Books of Kings: A Critical and Exegetical Commentary* (ICC, 10; Edinburgh: T. & T. Clark, 1951), pp. 201-202; E. Würthwein, *Das Erste Buch der Könige* (ATD, 11; Göttingen: Vandenhoeck & Ruprecht, 1977), p. 96.

9. See J. Trebolle Barrera, '4QKgs', in E.C. Ulrich (ed.), *Qumran Cave 4. IX. Deuteronomy, Joshua, Judges, Kings* (DJD, 14; Oxford: Clarendon Press, 1995), pp. 171-83 (177).

10. See also 1 Kgs 14.21b//2 Chron. 12.13b.

Chronicler has not just cited his source, but 'he has expanded it and given it a more emphatic sense'. He continues (the italics are mine):

> Where Kings put the choice of Jerusalem negatively ('I did not choose any city among any of the tribes of Israel to build a house there for my name'), the Chronicler *adds a positive complementary phrase*: 'But now I have chosen Jerusalem for my name to be there.'

Accordingly, Selman concludes incorrectly:

> The reason for the addition is that for the Chronicler, the election of Jerusalem has a more specific meaning than in the Deuteronomistic history, which is related to the broader theme of election in Chronicles.[11]

For the same reasons one must also reject Mulder's understanding of 1 Kgs 8.16:

> In 2 Chr. 6:5 something is *added* to this sentence: 'Nor had I chosen a man to be prince (= נגיד) over my people Israel'... In 2 Chr. 6:6 (cf. also LXX) one finds a similar development, inasmuch as 'and I have chosen Jerusalem that my name may be there' is *added* to our verse from Kings.[12]

It is important to note that the uniqueness of Jerusalem consists in its having been chosen not only from among 'all the tribes of Israel' (2 Chron. 33.7//2 Kgs 21.7; cf. 2 Chron. 6.5-6//1 Kgs 8.16), but in fact from among all the cities of the entire world. Moreover, the Chronicler omitted from his composition the deuteronomistic evaluation: 'And the Lord said, "I will...*cast off this city Jerusalem which I have chosen*, and the house of which I said, My name shall be there' (2 Kgs 23.27). The omission may be interpreted to indicate that contrary to DtrH, in Chronicles the concept of Jerusalem as an elected city by the Lord is *unconditional* and permanent. It means that Jerusalem continued to be the Lord's chosen city even in the time of the Chronicler himself. The devastation of Jerusalem by King Nebuchadnezzar of Babylon does not negate its divine election. The small size of Jerusalem in the Chronicler's era and its poor condition did not affect its spiritual superiority as the only legitimate cult-place of God! He chose unconditionally not only the city of Jerusalem, but also its *temple site* (1 Chron. 21.26 and 22.1—'additions' to 2 Sam. 24.25), Solomon the *temple-builder* (1 Chron. 28.6, 10; 29.1) and the *temple itself*: 'Now I have chosen (בחרתי) and consecrated this temple that my name should be there

---

11. See Selman, 'Jerusalem in Chronicles', p. 47.

12. See M.J. Mulder, *1 Kings. I. 1 Kings 1–11* (HCOT; Leuven: Peeters, 1998), pp. 406-407 (my emphasis).

forever, my eyes and my heart there for all time' (2 Chron. 7.16).[13] Does the concept under review originate from a hidden polemic against the Samaritans, who claimed that Mt Gerizim was the only legitimate cult-place of God?[14]

c. *The Location of the Temple and the* Aqedah
Although the location of the temple is absent from the story of its construction in 1 Kgs 5.15–9.25 (EVV 5.1–9.25),[15] it is described in the greatest detail in 2 Chron. 3.1. The description is given in a tripartite form that moves from the general to the specific. The first detail to be given is the name of the city in which the temple was built—'Jerusalem'; next, the name of the mountain in Jerusalem is given—'on Mt Moriah'; and finally, the exact location on the mountain is specified—'at the place which David had designated, at the threshing floor of Ornan the Jebusite'.[16]

The description of the temple's site forms a natural part of the account of its construction, which not only gives the date of its construction (1 Kgs 6.1 and 37), but also describes its size, the materials needed for it, the vessels used in it, and so on. It comes as no surprise, therefore, that the Chronicler noticed that this item of information was missing in the text of Kings and affixed it, as he did in a number of other passages parallel to texts in Samuel–Kings.[17]

13. See also v. 12c. The phrase, 'I have chosen', is an addition to the parallel text in 1 Kgs 9. Cf. Selman, 'Jerusalem in Chronicles', pp. 47-48.
14. On the polemic with the Samaritans, see I. Kalimi, 'The Affiliation of Abraham and the Aqedah with Zion/Gerizim in Jewish and Samaritan Sources', in *idem*, *Early Jewish Exegesis and Theological Controversies: Studies in Scriptures in the Shadow of Internal and External Controversies* (Jewish and Christian Heritage, 2; Assen: Van Gorcum, 2002), pp. 33-58.
15. On this issue, see in detail I. Kalimi, 'The Land/Mount Moriah, and the Site of the Jerusalem Temple in Biblical Historical Writing', in *idem*, *Early Jewish Exegesis and Theological Controversies: Studies in Scriptures in the Shadow of Internal and External Controversies* (Jewish and Christian Heritage, 2; Assen: Van Gorcum, 2002), pp. 9-32.
16. See Kalimi, 'The Land/Mount Moriah', p. 26. This resoning solves Williamson's problem (*1 and 2 Chronicles*, p. 204) that the verse 'involves the absurd implication of identifying the whole of Mount Moriah with the threshing floor'.
17. Thus, e.g., 2 Kgs 16.3 and 21.6 mention Kings Ahaz and Manasseh consigning their sons to the fire without giving details of the place, while the parallel passages in 2 Chron. 28.3 and 33.6 add that it happened in 'the Valley of Ben-hinnom'. This phenomenon is discussed at length in Kalimi, *Geschichtsschreibung*, pp. 73-79, and *idem*, *Book of Chronicles*, pp. 80-86.

Indeed, the use of the word 'Moriah' (this is the only place in the Hebrew Bible, besides Gen. 22.2 where this name is mentioned) and 'at the place which David had designated, at the threshing floor of Ornan the Jebusite' draw analogies both to the narrative of the binding of Isaac (*Aqedah*)[18] and to the account of the construction of an altar on the threshing floor of Ornan (1 Chron. 21.1–22.1//2 Sam. 24).[19] But why did the Chronicler add the words 'in Jerusalem' here? There was no need to mention it, since it was known to all that the temple was built in Jerusalem.

The purpose of mentioning Jerusalem as well as the analogies might have been to enhance the sanctity of the city and the temple in the Chronicler's day. The author attempted to endow Jerusalem and its temple with traditions deeply rooted in the history of the Israelite people.[20] The poor condition of Jerusalem and its (second) temple, which was certainly constructed on the ruins of Solomon's temple, at that time[21] indicated that Jerusalem and the temple were in need of such support. The temple was not of an impressive size and was poorly built, particularly when compared to the First Temple (Hag. 2.3; cf. Ezra 3.12-13). Haggai even went as far as to make promises concerning the future wealth and splendor of the temple (Hag. 2.6-9).

3. *Comparison of the Representation of Jerusalem in Chronicles with that in Prophetic and Post-Biblical Literature*

a. *Jerusalem in the Exilic and Postexilic Prophetic and Jewish Apocalyptic Writings*
The representation of Jerusalem in chronistic history differs markedly from what is found in the exilic and postexilic prophetic and apocalyptic literatures. In the exilic and postexilic prophetic writings, such as Ezekiel

---

18. The Chronicler does not retell the story of the binding of Isaac. He refers to it, assuming that it is familiar to his readers. A similar assumption underlies the text of Chronicles in other places too (see, e.g., 1 Chron. 2.7, which is a reference to Josh. 7, although the story is not retold in Chronicles). This phenomenon is also discussed in Kalimi, *Geschichtsschreibung*, pp. 172-90; *idem, Book of Chronicles*, pp. 191-210.

19. For details, see Kalimi, 'The Land/Mount Moriah', p. 27. The Chronicler's line of thought here was developed later in Rabbinic literature, see *idem*, 'The Land/ Mount Moriah', p. 27 n. 53. Similar things were said by the Samaritans about the site of their temple on Mt Gerizim. See Kalimi, 'The Affiliation of Abraham, pp. 48-54.

20. For a similar approach, cf. Williamson, *1 and 2 Chronicles*, p. 205.

21. See, e.g., Hag. 1.4, 8-9, 14; 2.3; Ezra 2.68; 3.3, 12; 6.3; 9.9 and also the tradition mentioned in *b. Zeb.* 62b.

(chs. 40–48), Deutero-Isaiah (Isa. 54.11-12), Trito-Isaiah (Isa. 60.13; 65.17-25; 66), as well as Haggai (2.6-9), there are eschatological visions of a new and ideal Jerusalem and its temple, a utopian holy city that was never realized.[22] The same can be said concerning the representation of Jerusalem in Jewish apocalyptic literature. This literature flourished specifically around the Maccabean crisis, as is revealed in Daniel, *1 Enoch* and the Dead Sea Scrolls.[23] Visions of a new Jerusalem flourished also in literature written after the destruction of the Second Temple, towards the end of the first century CE,[24] for instance in *4 Ezra* (7.26; 10.27), *2 Baruch* (= the *Syriac Apocalypse of Baruch*)[25] and *3 Baruch* (= the *Greek Apocalypse of Baruch*). The authors of these compositions were not satisfied with Jerusalem, especially with the size, quality and function of its temple. They dreamed rather about a new, ideal city and temple that would appear in the future, and they directed their attention from the earthly ones to the heavenly or spiritual ones.[26]

b. *Jerusalem in the Jewish Hellenistic Literature and Other Writings*
The Jerusalem that is portrayed in Chronicles also differs quite markedly from the representations of Jerusalem by some Jewish Hellenistic writers.

22. See J.J. Collins, *Jerusalem and the Temple in Jewish Apocalyptic Literature of the Second Temple Period* (International Rennert Guest Lecture Series, 1; Ramat-Gan: Bar-Ilan University Press, 1998), pp. 4-8, and the bibliography cited there.

23. See, for example, the Temple Scroll and the New Jerusalem Scroll from Qumran, and L.H. Schiffman, 'Jerusalem in the Dead Sea Scrolls', in M. Poorthuis and Ch. Safrai (eds.), *The Centrality of Jerusalem: Historical Perspectives* (Kampen: Kok, 1996), pp. 73-88 (83-88, 'The Eschatological Jerusalem'); M. Chyutin, *The New Jerusalem Scroll from Qumran: A Comprehensive Reconstruction* (JSPSup, 25; Sheffield: Sheffield Academic Press, 1997).

24. See also the fifth Sibylline Oracle and Rev. 21.1–22.5. For the authorship and date of the book of Revelation, see G.R. Beasley-Murray, *The Book of Revelation* (NCB; Grand Rapids: Eerdmans, 1983), pp. 32-38. On the view that its author was a Jew, see E. Vischer, *Die Offenbarung Johannis. Eine jüdische Apokalypse in christlicher Bearbeitung* (Leipzig: J.C. Hinrichs, 1886).

25. See R. Nir, '"This is not the City which I have Carved on the Palms of My Hand": The Heavenly Jerusalem in II Baruch', *Zion* 65 (2000), pp. 5-44 (Hebrew).

26. See Kalimi, 'The Land/Mount Moriah', pp. 27-31; Collins, *Jerusalem and the Temple in Jewish Apocalyptic Literature*, pp. 1-31. Most recently P. Söllner published a comprehensive study on the topic, *Jerusalem, die hochgebaute Stadt. Eschatologisches und Himmlisches Jerusalem im Frühjudentum und im frühen Christentum* (TANZ, 25; Tübingen/Basel: A. Francke Verlag, 1998). He discusses in detail early Jewish and New Testament sources, which encompass a time span from the third century BCE to the first century CE.

Philo of Alexandria, for example, referred to Jerusalem as a mythical and symbolic concept, rather than as a geographic location in the land of Israel.[27] The greater the geographical distance between Jews and Jerusalem, the more the city became an abstraction for them. This phenomenon finds expression specifically in the literature written by Jewish authors after the devastation of Jerusalem and the temple by Titus (70 CE) and continued almost through the last nineteen centuries, until the establishment of the modern State of Israel in May 1948, or even until the reunification of the city in June 1967.[28]

c. *Jerusalem in the Chronistic Writing*

Contrary to all the exilic and postexilic prophetic and post-biblical literature mentioned above, Jerusalem is represented in Chronicles *essentially* in realistic terms. Indeed, the Chronicler represents Jerusalem as the chosen city of God and the capital of the 'kingdom of the Lord', the site of his throne and sanctuary. However, this pragmatic treatment of the city follows the practice in most of the rest of the Hebrew Bible. The Chronicler describes the city basically as a monarchic capital. The postexilic temple-city of his day (c. 400–375 BCE),[29] the poor and provincial

27. See I.L. Seeligmann, 'Jerusalem in Jewish-Hellenistic Thought', in *Judah and Jerusalem: The Twelfth Archaeological Convention* (Jerusalem: Israel Exploration Society, 1957), pp. 192-208 (194-97) (= Seeligmann, *Studies in Biblical Literature* [Jerusalem: Magnes Press, 1992], pp. 396-410, both in Hebrew); J. Heineman, 'The Relationship Between the Jewish People and their Land in Hellenistic-Jewish Literature', *Zion* 13–14 (1948–49), pp. 1-9 (8) (Hebrew); D. Flusser, 'Jerusalem in the Literature of the Second Temple', in A. Eben-Shushan *et al.* (eds.), *Ve'im Bigvuroth: Fourscore Years, A Tribute to Rubin and Hannah Mass on their Eightieth Birthdays* (Jerusalem: Yedidim, 1974), pp. 263-94 (Hebrew). However, Flusser does not refer specifically to the Chronistic literature.

28. See B.Z. Dinur, 'The Concept of Zion and Jerusalem in Jewish Historical Thought', *Zion* 16 (1951), pp. 1-16 (Hebrew); E.E. Urbach, 'Heavenly and Earthly Jerusalem', in J. Avisam (ed.), *Jerusalem Through the Ages: The Twenty-Fifth Archaeological Convention* (Jerusalem: Israel Exploration Society, 1968), pp. 156-71; G. Shaked, 'Jerusalem in Hebrew Literature', *Jewish Studies* 38 (1998), pp. 15-32 (Hebrew).

29. For the dating of Chronicles, see I. Kalimi, 'Die Abfassungszeit der Chronik— Forschungsstand und Perspektiven', *ZAW* 105 (1993), pp. 223-33; *idem*, 'Könnte die aramäische Grabinschrift aus Ägypten als Indikation für die Datierung der Chronikbücher fungieren?', *ZAW* 110 (1998), pp. 79-81; *idem*, 'The Date of the Book of Chronicles: The Biblical Text, the Elephantine Papyri and the El-Ibrahimia's Aramaic Inscription', in J.H. Ellens, D.L. Ellens, R.P. Knierim and I. Kalimi (eds.),

Jerusalem of the Persian province, *Jehud Madinta* (Neh. 11.1; 1 Chron. 9.2-18// Neh. 11.3-19) and the poorly built temple of Zerubbabel[30] did not motivate him to illustrate Jerusalem and its temple in eschatological terms or to allude to the utopian visions of the exilic and postexilic prophets. Moreover, by way of contrast to Ezekiel, who described the heavenly plans of the future temple and Jerusalem (Ezek. 40–42; 43.10-27), the Chronicler spoke in detail about the heavenly *planned* structure of the Solomonic temple only:

> Then David gave Solomon his son the plan of the porch and its rooms…and the plan of everything which was in mind with him for the court of the house of YHWH and all the chambers round about, for the treasuries of the house of God… All this in writing from the hand of YHWH. (1 Chron. 28.11-19, no parallel)[31]

Such a paragraph is not found in Chronicles regarding Jerusalem itself. Moreover, no visionary description of Jerusalem as can be found later in the apocalyptic writings occurs here. The huge gap between the city of his own period and that of the monarchic period did not cause him to idealize and glorify Jerusalem, not to refer to it in a symbolic fashion. The Chronicler might have glorified some kings such as David, Solomon, Abijam/ Abijah, Hezekiah and Josiah (1 Chron. 11–29; 2 Chron. 1–9; 13; 29–32; 34–35), but never their royal city. Throughout his work the Chronicler treats Jerusalem in realistic, earthly, geographic terms, rather than according to some heavenly ideal.

The geographical reality of Jerusalem in the Chronicler's time could be depicted—more or less—from the description of Neh. 2.11-18; 3; 4.1, and from some archaeological excavations.[32] Usually, the Chronicler does not describe the pre-exilic city and temple in terms of the city and temple of his own day. In other words, when giving a 'physical' description of

God's Word for Our World: Biblical Studies in Honour of Simon John De Vries (JSOTSup, 352; London/New York: Continuum, forthcoming).

30. On this issue, see in detail Kalimi, 'The Land/Mount Moriah', pp. 27-29.

31. The plan of the temple is here patterned on the tabernacle of Moses (Exod. 25.9, 40; 26.30; 27.8). See R.L. Braun, *1 Chronicles* (WBC, 14; Waco, TX: Word Books, 1986), pp. 271-72. Later, it appears also in Wisd. 9.8 in reference to the Solomonic temple. P.B. Dirksen ('1 Chronicles xxviii 11-18: Its Textual Development', *VT* 47 [1997], pp. 429-38) argues unsuccessfully that 1 Chron. 28.12b-18a is a later addition.

32. See, e.g., B. Mazar, 'Jerusalem in the Biblical Period', in Y. Yadin (ed.), *Jerusalem Revealed: Archaeology in the Holy City 1968–1974* (New Haven: Yale University Press, 1976), pp. 1-8.

Jerusalem or the temple, the Chronicler essentially follows the biblical sources that were available to him without making anachronistic emendations.[33]

d. *The View of Jerusalem: Between the Chronicler and Other Writers*
The differences in the description of Jerusalem between Chronicles and all the other works probably derive from the intentions of their authors. Contrary to Keil and von Rad,[34] for example, Chronicles does not show any indications of 'messianic' expectations or 'eschatological' features—not even in Nathan's dynastic prophecy (1 Chron. 17//2 Sam. 7)—that these

33. It is striking that some geographical terms that the Chronicler uses with regard to the temple do not appear—at least verbally—in any other source. For example, 'the court of the priests' (2 Chron. 4.9—an 'addition' to 1 Kgs 7.39; perhaps identical with the 'inner court' of 1 Kgs 6.36; 7.12 and/or the 'upper court' of Jer. 36.10, as assumed by J. Goettsberger [*Die Bücher der Chronik oder Paralipomenon übersetzt und erklärt* (Die Heilige Schrift, 4.1; Bonn: Peter Hanstein Verlagsbuchhandlung, 1939), p. 215]); 'the new court' (2 Chron. 20.5—also an 'addition'; perhaps really the same that is mentioned in 2 Chron. 4.9, as stated by Goettsberger [*Bücher der Chronik*, pp. 215, 288]). It is unclear whether these terms reflect circumstances in the Chronicler's own day. His depiction of the location of the First Temple as surrounded by a wall with four gates, at the north, south, west and east (1 Chron. 9.24, 26—an 'addition'), could be based on Ezek. 42.15-20 and so does not necessarily reflect the Second Temple in his own day. Jerusalem's בית מהפכת (= a prison?), in which King Asa imprisoned Hanani the seer (2 Chron. 16.10—an 'addition'), could be borrowed from a similar story in Jer. 20.2-3; 29.26. The name 'Fish Gate' (2 Chron. 33.14—an 'addition') is mentioned not only in Neh. 3.3 but also in Zeph. 1.10b (Josiah's time). שער היסוד in 2 Chron. 23.5, instead of שער סור in the parallel verse in 2 Kgs 11.6, seems to be a textual corruption (the interchange of ד/ר and later an addition of הי). Cf. Dillard, *2 Chronicles*, p. 182 (but see his note on 23.5, p. 178). The change, 'she went into the *entrance of the Horse Gate*'//'she went into the *Horse entrance*' (2 Chron. 23.15//2 Kgs 11.16), was made by the Chronicler on the basis of Jer. 31.40 ('the corner of the Horse Gate'); cf. also Neh. 3.28. The only term that the Chronicler may have used anachronistically is 'the Valley Gate' (שער הגיא; i.e., the gate leading to the Hinnom Valley) in the description of Uzziah's building projects (2 Chron. 26.9—an 'addition'). This term is mentioned here and in the description of Jerusalem in Neh. 2.13a, 15; 3.13a only; see J. Becker, *2. Chronik* (NEBAT, 20; Würzburg: Echter Verlag, 1988), p. 87.

34. See C.F. Keil, *Biblischer Commentar über die nachexilischen Geschichtsbücher: Chronik, Esra, Nehemia und Esther* (BCAT, 1; Leipzig: Dörffling & Franke, 1870), p. 164; G. von Rad, *Das Geschichtsbild des Chronistischen Werkes* (BWANT, 54; Stuttgart: W. Kohlhammer, 1930), pp. 122-27, 135; *idem, Theologie des Alten Testaments* (Einführung in die evangelische Theologie, 1; 2 vols.; Munich: Chr. Kaiser Verlag, 1969), I, p. 362.

scholars detected.[35] Neither does Chronicles present any 'theocratic expectation'.[36] It seems that the Chronicler does not intend to present any particular hope for the future.[37] The future of the nation and its beloved chosen city depends on the quality of their day-by-day religious behavior, and relationship with God, his temple, and its servants and cults.[38] Moreover, the exilic and restorative prophets witnessed the trauma of the destruction of the city and its temple by the Babylonians (587/6 BCE). The apocalyptic literature originated especially in reaction to the hellenization of the city and its temple in the first half of the second century BCE and the ruin of Jerusalem and its shrine in the second half of the first century CE (70 CE; see Rev. 21.1–22.5).[39] Most of the authors who wrote in bitter exile about the city during the last 1900 years spoke about Jerusalem in imaginary terms, as did some prophets and apocalypticists. In contrast to

35. See the bibliography on this issue cited in I. Kalimi, *The Books of Chronicles: A Classified Bibliography* (SBB, 1; Jerusalem: Simor, 1990), pp. 104-105 (see items 715-726, 'Eschatology and Messianism'). For a survey of the topic, see H.G.M. Williamson, 'Eschatology in Chronicles', *TynBul* 28 (1977), pp. 115-54; B.E. Kelly, *Retribution and Eschatology in Chronicles* (JSOTSup, 211; Sheffield: Sheffield Academic Press, 1996), pp. 135-55; and, most recently, P.B. Dirksen, 'The Future in the Book of Chronicles', in P.J. Harland and C.T.R. Hayward (eds.), *New Heaven and New Earth Prophecy and the Millennium: Essays in Honour of Anthony Gelston* (VTSup, 77; Leiden: E.J. Brill, 1999), pp. 37-51 (37-44).

36. *Contra* E.M. Dörrfuss, *Mose in den Chronikbüchern: Garant theokratischer Zukunftserwartung* (BZAW, 219; Berlin: W. de Gruyter, 1994), p. 282. For a critical review of a 'royalistic' expectation in Chronicles, which was assumed by Williamson and adopted by Oeming and (most recently by) Kelly, see Dirksen, 'The Future in the Book of Chronicles', pp. 39-42. Dirksen also discusses (pp. 42-43) the view of Rudolf, which has been developed by Plöger and, most recently, by Riley.

37. See Dirksen, 'The Future in the Book of Chronicles', p. 44. Dirksen notices correctly (p. 43) that although Japhet states, 'The book of Chronicles cannot be defined as eschatological in any sense of the word' (S. Japhet, *The Ideology of the Book of Chronicles and its Place in Biblical Thought* [BEATAJ, 9; Frankfurt: Peter Lang, 1989], p. 501), a few pages later (pp. 503-504) she erroneously comments, 'They are concrete hopes that the land will be redeemed and Israel's greatness and glory will be restored...the Chronicler...awaited the restoration of Israel's fortunes'.

38. Cf. D.F. Murray, 'Dynasty, People, and the Future: The Message of Chronicles', *JSOT* 58 (1993), pp. 71-92.

39. For the new Jerusalem in this book, see the detailed study of U. Sim, *Das himmlische Jerusalem in Apk 21,1–22,5 im Kontext biblisch-jüdischer Tradition und antiken Städtebaus* (Bochumer Altertumswissenschaftliches Colloquium, 25; Trier: Wissenschaftlicher Verlag, 1996).

all these writers, the Chronicler lived in an era that, as far as we know, was not distinguished by any dramatic events. The existence of Jerusalem and its temple, although a small and poor town and sanctuary, were evident. In other words, his environment did not provide the appropriate historical context to develop a completely new Jerusalem, as did those authors who wrote before and after his time. Although he attempts to enhance the holiness of his own temple,[40] he avoids ascribing any visionary description to it.

e. The Centrality of Jerusalem in the Chronistic Writing

The Chronicler was interested above all in the history of the Davidic dynasty, that is, specifically in the United Kingdom and in the Kingdom of Judah. Therefore, he fundamentally ignores the Northern Kingdom. His writing concentrates on the religious–theological aspects of the Southern Kingdom, precisely the Jerusalem temple, its building, vessels, staff and the rite(s) of worship practiced there (things that had been re-established, in one form or another, in his own time). Let us turn our attention now to this matter in some detail.

The reign of David is described in 1 Chronicles 10–29, but chs. 22–29 deal exclusively with David's preparations for the building of the temple in Jerusalem. 2 Chronicles 1–9 treats the reign of Solomon, but chs. 2–7 describe the temple itself, its location, date of construction, structure, personnel, liturgy, and so on. 2 Chronicles 10–36 covers the history of the kings of Judah, with special interest in the kings' attitudes towards the temple, its worship and the maintenance of its building (2 Chron. 24.1-14// 2 Kgs 12; 2 Chron. 34.8-17//2 Kgs 22.3-10). Some of these issues do not appear at all in the parallel texts in the book of Kings.[41] Thus, the House of God and the House of David both occupy a central place in Chronicles. Just a brief glance at the book indicates that the author devotes much space to these issues. Out of 65 chapters of the book, 56 deal directly with kings from David and Solomon through to their successors who sat on the throne of Judah (1 Chron. 10–29; 2 Chron. 1–9; 10–36).[42] Here should be added also 1 Chronicles 3, which lists the sons of David and the kings of the Davidic dynasty and royal lineage. This means that about 85 per cent of

40. See Kalimi, 'The Land/Mount Moriah', p. 27.
41. See, e.g., 2 Chron. 24.14b-24 (esp. vv. 18, 21); 26.16-21; 28.24-25; 29.
42. The exceptions are some necessary paragraphs on the northern kings, such as Jeroboam and Ahab.

the book is connected somehow with kings who reigned in Jerusalem. Almost 32 chapters, that is, nearly 50 per cent of the entire composition, are associated somehow with the temple,[43] which was founded in the heart of the city.

In the monarchic period the two most important Israelite institutions, the temple and the Davidic dynasty, were located in Jerusalem. On the other hand, in the Persian period the city included the temple, but this was also the center of *Jehud Medinta*—and most probably held the residence of the Chronicler himself. There is no wonder, therefore, that Jerusalem occupies an essential place in the book of Chronicles. Almost everything the Chronicler discusses as happening in or around Jerusalem is related to whomever ruled from or served in or somehow was associated with the city. Accordingly, there is no surprise that the name 'Jerusalem' appears very frequently in Chronicles,[44] both as a result of its mention in the Chronicler's sources, and even more in the material that the Chronicler added to his sources.[45] Just a little less than one fourth of the references to Jerusalem in the entire Hebrew Bible occur in the chronistic writing (151 times out of 669).[46] In other words, about 23 per cent of the appearances of the name 'Jerusalem' in the Hebrew Bible are found in Chronicles, which comprises about eight per cent of the biblical corpus.[47] In addition, the city is also mentioned in the book 19 times by other names such as 'the city of David'

43. See 1 Chron. 5.27–6.66 [EVV 6.1-81]; 13.1–16.3; 21.1–29.19; 2 Chron. 2–7; 15.3-18; 20.14-17; 23.1–24.22 [//2 Kgs 11.1–12.17]; 26.16-21; 27.2-3; 28.24-25; 29–31; 33.4-8 [//2 Kgs 21.4-8]; 34 [//2 Kgs 22]; 35; 36.14-19.

44. The exceptions are 2 Chron. 25.1 and 32.9 (cf. also Jer. 26.18; Esth. 2.6) always without ' after the ל (ירושלם), as in the rest of the Hebrew Bible.

45. See, e.g., 2 Chron. 32.9, 10 (an 'addition' to 2 Kgs 18.17, 19//Isa. 36.2, 4); 2 Chron. 32.33 (an 'addition' to 2 Kgs 20.21); 2 Chron. 34.3, 5 (an 'addition' to 2 Kgs 22.2); 23.16; 35.1, 18 (an 'addition' to 2 Kgs 23.18). According to P.C. Beentjes ('Jerusalem in the Book of Chronicles', in M. Poorthuis and Ch. Safrai [eds.], *The Centrality of Jerusalem: Historical Perspectives* [Kampen: Kok, 1996], pp. 15-28 [17-18]), in 86 instances the references to 'Jerusalem' appear in the 'additional texts' of Chronicles, that is, 57 per cent (rather than 'seventy-five per cent', as he stresses), while only in 65 instances did the Chronicler depend on his sources.

46. For the statistical data concerning the name 'Jerusalem', see Beentjes, 'Jerusalem', p. 17. Beentjes does not discuss other names of the city, nor does he take them into account in his statistical data.

47. For the percentage of the text of Chronicles in the entire Bible, see the 'Statistical Appendix', in E. Jenni und C. Westermann (eds.), *Theologisches Handwörterbuch zum Alten Testament* (München: Chr. Kaiser Verlag/Zürich: Theologischer Verlag, 1984), II, p. 540 (= *TLOT*, III, p. 1445).

or 'the city of Judah', thus altogether 170 times. Obviously, the numerous occurrences of the city's names in Chronicles bear witness as well to its cardinal importance in the chronistic literature.

The centrality of Jerusalem in the chronistic history is indicated also by several passages specifically dealing with the city. It seems that in spite of all that statistical evidence, the Chronicler did not presume this issue to be self-evident. He made a special literary effort to reveal the importance of the city by means of literary creativity. He made several emendations, additions and omissions in his sources from the earlier biblical books, Samuel and Kings, which profoundly affected his narratives about Jerusalem. Indeed, a variety of texts in Chronicles reveal its author's attitude towards Jerusalem and stress the city's fundamental place in the chronistic theology and history during the monarchic period.[48] So, for instance, in another study I have concluded that the main purpose of 1 Chron. 11.6 is to emphasize the difficulties that were faced in the capture of Jerusalem in order to create suspense and anticipation of a significant impending event in Israel's national life.[49]

4. *Conclusion*

Jerusalem emerges in Chronicles as the only capital of 'the kingdom of the Lord' and as the location of his throne. It hosted all the kings of the Davidic dynasty, those chosen to represent God on earth. God's presence in the city is timeless, for his name dwells in Jerusalem's temple continually. Jerusalem is his chosen city, and within it is located his only legitimate temple. The election of the city is permanent, and it continues to be the Lord's chosen city, even in the Chronicler's time and in spite of its small size and poor condition. These circumstances do not affect the city's spiritual superiority and holiness. The Chronicler outlines in detail the location of the temple, while drawing analogies to the *Aqedah* and the construction of the altar by David on the threshing floor. This was done, presumably, to enhance the sanctity of the city and the temple of his time, which were in critical need of such support.

48. Some of these texts are mentioned earlier in this study; others are analyzed separately in my article, 'The View of Jerusalem in the Ethnographical Introduction of Chronicles (1 Chr 1–9)', *Bib* 83 (2002), pp. 556-62, and in the item in the next footnote.

49. See I. Kalimi, 'The Capture of Jerusalem in the Chronistic History', *VT* 52 (2002), pp. 66-79.

The portrayal of Jerusalem in the chronistic history differs from that in DtrH and that in the exilic and postexilic prophecy, apocalyptic and some Jewish Hellenistic writings. In the latter, Jerusalem and the temple are described in eschatological visions, a new and ideal holy city that would appear in the future. This phenomenon finds expression also in Jewish literature written after the Roman destruction of Jerusalem, and it continued for almost 1900 years. In Chronicles, however, Jerusalem is represented *essentially* in realistic terms and designated as an earthly city, the capital of the Davidic dynasty, and it is not referred to in heavenly, utopian terms. Though the Chronicler represents Jerusalem as the chosen city of God and the capital of the 'kingdom of the Lord', generally the city is presented from a pragmatic viewpoint. The striking differences between the poor, provincial Jerusalem and its poorly built temple of the Persian period and that of the monarchic era did not cause him to idealize and glorify Jerusalem (and its temple) in eschatological terms. He did not allude to the utopian visions of the exilic and postexilic prophets, and he certainly did not refer to them in symbolic or mystical language. He did not describe the city and the temple of the monarchic time in terms of the city and temple of his own day.

The differences in the description of Jerusalem in the chronistic and all the other literature probably originated in the specific intentions of the authors. The exilic and postexilic prophets witnessed the trauma of the city and the destruction of its temple by the Babylonians; and later the apocalyptic literature developed as a reaction to the hellenization of the city and the temple, and then the ruin of the city and the temple by the Romans. They wrote in light of these events, and are comparable to the authors who wrote about the city later on, in the bitter and long exile. In contrast to these other works, however, Chronicles does not show any 'messianic' or 'eschatological' expectations, and its environment did not provide the appropriate historical context to stimulate him to develop 'another' Jerusalem. Though he attempts to enhance the holiness of his own temple, he avoids visionary descriptions.

In the monarchic period the important Israelite institutions (the temple and the Davidic dynasty) on which the Chronicler's attention was focused were located in Jerusalem. In the Chronicler's own day, however, Jerusalem hosted the temple, was the center of *Jehud Medinta*, and was probably the home of the Chronicler himself. All of this points to the city's cardinal importance for the author of Chronicles, a point underscored by frequent explicit references to Jerusalem and his creative use of literary technique to illustrate the important place of the city in theology and history. It is no exaggeration to conclude that in Chronicles little happens without some connection to Jerusalem.

'RETRIBUTION' REVISITED: COVENANT, GRACE AND RESTORATION

Brian E. Kelly

In retelling the history of Israel from the foundation of the monarchy down to the destruction of Jerusalem and the eve of restoration, the author of Chronicles employed a number of distinctive theological motifs. One of the most salient and widely recognized of these is a concern with divine blessing and punishment in the history of the people and their kings. This concern is most evident in the account of the post-Solomonic monarchy (2 Chron. 10–36), although the same principles and motifs can be discerned throughout the earlier sections as well. How is this dimension of the writer's thought to be characterized and understood? The following study begins by reviewing my initial research into this question and then extends these findings in the light of subsequent discussions and interpretations.[1]

The Scholarly Consensus

The mid-twentieth century consensus is well represented in Weiser's *Introduction*, where he states, 'The dominating viewpoint of the Chronicler's presentation of history is the idea of retribution carried through mechanically and, as regards each individual, down to the smallest details; when history does not fit in with it, it is usually distorted'.[2] Many similar statements from this time could be adduced,[3] in which the Chronicler is

1. See my *Retribution and Eschatology in Chronicles* (JSOTSup, 211; Sheffield: Sheffield Academic Press, 1996), pp. 29-110. An earlier form of this essay was presented as a paper at the SBL Annual Meeting in Nashville in November 2000. For the sake of this essay, discussion is confined largely to 2 Chron. 10–36.

2. A. Weiser, *Introduction to the Old Testament* (London: Darton, Longman & Todd, 1961), p. 324.

3. Besides the illustrative examples considered below, the broad consensus on 'retribution' is reflected in the following discussions: E.L. Curtis and A.A. Madsen, *A Critical and Exegetical Commentary on the Books of Chronicles* (ICC; New York:

regularly criticized for allegedly holding to a rigid and extreme doctrine of divine retribution. This is generally depicted as 'individual' and 'immediate'; that is, punishment comes hard on the heels of transgression in the form of sickness, death, military defeat or exile for the disobedient, while God's concrete blessings follow quickly in the lives of pious kings and people in the form of building projects, large families for the king, military success, tribute from the surrounding nations, and 'rest' for the land. To many commentators, the Chronicler's presentation (in particular his account of the post-Solomonic kings in 2 Chron. 10–36) has appeared contrived and theologically reductionistic, and in numerous cases, at odds with the portrayal in Kings. Most of the Chronicler's additional material in this section appears to be in the service of this outlook, and because his theological tendency is so often evident, the historical value of this non-synoptic material has frequently been deprecated.[4] While the question of

Charles Scribner's Sons, 1910), p. 9 (the Chronicler treated Israel's life as 'a church with constant rewards and punishments through signal divine intervention... He made more universal the connection between piety and prosperity, and wickedness and adversity, heightening good and bad characters and their rewards and punishments, or creating them according to the exigencies of the occasion'); W.A.L. Elmslie, *The Book of Chronicles* (CBSC; Cambridge: Cambridge University Press, 2nd edn, 1916), p. lv; R.H. Pfeiffer, *Introduction to the Old Testament* (New York: Harper & Brothers, 1948), pp. 778-89; W. Eichrodt, *Theology of the Old Testament* (OTL; 2 vols.; Philadelphia: Fortress Press, 1961), II, pp. 307, 487; E.J. Bickerman, *From Ezra to the Last of the Maccabees: Foundations of Post-Biblical Judaism* (New York: Schocken Books, 1962), pp. 24-26; C. Westermann, *Handbook to the Old Testament* (London: SPCK, 1969), p. 256; O. Eissfeldt, *The Old Testament: An Introduction* (Oxford: Oxford University Press, 1965), pp. 535-37; G. Fohrer, *Introduction to the Old Testament* (London: SPCK, 1970), p. 247; O. Kaiser, *Introduction to the Old Testament: A Presentation of its Results and Problems* (Oxford: Basil Blackwell, 1975), p. 186; S.B. Berg, 'After the Exile: God and History in the Books of Chronicles and Esther', in J.L. Crenshaw and S. Sandmel (eds.), *The Divine Helmsman: Studies on God's Control of Human Events, Presented to Lou. H. Silberman* (New York: Ktav, 1980), pp. 107-27 (the Chronicler's doctrine is an expression of God's active ['manipulative'] control of history which contrasts with the 'secular' view of Esther that stresses human responsibility); R.L. Braun, *1 Chronicles* (WBC, 14; Waco: Word Books, 1986), pp. xxxvii-xxxix; S.J. De Vries, *1 and 2 Chronicles* (FOTL, 11; Grand Rapids: Eerdmans, 1989), pp. 119-21. This is also the dominant approach in R.B. Dillard, *2 Chronicles* (WBC, 15; Waco, TX: Word Books, 1987), pp. 76-81 and *passim*, in his discussion of 2 Chron. 10–36, although he does seek to be more appreciative of the theology he discerns in this theme.

    4.   On the changing perceptions of Chronicles as historiography, see most recently K. Peltonen, *History Debated: The Historical Reliability of Chronicles in Pre-Critical*

historicity lies outside the scope of this study, it should be noted in passing that a negative estimation of the historical value of Chronicles has often coloured judgments of its theological value, particularly as this is expressed in its presumed 'doctrine of retribution'.

This understanding derives in large measure from Wellhausen, who perceived Chronicles as teaching that 'a divine pragmatism' governed the fate of Judah and its rulers, strictly in terms of their fidelity to the Mosaic Law, which the Chronicler believed had always been in force.[5] Thus in 2 Chronicles 10–36 the writer presented (or invented) moral grounds for each misfortune that was recounted but not explained in Kings (such as Asa's foot disease [2 Chron. 16.12] or Uzziah's leprosy [2 Chron. 26.16-20]) and ascribed God's blessings in the form of armies, wealth and progeny only to those kings he considered faithful to the Mosaic Law (including Rehoboam and Abijah, contrary to the estimate of Kings). Similarly, Manasseh's 55-year reign (2 Chron. 33) was explained by the fictional device of a personal exile in Babylon, where he atoned for his guilt through temporary imprisonment, to be followed by cult reform and building works in Jerusalem. This diverges from the more contemporary reports of Kings (2 Kgs 23.26) and Jeremiah (Jer. 15.4), where Manasseh is condemned as the chief catalyst of the exile.

It appears that most scholars have accepted Wellhausen's basic interpretation of the work at this point, as well as extending it in different ways. Von Rad[6] identified in the Chronicler's 'retributionist' outlook two particular concerns: (1) a special interest in theodicy, which sought to show over against the portrayal in Kings that God's justice was entirely rational and unambiguous, though tempered with mercy; and (2) the writer's own theological contribution to 'the question of the share of the individual in

and Critical Research (Publications of the Finnish Exegetical Society, 64; Helsinki: The Finnish Exegetical Society, 1996) and M.P. Graham, K.G. Hoglund and S.L. McKenzie (eds.), *The Chronicler as Historian* (JSOTSup, 238; Sheffield: Sheffield Academic Press, 1997). W. Johnstone (*1 and 2 Chronicles*. I. *1 Chronicles 1–2 Chronicles 9: Israel's Place among the Nations*; II. *2 Chronicles 10–36: Guilt and Atonement* [JSOTSup, 253, 254; Sheffield: Sheffield Academic Press, 1997]) prescinds from considering Chronicles as historiography.

5.   J. Wellhausen, *Prolegomena to the History of Israel* (Edinburgh: A. & C. Black, 1885; trans. from the 2nd German edn, 1883), p. 224.

6.   G. von Rad, *Das Geschichtsbild des chronistischen Werkes* (BWANT, 54; Stuttgart: W. Kohlhammer, 1930); *idem*, *Old Testament Theology* (2 vols.; London: SCM Press, 1962), I.

Jahweh'.[7] Von Rad believed that the issue of the individual's faith and its recompense had become more pressing in later biblical thought (a concern also attested in the contemporaneous Wisdom literature). In contrast to an earlier, more collectivist understanding of the people in their standing before God, and with no belief in post-mortem retribution, the Chronicler insisted 'that Jahweh confronted each generation quite immediately and with his whole revelation'.[8]

A supplement to this view was proposed by North,[9] who understood the Chronicler as a theological traditionalist confronted with new ideas that were entering Judaism from Persian or Alexandrian contacts. The writer's 'short-term retributionism' was 'the last-ditch credo of a conservative' who refused to allow the question of rewards and punishments to be deferred (as in other Jewish literature of the time) into an afterlife of the soul or an eschatological future. Since the same destiny awaited all people in Sheol, God's justice in this life had to be shown to be unimpeachably fair.[10]

The most highly developed interpretation of theodicy in Chronicles is proposed by Japhet.[11] In her view the Chronicler expounds a systematic 'historiosophy' or philosophy of history, according to which the historical process is governed by the principle of absolute divine justice. Japhet contends in fairly categorical terms that the Chronicler's outlook contrasts sharply with that of DtrH: for the Chronicler 'Reward is mandatory,

---

7. Von Rad, *Old Testament Theology*, I, p. 349.

8. Von Rad, *Old Testament Theology*, I, p. 350.

9. R. North, 'Theology of the Chronicler', *JBL* 82 (1963), pp. 369-81.

10. On the question of post-mortem retribution (of whatever form), it must fairly be said that the Chronicler's views on this matter are unknown, and the book nowhere addresses the question directly. The burial notices do not constitute 'reward' (*pace* von Rad) but signify the author's theological judgment on the reigns. Nothing in principle precludes the Chronicler from entertaining some post-mortem hopes, since the evidence of certain psalms places such beliefs much earlier than was previously believed (see, e.g., Philip S. Johnston, *Shades of Sheol: Death and Afterlife in the Old Testament* [Leicester: Apollos, 2002], pp. 199-217); while P.R. Ackroyd (*Studies in the Religious Tradition of the Old Testament* [London: SCM Press, 1987], pp. 176-80), suggests that the portrayal of Hezekiah's death in 2 Chron. 32.33 is hinting in such a direction. But the question is inconclusive and does not really touch on the writer's concern.

11. S. Japhet, *The Ideology of the Book of Chronicles and its Place in Biblical Thought* (BEATAJ, 9; New York: Peter Lang, 2nd edn, 1997); *idem, I and II Chronicles: A Commentary* (OTL; Louisville, KY: Westminster/John Knox Press, 1993).

immediate and individual',[12] with no accumulated guilt across the genera-tions of Israel's existence, no deferment of punishment for one generation's sins into the lifetime of another, and no accruing of 'merit' from the past. According to such a system, God's warning before punishment, in the form of prophetic oracles and rebukes, is 'a mandatory element in the judicial procedure', and God always responds positively to repentance.[13]

In re-evaluating the scholarly consensus, I must agree at least with Japhet's last observation, since in Chronicles whenever kings or people show repentance, punishment is indeed mitigated or even remitted in whole. However, Japhet does not give sufficient force to the theological significance of this fact, that God's response to repentance is not so much an issue of divine *justice* as of *grace* and his restorative will towards his guilty people. Already Rudolph had observed that repentance in Chron-icles mitigated the effects of retribution[14] (although he broadly accepted Wellhausen's view), and the same point is made more emphatically by Williamson in his discussion of the special chronistic vocabulary of repentance in 2 Chron. 7.14.[15] These points are taken up and developed in the following discussion, where the theme of repentance and restoration is highlighted, rather than retribution.

Among the most recent treatments of the question, the theological read-ing adopted by Johnstone is of particular note.[16] He presents Chronicles in the first instance as a 'midrash' on Israel's traditions, grappling with the problem of the broken relationship between God and humanity. The solution to this problem is to be found only in the eventual recognition of God's sovereignty on earth, and to this end Israel was appointed to a life of holiness to Yahweh under the tutelage of the Levites. The Davidic

12. Japhet, *I and II Chronicles*, p. 44.

13. To be fair, Japhet (*Ideology*, p. 190) also recognizes the role of divine mercy as this is explicitly stated in 2 Chron. 30.6-9; 36.15; but this is a very minor theme in her presentation.

14. W. Rudolph, *Chronikbücher* (HAT, 21; Tübingen: J.C.B. Mohr [Paul Siebeck], 1955), p. xix.

15. H.G.M. Williamson, *1 and 2 Chronicles* (NCB; London: Marshall, Morgan & Scott, 1982), pp. 225-26.

16. W. Johnstone, *1 and 2 Chronicles*, I-II. See also his programmatic essay 'Guilt and Atonement: The Theme of 1 and 2 Chronicles', in J.D. Martin and P.R. Davies (eds.), *A Word in Season: Essays in Honour of William McKane* (JSOTSup, 42; Shef-field: JSOT Press, 1986), pp. 113-38 (repr. in W. Johnstone, *Chronicles and Exodus: An Analogy and its Application* [JSOTSup, 275; Sheffield: Sheffield Academic Press, 1998], pp. 90-114).

monarchy under Solomon, 'the flawless executor of the ideal',[17] is initially presented as the means whereby God's sovereignty may be realized among the nations, but for the most part the subsequent Davidic kings fail to live up to this ideal. Israel as a people also shares in this failure. Despite Israel's high calling within the world of the nations, its existence in the land is marked from beginning to end (1 Chron. 2.7; 2 Chron. 36.14) by מעל, traditionally rendered 'unfaithfulness'. Taking his cue from Lev. 5.14-26 (EVV 5.14–6.7), Johnstone understands this as a specifically sacral offence of defrauding God of his due, both in holy living and worship, as prescribed in the Law of Moses. Johnstone thus takes guilt and atonement to be the central theme of 2 Chronicles 10–36, a narrative that culminates in the exile of the people and the forfeiture of the land as the penalty for מעל, in keeping with the covenant curses of Leviticus 26. According to this view, Chronicles presents Israel, though physically present in the land, as still in spiritual 'exile' and awaiting a divine consummation or 'return', presumably to its intended relationship with God.[18] The final word of the book, ויעל ('Let him go up'), is taken not as an invitation to a physical return to Jerusalem but as a pointer to the Chronicler's eschatological hope in such a consummation. Johnstone observes that Leviticus 26 itself holds out the hope of restoration to the land following repentance, and the Chronicler explicitly picks up this note at the close of his book in 2 Chron. 36.21, which alludes to Lev. 26.40-45. Moreover, immediately prior to Leviticus 26 we have the chapter on the year of Jubilee (Lev. 25.8-55), mandating a return of the Israelites to their land 'in the fiftieth year', and the Chronicler is said to equate his generation with the one to whom this invitation is made—ostensibly the fiftieth generation since Adam, according to his chronological scheme.

In the interim of waiting, Israel must avail itself of the Levitical institutions as the counterpoise to judgment and the means whereby the people may once again consecrate its life to God. These institutions include the temple, priesthood and altar of atonement centred in Jerusalem, as well as the Levites distributed throughout the land as teachers of the Law and 'monitors of Israel's practice of holiness'.[19]

Johnstone presents a stimulating reading of the book and is often helpful in highlighting intertextual aspects of the work, in particular how the

---

17. Johnstone, *1 and 2 Chronicles*, II, p. 11.
18. Johnstone, *1 and 2 Chronicles*, I, p. 16.
19. Johnstone, *1 and 2 Chronicles*, I, p. 82.

author echoes and reuses language and themes from Israel's scriptural traditions. However, it is not clear that the Levitical institutions and the rites of atonement have the primacy that Johnstone affirms or that the Chronicler is working in such a thoroughgoing typological way. First, guilt and atonement are certainly a matter of great importance in the work, but מעל should not be taken as *the* overarching conception. As I argue below, within the overall structure of the book, a more fundamental role is played by the Davidic covenant. This is presented as a concept that embraces and consolidates within an ideal unity the monarchy, the temple and its institutions, and the people. It is within this covenant that the Levites have a vital, *subsidiary* function in sustaining temple worship (1 Chron. 9.28-32; 23.28-32; 2 Chron. 8.13) and leading Israel in praise under the directions given by David (1 Chron. 6.31-32; 15.16-22; 16.4-6, 37-42; 2 Chron. 7.6). The authority of the Davidic kings over the organization of the temple personnel and in instigating and overseeing cult reform is emphatically affirmed throughout the book, and it is never subordinated to the priests and Levites. Naturally this raises the question, what has become of the promise to David in an age without kings?' Is it subsumed into the cult (and people), or is it still latent and capable of a new form of fulfillment?

Second, Williamson's review of Johnstone's commentary[20] finds a measure of over-interpretation in the chronological and typological scheme that Johnstone discerns within the book. Johnstone argues that the Chronicler understood the generations from Adam to Josiah to number 49 and the exile to begin with the death of Josiah. Thus the exilic generation to whom Cyrus' invitation to return was made was the fiftieth. By extension, this generation is said to include all who were born from that time down to the Chronicler's own period, about 200 years later: they remain 'in "Exile"', awaiting 'the definitive "Return" in God's future'.[21] Cyrus' edict is understood as the 'proclamation of eschatological jubilee',[22] an event that is still outstanding in the experience of the Chronicler's audience.

This reading is open to several objections. First, the interpretation depends in part in equating 'the fiftieth year' of Jubilee with 'the fiftieth generation' since Adam. Yet the Chronicler does not draw attention to the number of generations in his scheme,[23] and no reason is given for a shift

20. *JTS* 51 (2000), pp. 203-208.
21. Johnstone, *1 and 2 Chronicles*, I, p. 16.
22. Johnstone, *1 and 2 Chronicles*, I, p. 17.
23. Contrast the explicit schematic use of numbers and generations in Mt. 1.

from 50 *years* in Lev. 25.10 to a putative 50 *generations* since Adam. The (possible) coincidence of numbers aside, there is no evidence in the text that the Chronicler symbolically understood 'year' as 'generation'. Second, there is no textual evidence that the author understood exile and return as symbolic or spiritual states rather than historical facts. Williamson notes that Johnstone's discussion usually capitalizes these words or places them in quotation marks,[24] but again, there is no textual warrant for this inter-pretation. Third, it is not explained why the book's presumed generational scheme should start with *Adam* (1 Chron. 1.1) rather than with Israel's entry into the land—the point at which the history of מעל begins (1 Chron. 2.7).

On the more general question of retribution in the work, some prelimi-nary comments are necessary. First, it is evident that the Chronicler under-stands Yahweh to be personally active in the history of Israel, blessing the people and requiting their deeds. Yahweh is depicted as Israel's righteous judge (2 Chron. 12.6; 20.12) and king (1 Chron. 29.11), and so his actions are properly juridical. Blessing and woe are usually depicted as coming from God's own personal decision and action and not simply from an impersonal moral order in the world, which God superintends and sees through to its fulfillment.[25] Thus, the requiting of human deeds is not 'mechanical' in the strict sense (as, for example, in the conventional under-standing of the Buddhist and Hindu law of *karma*)—however this divine requiting may appear in the Chronicler's presentation—but is always grounded in God's personal decision and direct activity. By the same token, 'seeking Yahweh', one of the key theological motifs of the work, is not to be understood simply in cultic terms. While faithful worship accord-ing to the Mosaic Torah is one of the principal expressions of this concept,

24. Johnstone, *1 and 2 Chronicles*, I, pp. 16, 129; *idem*, *1 and 2 Chronicles*, II, pp. 274-75.

25. K. Koch's influential essay 'Gibt es ein Vergeltungsdogma im Alten Testa-ment?', *ZKT* 52 (1955), pp. 1-42, argued (on the basis of certain texts from Psalms and Proverbs) that there was no doctrine of retribution in the strict juridical sense of the word in the Old Testament, but rather an 'act–consequence relationship' overseen by Yahweh, rather like a midwife, in which the seed of an action yielded its own fruit. However, this is plainly not the understanding of Chronicles, in which Yahweh is expressly depicted as the personal subject dispensing blessing or punishment (cf. 1 Chron. 2.3; 4.10; 5.20, 26; 10.14; 13.14; 18.6, 13; 21.7, 14; 22.18; 2 Chron. 1.1, 12; 10.15; 12.5, 7; 13.16, 20; 14.12; 15.6; 17.5; 18.31; 20.22; 21.16; 22.7; 24.24; 25.16, 20; 26.7, 20; 28.5, 9; 29.36; 30.20; 32.22; 33.11, 13; 36.17), even in describing actions accomplished through his human agents.

more fundamentally the term describes an orientation of the whole of life towards God within a personal covenantal faith.[26]

Second, the term 'retribution' (*Vergeltung*) is problematic. Although it has an established place in the history of research, strictly speaking, this word (from the Latin *retribuere*, 'to give as due') denotes recompense according to merits or desserts. This is more than just a semantic quibble. While the Chronicler believes that the punishment that befalls Israel and Judah is proportionate and properly deserved for covenant-breaking (and is therefore 'retribution'), it should not be assumed that the converse blessings that befall the kings and people are necessarily deserved or earned. While there is a clear correspondence between observing the divine law and blessing in the Old Testament, this connection is not based on human merit but on Yahweh's electing love for his people,[27] and the Chronicler is no exception to this understanding. He is, however, concerned to show that God *consistently* bestows on his faithful people blessings that flow from the grace of his covenant (rather than from their merit), as well as showing favour and forbearance at particular times to the undeserving. These points, which are explicated below, pose serious problems for the conventional scholarly understanding of 'immediate and individual retribution' in this work.

The Davidic Covenant in Chronicles

The centrality of the Davidic covenant in the work is brought out most clearly by Selman,[28] who draws attention to the significance of the two divine addresses in the book, both for the structure of the work and for its underlying theology. These passages are the dynastic oracle to David (1 Chron. 17.3-15), and Yahweh's word to Solomon (2 Chron. 7.12-22) in reply to his prayer made at the dedication of the temple. The Chronicler wishes to show that God's word is active and effectual within the history

---

26. M.J.D. Selman, *1 Chronicles* (TOTC, 10a; Leicester: Inter-Varsity Press, 1994), p. 54; cf. 1 Chron. 28.9.

27. A point made forcibly by J.R. Vannoy, 'Retribution: Theology of', in W.A. VanGemeren (ed.), *New International Dictionary of Old Testament Theology and Exegesis* (Carlisle: Paternoster Press, 1997), IV, pp. 1142-43, with reference to covenant blessings.

28. M.J.D. Selman, *1 Chronicles: An Introduction and Commentary* and *2 Chronicles: An Introduction and Commentary* (TOTC, 10a and b; Leicester: Inter-Varsity Press, 1994).

of his people, as it establishes a dynastic line and commands the building of a temple for his name. These addresses, therefore, appear at climactic liturgical moments within the narrative of the united monarchy of David and Solomon: when David is established in Jerusalem and the ark of the covenant has been installed in the city; and when Solomon has completed his task of building and dedication. Moreover, these two addresses are the only divine oracles in the book that are recounted *in extenso* and in collocation with prayer, a fact that further highlights their programmatic theological importance for the work.

Both divine addresses are concerned with the meaning of the Davidic covenant as the foundation of God's relationship with Israel.[29] In the Chronicler's understanding this covenant does nothing less than constitute Israel as the earthly manifestation of Yahweh's kingdom, a reality with a twofold expression in the interrelated institutions of the Davidic dynasty and the Solomonic temple. The mutual relationship of dynasty and temple is underlined by the wordplay in 1 Chron. 17.10, 12. Here Yahweh promises to '*build* a house' for David (that is, to establish a dynasty; note the change from 2 Sam. 7.11, יעשה), while David's son in turn will '*build* a house' (that is, construct a temple) for Yahweh. In the Chronicler's presentation the fulfillment of this task by Solomon (in the form of a fully operational cultus of worship and sacrifice, 2 Chron. 8.16) is the most significant purpose of his reign and the principal act of obedience in the establishment of the divine promise. The concept of Yahweh's kingdom actually realized in Davidic Israel is then expressed through some textually minor but theologically significant changes that the author makes to his *Vorlage* (2 Sam. 7.16) in 1 Chron. 17.14. The earlier statement '*your* house and *your* kingdom shall be made sure forever before me' is transformed into 'I will establish him in *my* house and in *my* kingdom forever'. Thus both the temple and the dynasty are the signs and witnesses of God's kingdom concretely realized in Israel, an idea that is further expressed in a range of later texts.[30]

29. The Davidic covenant in Chronicles is in turn closely related to the earlier Sinaitic and Abrahamic covenants. Obedience to the law of Moses is basic to the life of the community (cf. 1 Chron. 22.13; 28.7; 2 Chron. 6.16; 7.17; 23.18; 33.8) and is implicit in its restoration to God (cf. 2 Chron. 17.7-9; 19.4-11; 30.15-16; 35.6, 12). The Abrahamic covenant with its grant of land finds its fulfillment in the establishment of the temple (2 Chron. 20.7-8; cf. 1 Chron. 16.15-18).

30. See also 1 Chron. 28.5; 29.23; 2 Chron. 9.8; 13.8.

The focus of the first divine address is primarily upon the dynastic promise made to David and Solomon, although the author does retain the note that the election of David is for the benefit of 'my people Israel' (1 Chron. 17.9). The second divine address, to Solomon, also takes up the matter of the confirmation of the dynastic promise in 2 Chron. 7.17-18,[31] but the principal concern here is the significance of the temple to a people under judgment. Although in a strictly temporal sense this divine response would have come 13 years after the temple dedication (2 Chron. 7.11; cf. 1 Kgs 6.31–7.1; 9.10), here, as in Kings, it is intended narratively as the immediate answer to Solomon's prayer (2 Chron. 6.14-40//1 Kgs 8.23-53) that the temple may be accepted as the place where Israel may offer effectual prayer for forgiveness and restoration. However, the emphasis in Kings rests more squarely on a repeated challenge to obedience to the Sinaitic covenant, both in Solomon's exhortation to the people (1 Kgs 8.55-61, no parallel) and Yahweh's response to the prayer (1 Kgs 9.3-9), where there is no reference to forgiveness. Selman[32] draws attention to a significant change of emphasis in the Chronicler's version of the divine response, which is due chiefly to the insertion of a chiastic unit in 2 Chron. 7.12b-16a. The concentric ring structure in language and ideas can be seen from this arrangement of the unit, where the centre of emphasis falls on v. 14:

A (v. 12)   I have heard your prayer (שמעתי את תפלתך) and chosen (בחרתי) this place (במקום הזה) for myself as a house of sacrifice (לבית זבח).

B (v. 13)   When I shut up the heavens (השמים) so that there is no rain, or command the locust to devour the land (לאכול הארץ) or send plague among my people (בעמי),

C (v. 14a)   if my people will humble themselves (ויכנעו עמי)— they who are called by my name—and pray (ויתפללו) and seek (ויבקשו) my face and turn (וישבו) from their evil ways,

B' (v. 14b)   I will hear from heaven (אשמע מן השמים) and forgive (ואסלח) their sin and heal their land (וארפא את ארצם).

A' (vv. 15-16a)   Now my eyes will be open and my ears attentive to the prayer of this place (לתפלת המקום הזה). For now I have chosen (בחרתי) and consecrated this house (הבית הזה)...

31. The covenantal significance of this verse is slightly strengthened through its modification to read 'as I covenanted (כרתי)' against 1 Kgs 9.5, 'as I promised (דברתי)'.

32. Selman, *2 Chronicles*, p. 333.

This insertion picks up in v. 13 motifs of divine chastisement and human repentance from Solomon's prayer (cf. 2 Chron. 6.26, 28-30, 36-39) and in v. 14 assures Israel of Yahweh's certain will to forgive his penitent and prayerful people and to heal their land from the punishment of drought and pestilence. Thus DtrH's challenge to maintain covenantal *obedience* (no less a concern for the Chronicler)[33] is enlarged by the Chronicler into a divine invitation to a *disobedient* people to turn and pray in the sure expectation of receiving God's salvation. The chapter then concludes in vv. 19-22 by balancing the offer of the gift of restoration in v. 14 with the threat of divine judgment and rejection for those who refuse to repent. Thus the distinction between restoration and retribution does not depend upon merit (since the same people are in view) but upon the presence or absence of repentance.

This message of prayer, repentance and restoration is the central theme of the subsequent presentation in 2 Chronicles 10–36, rather than a supposed theory of divine rewards and punishment. The key vocabulary of 2 Chron. 7.14—both the human attitude enjoined (בקש/שדרש, 'seek'; התפלל, 'pray'; niphal כנע, 'humble oneself'; שוב, 'turn') and the divine response assured (שמע, 'hear'; סלח, 'forgive'; רפא, 'heal')—is distributed throughout these chapters to show the explicit fulfillment of this promise.[34] The validity of such prayer in or toward the Solomonic Temple is, moreover, to be understood as a benefit that Israel derives directly from its constitution by the Davidic covenant as Yahweh's people and the earthly manifestation of his kingdom. In 1 Kgs 8.52, Solomon pleads that Yahweh may hear Israel's supplications made in a variety of situations of

33. See n. 29 above, on the relationship of the Mosaic covenant to the Davidic. E.M. Dörrfuss, *Mose in den Chronikbüchern. Garant theokratischer Zukunftserwartung* (BZAW, 219; Berlin: W. de Gruyter, 1994), argues that all references to Moses (apart from 1 Chron. 5.29 [EVV 6.23]) are secondary expansions of the text from the second century BCE, intended to undermine David's authority as the cult founder. However, the textual evidence for such late expansions is lacking, and none of the texts really lends itself to an anti-Davidic interpretation. See the review of Dörrfuss's work by G.N. Knoppers in *CBQ* 58 (1996), pp. 705-707.

34. See, e.g.: דרש in 2 Chron. 14.3, 6; 15.2, 12, 13, 15; 17.4; 19.3; 20.3-4; 31.21; 34.3; התפלל (or its equivalent terms 'cry out' or 'call') in 2 Chron. 13.14; 14.11; 20.5-12; 30.18; 32.20; 33.13; niphal כנע in 2 Chron. 12.12; 33.12, 23; 34.27; שוב in 2 Chron. 15.4; 30.6, 9; 36.13. For the divine responses שמע and רפא see 2 Chron. 30.20; 33.13; 34.27; 36.16. Of course, the same *ideas* may be expressed in different language in passages where this vocabulary is not used, or they may be implied through the narrative.

distress, basing this appeal on the divine mercy shown in the exodus and the covenant with Moses (v. 53). The Chronicler, however, modifies his *Vorlage* to omit the reference to the exodus and instead connects such supplication directly to the *temple* (לתפלת המקום הזה, 2 Chron. 6.40), and hence to the Davidic covenant to which the temple testifies.[35] This petition is reproduced almost verbatim in Yahweh's reply in 2 Chron. 7.15. The Chronicler's conviction that God hears and responds positively to his people is then demonstrated throughout 2 Chronicles 10–36, where prayer is shown to be consistently effectual.[36]

Israel's Unfaithfulness

An overview of the post-Solomonic history brings out further aspects of the basic theological conviction articulated in the two divine addresses. First, there is the recognition of Israel's persistent unfaithfulness, such that every reign is marked to some degree by disobedience to God, even those that approximate the Chronicler's ideal and are generally evaluated positively. Thus Jehoshaphat, who commands the teaching of Yahweh's *torah* and its legal enforcement in the land (2 Chron. 17.7-9; 19.4-11), is rebuked for his alliances with the ungodly Ahab and Ahaziah (2 Chron. 19.2; 20.35-37), leading to the threat or fact of divine punishment. Hezekiah, the reforming king who repairs the damage caused by Ahaz and restores the temple worship to the manner of the days of David and Solomon (2 Chron. 29.25-30; 30.26), nevertheless succumbs to a pride that threatens Judah and Jerusalem with wrath (2 Chron. 32.25). Even Josiah, who is exemplary in his piety from his early years (2 Chron. 34.3), fails to heed God's word through Neco and so dies in battle (2 Chron. 35.22-24).

The Chronicler insists, then, that 'all have sinned' (cf. 2 Chron. 6.36) and have contributed to the final failure of the kingdom. Even the reforms and godly conduct of Hezekiah and Josiah can only delay and not avert the final outcome of destruction and exile. Thus, while 2 Chron. 32.26 states that Hezekiah repented of his pride so that 'Yahweh's wrath did not come

---

35. The same point is made in the concluding prayer in 2 Chron. 6.42, where the petition that God will remember the חסדי דוד is best understood as a reference to the Davidic covenant (taking the phrase as an objective genitive; Kelly, *Retribution and Eschatology in Chronicles*, p. 145).

36. Examples of answered prayer abound in the work, beginning in 1 Chron. 4.10. Prayer in Chronicles does not work *ex opere operato*, but is always a sign of faith and repentance in the one who prays (cf. Japhet, *Ideology*, p. 255 n. 185).

upon [the people of Jerusalem] during the days of Hezekiah', the clear implication is that the penalty has been stayed but not permanently set aside.[37] Hereafter Judah lives under the lengthening shadow of exile, exemplified certainly by Manasseh (2 Chron. 33.11-13) and possibly also by Josiah, if Johnstone is right in arguing that the Chronicler sees the exile as beginning in principle with the death of that king.[38] This view contrasts sharply with Japhet's insistence that 'Only Zedekiah and his generation are responsible for the disaster that occurred in his time'.[39] That is how she understands 2 Chron. 36.15-16, but Johnstone is surely right to counter that 'the verses are most naturally understood in terms of a long process of events: Zedekiah is not alone in his culpability, but marks the climax of an age-long process'.[40] Von Rad also contrasted Chronicles with Kings, which he saw as depicting 'a constantly mounting guilt' issuing in a collective judgment of the nation, over against the Chronicler's portrayal of individual generations each discretely considered,[41] but it seems instead that the two works are essentially in agreement here.

The Role of the Prophets

Another reason for disputing the traditional consensus on retribution in Chronicles is the fact that within this work Yahweh *always* responds in blessing to those who 'seek' him, but his response to the disobedient is more complex. Attention has already been drawn to a second motif, the role of warning prophets or equivalent figures.[42] Wellhausen believed that the function of the chronistic prophets was 'to connect the deeds of men with the events of the course of the world' with prophecies that 'always come exactly true' and therefore demonstrate the principle of retribution: 'never wherever misfortune occurs is guilt wanting', and 'merit is always the obverse of success'.[43] Japhet, however, points out against Wellhausen

---

37. Cf. Johnstone, *1 and 2 Chronicles*, II, p. 220.

38. This is, of course, an inference from the text and is not explicitly stated by the author.

39. Japhet, *Ideology*, p. 163.

40. Johnstone, *Chronicles and Exodus*, p. 123.

41. Von Rad, *Geschichtsbild*, p. 13.

42. Prophetic words and admonitions are given in 2 Chron. 12.5; 15.1; 16.7; 18.5, 16-17; 19.2-3; 20.14-17, 37; 21.12-15; 24.19-22; 25.7-9, 15; 26.18; 33.10; 34.23-24; 36.12-13.

43. Wellhausen, *Prolegomena*, pp. 203, 209.

that the prophets' role in Chronicles is not to offer an interpretation of history but to preach repentance;[44] and Williamson observes that it is only when the warnings are rejected that the punishment is forthcoming.[45] A notable example of this is Uzziah's act of hubris in attempting to make an offering at the altar of incense (2 Chron. 26.16-20). His affliction with 'leprosy' comes only *after* his angry defiance of the priests who opposed him.

This is a point of signal importance for understanding the author's outlook. It indicates that the decisive issue in the imposition of punishment is *not* the original offence itself but rather the *rejection of the divine word of warning*. Above all, this feature demonstrates that, for the Chronicler, the critical question is not the requiting of evil but rather the awful consequences of spurning the offer of divine grace. Other illustrations of this motif are found in the examples of Asa (2 Chron. 16.7-10), Joash (2 Chron. 24.17-22) and Amaziah (2 Chron. 25.15-23). When punishment *is* exacted, this happens regularly according to the principle of 'measure for measure'. The author illustrates God's justice through a punishment that corresponds closely in character with the offence (cf. 2 Chron. 12.5; 15.2; 24.20, 22, 25).[46]

As was noted above, repentance in Chronicles in the face of the prophetic word has the capacity to mitigate or even set aside a punishment that has been decreed.[47] In every case, then, retribution (in contrast to blessing) is never 'immediate', nor is it always exacted. The Chronicler's own understanding of the role of the prophets is explicitly stated in 2 Chron. 20.20, where faith in the prophets is enjoined so that the people

---

44. Japhet, *Ideology*, pp. 177-78. Johnstone (*Chronicles and Exodus*, p. 118 n. 8) rightly glosses Japhet's observation with the comment that the prophets' function is a 'continuous and cumulative raising of consciousness through the generations to bring to repentance and in order to display the long-suffering patience of God...rather than merely "warning" delivered *seriatim* to each generation', since no prophetic warning is mentioned for a number of reigns that were marked by sin, as Japhet (*Ideology*, p. 191 n. 561) concedes.

45. Williamson, *1 and 2 Chronicles*, p. 32.

46. Cf. Japhet, *Ideology*, p. 170 n. 493; I. Kalimi, *Zur Geschichtsschreibung des Chronisten. Literarisch-historiographische Abweichungen der Chronik von ihren Paralleltexten in den Samuel- und Königsbüchern* (BZAW, 226; Berlin: W. de Gruyter, 1995), pp. 165-71.

47. 1 Chron. 21.15 contains a striking example of God's mercy, leading God to relent from a punishment he had already decreed. 2 Chron. 12.7-8 also describes the tempering of judgment in response to repentance.

'will be successful', and in his comment in 2 Chron. 36.15, that Yahweh 'sent word to them through his messengers again and again, because he had pity on his people and on his dwelling-place'. Divine pity rather than strict justice is the controlling motif; and since the chronistic prophets summon kings and people to repentance at the explicit behest of Yahweh, the *opportunity* to repent is itself a divine gift of grace. The catalyst to human repentance originates in Yahweh, not in any autonomous human will. Chronicles thus provides us with instances of what traditional theology has come to term 'prevenient grace'.

Mercy to the Undeserving

A third matter concerns the Chronicler's presentation of a number of reigns, namely, those of Solomon, Rehoboam, Abijah, Asa and Manasseh. These accounts differ significantly from the *Vorlage* through the inclusion of additional material detailing Yahweh's blessing upon these kings and their acts of repentance, or in Solomon's case, the omission of material that reflected negatively upon him.[48] This fact has led many commentators to conclude that the Chronicler, following an assumed principle of divine reward for faithfulness, viewed the piety of these individuals differently than the negative judgment found in Kings.[49] However, rather than dissenting from Kings, the Chronicler is more probably stressing Yahweh's faithfulness to the Davidic covenant and his goodness even to those

---

48. Especially 1 Kgs 11.1-40, although it must be stated that there are allusions to this in 2 Chron. 9.29; 10.4, 10, 14, and material that reflects *positively* on Solomon has also been omitted (cf. 1 Kgs 3.16-28; 4.1-34). See Selman, *2 Chronicles*, p. 350.

49. This interpretation appears to have begun with Wellhausen, and most commentators down to the present have generally agreed with him. Thus, on Solomon: Wellhausen, *Prolegomena*, pp. 184-85; Curtis and Madsen, *Books of Chronicles*, p. 313; Rudolph, *Chronikbücher*, pp. 135, 225-26; R. Mosis, *Untersuchungen zur Theologie des chronistischen Geschichtswerkes* (FTS, 92; Freiburg: Herder, 1973), *passim*; Braun, *1 Chronicles*, pp. xxxii-xxxv; Dillard, *2 Chronicles*, pp. 1-2; Japhet, *I and II Chronicles*, p. 48; Johnstone, *1 and 2 Chronicles*, I, pp. 298-99; on Rehoboam: Wellhausen, *Prolegomena*, p. 209; Curtis and Madsen, *Books of Chronicles*, pp. 362-63; P. Welten, *Geschichte und Geschichtsdarstellung in den Chronikbüchern* (WMANT, 42; Neukirchen–Vluyn: Neukirchener Verlag, 1973), p. 127; with some qualification, Dillard, *2 Chronicles*, p. 94; Japhet, *I and II Chronicles*, p. 664; on Abijah: Wellhausen, *Prolegomena*, p. 193; Curtis and Madsen, *Books of Chronicles*, pp. 373-74; Welten, *Geschichte und Geschichtsdarstellung*, p. 127; Dillard, *2 Chronicles*, pp. 104-105; on Manasseh: Wellhausen, *Prolegomena*, pp. 207-209.

disobedient members of the Davidic line who were not punished as their sins deserved.

Although it is common to see blessings and punishment in Chronicles as strictly periodized according to the times of faithfulness and apostasy,[50] the blessings that Rehoboam received in the form of buildings and a large family (2 Chron. 11.5-12, 18-23) were evidently not confined to the three-year period when he and his kingdom obeyed the Law of Moses, while the overall assessment of Rehoboam is clearly negative (2 Chron. 12.14). The same is true of Manasseh, whose prayer in exile and restoration to the land (2 Chron. 33.11-13) are recounted, not to number him among the pious but for the parenetic purpose of affirming that Yahweh's mercy may come even to the worst of sinners, once the step of repentance is taken.

The presentation of Abijah and his reign (2 Chron. 13) is rather more complex. Here, while Yahweh's faithfulness to the Davidic covenant and Judah's *corporate* fidelity to the Mosaic cultic law are strongly affirmed (cf. vv. 8-12), reading between the lines, we may detect a certain reserve on the author's part on the question of King Abijah's personal piety.[51]

Innocent Suffering

Finally, consideration must be given to those cases where misfortune or affliction cannot be readily coordinated with some preceding sin by those who suffer. There are some five or six examples of trouble or distress in the book that militate against Wellhausen's assertion, quoted above, that 'never where misfortune occurs is guilt wanting'.[52]

First, the three accounts of stylized 'Yahweh war' in which Judah is victorious in defending itself against its aggressive enemies (2 Chron. 13.3-20; 14.9-15; 20.1-30) must be distinguished from the more usual presentation in Chronicles, where invasion is explicitly depicted as punishment for covenant-breaking.[53] In each case the attack comes *after* some

---

50. Cf. Dillard, *2 Chronicles*, p. 78.

51. See D.G. Deboys, 'History and Theology in the Chronicler's Portrayal of Abijah', *Bib* 71 (1990), pp. 48-62. Abijah is no 'preacher of righteousness', as Dillard (*2 Chronicles*, p. 110) proposes.

52. Wellhausen, *Prolegomena*, p. 203. This remark is immediately preceded by the comment that 'Never does sin miss its punishment', but the examples adduced above demonstrate how inaccurate that comment is.

53. Cf. 2 Chron. 12.4; 21.8-10, 16-17; 24.23-24; 25.22-24; 28.5, 17-20; 33.11; 36.17.

cult reform (or, as in 2 Chron. 13.1-12, in conjunction with a statement affirming Judah's cultic faithfulness). It is significant that Jehoshaphat's temple prayer in 2 Chron. 20.3-12 (a mouthpiece for the Chronicler's own theology)[54] contains no confession of wrongdoing, but rather perceives that invasion as an unjustified act. To these accounts must be added as well the Chronicler's version of Sennacherib's threat against Jerusalem (2 Chron. 32.1-23), which is prefaced by the comment on Hezekiah's great acts of cult reform (2 Chron. 29–31), 'after these faithful deeds'.[55] Japhet is surely correct to understand these cases not as retribution but as opportunities for testing the genuineness of the leaders' faith.[56] The Chronicler recognizes that the piety of these leaders does not exempt them from the serious difficulties that confront Judah in the world but rather throws them again on the divine promises made in the Davidic covenant.[57]

Second, innocent suffering is in view in 2 Chron. 25.6-13, in the account of the Ephraimite mercenaries who carried out plunder and massacred 3000 Judahites when Amaziah sent them home—and this at the behest of a man of God. Japhet argues that 'the narrative as a whole remains in some tension with the Chronicler's theological system', because 'in terms of the chronistic theory of divine retribution, Amaziah is actually punished for his proper conduct in hearing the prophet's demand. We look in vain here for some account of transgression by Amaziah, or by the inhabitants of the spoiled cities.'[58] However, the tension only arises when such a rigid 'theological system' is assumed. Moreover, Amaziah himself is scarcely an exemplary figure of faith. He is presented as a rather venal king (v. 9) who engages in idolatry immediately after a God-given victory (v. 14).

A similar issue arises in David's confession of responsibility in 1 Chron. 21.17, following the plague that kills 70,000 Israelites and now threatens Jerusalem: 'I am the one who sinned and did wrong. But these sheep, what

54. This is demonstrated generally for the book in M.A. Throntveit, *When Kings Speak: Royal Speech and Royal Prayer in Chronicles* (SBLDS, 93; Atlanta: Scholars Press, 1987).

55. Linking this verse with the preceding 2 Chron. 32.20 and taking הדברים והאמת האלה as a hendiadys (Dillard, *2 Chronicles*, p. 253).

56. Japhet, *I and II Chronicles*, pp. 783, 980. Contrast Wellhausen (*Prolegomena*, p. 204), who maintained that the invasion in 2 Chron. 20 was in consequence of Jehoshaphat's disobedience (cf. 2 Chron. 18.20).

57. Thus Jehoshaphat's prayer in 2 Chron. 20.9 makes explicit allusion to Solomon's temple dedication prayer (cf. 2 Chron. 6.28).

58. Japhet, *I and II Chronicles*, p. 858.

have they done?'[59] David's culpability and the people's innocence are plainly stated in this verse, which replicates and intensifies the statement in the *Vorlage* (2 Sam. 24.17); but the Chronicler also has Joab protest: 'Why should [it/he?] be לאשמה upon Israel?' (1 Chron. 21.3b). This sentence is conventionally translated as something like 'Why should (David) *bring guilt* upon Israel?',[60] raising a problem that Bailey articulates: 'There is no obvious reason for the people becoming a target for retribution because of *David's* actions, and the commentaries generally exhibit confusion about this'.[61]

The difficulty seems to arise mainly from the traditional rendering of אשמה as 'guilt'. A contextual study of the occurrences of this noun elsewhere in Chronicles and the Hebrew Bible[62] suggests to me that it may equally denote '*consequence of* guilt' as much as the state of moral culpability itself. Thus 2 Chron. 24.18c may be rendered 'and there was wrath upon Judah and Jerusalem as a consequence of their guilt (באשמתם)'; while the 'fierce anger against Israel' in 2 Chron. 28.13 explicates the sense of כי רבה אשמה לנו. Similarly, the account of Amon's assassination in 2 Chron. 33.24 may complete the sense of the statement about the king in the preceding verse, אשמה הרבה.

This suggestion is supported by Jay Sklar's new study of the verb אשם in Leviticus, which includes reference to the cognate noun אשמה in Lev. 4.3.[63] Sklar reviews the main understandings of אשם proposed by the RSV

---

59. See N. Bailey, 'David and God in 1 Chronicles 21: Edged with Mist', in M.P. Graham and S.L. McKenzie (eds.), *The Chronicler as Author: Studies in Text and Texture* (JSOTSup, 263; Sheffield: Sheffield Academic Press, 1999), pp. 337-59.

60. Cf. NEB, GNB, NIV, NRSV.

61. Bailey, 'David and God', p. 338 (my emphasis). Insofar as they discuss Joab's statement that David's action will involve Israel; most do not. Japhet (*I and II Chronicles*, p. 377), however, believes that the Chronicler was responding to the problem of innocent suffering raised by 2 Sam. 24.17: 'In Chronicles the answer is given here: by his decision David makes transgressors of the people as well, for to submit to a census is in itself a sin!' This is scarcely convincing: did the people have a choice in the matter?

62. Lev. 5.24 (EVV 6.5), 26 (EVV 6.7); 22.16; Ps. 69.6 (EVV v. 5); Ezra 9.6, 7, 13, 15; 10.10, 19; 2 Chron. 24.18; 28.10, 13; 33.23. J. Milgrom (*Leviticus 1–16* [AB, 3; New York: Doubleday, 1991], p. 231), commenting on Lev. 4.3, states: 'It connotes both the wrong and the retribution'.

63. J. Sklar, 'Sin, Impurity, Sacrifice and Atonement' (PhD dissertation, Cheltenham and Gloucester College, 2001), pp. 22-38. Sklar's discussion is confined to priestly texts but is supported by other uses of אשם; see the following note.

and related versions ('to be/become guilty'), Milgrom ('to feel guilt'), and Kiuchi and the NJPS ('to realize guilt'), before arguing that 'to suffer guilt's consequences' best fits the sense of Lev. 4.3, 13-14, 22-23, 27-28; 5.21-23 (EVV 6.2-4).[64] As Bailey observes, 'There is certainly an iconic and verbal similarity between Lev. 4.3 and 1 Chron. 21.3, especially in the collocation of אשמה with the verb הסא' (cf. 1 Chron. 21.8, 17).[65] Sklar's rendering of Lev. 4.3, 'If it is the anointed priest who sins so that the people suffer guilt's consequences', is a proposal with a direct parallel in 1 Chron. 21.3.[66]

A supporting argument may be offered from the related semantic field of עון, which figures into this pericope. This word is variously rendered 'iniquity', 'guilt' or 'punishment for guilt', according to context.[67] In 1 Chron. 21.8 (//2 Sam. 24.10) David prays with reference to his action:

64. That the verb אשם may have this meaning in non-priestly texts is accepted by the translators of the RSV and the NIV in Hos. 10.2; 14.1 (EVV 13.16); Isa. 24.6; Ps. 34.22 (EVV v. 21); Jer. 2.3. Hos. 4.15 and 5.15 can also bear this meaning; cf. A.A. Macintosh, *Hosea* (ICC; Edinburgh: T. & T. Clark, 1997), p. 161: 'The verb אשם comprehends the meanings (1) to commit an offence, (2) to be or become guilty, and (3) to be held guilty, bear punishment'. The NEB, following ibn Ezra and Kimchi, prefers to emend to שמם ('to be desolate'), or it follows G.R. Driver's suggestion that a second root אשם means 'to be desolate' (see B. Schindler and A. Marmorstein [eds.], *Occident and Orient: Gaster Anniversary Volume* [London: Taylor's Foreign Press, 1936], pp. 75-76; cited in Macintosh, *Hosea*, p. 214), but these conjectures seem unnecessary.

65. Bailey, 'David and God', p. 339

66. Sklar, 'Sin, Impurity, Sacrifice and Atonement', p. 339. Bailey is pointing in the same direction when he suggests: 'Perhaps...the people in 1 Chronicles 21 do not become guilty themselves; instead, David's activity has the facility of drawing the people into its orbit' ('David and God', p. 340). In other words, innocent people can be enmeshed in the consequences of the sins of others. This is not a remarkable point, but it is strange that commentators in the past have denied that the Chronicler could make this basic distinction. At the risk of belaboring the point, it is obvious that the chronistic prophets who suffer for declaring Yahweh's word (2 Chron. 16.10; 24.21; 36.16) do so as innocents. However, Bailey does point out that the people, rather than David's own person, are the immediate object of *divine* chastisement (rather than simply victims of sin). In what sense is this punishment for *David*? Perhaps in the decimation of his kingdom, and his subsequent exclusion from temple building for this sin; see my 'David's Disqualification in 1 Chronicles 22.8: A Response to Piet B. Dirksen', *JSOT* 80 (1998), pp. 53-61.

67. R.L. Harris *et al.* (eds.), *Theological Wordbook of the Old Testament* (Chicago: Moody, 1980), II, pp. 650-51. See, e.g., Isa. 30.13 (= 'sin'); 1 Sam. 25.24 (= 'blame'); Jer. 51.6 (= 'punishment').

'Please take away the עָוֹן of your servant'. English versions typically translate the word rather precisely (RSV, 'iniquity'; NIV, 'guilt'), but Hebrew
usage suggests that sin and its punishment are connected notions, rather
than separate.

Finally, a tangential matter here concerns the possible significance of
sickness as retribution. It is usually held that the Chronicler inserted the
Hanani episode (2 Chron. 16.7-11) to provide a theological rationale for
Asa's foot disease (v. 12), reported in 1 Kgs 15.23.[68] While this is a possible deduction (strengthened by the addition of a chronological notice in v.
12), it is not expressly stated here that the illness is a punishment, in
contrast to the writer's practice in 2 Chron. 21.18-19; 26.20. War (v. 9)
rather than illness is the threatened retribution for the alliance; thus Japhet
concludes that 'Asa's present illness must be due to another specific error,
i.e. his treatment of the prophet',[69] whom he threw into prison. But if so,
the Chronicler has not made explicit the connection here between abuse of
the prophet and the king's suffering, as he does in the case of Joash, who
dies for his complicity in the murder of Zechariah ben Jehoiada (2 Chron.
24.21, 24-25).[70]

Conclusion

The argument of this study has been that the traditional understanding of
retribution in Chronicles is in many respects a chimera that has distorted a
proper understanding of the author's theology and message. Retribution
for *persistent and impenitent evil* is certainly one of the book's themes, but
such punishment is never 'immediate', nor is it always inevitable. Far
from stressing the outworking of a strict theodicy in the world, the Chronicler is concerned primarily to highlight the offer of God's prevenient and
undeserved mercy to a sinful yet penitent people—an offer, moreover, that
is tied to the concrete form of the Jerusalem temple and its cultus of prayer
and sacrifice.[71] This gift is a reflex of the Davidic covenant which has

68. See, e.g., Dillard, *2 Chronicles*, p. 126; De Vries, *1 and 2 Chronicles*, p. 306:
Asa 'suffered the most personal form of retribution from God, viz. a gangrenous
sickness in his feet'.

69. Japhet, *I and II Chronicles*, p. 737.

70. See also n. 25 above, detailing cases where the Chronicler makes divine agency
explicit.

71. The general thrust of this essay is paralleled by D.F. Murray, 'Retribution and
Revival: Theological Theory, Religious Praxis, and the Future in Chronicles', *JSOT* 88

abiding religious significance in the postexilic period, despite the absence of a reigning Davidide. The grace of this covenant is extended far beyond that particular family line potentially to embrace all Israel within the scope of God's forgiveness and restoration (though the extent and precise form of that expected restoration remain a matter of debate). In pointing the way to the future for the people, the Chronicler's message of grace places this work firmly in the mainstream of the biblical tradition.

(2000), pp. 77-99, who likewise holds that 2 Chron. 7.13-15 (as the *locus classicus* of chronistic theology) sets out 'not a programme that distances YHWH from Israel as the dispassionate dispenser of a precisely measured retribution, but one that involves him with *his people* personally, one in which he takes the initiative to move their hearts towards repentance and restoration' (pp. 95-96 [emphasis in original]). Murray rightly characterizes this programme—represented above all in the idealized depiction of the reign of David and Solomon, but also in the time of Asa and Jehoshaphat—as a concern with religious *revival* in the sense of rekindling the people's 'deep personal commitment to YHWH through the praxis of the temple and its cult' (p. 86), so that they may face the future with joy. Murray concludes (p. 96): 'The roots of this theological theory lie not in a rationalizing retributivist analysis of history, but in a deep religious conviction that stems from committed religious praxis'.

THE EVOLUTION OF NAME THEOLOGY

William M. Schniedewind

Reverence for the divine name is a well-known feature of Judaism. The question remains, however, when and why did this reverence develop? A turning point in the development of Name Theology occurs during the exile. It is an honor to dedicate this essay to Ralph Klein, whose monograph, *Israel in Exile: A Theological Interpretation*,[1] addressed the seminal importance of the exile in the theology of ancient Israel. Another of Ralph Klein's contributions to biblical scholarship has been the work on the book of Chronicles, in which we shall see that Name Theology further develops. My hope is that this study will contribute specifically to the understanding of how Name Theology evolved in ancient Israel.

In this article I shall argue that Name Theology first arises with political and religious nationalism in the seventh century BCE and was intended to project Yahweh's exclusive claim to the city of Jerusalem and its temple as Yahweh's physical dwelling place. Unfortunately, the Babylonian destruction of Jerusalem and the temple left Yahweh homeless. As a theological solution to this social crisis, the name of God was personified and abstracted; Yahweh did not actually live in the Jerusalem temple, only his name. When Yahweh returned to a rebuilt temple in the late sixth century BCE, would only his name dwell there? Yes, but the name of God became a hypostasis of Yahweh himself, and thereby God was returned to his temple. For the postexilic writer of Chronicles it was assumed that God's name—and thereby God himself—came to rest in the temple.

It will be useful to begin with an aside. A quick gauge of the changing use of the divine name is to look at its incorporation into personal names. The divine name was used regularly in personal names in ancient Israel before the exile—just as theophoric names were used throughout the Near East. In pre-exilic inscriptions (primarily seals and seal impressions)

---

1.   R.W. Klein, *Israel in Exile: A Theological Interpretation* (OBT; Philadelphia: Fortress Press, 1979).

personal names regularly use the theophoric element *yah* or *yahu* (abbreviated forms of *Yahweh*).[2] The same pattern holds for biblical literature, where predominant theophoric elements of personal names of people located in the narrative history of the kingdom of Judah derive from *Yahweh*. The theophoric element is used as both a prefix (as in *Jo*shua) and a suffix (as in Isa*iah*). There is a sharp decline in the use of the theophoric *Yahweh* in personal names in postexilic texts. A quick perusal of the list of returnees' names in Ezra 2 finds that only nine names use Yahwistic theophoric elements. By the end of the Second Temple Period, theophoric elements based on *Yahweh* will have been virtually eliminated from Jewish names.[3] In short, the use of *Yahweh* as the basis of a theophoric name probably reflects its general sacral evolution, with the reverence of the divine name developing especially in the Persian Period and later.

Within Qumran literature there is evidence for the rising reverence for the name of God. This is graphically illustrated by the different ways that the Qumran scribes avoid or encode the divine name. It is certainly noteworthy, for example, that the Great Isaiah Scroll (1QIsaᵃ) regularly employs the divine name with no special attention; however, when a scribe makes a correction, restoring a verse of Isaiah 40 apparently lost through haplography, the correcting scribe writes the divine name as four dots. In the Pesher to Habakkuk, the commentary on the biblical text never uses the tetragrammaton, and when the commentary quotes the divine name from the biblical lemma, it reverts it into paleo-Hebrew script rather than using the standard Herodian Aramaic script. These are small indications that the name of God had already taken on a special significance towards the end of the Second Temple Period.

Name Theology in Deuteronomic Literature

Deuteronomic literature is at the heart of Name Theology. As this pretends to be a historical approach, it begs the question of dating deuteronomic

---

2.   See J.H. Tigay, *You Shall Have No Other Gods: Israelite Religion in the Light of Hebrew Inscriptions* (Harvard Semitic Studies, 31; Atlanta: Scholars Press, 1986).

3.   See R. Hachlili, 'Hebrew Names, Personal Names, Family Names and Nicknames of Jews in the Second Temple Period', in J.W. van Henten and A. Brenner (eds.), *Families and Family Relations: As Represented in Early Judaisms and Early Christianities; Texts and Fictions. Papers Read at a Noster Colloquium in Amsterdam, June 9-11, 1998* (Studies in Theology and Religion, 2; Leiden: Deo Publishing, 2000), pp. 83-115.

literature. Increasingly, scholars will not be able to get around the fact that the late Judaean monarchy was a period of great literary production. This is suggested, first of all, by growing archaeological, epigraphic and anthropological evidence that point to an explosion in writing during the late Judaean monarchy.[4] It is not coincidental then that the great writing prophets are located within the period of the late Judaean monarchy. Neither is it coincidental that the Josianic 'Book of the Covenant' is associated with Deuteronomy and the DtrH during this historical period. At the same time, it is clear that deuteronomic literature was collected and edited in the exilic period and later. For the present purposes, both the Josianic and exilic contexts will be part of this historical analysis. Yet, it must be emphasized that the social and historical context best suited for the initial formation of the biblical canon, and particularly, the deuteronomic corpus, is the late Judaean monarchy.

The DtrH uses a variety of phrases to express Name Theology.[5] These include 'the place that Yahweh your God shall choose to put his name' (הַמָּקוֹם אֲשֶׁר יִבְחַר יהוה אֱלֹחֵיכֶם בּוֹ לְשַׁכֵּן שְׁמוֹ שָׁם, Deut. 12.11; 14.23; 16.2, 6, 11; 26.2; also cf. Jer. 7.12; Neh. 1.9; Ezra 6.12), 'to put his name there' (לִהְיוֹת שְׁמִי שָׁם, Deut. 12.5, 21; 14.24; cf. 1 Kgs 9.3; 11.36; 14.21; 2 Kgs 21.4, 7), 'so that his name shall be there' (לִהְיוֹת שְׁמִי שָׁם, cf. 1 Kgs 8.16, 29; 2 Kgs 23.27), 'to build a house for his name' (לִבְנוֹת בַּיִת לְשֵׁם), cf. 2 Sam. 7.13; 1 Kgs 3.2; 5.17-19 [EVV vv. 3-5]; 8.17, 18, 19, 20, 44, 48), and 'to dedicate a house for the name of Yahweh' (הַקְדִּישׁ בַּיִת לְשֵׁם יהוה, cf. 1 Kgs 9.7).[6] The expression 'the house/ city which is called by my name' (הַבַּיִת/הָעִיר אֲשֶׁר נִקְרָא שְׁמִי עָלָיו), 1 Kgs 8.43; Jer. 7.10, 11, 14, 30; 25.29; 32.34; 34.15) appears in exilic or postexilic literature

---

4.   I. Finkelstein and N.A. Silberman (*The Bible Unearthed: Archaeology's New Vision of Ancient Israel and the Origin of its Sacred Texts* [New York: Free Press, 2001]) are certainly correct in reading the archaeological evidence as pointing to the late Judaean monarchy as the formative period for the composition of biblical literature. I presented similar evidence in a talk entitled, 'Jerusalem, the Late Judaean Monarchy and the Composition of Biblical Texts', at the SBL annual meeting, November 1998 (to be published in *Essays in the History, Literature and Archaeology of Jerusalem* [SBL Symposium Series; Atlanta: Scholars Press, forthcoming]), and my book, *How the Bible Became a Book: The Textualization of Ancient Israelite Culture* (Cambridge University Press, forthcoming), will address this in more detail.

5.   For a recent review of Name Theology, see I. Wilson, *Out of the Midst of the Fire: Divine Presence in Deuteronomy* (SBLDS, 151; Atlanta: Scholars Press, 1995).

6.   See M. Weinfeld, *Deuteronomy and the Deuteronomic School* (Oxford: Clarendon Press, 1972), pp. 191-209, 324-25.

and is influenced by Deuteronomy. As Moshe Weinfeld observes, how-ever, this expression 'to attach a name to X (קרא שם על־X)' appears in earlier literature (e.g. 2 Sam. 6.2; 12.28; Isa. 4.1; Ps. 49.12 [EVV v. 11]) and cannot be considered exclusively deuteronomic. Rather, it is the use of this language particularly about Jerusalem and the temple that indicates deuteronomic influence.

Deuteronomic Name Theology, like the structure of the book of Deu-teronomy itself, can be traced to Near Eastern antecedents. For example, the Amarna letters (c. 1400 BCE) reflect this concept: 'As the king has placed his name (*šarri šakan šumšu*) in Jerusalem forever, he cannot abandon it—the land of Jerusalem' (EA 287.60-63).[7] The language of putting a name in a place is also typical of royal inscriptions and parti-cularly of erecting a stele, where the king is said to place his name.[8] Every-where the king places his name, he claims exclusive ownership. Even in biblical literature, the attaching of a name to a place claims ownership; for example, we read in Deut. 3.14, 'Jair the Manassite took the whole region of Argob as far as the border of the Geshurites and the Maacathites, and he *named* them—that is, Bashan—after himself, Havvoth-jair, as it is to this day'. Likewise, when David conquers Jerusalem, he renames it 'the City of David' (2 Sam. 5.9). The concept of the name in both Near Eastern and biblical literature indicates that to put one's name somewhere meant to claim exclusive ownership. Kings, in particular, put their names on monu-ments, stele, and border inscriptions to claim exclusive ownership of things. It is not a coincidence that Semitic royal inscriptions often begin with the expression, 'I am X, son of Y, King of Z'. The king puts his name in a place and thereby claims ownership and exclusive dominion. Indeed, this was the thrust of the Josianic reforms: the exclusive worship of Yahweh in a temple that Yahweh shared with no other gods. There is no implication that Yahweh's name was an abstraction of the deity. Rather, the abstraction of Yahweh's name was most likely a later exilic reflection; originally, the claim that Yahweh 'put his name' in Jerusalem and in the temple expressed Yahweh's exclusive claims.[9] In this respect, Name

7.   W.L. Moran (ed.), *The Amarna Letters* (Baltimore: The Johns Hopkins Uni-versity Press, 1992), p. 328.

8.   W. Von Soden, *Akkadisches Handwörterbuch* (3 vols.; Wiesbaden: Otto Har-rassowitz, 1981), III, pp. 1274-75.

9.   The exilic prologue to Deuteronomy (chs. 1–4) will articulate this abstrac-tion of God's name (cf. S.A. Geller, *Sacred Enigmas: Literary Religion in the Hebrew Bible* [London: Routledge, 1996], pp. 30-61), but this is a radical hermeneutical

Theology was simply another expression of the religious centralization of the Josianic reforms. Borrowing from Near Eastern practice, the ancient Josianic 'theologians' made an exclusive claim to Jerusalem and the temple by making it the place where Yahweh put his name.

Deuteronomic Name Theology has been understood as opposing the patently anthropomorphic priestly viewpoint that derived from early sacral conceptions (e.g. 1 Sam. 4.4; 2 Sam. 6.2; Ps. 80.2).[10] Von Rad, for example, argued that the deuteronomic terminology intended to combat the popular belief that Yahweh actually dwelled in the temple.[11] In fact, the idea of a name being associated with a place is well-attested in the ancient Near Eastern literature. The language derives from royal inscriptions in which the king establishes his name in a particular locale. As such, it maintains the king's dominion and exclusive claim over the place. The abstraction of the name was a development within the biblical literature. The idea of the temple as a place for Yahweh's name within the context of the Josianic religious reforms was undoubtedly intended to affirm Yahweh's exclusive right against other deities. We read, for example, in 2 Kgs 21.7: 'The carved image of Asherah that [Manasseh] had made he set in the house of which Yahweh said to David and to his son Solomon, "In this house, and in Jerusalem, which I have chosen out of all the tribes of Israel, I will put my name forever".' The sin of Manasseh is depicted as abrogating Yahweh's exclusive claim to Jerusalem and the temple. Josianic reforms thus asserted Yahweh's exclusive presence in the temple, and they did not abstract Yahweh's presence in the temple.

The significance of the deuteronomic phrase 'a house for Yahweh's name' thus lies in the exclusivity of worship and not its abstraction. Gerhard von Rad's classic *Studies in Deuteronomy* popularized the idea that the deuteronomic Name Theology reflected an abstract theological concept that intended to subvert the prevalent Priestly conception, which depicted the temple as the deity's actual dwelling place.[12] It is important to contextualize von Rad's argument by one of his premises: namely, Deuteronomy comes together in the exilic period. The force of this premise for

innovation. Ironically, the books of Chronicles hypostatized God's name so that eventually we come full circle in Rabbinic literature where 'the name' (השם) is God.

10. See Weinfeld, *Deuteronomy and the Deuteronomic*, pp. 191-209.

11. See G. von Rad, *Studies in Deuteronomy* (SBT, 9; Chicago: Regnery, 1953), pp. 38-39.

12. See von Rad's third chapter on 'Deuteronomy's "Name" Theology and the Priestly Document's "Kabod" Theology', in his *Studies in Deuteronomy*, pp. 37-44.

shaping von Rad's argument is explicit in the very first sentence of his thesis: 'Deuteronomy makes its appearance at a definite point in the history of Israel's faith'.[13] Even though von Rad accepted the arguments of W.M.L. de Wette that the book discovered in the temple was at least the kernel of the book of Deuteronomy, he was also working under Noth's premise of a deuteronomic historical work composed in the exilic period. This meant for von Rad that Deuteronomy and, more importantly, DtrH crystallized after the destruction of the temple during the Babylonian exile. It is only natural with such a premise to understand Name Theology as an abstraction that was necessitated by the destruction of the temple. To be sure, the deuteronomic abstraction of the name of God would be precipitated by the destruction of the temple, but I believe this abstraction is one exilic interpretation of Name Theology. Another interpretation of the destruction of the temple, however, would be to eliminate the need for it entirely (e.g. Isa. 66.1-2). Even if Name Theology came to be understood as an abstraction—especially by Protestant theologians—it is unlikely to have been *invented* as one.

The theme of a 'house for the name of Yahweh' is quite pervasive in the DtrH. It begins with 2 Sam. 7.13, where God promises that David's son 'shall build a house for my name'. This verse is widely acknowledged as a deuteronomic comment that was added to the promise to David.[14] This theme is picked up in several places in Kings. 1 Kings 3.2 sets the stage for the fulfillment of this promise: 'The people were sacrificing at the high places, however, because no house had yet been built for the name of the LORD'. 1 Kings 5.3-5 (cf. 8.17-20) explicitly comments on the promise when Solomon informs King Hiram of Tyre that 'My father David could not build a house for the name of the LORD his God because of the warfare with which his enemies surrounded him, until the LORD put them under the soles of his feet' (v. 3), and that 'I intend to build *a house for the name of the LORD* my God, as the LORD said to my father David, "Your son, whom I will set on your throne in your place, shall build the house for my name"' (v. 4).

The importance of this theme is indicated by the foreshadowing in 1 Kgs 3.2, namely that the temple would replace the sacrificing at the high places. This was, of course, a focus of the Josianic reforms. It is difficult to

---

13. Von Rad, *Studies in Deuteronomy*, p. 37.

14. See my *Society and the Promise to David: The Reception History of 2 Samuel 7.1-17* (New York: Oxford University Press, 1999), pp. 33-39.

imagine such a theme originating in the exilic period when the temple already had been destroyed.

The Name of God in Exile

The destruction of the temple and the loss of the temple treasures created a serious theological crisis.[15] It is precisely at this moment of disaster, when the temple lies in ruins (Lam. 5.17-18), that a poet confesses, 'But you, Yahweh, sit enthroned forever; your throne lasts generation after generation' (5.19).[16] This lament alludes to both the supposed promise to David that his descendants would be on the throne in Jerusalem forever and the problem of Yahweh's dislocation. It is Yahweh, rather than David's seed, who would sit enthroned forever. Although Yahweh was supposed to sit enthroned between the cherubim in the Jerusalem temple, jackals prowled God's earthly dwelling place. Hence, the poet proclaims that Yahweh dwells in heaven. In doing so, the poet of Lamentations addresses a physical and ultimately theological crisis that resulted from the Babylonian destruction of Jerusalem and the temple and left Yahweh homeless. But Yahweh was not homeless. Yahweh dwelled in heaven. Only his name dwelled in the temple.

The classic exilic exposition on Yahweh's heavenly dwelling place is in Solomon's prayer in 1 Kings 8.[17] In the narrative, the prayer takes its occasion at the completion of Solomon's temple, which is the fulfillment of David's vision 'to build a house for Yahweh to dwell in' (2 Sam. 7.5). Yet, the prayer foresees the exile in a way that belies its exilic composition (1 Kgs 8.46-53). The first part of the prayer (vv. 14-21) closely echoes the themes of the promise to David in 2 Sam. 7.1-17. The second part, however, turns to distancing the temple from Yahweh's presence.

Exilic literature relocates the homeless God of Israel. In Ps. 103.19, for example, we read, 'Yahweh has established his throne in the heavens'. In spite of the destruction of Jerusalem, God's home is unscathed. In Ezekiel the presence is mobile (especially ch. 1); God does not dwell in one place on earth. There is, however, a heavenly sanctuary (chs. 40–48) that makes

15. Klein, *Israel in Exile*, pp. 10-11.
16. Cited by Klein, *Israel in Exile*, p. 17.
17. For the exilic dating of this relevant part of the prayer, see J.D. Levenson, 'From Temple to Synagogue: 1 Kings 8', in B. Halpern and J.D. Levenson (eds.), *Traditions in Transformation: Turning Points in Biblical Faith* (Winona Lake, IN: Eisenbrauns, 1981).

an earthly sanctuary irrelevant. Not surprisingly, Qumran literature seized on Ezekiel's visions in justifying the community's rejection of the 'human' temple and looking forward to an eschatological temple (cf. 4Q174.3). In Lamentations, the heart of the people is sick because Mt Zion lies desolate, 'yet you, O Yahweh, reign forever; your throne endures for all generations' (5.19). Fortunately for Yahweh, only his name was located in the Jerusalem temple and therefore Yahweh's real heavenly throne remained untouched by the Babylonian exile—at least, this would be the explanation of exilic authors. Of course, if Yahweh dwelled in heaven, some would ask why a temple in Jerusalem was needed at all.[18]

Name Theology in the Postexilic Period

The first hint that the name of God becomes equated with Yahweh himself comes from so-called Third Isaiah (chs. 56–66). There, Yahweh and his name appear in parallelism (e.g. 56.6; 60.9). In Isa. 56.6, the oft-used expression 'to love the LORD', which is perhaps best known from its use in Deut. 6.5 but occurs over 40 times in the Hebrew Bible, is replaced by the expression 'to love *the name of* the LORD'. This unique occurrence, replacing as it does the more typical expression, hints at the hypostasization of the name of the LORD. In Isa. 60.9, the 'name of God' is in synonymous parallelism with 'the Holy One of Israel'.

The unification of Yahweh with his name is part of the eschatological vision. The last chapter of Zechariah envisions the coming day of Yahweh: Jerusalem will be destroyed by the nations, but Yahweh will come forth and restore Jerusalem. On that day, the prophet relates, 'Yahweh will become king over all the earth; on that day Yahweh will be one and his name one' (והיה יהוה למלך על כל הארץ ביום ההוא יהיה יהוה אחד ושמו אחד, Zech. 14.9).

Name Theology might have been one of the main arguments against the rebuilding of the Jerusalem temple. After all, if Isaiah 66 or Solomon's prayer (1 Kgs 8.27) were correct, then the Jerusalem temple certainly could not contain Yahweh. Therefore, Yahweh promised that 'my Name would abide there' (2 Kgs 8.29), because Yahweh would not fit. Key to relocating Yahweh in the temple (and thereby in Jerusalem) would be equating his name with Yahweh himself. Although Chronicles does not explicitly develop the name motif, it does carefully restructure and rewrite

18. This may be what lies behind the reticence to rebuild the Jerusalem temple, which is seen in literature such as the book of Haggai.

the narratives concerning the selection of Jerusalem, the ark's movement to Jerusalem, the promise of a temple, and the building of the temple. Chronicles also reflects aspects of Name Theology by its own use of the divine name.

The book of Chronicles essentially reproduces most occurrences of the name *Yahweh* found in Samuel–Kings. Chronicles does not actively develop the name of God as a motif. Still, there are a few original passages (without parallel in Samuel–Kings). These include the speech of David in 1 Chronicles 22, the speech of Asa in 2 Chron. 14.10 (EVV v. 11), and the speech of Jehoshaphat in 2 Chron. 20.8-9. Moreover, the book of Chronicles reflects a new understanding and role for the name of God within an emerging Judaism.

Figuratively speaking, *God* replaces *Yahweh* in the Second Temple Period, as we may suggest from an examination of the book of Chronicles. In particular, the term 'the house of *God/Elohim*' (i.e. בית אלהים) becomes standard in Chronicles, replacing 'the house of *Yahweh*' (i.e. בית יהוה) and reflecting on aspects of Name Theology in the Second Temple Period. 'House of God' occurs 33 times in Chronicles but never occurs in Kings. Moreover, 'house of God' never occurs in a certain Standard Biblical Hebrew text as a technical term for the Jerusalem temple.[19] 'House of God' is found 18 times in the late texts of Ezra, Nehemiah and Daniel. Robert Polzin is quite correct in judging 'house of God' to be Late Biblical Hebrew, replacing the older 'house of Yahweh, as the technical term for the Jerusalem temple.[20] 'House of Yahweh' is found in Chronicles 70 times; however, over half of these directly reflect synoptic sources. 'House of Yahweh' also appears in Hebrew ostraca (e.g. Arad ostracon 18 l. 9; 'Three Shekel Ostracon'[21]), whereas 'House of God' never occurs. The preference for using 'House of God'—as opposed to 'House of Yahweh'—is also reflected in other postexilic sources.[22] In accordance with

19. In Genesis, Joshua, Judges and Hosea, we find 'House of God' referring to various other temples. Judg. 18.31 refers to the temple at Shiloh.

20. R. Polzin, *Late Biblical Hebrew: Toward an Historical Typology of Biblical Hebrew Prose* (HSM, 12; Missoula, MT: Scholars Press, 1976), p. 30.

21. P. Bordreuil, F. Israel and D. Pardee, 'King's Command and Widow's Plea: Two New Hebrew Ostraca of the Biblical Period', *Near Eastern Archaeology* 61 (1998), pp. 2-13.

22. 'House of Yahweh' occurs nine times in Ezra–Nehemiah among the postexilic books. The phrase in the exilic books 'House of Yahweh of Hosts' (Hag. 1.14; Zech. 7.3; 8.9; 11.13; 14.21) is a frozen form, which suggests that 'House of Yahweh' became a more lofty and archaic term in Late Biblical Hebrew. The use of 'House of

Late Biblical Hebrew, the Chronicler often exchanged *Yahweh* in his sources for *Elohim*. This is a general tendency that we also witness for the expression 'the ark of Yahweh' that becomes 'the ark of God' in Chronicles (cf. 1 Chron. 13.14//2 Sam. 6.11; 1 Chron. 13.12//2 Sam. 6.10; 1 Chron. 16.1//2 Sam. 6.7; 1 Chron. 15.25//2 Sam. 6.12; 2 Chron. 5.5// 1 Kgs 8.4). The Chronicler changes 'House of Yahweh' to 'House of God' twelve times,[23] and the Chronicler's reliability with regard to his preference for *Elohim* reaches even the textual variants. Thus, in 2 Kgs 22.9 we find the absolute הבית ('the house'), while in the parallel text in 2 Chron. 34.17 we find בית יהוה ('the house of Yahweh'). According to the tendencies illustrated with regard to the Chronicler's use of *Yahweh* and *Elohim*, we would expect him not to employ *Yahweh* in his own creative activity, where it was not first present in his source. Thus, we should not be surprised that the LXX of 2 Kgs 22.9 retains *Yahweh* with 2 Chron. 34.17 and against the MT of Kings. Again, where we find דבר אלהים ('the word of God') in 1 Kgs 12.22, we find that the LXX agrees with the parallel in 2 Chron. 11.2, דבר יהוה ('the word of Yahweh') against the MT of Kings (also note 2 Sam. 6.12 [MT]//[LXX]//1 Chron. 16.25). In sum, Chronicles shows a marked preference for *Elohim* over *Yahweh* that must reflect something of the increasing reverence for the divine name itself.

Finally, we must look into the Ark Narratives, by which Yahweh's name comes to reside in the temple.[24] In general, the Chronicler structures his narrative to justify the rebuilt temple.[25] The largest and perhaps most

---

Yahweh' six times in Ezekiel (8.14, 16; 10.19; 11.1; 44.4, 5) alongside 'House of God' also accords well with Avi Hurvitz's argument that Ezekiel represents exilic Hebrew and a transition period between Standard Biblical Hebrew and Late Biblical Hebrew. See A. Hurvitz, *A Linguistic Study of the Relationship between the Priestly Source and the Book of Ezekiel* (Cahiers de la Revue biblique, 20; Paris: J. Gabalda, 1982).

23. Compare 2 Chron. 3.3//1 Kgs 6.1; 2 Chron. 4.11//1 Kgs 7.40; 2 Chron. 4.19// 1 Kgs 7.48; 2 Chron. 5.1//1 Kgs 7.51; 2 Chron. 5.14//1 Kgs 8.11; 2 Chron. 7.5//1 Kgs 8.63; 2 Chron. 15.18//1 Kgs 15.15; 2 Chron. 22.12//2 Kgs 11.3; 2 Chron. 23.3//2 Kgs 11.4; 2 Chron. 23.9//2 Kgs 11.10; 2 Chron. 25.24//2 Kgs 14.14; 2 Chron. 34.9//2 Kgs 22.4.

24. Ralph Klein delivered a (still unpublished) paper ('Redactional and Text-Critical Issues in the Ark Narrative') at the 1987 SBL meeting in Boston that detailed the differences between Chronicles' and 1–2 Samuel's accounts of the Ark Narrative. A succinct analysis of the changes and their significance can be found in R.L. Braun, 'Solomonic Apologetic in Chronicles', *JBL* 92 (1973), pp. 503-16.

25. See R.L. Braun, 'The Message of Chronicles: Rally 'Round the Temple', *CTM* 42 (1971), pp. 502-14; also see H.G.M. Williamson, 'The Temple in the Books of

significant change occurs with the repositioning and editing of David's census. In the DtrH, David's census appears as an afterthought tacked on to the end of the book of Samuel (2 Sam. 24). In Chronicles, David's census becomes central to its development of the temple. It is in the Chronicler's account of the census that David sees the angel of Yahweh 'standing between heaven and earth' at the threshing floor of Araunah (1 Chron. 21.16), where the temple would later be built (2 Chron. 3.1). This vision certainly confirms that the Jerusalem temple is the nexus point between heaven and earth. As a result, David knows that this special place should be the site of 'the house of Yahweh and the altar of the burnt offerings for Israel' (1 Chron. 22.1). The significance of these two particular additions of the Chronicler is (1) to emphasize the temple site as the place where God comes down to earth and (2) to justify the selection of this site for Yahweh's home on earth.

The completion and dedication of the temple is narrated in 1 Kings 8 and retold in 2 Chronicles 5–6. Chronicles closely parallels the DtrH, but appends an excerpt from Psalm 132 onto the end of Solomon's dedicatory prayer. This psalm is an old processional hymn, probably used in the annual liturgy celebrating the New Year.[26] The ancient festival must have included the ritual procession of the ark into the temple, thus symbolizing Yahweh's actual presence in the temple. Why does Chronicles choose to add this psalm to the ark narrative? This is a proactive addition by the Chronicler to the DtrH. The excerpt from Ps. 132.8-10 (//2 Chron. 6.41-42) emphasizes Yahweh's physical presence in the temple: 'Advance, O Yahweh God, to your resting place, you and your mighty ark'. Does the Chronicler understand this literally? This processional song celebrates the advance of both the ark and Yahweh himself into the temple. In this old hymn the actual presence of God is enjoined to enter his *resting place* in the temple. It may be this hymn, in fact, that the Chronicler draws upon when he characterizes the temple as a 'house of rest' (1 Chron. 28.2). It is the place where Yahweh and his wandering ark come to rest. Chronicles apparently underscores the importance of the temple by re-emphasizing the physical presence of Yahweh in the face of the theology of the name, which implied that only God's name dwelt in the temple.

Chronicles', in W. Horbury (ed.), *Templum Amicitiae: Essays on the Second Temple Presented to Ernst Bammel* (JSNTSup, 48; Sheffield: Almond Press, 1991), pp. 15-31.

26. See T.E. Fretheim, 'The Cultic Use of the Ark in the Monarchial Period' (PhD dissertation, Princeton University, 1967).

Finally, it is important to realize that the Chronicler's presentation of the construction of the Solomonic temple was paralleled by the rebuilt temple described in Ezra. It has not been lost on commentators that the Chronicler's short addition to his synoptic source in 2 Chron. 3.1-2 is pivotal for his understanding of the temple:

> Then Solomon began to build the House of Yahweh in Jerusalem on Mt. Moriah, where Yahweh had appeared to his father David, at the place that David had designated, at the threshing floor of Ornan the Jebusite. He began to build on the second day of the second month of the fourth year of his reign.

Most striking is the identification of the temple site with Mt Moriah of Genesis 22. Just as in the Chronicler's account of David's census, the association with Mt Moriah emphasizes the temple site as the place where the divine and human meet. As such, it makes a suitable place for God's special presence on earth. It should also be noted that the construction of the Second Temple began at the same time of year (Ezra 3.8). The type of parallelism that is retained in the tradition of the destruction of the First and Second Temples on the ninth of Av is also suggested in the building of the temple. The Second Temple was like the First Temple according to the Chronicler. By implication God, through his name, would come to rest in the Second Temple as he had in the First Temple.

BEYOND TRANSCENDENCE AND IMMANENCE:
THE CHARACTERIZATION OF THE PRESENCE AND ACTIVITY OF GOD
IN THE BOOK OF CHRONICLES*

John W. Wright

In the once widely used textbook on the rise of 'Palestinian Judaism', Werner Foester postulated a development within 'postexilic' Judaism in which God was perceived as becoming increasingly 'transcendent' as Judaism became increasingly apolitical. Foester wrote concerning God in this 'Judaism':

> God was silent, and instead of the God whose guiding hand could be traced in Israel's history, instead of the prophets who caused the divine summons to resound again and again in relation to public and private life, there now stood the Law, i.e. the account of Israel's special history in the past, and the provisions established once and for all in relation to political, legal, ceremonial and private life. The former introduced a retrospective feature into the piety of Judaism, the latter led to a tension: for the Law reckoned with a political independence which now no longer existed.[1]

According to Foester, the promulgation of Torah and the practice of the temple cult replaced the direct divine presence in history through the prophetic word over the nation of Israel.

Foester here stood within an interpretive tradition of Second Temple Judaism, one fraught with intellectual and moral problems, though still present in recent scholarship.[2] This interpretive grid runs into and through

---

* It is an honor to offer this essay in celebration of the life, character, and career of Ralph Klein. Ralph's wisdom, truthfulness, and guidance came to me as an important gift as I learned to write as a member of the professional guild. For such a gift, I will always be thankful.

1. W. Foester, *From the Exile to Christ: A Historical Introduction to Palestinian Judaism* (Philadelphia: Fortress Press, 1964), p. 5.

2. J.H. Charlesworth identifies 'stresses upon God's transcendence' as one of 'at least four significant theological concerns' in the Old Testament Pseudepigrapha; see his 'Introduction for the General Reader', in *OTP*, I, p. xxix. He further explains,

the influence of Julius Wellhausen's reconstruction of Israelite religion in his *Prolegomena*. Near the end of his book, Wellhausen remarked concerning Israel's religion after exile:

> Worship no longer springs from an inner impulse, it has come to be an exercise of religiosity. It has no natural significance; its significance is transcendental, incomparable, not to be defined; the chief effect of it, which is always produced with certainty, is atonement. For after the exile the consciousness of sin, called forth by the rejection of the people from the face of Jehovah, was to a certain extent permanent: even when the hard service of Israel was accomplished and the wrath really blown over, it would not disappear.[3]

Wellhausen's perspective was anchored in German Romanticism, a romanticism fully in concert with his anti-Semitism and anti-Catholicism. As Joseph Blenkinsopp has noted, 'It is the Romantic glorification of natural man living a spontaneous existence close to the soil and to the cycles of nature which lies beneath Wellhausen's admiration for both the religion of ancient Israel and the untrammeled individualism of the prophets.'[4] The perceived emphasis on the transcendence of God in the 'postexilic period', therefore, was seen as a degradation of the 'closeness' or immanence of God in early Israelite religion. In such a romantic system, divine immanence and divine transcendence lay on opposing ends of a single continuum, with divine immanence good, and transcendence bad.

'After the exile God is usually perceived as one who is above... He has withdrawn from the world and no longer acts in its history; he will, however, act again, probably through intermediaries... Most pseudepigrapha, in contrast to earlier Jewish writings, are characterized by an increasing claim that God is thoroughly majestic and transcendent' (p. xxxi). Interestingly, Charlesworth immediately recognizes the problems with such categories. He writes, 'The contrast between ideas or tendencies in early documents, such as Genesis, and those in the Pseudepigrapha should not be exaggerated... As the hymns, odes, and prayers in the apocalypses themselves demonstrate, the Jew [*sic*?] continued to affirm efficacious and personal communion with God' (p. xxxi). Even though the texts do not fit, Charlesworth nevertheless stays with the old categories of scholarly tradition.

3. J. Wellhausen, *Prolegomena to the History of Ancient Israel* (Gloucester, MA: Peter Smith, 1973), p. 424.

4. J. Blenkinsopp, *Prophecy and Canon: A Contribution to the Study of Jewish Origins* (University of Notre Dame, Center for the Study of Judaism and Christianity in Antiquity, 3; Notre Dame: University of Notre Dame Press, 1977), p. 20. See also *idem*, 'Tanakh and the New Testament: A Christian Perspective', in L. Boadt *et al.* (eds.), *Biblical Studies: Meeting Ground of Jews and Christians* (Studies in Judaism and Christianity; New York: Paulist Press, 1980), pp. 96-119.

The book of Chronicles played an important role in the development of this interpretive tradition. As a central document in the development of 'Judaism' after the exile, the perceived increasing transcendence of God in the postexilic period both influenced and was shaped by readings of divine activity in the book of Chronicles. Wellhausen, for instance, wrote,

> The alterations and additions of Chronicles are all traceable to the same fountain-head—the Judaising of the past, in which otherwise the people of that day would have been unable to recognize their ideal. It was not because tradition gave the Law and the hierocracy and the *Deus ex machina* as sole efficient factor [*sic*] in the sacred narrative, but because these elements were felt to be missing, that they were thus introduced.[5]

Later scholars picked up and developed Wellhausen's understanding of God as '*ex machina*' in Chronicles.

Gerhard von Rad's *Das Geschichtsbild der chronistischen Werkes* represents a mature articulation of this interpretative tradition. While not exhibiting Wellhausen's negative evaluation of the theology of Chronicles, von Rad argued nonetheless that the 'Chronicler' had consistently emphasized Yahweh's 'transcendence'. From the 'frequent substitution' of 'Elohim' for 'Yahweh' (p. 5), and the increased use of the theology of the 'name of Yahweh' (p. 8) to the role of 'Satan' in 1 Chronicles 21 (p. 9), von Rad found in Chronicles a 'high concept of the transcendentalization of Yahweh' (p. 8).[6]

The reading of God as 'transcendent' in the book of Chronicles, however, has not gone uncontested. In her magisterial *The Ideology of the Book of Chronicles*, Sara Japhet surveys the same data as von Rad, but continually arrives at opposite conclusions.[7] Japhet concentrates especially on the battle reports in Chronicles, data that von Rad saw related to divine transcendence through the Chronicler's doctrine of retribution. In these passages Japhet argues that God in Chronicles is immanent, directly active in history: 'It is God who is active. Even the concept of double causality,

---

5.   Wellhausen, *Prolegomena*, p. 223.

6.   G. von Rad, *Das Geschichtsbild des chronistischen Werkes* (BWANT, 54; Stuttgart: W. Kohlhammer, 1930).

7.   For instance, S. Japhet (*The Ideology of the Book of Chronicles and Its Place in Biblical Thought* [BEATAJ, 9; Frankfurt: Peter Lang, 1989], p. 37) ascribes the shift from 'Yahweh' to 'Elohim' to the manuscript tradition, rather than the Chronicler's own work: '…the transition in Chronicles from "YHWH" to "Elohim" was, first and foremost, the result of the process of manuscript transmission and not the work of the actual author of the book'.

whereby God controls events via natural, human deeds, does not describe divine involvement in Chronicles. YHWH intervenes directly and immediately, and He alone is active.'[8] For Japhet, Chronicles does anything but depict God as beyond the sphere of creation: '…the Chronistic narrative illustrates a theological principle: YHWH's action is direct and immediate'.[9]

What is interesting about Japhet's reading is how she too understands God's transcendence and immanence as opposing theological affirmations, overcome only within human 'religious' experience:

> …two conflicting premises underlie the passages which refer to this subject [God's relationship to the world]: on the one hand, God is the far-off, omnipotent master of the universe, dwelling above and beyond the world He created; on the other, He is not distant, but near, and those who believe in Him find Him everywhere. Both approaches are part of the believer's religious experience, an experience that encompasses faith in a sublime, transcendent deity, distant and unattainable, as well as a sense that God is nearby, protectively watching over his faithful and answering their prayers.[10]

By collapsing affirmations about God into statements expressing human experience, Japhet translates God's 'transcendence' into God's 'immanence':

> The passages from Chronicles in which God is depicted as dwelling in heaven prove that the increase in distance is only physical; there is no disruption of the spiritual link or the experience of divine presence… That God dwells in heaven expresses, above all, his supremacy and omnipotence, not his distance. There is no gap or separation between Him and human beings; from heaven, He rules them and answers their prayers.[11]

Romanticism has grasped Japhet as it did Wellhausen; yet, *contra* Wellhausen, in this romanticism she finds 'Chronicles' an ally, rather than an enemy.

---

8.   Japhet, *Ideology*, p. 136.

9.   Japhet, *Ideology*, p. 135. Japhet emphasizes this point throughout her work and summarizes her position as follows: 'The book of Chronicles, however, emphasizes God's direct and immediate intervention in history and describes that intervention in one of two ways. Either the wording conveys a clearly causal relationship…or the objective historical account is supplemented with explanatory statements indicating that YHWH brought about this particular event' (p. 57).

10.   Japhet, *Ideology*, pp. 59-60.

11.   Japhet, *Ideology*, pp. 84-85.

From the perspective of the history of theology, Jewish, Christian and Islamic, however, the terms of this debate seem curious. Quite simply, a conceptuality that places divine transcendence at the opposite end of a continuum from divine immanence only arises with modernity. Beginning in seventeenth-century Europe, the concept of 'transcendence' shifted in language concerning God as confidence grew that human language could accurately describe God. William Placher has written:

> Increasingly, Christian writers in the seventeenth century, since they did not want to think of God as utterly beyond their comprehension, thought of God's otherness in terms of distance and remoteness from the world. Though they did not use the terms, they were in effect contrasting *transcendence* with *immanence*. Such a 'contrastive' account of transcendence... makes divine transcendence and involvement in the world into a zero-sum game: the more involved or immanent, the less transcendent, and vice versa.[12]

Such a mode of thought possesses serious theological problems. It tends either to place God within creation as another 'force' or to deny activity to God within creation altogether. Such thought was utterly foreign to medieval concepts of God, whether Jewish, Christian, or Islamic.[13] The concepts that have framed the twentieth-century academic discussion about divine activity in Chronicles, therefore, seem entrapped within Modernist convictions and presuppositions.

Previous treatments of God in the book of Chronicles have tended to abstract stable doctrinal propositions from the Chronicles narrative in order to describe the presence and activity of God within the text. Yet one does not find propositions about God in Chronicles; one meets a character, one who appears within the narrative, is talked about by others, and whose activity the narrator describes when otherwise not evident within the text. Concrete characterization, not abstract conceptuality, may best describe the divine presence and activity in Chronicles. Narratological questions, therefore, can help overcome the 'transcendence–imminence' dichotomy that has shaped twentieth-century academic discussions.

12. W.C. Placher, *The Domestication of Transcendence: How Modern Thinking about God Went Wrong* (Louisville, KY: Westminster/John Knox Press, 1996), p. 111. See also, D.B. Burrell, *Freedom and Creation in Three Traditions* (Notre Dame, IN: University of Notre Dame Press, 1993), pp. 1-6.

13. See D.B. Burrell, *Knowing the Unknowable God: Ibn-Sina, Maimonides, Aquinas* (Notre Dame, IN: University of Notre Dame, 1986).

To develop a more precise understanding of God in Chronicles, I will examine 'God's activity' from various perspectives within the narrative: the perspective of 'direct' divine activity within the narrative; the perspective on the activity of God by other characters; and finally, the narrator's interpretation of divine activity. At the very least, I will argue that the categories of 'transcendent' and 'immanent' are inadequate to describe the characterization of God in the book of Chronicles. Indeed, there is no fixed 'doctrine' of God's presence and activity in Chronicles; rather, there are contesting levels, at times reinforcing, at other times undercutting each other.

Direct Divine Activity in the Book of Chronicles

God is a rather slippery character in the book of Chronicles. In some ways ever-present, in other ways God is usually absent within the narrative. While the reader receives all information concerning God in Chronicles from the words of the narrator, there are occasions where God's direct activity is not merely attributed by the narrator, but described as visually and/or audibly directly present within the narrative world. Here, at the level of direct characterization, God is epiphanally present, a presence on earth that is largely—and increasingly as the narrative progresses—marked by absence.

God remains remarkably 'physically' absent from the book of Chronicles. Only in four cases—all in 2 Chronicles—does God explicitly appear as a character within the book. In three of the cases God's visual appearance is asserted but not described; the fourth describes God 'in heaven'. Only in heaven does God 'physically' appear, and even then that physical presence is extremely non-descript. In 2 Chronicles 18, the prophet Micaiah reports seeing 'the Lord sitting on the throne, with all the hosts of the heaven standing to the right and to the left of him' (v. 18). In contrast to the book of Ezekiel, Micaiah offers no ornate description of God's presence. Instead, God speaks. God's presence in heaven is marked in the narrative by divine speech. God commissions the spirit (הרוח) to lead Ahab to his death in battle and does nothing to stop the spirit from fulfilling the task by becoming the 'lying spirit in the mouth of all the prophets' (v. 21). The passage vividly depicts God residing in heaven, relating to events on earth through 'spirits' who take the divine word, spoken in heaven, to the earth so that it might be disseminated through prophetic oracles. Only in heaven is God fully and physically manifest; the heavenly presence appears on earth as a deceptive prophetic word.

In three cases, God directly appears within the narrative world of Chronicles. All occur in the Solomon narrative. The first occurs at Gibeon at the beginning of Solomon's reign. Following a formal convocation of 'all Israel' with abundant sacrifices offered to Yahweh, 'that night God appeared (נראה) to Solomon' (2 Chron. 1.7). The appearance, however, is not visible, but audible, for God 'appears' only in God's dialogue with Solomon (vv. 7-12). Similarly, 'the Lord appeared to Solomon in the night' immediately following the dedication of the temple, again, after a formal convocation of Israel with generous sacrifices (7.12). Though a visual term introduces the scene (וירא), God's 'appearance' is again audible: God 'appears' in God's word, here a long monologue exhorting Israel to keep the covenant upon threat of exile (vv. 12-22).

A third, and unique, theophany occurs to all Israel at the dedication of the temple. 'The glory of the Lord' (כבוד יהוה) fills the temple (2 Chron. 5.13-14; 7.1), the 'cloud' (ענן) that prohibits the priests from entering into the temple. The text is interesting, not only in what it says, but in what it does not say. First, the presence of the Lord is also God's absence—*God* is not present, only God's *glory*. Second, even though the text states that the glory fills (מלא) the temple, it simultaneously places the glory 'upon' or 'above' the temple, not in it—'the Israelites saw...the glory of the Lord above the temple' (על הבית, 7.3). Finally, the narrator first introduces the 'glory' as 'a cloud' (ענן)—and it is the cloud, not the glory, that prohibits priests from entering into the temple (5.13-14). The text is full of affirmations and denials, God's presence amid God's absence, a cloud that is simultaneously (or is it?) God's glory. The visible manifestation of God evaporates in its giving, from God's very presence, to God's glory, to a cloud. Once given in the temple at its dedication, God's glory never explicitly enters the narrative world of Chronicles again.

Both—and neither—immanence or transcendence accounts for these texts adequately. God is 'in heaven'—and thereby, transcendent; God 'appears' to Solomon—and is thereby imminent. Yet God's absence from the earth in 2 Chronicles 18 nonetheless leads to God's will occurring on earth, and God's presence in the world remains an absence. Hidden under the guise of nightfall, God 'appears' in divine speech and in a cloud. Rather than transcendence or immanence, God's direct manifestations in Chronicles are epiphanal—sporadic manifestations of the divine within the human realm. These epiphanies are not open to all. A prophet has access to the epiphany of the divine in heaven; the Davidic king, Solomon, to the epiphany on earth—an epiphany that seemingly depends on direct solicitation of the divine, sacrifices made at the temple for its dedication. God directly 'appears' on earth through divine speech and in 'God's glory'. One 'sees' God on earth only in the hearing of the divine word and in the dedication of the temple cult.

Direct divine speech in Chronicles, however, does not occur only in God's 'appearance'. Usually God's direct speech occurs in the text without the explicit appearance of the divine. Reported divine speech represents the most common (in)direct manifestation of divine activity in Chronicles. God speaks, but God speaks from nowhere.

In three cases direct divine speech occurs when the 'spirit of God' is 'upon' or 'clothes' groups or individuals (2 Chron. 15.1-7; 20.14-17; 24.20). Unlike the direct epiphanies, in each case these words spoken 'from God' speak of God in the third person, implying a distinction between the spirit/speaker and God. This is in concert with 2 Chronicles 18. While the subsequent words have divine authorization, they are, strictly speaking, not the direct words of the one whom Micaiah saw sitting on the throne within the narrative world of Chronicles.

The use of the third person within reported divine speech in Chronicles corresponds to 'divine words' uttered by the prophets after the reign of Rehoboam. Prophetic speech occurs throughout the episode of Jehoshaphat's meeting with Ahab in 2 Chronicles 18. The 'lying spirit' speaks in 2 Chron. 18.11-12, in a third-person reference to God (v. 12). Divine speech in Micaiah's report to the kings is complex. Micaiah's report itself refers to God in third person (vv. 16, 18-22), reflecting the visionary nature of his report. His reference to the divine words, however, is given as a direct quotation of a heavenly dialogue. The speech is attributed to God, but God speaks of God's self in third person in the voice of the prophet. The Chronicles text, thereby, calls into question, but does not annul, direct divine activity in the 'mouths of the prophets'. An ambiguity inheres in reported divine activity in the words of the prophets. Not only is God's self not present—only God's word is—but God's word itself is spoken in another's mouth, with references to God in third person.

The absence of God in the presence of the prophetic 'word of the Lord' unsettles the narrative as the 'history of Israel'. After the reign of Rehoboam, prophets speak the third-person divine word. In one instance, the divine word even withdraws God's presence farther from the narrative world. When Jehoram receives a letter from the prophet Elijah, God is doubly absent from the direct divine word—absent in the withdrawal of the body of the prophet from the scene and absent in third-person references to God in the letter (2 Chron. 21.12-15). God's word is textualized. God is active in giving his/her word, but absent in its giving.

The hiddenness of God's presence in the prophetic word stands in marked contrast to the divine activity attested in direct divine speech in the reigns of David, Solomon, and Rehoboam. God speaks to David and Solomon as God does to the divine council in the heavens. 'All Israel' reports Yahweh's election of David as king in direct divine speech spoken to David in the past—'The Lord your God said to you, "You shall shepherd my people Israel, and you shall be a prince over my people Israel"' (1 Chron. 11.2). The speech presents itself as a direct divine speech to David, even though a third party reports the speech. Even if from nowhere, God speaks directly to David. David himself quotes divine speech in the past, always with the deity speaking in first person. Whether addressed directly to him (28.3; see also 22.8-10; 28.6-7) or amid a psalm concerning what God had said to Israel or foreign kings (16.18, 22), David repeats direct past divine speech as first-person quotation. The divine speech in the past, as reported by the founding king, needs no mediation. In none of these cases does the reader have access to the direct divine word, except through the word of the king.

In two cases God speaks directly to David within the narrative (1 Chron. 14.10, 14-15). God speaks in response to the king consulting an oracle. In the first case God refers to him/her in the first person; in the second, however, God speaks immediately, but refers to him/her in the third person (v. 15). God is directly present in the divine word to David, though even God withdraws in the process of speaking to the king.

Despite this direct line of communication between David and the king, God does not always speak directly to David but speaks to him through the prophet as the narrative progresses. God speaks directly to Nathan (at night) to relate a word to David (1 Chron. 17.4-14). Interestingly, however, the narrative only briefly reports that Nathan gave the words to David. The text, therefore, emphasizes the direct activity of God in the giving to Nathan, rather than Nathan's passing the message on to David. Similarly, in 1 Chron. 21.10-12 God speaks to David through the seer Gad. Gad, however, does not report the divine word verbatim, but expands the divine word when he speaks to the king, indicated as well in the shift from the divine first (v. 10) to the divine third person (v. 12). The divine word directly given to the prophet is withdrawn, as it is given to the king.

The pattern continues with Solomon. As discussed above, the 'appearances' of God to Solomon are auditory, not visual. In the first appearance God enters a direct dialogue with Solomon to grant him a favor (2 Chron.

1.7-12), using first person throughout. Likewise, in the epiphany after the dedication of the Jerusalem temple, Yahweh speaks in a monologue in the presence of Solomon—Solomon himself never speaks. Yet the mono-logue has various voices within it. God's voice directly addresses Solomon (2 Chron. 7.12-18a, 19-21a), yet God also quotes him/her in the past (v. 18b) as well as the future voice of anonymous people who pass by the temple site (vv. 21b-22). The divine voice remains in the first person, except when God quotes others referring to God at the end of the passage.

Solomon also quotes direct divine speech in the past. As David quoted Yahweh's direct word concerning Solomon to legitimate Solomon's succession, so Solomon quotes Yahweh's word to David to legitimate Solomon's project of building the temple (2 Chron. 6.5-6, 8-9, 16). No prophet is ever needed to mediate the divine word to Solomon. Solomon has access to divine presence as no other character in Chronicles.

The contrast between the manifestation of the divine to David and especially Solomon and all others in the history of Israel becomes apparent as the narrative continues into Rehoboam's reign. During the time of Rehoboam, the divine word speaks only through Shemaiah, 'the man of God' (2 Chron. 11.2). Deity speaks in first person, giving unsolicited instructions 'to Rehoboam of Judah, son of Solomon, and to all Israel in Judah and Benjamin' (11.3-4), and later, in judgment for forsaking the Law, a condemnation ameliorated by the passive acceptance of the divine judgment by the people (12.5-8). The divine word appears in the first person throughout, even though the word comes in the mouth of Shemaiah the prophet (12.5).

Analyzing the activity of God at the level of direct visible and audible presence within the Chronicles narrative, the inadequacy of the categories of transcendence and immanence is apparent. Visibly manifest in heaven, God is nonetheless present on earth as divine word. Yet divine presence as word without body is inherently unstable, epiphanal. The activity of God in Chronicles is not static, but constantly changing within the narrative world. God's audible or visible presence within the human realm fluctu-ates according to the chronological development of the narrative. Reho-boam's reign emerges as pivotal in a transition in the divine word's direct presentation to David and Solomon to the third-person speech of the later prophets.

God's epiphanies in Chronicles center upon the characters of David and Solomon. The rate and directness of the divine manifestation begins high with David and climaxes in Solomon. Even here with the founding kings of nation and temple, direct divine presence is marked by word, not body, an absence even amid presence. After Solomon's reign, however, the divine word ceases speaking directly to the Davidic king. As the word/ activity of God narrows to the prophets, the relationship of the prophetic word to divine activity itself becomes ambiguous and questionable. When Neco claims divine authorization for his activities, he quotes no direct divine words. Josiah does not regard the speech as authentic (35.20-22) and the results are tragic. The divine epiphany had become characterized more by absence than presence.

Yet divine activity in the past remains, unmarked by ambiguity. David, Solomon, even the narrator (2 Chron. 25.4) can quote God's speech in the past with confidence as the place for the manifestation of God. This becomes especially clear in the one post-Rehoboam narrative where God speaks in the first person. In the divine/prophetic authorization of the Book of the Law found in the temple, God speaks in first person (34.23b-28) through Huldah the prophetess. The speech begins in third person and moves to first as it directly addresses Josiah. Even God can quote the divine word in the Torah as an enduring locus of the divine epiphany.

Immanence and transcendence inadequately describe God's activity as marked by direct character presence and words within the narrative by saying both too little and too much. The categories do not trace with sufficient precision the narrative dynamics of the divine character in its relationship to the narrative world, nor is the character marked by a simple immanent–transcendent dichotomy. Even at the height of the divine presence in the epiphany to Solomon, the divine word still comes up short in revealing the divine character. The direct presence of God and God's activity in Chronicles is marked by ambiguity—an ambiguity of presence marked by absence, an absence that increases as history moves away from the founding reigns of David and Solomon. With the division of the kingdom into Judah and Israel during the reign of Rehoboam, the divine presence slips from king to prophet, from first-person quotation to third-person citation.[14]

14. On the particular significance of the Rehoboam narrative in Chronicles, see G.N. Knoppers, 'Rehoboam in Chronicles: Villain or Victim?', *JBL* 109 (1990), pp. 423-40; *idem*, 'Battling against Yahweh: Israel's War against Judah in 2 Chr 13.2-20', *RB* 100 (1993), pp. 511-32.

*Divine Activity in the Perspective of Characters' Speech
in Chronicles*

If epiphany and ambiguity and post-Solomonic withdrawal mark the direct 'presence' of God in Chronicles, characters who speak of divine activity offer a markedly different perspective. Election replaces epiphany; predictability of judgment overrides ambiguity. Characters other than God make much more extravagant claims for God's presence and activity than the text of Chronicles actually shows. Yet not just anyone is allowed to speak of divine activity. Royalty and prophets have special authority to speak directly of the divine in Chronicles. It is a special prerogative of David and Solomon, yet other royalty, even non-Israelites or non-Judeans such as Hiram of Tyre and the Queen of Sheba, also recognize the work of the God of Israel. Even negative words about God are spoken by a royal figure. The Assyrian king Sennacherib contests the superiority of Israel's God, not only in word, but also in writing.

Only in six places do non-royalty speak of the divine. 'All Israel' is the first character to speak of God's activity—yet they speak merely to affirm that God had spoken to David in order to make him king (1 Chron. 11.2). Joab speaks twice of God, yet in a very general manner that hopes for— but strictly speaking, does not describe—God's presence (1 Chron. 19.13; 21.3). Finally, in three places, Levites and/or the people speak of the divine nature: 'He is good; his love endures forever' (2 Chron. 5.13; 7.3; cf. also 20.21). Yet these are not their own words, but the words of David (cf. 1 Chron. 16.34). Within the narrative world of Chronicles, royalty (especially Davidic royalty) and prophets speak of the divine to the people and readers.

Within this speaking, divine activity is not stable throughout the text. Characters speak differently about God and God's activity, depending on their place in the narrative. Who speaks of the divine, how much is spoken, and the contents of the speech develop as the narrative progresses. The particularities of these utterances reveal patterns of divine activity within the perspective of the characters in Chronicles.

David dominates talk of God in 1 Chronicles. Even when other characters speak of God's activity in the narrative, they speak with unquestionable certainty of God's election of and presence with David.[15] David, of

---

15. See, e.g., 1 Chron. 11.2; 12.18. There is a certain irony in 1 Chron. 17.2. Nathan unconditionally approves David's decision to build a temple, based upon the fact that 'God is with you', only to have God immediately reject David's plan.

course, does nothing but reinforce this perception of divine activity. He responds effusively to Nathan's oracle (1 Chron. 17.16-27). Although God prohibits him from building the temple, David only refers to his divine election as a dynastic founder. God 'has brought me this far' (v. 16), has regarded 'me as someone of high rank' (v. 17). 'For your servant's sake, O Lord, and according to your own heart, you have done all these great deeds, making known all these great things' (v. 19). From David's perspective, his own divine dynastic election provides a basis for noting the wider divine election and activity of God for Israel in the past. After receiving the dynastic oracle, David states,

> Who is like your people Israel, one nation on the earth whom God went to redeem to be his people, making for yourself a name for great and terrible things, in driving out nations before your people whom you redeemed from Egypt? And you made your people Israel to be your people forever; and you, O Lord, become their God. (vv. 21-22)

David therefore has no qualms or hesitancy about claiming divine activity for and presence with himself or Israel. He accepts completely the divine word mediated through the prophet. He then affirms God's activity for Israel in the past as evidence for a divine promise for the future. David's own divine election becomes the basis for the blessing that God will be with Solomon and grant him rest to build the temple. David thus places himself at the center of God's activity in the world for the sake of Israel, the temporal divide between God's activity for Israel in the past and in the future.

David's interpretation of divine presence and activity, however, stretches beyond Israel. In formal gatherings of 'all Israel', David proclaims audaciously the universal presence and activity of God among all the nations. After the ark is brought into Jerusalem, David proclaims: 'All the gods of the peoples are idols, but the Lord made the heavens' (1 Chron. 16.26). According to David, the nations should proclaim: 'The Lord is king!' (16.31). The activity of God on behalf of Israel does not limit God to Israel. In his final speech before Israel, David extends the rule of God to encompass explicitly all creation:

> Yours, O Lord, are the greatness, the power, the glory, the victory, and the majesty; for all that is in the heavens and earth is yours; yours is the kingdom, O Lord, and you are exalted as head above all. Riches and honor come from you, and you rule over all. In your hand are power and might; and it is in your hand to make great and to give strength to all. (1 Chron. 29.11-12)

According to David, the God who chose him is the Sovereign God, active in all nations, indeed in all creation.

In extent and clarity, David's claims concerning God's presence and activity markedly exceed the claims made by the divine character's direct 'presence' and activity in the text of Chronicles itself. While not necessarily contradictory, a fissure nonetheless opens in the text, a fissure that the character David attempts to fill with his own character as the manifestation of the 'great deeds' of God. In speaking of God, David presents himself as evidence of the unambiguous, continuous sovereign presence of God amid Israel and, thereby, the nations.

Though he does not speak of God as much, Solomon continues themes found in his father's speech about God. Each time he speaks to or before all Israel, similar themes to those found within the David narrative. When Solomon speaks to God in the opening epiphany—his first speech in the book—he refers to God's election of David and his own enthronement by the divine will (2 Chron. 1.8). Upon the completion of the temple, he states:

> Blessed be the Lord, the God of Israel, who with his hand has fulfilled what he promised with his mouth to my father David... Now the Lord has fulfilled his promise that he made; for I have succeeded my father David, and sit on the throne of Israel, just as the Lord promised, and have built the house for the name of the Lord, the God of Israel' (2 Chron. 6.4, 10)

The same themes emerge in Solomon's dedicatory prayer, even as Solomon seeks future divine blessings for the Davidic dynasty (2 Chron. 6.14-17). The divine election of and presence with David moves directly into the divine election of and presence with Solomon.

Solomon's words subtly but clearly declare himself as the locus of divine activity. God has fulfilled God's promises in the construction of the temple—the temple that Solomon claims to have built. Solomon himself is evidence of God's faithfulness to God's promises to Solomon! This is not apparent to Solomon alone, however. King Hiram of Tyre concurs with the Davidic house's perspective on divine activity. In his letter replying to Solomon, he declares that the Lord God of Israel, 'who made heaven and earth', 'loves his people' through making Solomon their king. God 'has given King David a wise son' (2 Chron. 2.11-12). As did David, Solomon embodies evidence for the presence and activity of God in the world.

While Solomon's words about God leave no doubt about his understanding of God's activity and presence with him, his words about God in relationship to the temple pose an interesting tension. Solomon declares that 'the house that I am about to build will be great, because our God is greater than all other gods' (2 Chron. 2.5). Yet he immediately continues, 'But who is able to build him a house, since heaven, even the highest heaven, cannot contain him?' (v. 6). The temple, therefore, is not a residence for the divine. It is not the divine house, for God exceeds the ability of the house to contain God. The temple instead is a place of sacrifice to God (2.6).

The temple is not really a locus of the divine presence, even though the Lord's glory appears there following the dedication. In his dedicatory speech, Solomon explicitly states the tension inherent in his task: 'The Lord said that he would reside in thick darkness. I have built you an exalted house, a place for you to reside in forever' (6.1-2). In his dedicatory prayer the same theme emerges: 'But will God indeed reside with mortals on earth? Even heaven and the highest heaven cannot contain you, how much less this house that I have built!' (6.18). Solomon develops a sense of the excessive presence of God, an excessiveness that leaves God absent from the temple. Instead, God's self does not dwell there, though God's 'name' does. In light of the divine absence, Solomon prays that God's eyes be opened 'day and night toward this house, the place where you promised to set your name' (6.20). Solomon clearly struggles to articulate how God's presence relates to the temple. His speeches stagger under the weight of the subject.

Solomon does not equate the temple with the presence of God, nor at the same time, deny God's presence in the temple. God's transcendence does not annul God's immanence, but renders it allusive—present and absent simultaneously. God's immanence does not annul God's transcendence—indeed, it makes it known. An epiphanal elusiveness enters into Solomon's characterization of God in relationship to the temple that was not found in David's speech. In relationship to the temple, God indeed does dwell in a dark cloud.

An interesting contrast, then, is found in Solomon's language concerning the presence and activity of God. God's presence and activity are clear in relationship to David and Solomon. In Solomon's speech, God is unambiguously present and active with and for him, even when not otherwise seen in the narrative. In relationship to the temple, however, Solomon's language bends, if not breaks. God's presence is not denied, though God's excessiveness renders speaking about this presence difficult. As a result, a link is formed between Solomon's speaking of divine activity and his own royal self-interests. As with his father, so the Davidic kingship is the sure, unambiguous location of the divine presence and activity, even in relation to the temple. Thus, the Queen of Sheba is the last character to speak of God's activity in the Solomon narrative. She does not remark about the temple, but rather, God's activity in Solomon: 'Blessed be the Lord, your God, who has delighted in you and set you on his throne as king for the Lord your God. Because your God loved Israel and would establish them forever, he has made you king over them, that you may execute justice and righteousness' (2 Chron. 9.8).

When we leave the David and Solomon narratives behind, the frequency of speaking about God's presence and activity slackens and changes in nature. Prophets, rather than kings, usually speak. While God's promise to David is periodically affirmed, the nature of speaking about divine activity changes. Almost as a response to Solomon's dedicatory prayer in the temple, God acts as the predictable arbiter of reward and punishment— hearing those who ask for forgiveness and bringing wrath upon those who turn away from God. As the narrative progresses chronologically, characters speak of God's activity as increasingly the activity of judgment.

As the narrative moves into the post-Solomon era, Rehoboam's successor, Abijah, invokes language about God found in earlier characters' mouths: 'Do you not know that the Lord God of Israel gave the kingship over Israel to David and his sons by a covenant of salt?... See, God is with us at our head' (2 Chron. 13.5, 12). David and Solomon and their heirs are still the locus of divine activity, the evidence of God's presence with Judah. Yet the presence of God is now a warrant for divine protection and success in battle. To fight a faithful Judah is now to fight directly against the Lord: 'O Israelites, do not fight against the Lord, the God of your ancestors; for you cannot succeed' (13.12). Later Asa evokes God's activity in response to Judah's faithfulness to inquire of God: 'The land is still ours because we have sought the Lord our God; we sought him and he has given us peace on every side' (14.7).

A subtle but significant shift has taken place in the characters' speaking of the divine. David and Solomon's language of God's activity during their reigns becomes the basis for the prediction of God's activity in the post-Solomon era. On the basis of God's promise to David and Solomon's dedicatory prayer, characters speak of divine presence and activity as a predictable phenomenon. God is always Judah's God—that does not, nor can it change. God's activity will therefore always be on behalf of the interests of Judah as long as they seek him, just as Solomon prayed in the dedicatory prayer. Thus, when the spirit comes upon Azariah to speak with

Asa, he states: 'The Lord is with you, while you are with him. If you seek him, he will be found by you, but if you abandon him, he will abandon you' (2 Chron. 15.2). The seer Hanani conveys the same message to Asa: 'Because you relied on the Lord, he gave them into your hand. For the eyes of the Lord range throughout the entire earth to strengthen those whose heart is true to him' (2 Chron. 16.9). In the characters' speech, God's activity becomes predictable in Judah, in light of the king and the people 'seeking' or 'forsaking' God, based upon the divine election of David and Solomon.

The characters' portrayal of divine activity suggests two different possibilities. If Judah seeks God appropriately, God will aid and sustain them in their cause. Yet the statement of positive divine action on their behalf implies the possibility of negative action against them as well. No character explicitly says that God has acted to judge Judah until Jehu the seer during the first part of Jehoshaphat's reign: 'Because of this, wrath has gone out against you from the Lord' (19.2). Jehoshaphat learns his lesson quickly. As he appoints judges, he articulates the principles of divine activity: 'Let the fear of the Lord be upon you; take care what you do, for there is no perversion of justice with the Lord our God, or partiality, or taking of bribes' (19.7). Similarly, he exhorts the levitical judges, stationed in Jerusalem: 'You shall instruct them so that they may not incur guilt before the Lord and wrath may not come on you and your kindred. Do so, and you will not incur guilt... Deal courageously, and may the Lord be with the good!' (19.10-11).

Jehoshaphat articulates a consistent principle underlying characters' perception of divine presence and activity from this point on in the narrative. The Chronicler's so-called 'doctrine of immediate retribution', therefore, emerges at a certain point in the chronological development of the story.[16] Characters consistently speak of God's activity in the past. Divine ability to intervene is presupposed and even articulated throughout. God's presence in heaven grants God power and authority to work on earth. As Jehoshaphat states, 'O Lord, God of our ancestors, are you not God in heaven? Do you not rule over all the kingdoms of the nations? In your hand are power and might, so that no one is able to withstand you' (2 Chron. 20.6). Yet, from the perspectives of kings and prophets, divine action in the narrative—present or near future—is predicated upon the sole

16. For the doctrine of retribution, see R.B. Dillard, 'Reward and Punishment in Chronicles: The Theology of Immediate Retribution', *WTJ* 46 (1984), pp. 164-72.

reliance to consult the oracles of the Lord in Jerusalem and abide by this alone. Thus, Eliezer prophesies against Jehoshaphat later in the narrative, 'Because you have joined with Ahaziah, the Lord will destroy what you have made' (2 Chron. 20.37). A nameless prophet speaks to Amaziah, 'I know that God has determined to destroy you, because you have done this and have not listened to my advice' (25.16). The prophet Oded explains to the Northern Kingdom, Israel, that 'Because the Lord, the God of your ancestors, was angry with Judah, he gave them into your hand' (28.9). Yet Israel's own sins come back to haunt them: 'the fierce wrath of the Lord is upon you' (28.11). Hezekiah and Josiah both recognize that God's judgment in Judah arises out of Judah's unfaithfulness: 'Do not be like your ancestors and your kindred, who were faithless to the Lord God of their ancestors, so that he made them a desolation, as you see' (30.7). Josiah states, 'The wrath of the Lord that is poured out on us is great, because our ancestors did not keep the word of the Lord' (34.21). Following Jehoshaphat, characters consistently articulate divine activity on the basis of retribution or reward for the behavior of the people.

A shift, then, occurs, in the narrative development of how characters speak of God within the text of Chronicles. The shift is not in whether or not God is involved in Judah, Israel, or the world—this seems presupposed throughout. While characters speak less of divine activity after David and Solomon, they nonetheless continue to speak of it. It is not a movement from transcendence to immanence or vice versa. From the character's language, God remains active. Yet there is a turn. Characters in the reigns of David and Solomon articulate God's activity in positive terms of promise, election, and faithfulness. God's presence brings election, blessing, honor, peace, and prosperity. As the book continues, divine activity becomes more predictable on the basis of a principle of reward and retribution. Solomon's dedicatory prayer in the temple seems to provide the crucial narrative transition point. Characters initially speak of the principle in terms of the opportunity of divine blessing. After Jehoshaphat's reign, however, characters largely use the retribution principle to speak of God's activity of judgment upon Judah and Israel. Characters' speech of divine activity, therefore, moves from articulating God's involvement in the world for the empowerment of Israel/Judah through the persons of David and Solomon to judgment and punishment. Only Hezekiah evokes the positive side of the retribution formula when he tells the people: 'Do not be afraid or dismayed before the king of Assyria and all the horde that is with him; for there is one greater with us than with him. With him is an arm of flesh; but with us is the Lord our God, to help us and to fight our battles' (2 Chron. 32.7-8). Hezekiah's words appear in a context that negates Sennacherib's aspersions on God's ability to intervene, an ability never in doubt from other characters' perspectives within the book.

Interestingly, the last character to speak of God in Chronicles is another foreign king. King Cyrus of Persia, invokes the language of Solomon in speaking of divine activity: 'The Lord, the God of heaven, has given me all the kingdoms of the earth and he has charged me to build him a house at Jerusalem' (2 Chron. 36.23). Yet Cyrus' claim for divine commissioning exceeds Solomon's. Cyrus has been granted rule over all kingdoms of the earth, a rule that matches God's own as expressed in other characters' language about God. The words of Cyrus state that the divine election breaks forth again in an expected fashion, breaking the formula of immediate retribution and reward to claim a royal prerogative as the result of divine activity. The book ends with a new royal character stating a new beginning. The tensions with earlier divine and royal proclamations concerning the line of David are not resolved, but maintained.

Character language of divine presence and activity in Chronicles focuses on the words of kings and prophets. Individual characters offer no global interpretation of divine activity but articulate without ambiguity their confidence in the divine presence and activity in specific situations. The tension in Solomon's description of the divine presence within the temple provides an exception to the rule. Yet even this exception fortifies the broader view. From the characters' speeches, God is active throughout the world, but especially in Judah and Israel, largely (but not exclusively) through the persons of the Davidic kings. God's election of David and Solomon, then, becomes the basis for the predictability of God's activity, a predictability that moves generally from the articulation of divine favor to divine judgment. Cyrus, king of Persia, however, shatters this predictability, making a 'Solomonic claim' of divine activity on his own behalf as ruler for over all the kingdoms of the earth. No assessment is made of the validity of his claim, however. God remains hidden, even as Cyrus speaks of the divine voice.

One recognizes in this pattern certain connections with the direct visible and direct manifestations of God in Chronicles. David and Solomon remain highpoints of divine activity, and a slow deterioration of divine activity emerges following Rehoboam's reign. The epiphanal presence of God remains associated with the temple, though kings are seen as the special locus of divine presence and activity—even beyond that of the temple. On both levels, 'transcendence' is not an opposite pole of 'immanence' in the divine's relationship with the world, but rather, transcendence is a necessary condition to express God's immanence. Only as God is 'in heaven' and rules the whole world, can characters claim the direct involvement of God in the narrative world of Chronicles.

Yet, certain significant differences emerge as well. Most significantly, the ambiguity and limited extent of direct divine activity in Chronicles differ from the directness, extent, and certainty by which the characters speak of the divine. The two levels of characterization of articulating God's presence and activity in Chronicles hang tenuously together in the slippage between what characters claim and what the reader actually 'sees' in the narrative. This gap continues in light of the comments and perspective that the narrator of Chronicles makes concerning God's presence and activity within the text of Chronicles.

The Narrator and the Presence and Activity of God in the Book of Chronicles

The narrator's voice is the one consistent—and dominant—voice throughout the book of Chronicles. Unembodied, ungendered, and anonymous, the narrator has the ability to discern and identify the divine presence and activity in the world, when it would otherwise be inaccessible to the reader. The narrator, therefore, interprets God's role globally within the narrative world for the reader. The narrator suffers no lack of confidence in ability to know when and where God is active in the world. At times, the means of divine activity is open only to the narrator, as it remains hidden from the reader. Yet the narrator especially identifies those cases where God is not visibly or audibly active within the narrative; where God is directly present, the narrator has no need to identify the activity for the reader. Thus, in Solomon's reign the narrator only refers to God's presence or activity twice, once at the beginning of the narrative and once at its end. The more God is 'present' in the narrative, the less the narrator provides theological commentary. The more God is 'absent' in the narrative, the narrator provides more, even abundant, theological commentary. Nonetheless the narrator's overall concern seems to define God's activity in the history of Israel. The narrator presents God actively involved in the events and affairs of the people of Judah and Israel, even if (or especially when) the means of that activity remains ambiguous.

The narrator does not begin the narration with God as a major actor. Chronicles, of course, begins with a series of genealogies. 'God' remains initially absent from the genealogical or chronological progression of the narrative. The story begins with humans, not God. God does not 'set the ball rolling', either for all creation or by singling out the descendants of 'Abram, that is, Abraham' as the ancestor of Israel (1.27). Chronicles first mentions God with the genealogy of the line of Judah. Here, the narrator 'introduces' Yahweh as a moral evaluator and executor of Er, the firstborn son of Judah. Er was 'wicked in the sight of the Lord' (2.3).

The reference, brief and unassuming as it is, unsettles the narrative. Up to this point, the narrative works on the surface—human actors beget human actors. All characters remain empowered for their own actions; they propagate and then die. Yet suddenly, with no forewarning, God emerges as a distinct character. Er is removed from an active role within the narrative, demoted to a mere recipient in the narrative's unfolding. Yet God's sudden presence here marks previous divine absence in the genealogy and raises a host of questions. Has Yahweh always been the power behind the progression of the genealogies? Is Yahweh a character solely related to the line of Judah? Does Yahweh merely bring death? Was Er the only one judged evil by Yahweh, or does this judgment lie behind the death of all?

God becomes what a narratologist might call a 'power': a class of actors 'who support the subject in the realization of its intention, supply the object, or allow it to be supplied or given'.[17] Throughout the narrator's discourse, God consistently responds to other characters, bringing weal or woe, shifting the course of events in the process. The narrator presents God as the arbiter of life and death, prosperity or disaster, particularly in battles. For a Judean to 'call out' to God is to bring divine favor to hand in a situation. During Abijah's reign, Judah 'cries out' to God, and the narrator comments that 'the people of Judah prevailed, because they relied on the Lord, the God of their ancestors' (2 Chron. 13.18). Even in the midst of an ill-planned battle, Jehoshaphat cried out, and according to the narrator, 'The Lord helped him. God drew them away from him' (18.31). It is the narrator who states concerning Uzziah, 'as long as he sought the Lord, God made him prosper' (26.5). Consistently, the narrator articulates God as a power, bringing aid to Judeans who ask for it.

---

17. M. Bal, *Narratology: Introduction to the Theory of Narrative* (Toronto: University of Toronto Press, 1985), p. 28.

Yet favorable divine activity is not always in the narrator's voice. As mentioned above, Er's wickedness led to his divine execution, as does Saul's seeking a medium (1 Chron. 10.13). God especially responds negatively to those who ignore God's communication: Manasseh and his people (2 Chron. 33.10), Josiah (35.22), and especially, Judah during the time of Zedekiah (36.15-21). The narrator presents God as a moral force in the universe, responding beneficially to Judeans who respond well to God, punishing severely those who (especially in Judah and Israel) ignore God. From the narrator's perspective, God always seems lurking behind the text, ready to respond for weal or woe in the morally/culticly appropriate situation. The narrator even grants a reason for the divine execution of Uzzah, while carrying the ark into Jerusalem. God 'struck him down because he put out his hand to the ark' (1 Chron. 13.10). The narrator's God responds rationally according to moral criteria, known (so it seems) to God and the narrator.

At times, the narrator suggests that God not only responds to characters and events, but even determines outcomes beforehand, outside the bounds of 'morality'. Divine favor adheres to select individuals, often without explicit justification. God is 'with' Phineas, son of Eleazar, 'prince' (נגיד) over the gatekeepers (1 Chron. 9.20). According to the narrator, 'the Lord his God was with him [Solomon] and made him exceedingly great' (1.1). The narrator relates that 'The Lord stirred the spirit (העיר יהוה את רוח)' of Cyrus king of Persia to proclaim his divine commission over all kingdoms and to rebuild the temple in Jerusalem (2 Chron. 36.22). Under Jehoram, the narrator explains that God restrains from destroying the Davidic heirs 'because of the covenant he [God] had made with David' (21.7), though God does plague Jehoram with an incurable bowel disease (21.18). Instead of responding to their obedience or disobedience, the narrator reports that God enables the people to obey Hezekiah's reforms: 'The hand of God was also on Judah to give them one heart to do what the king and the officials commanded by the word of the Lord' (30.12). Perhaps most interesting, however, is where the narrator seems to indicate that God closes Rehoboam's mind to the words of the people. The narrator depicts divine manipulation of a character, not as a response to the character's own activity, but so that God may remain true to the prophetic word: 'The king did not listen to the people, because it was a turn of affairs brought about by God (את היתה נסבה מעם האלהים) so that the Lord might fulfill his word, which he had spoken by Ahijah the Shilonite to Jeroboam son of Nebat' (10.15). In each case, God acts unilaterally.

Underneath the storyline, the narrator asserts that God works to bring about the ordained divine will.

The narrator's words come as an interpretive layer over events and characters. The narrator interprets events, not only as a means of divine response to a certain moral or cultic order, but also as a means of divine orchestration of events and characters. The narrator consistently interprets God as empowering or, at least at crucial times, interacting with the events in the narrative world. God directs events and characters in a certain way to uphold the divine will, especially as it relates to God's cultic and moral governance of Israel living amid the nations.

When one examines the means by which the narrator understands the presence and activity of God, one discovers that the narrator has at least three ways of speaking about divine activity in the world. First, the narrator interprets divine activity through the agency of others. Saul dies by suicide, falling on his own sword (1 Chron. 10.4); later, however, the narrator attributes his death directly to divine activity (10.13). In the Jehoshaphat narrative, 'The Lord set an ambush (נתן יהוה מארבים) against the Ammonites, Moab and Mount Seir' (20.22). Yet as the narrative continues, the nature of these 'ambushes' appears to be the violent dissolution of the invading coalition (cf. 20.23). In these cases, it might be said that the narrator operates with a notion of double causation. God is not merely one agent among others. Rather, both an agent within the world and God simultaneously and completely cause an event. Such a notion requires that God be conceived of as completely 'other'. God is 'not one of the things or agents among others in the world, to be located either closer or farther away, more involved in interactions or less. Rather, God transcend[s] all our ways of classifying, locating, and relating the things in the world.'[18] The narrator never develops this notion in any sustained way, but it seems required in order to articulate the text's dual affirmations about God's activity in the world with the primary actions of other characters.

The narrator also asserts divine agency as a result of earlier divine activity. In several cases the consequences of earlier events reach beyond those events to determine reactions of characters in the future. The narrator is not hesitant to attribute the later reactions to direct divine activity. Following David's military conquests, his 'fame spread throughout every land and the Lord made all the nations fear him' (1 Chron. 14.17). The narrator especially attributes 'rest' to God's activity as a consequence

---

18. Placher, *Domestication*, p. 111.

of earlier events. God grants Asa 'rest' following his victorious battles (2 Chron. 15.15). 'Fear' and 'rest' come together in an extended narratorial comment in the Jehoshaphat narrative:

> The Lord had enabled them to rejoice over their enemies... The fear of God came on all the kingdoms of the countries when they heard that the Lord had fought against the enemies of Israel. And the realm of Jehoshaphat was quiet (ותשקט מלכות יהושפט), for God had given him rest all around. (2 Chron. 20.27-30)

The narrator interprets the responses of the surrounding people as the immediate and direct result of the activity of God, while simultaneously tying the responses to early actions and events in the narrative. Dual causation seems involved; behaviors simultaneously result from both the psychological responses of characters to previous events and the direct activity of God.

Yet dual causation is not the only means by which the narrator sees God as being active in the world. The narrator occasionally attributes events solely to immediate divine agency. Thus, the narrator states at the end of 1 Chronicles, 'The Lord highly exalted Solomon in the sight of all Israel, and bestowed upon him such royal majesty as had not been on any king before him in Israel' (1 Chron. 29.25). God's activity here is asserted as a direct, unmediated act of God, with the precise means of the divine activity unspecified. The narrator even claims direct divine involvement in battles. During the reign of Asa, 'The Lord defeated the Ethiopians before Asa and before Judah...they were broken before the Lord and his army (מחנהו)' (2 Chron. 14.11-12 [EVV vv. 12-13]). The text is both suggestive and allusive. Who is the Lord's army (מחנהו)? Angels? Asa and Judah? The ambiguity lies heavy over the text in light of the unambiguous statement of direct divine activity. Similarly, the narrator claims direct divine activity in a battle between Judah and Israel during the reign of Abijah: 'The priests blew the trumpets. Then people of Judah raised the battle shout. And when the people of Judah shouted, God defeated (והאלהים נגף) Jeroboam and all Israel before Abijah and Judah' (2 Chron. 13.14b-15). Again, the ambiguity of narrative world undercuts the direct attribution of divine activity. How does God defeat Israel? No theophany is described; no account of battle ensues. The narrator stretches the imagination of the reader in the attempt to place the divine activity directly within the narrative flow of events. The narrator's silence on the precise means of divine agency seems to claim God's active presence, while declining to define the nature of that presence. The scene undercuts the clarity of the interpretive comment. Whether it is the Aramean army's success over Joash, Jehoram's bowels, Uzziah's success, Manasseh's return, or Cyrus' moved heart, the narrator claims direct divine activity, without any indication of how this activity is concretely experienced by the characters within the narrative world.

Third, the narrator depicts divine action through a heavenly mediator. The narrator, however, in at least two places, places divine activity in a heavenly emissary sent from God. Thus, 'the Lord sent an angel, who cut off (וישלח יהוה מלאך ויכחד) all the mighty warriors and commanders and officers in the camp of the king of Assyria' (2 Chron. 32.21). The scene invokes the memory of an angel who begins the destruction of Jerusalem in David's reign, until restrained by God (1 Chron. 21.15-27). In these stories the heavenly being seemingly appears physically amid the world to wreak havoc from God. The narrator depicts divine activity in the earth through these heavenly mediators. God's activity is direct in the sending of the angel, presumably from heaven, but not directly present within the scene.

The narrator's voice consistently speaks of divine involvement throughout the narrative. The different modes by which the narrator speaks of divine activity bear no discernable pattern, but move back and forth throughout the narrative—until the end of the book. From the return of Manasseh to the destruction of Jerusalem during the reign of Zedekiah, even the narrator stops speaking about divine activity. For instance, Solomon's temple dedication results in a theophany, and the narrator states explicitly that God heard the prayers of Hezekiah and the priests and Levites. Josiah's ceremonies, however, including a passover greater than any passover that had come before, result in no explicit manifestation of God, special prophetic word, or even narrator comment. The narrator ceases speaking of divine activity until the destruction of Jerusalem, but resumes in the divine activity in the heart of Cyrus.

In summary, only in the period from Amon through to Jehoiachin does the narrator fall silent about divine activity in the narrative portrayal of events. Otherwise, the narrator in Chronicles depicts God as directly involved in the events of Judah and Israel, as well as within select individuals and nations that come into contact with them. The narrator does not hesitate to ascribe events to the activity of God. Whether in dual causation, direct activity, or heavenly mediators, the narrator portrays God involved in the affairs of Judah and Israel and—through them—even the nations. God consistently intervenes according to the cultic or moral behavior of characters and even manipulates behavior to maintain the divine will. Yet this generously broad interpretation of divine presence and activity raises its own questions about divine agency. Is God's activity in one place a sign of God's absence in others, or is the divine presence or activity always at work just outside the range of the typical human perception, awaiting only the narrator's interpretative voice to bring it to bear? Is God present, then absent? Or is God's presence, even in the narrator's words, marked by God's absence?

Such may be the nature of a narrative 'power'. The narrator seems to portray God as the ultimate power within the narrative world of Chronicles, different from, though working amid, other powers in the narrative world. Simply stated, the narrator seems to use the character 'God' as an interpretive category to provide an overall explanatory unity to the direction and development of the narrative. The consistency of the interpretive perspective of the narrator even suggests God's presence in the narrative events, when the divine is explicitly absent. Yet despite the expressed clarity and conviction of the narrator's perspective, God's presence and activity remain elusive. The narrator's attribution of an event directly to divine activity is unclear with regard to its reference. The attribution of another agent in addition to the divine agency raises questions concerning the nature of the divine activity in the first place. Finally, the mediation of heavenly emissaries seemingly isolates direct divine activity from the earth. God's activity, so strongly and clearly embraced by the narrator, quivers when examined in detail.

Even with the narrator, God's presence in the book of Chronicles remains ambiguous. Both immanent and transcendent, God is also neither immanent nor transcendent. The character strains at coherence even within the discourse of the narrator itself, let alone in conjunction with the language of the characters and direct presence in the narrative world itself.

Conclusion: God in the Book of Chronicles

If nothing else, this study has argued that the characterization of divine activity in the book of Chronicles cannot be reduced to a simple choice between binary dogmatic categories such as immanence and transcendence. Relationships within the text implode such categories. Much more significant than God's transcendence or immanence is the where or when of the divine presence and activity, and how this presence and activity is simultaneously, at least to some degree, absence and silence. The text resists wrapping one's mind around 'God', even while it portrays the character as the major power within the narrative world. Whether within the direct presence of the divine character in the text, characters' speech about the divine, or the narrator's broad interpretive position, God is not simply immanent or transcendent, but epiphanal. God is manifest at certain times and places to the narrator and, in some cases, to certain characters, a manifestation that also obscures the full nature of the divine character, even as it reveals it.

God is a strange, different character in the narrative world of Chronicles. Seemingly embodied in the heavens (though a character states that the heavens cannot contain God), God never bodily enters the text. Nonetheless, this does not in any way lessen God's presence within the narrative world—though only God's 'glory' and 'word' are visibly and audibly manifest in the text. Characters seek to invoke God to promote a certain Davidic or Judean moral–cultic–political order. Yet 'God' ultimately eludes such an attempt at control, until the foreign king Cyrus claims his ascendancy on the basis of a divine commission. Even the narrator's sweeping interpretive framework falters in the breadth of the framework, and the vagueness of the precise means of the divine activity within the narrative world.

When one distinguishes between the characters' direct presence in the narrative and what characters and the narrator say about God, 'God' becomes more complex. Some things stay consistent between the three discourses: God seemingly bears a distinct interest and even presence with the line of Judah, especially David and Solomon. God therefore has a special interest in Judah—and thereby Israel, though not to the exclusion of other nations, especially as they interact with Judah. It is good for a character to remain on the positive side of this divine character, as God has no problem taking life—or granting prosperity. Finally, the text at all levels seemingly highlights divine presence and activity in the past, particularly David and Solomon. Yet God appears to withdraw from the narrative as it progresses, until the divine presence is made known anew in the destruction of the exile and the stirrings of Cyrus.

These large, consistent patterns are significant. Yet we have also seen substantial differences in the divine characterization among the following: the direct divine manifestation within the text, the characters' statements about God, and the narrator's interpretive framework. The interpretive framework remains consistent—God is involved throughout the story as its underlying power, even if this is manifested in several different ways.

Characters speak confidently about God in particular situations and, eventually, predict divine activity according to a religio-moral principle. Yet this principle itself seems undercut by the words of Cyrus, words that the narrator attributes to divine agency. The actual presence of God in the text, however, does not explicitly live up to the confidence of the characters and narrator. God is present, but not fully; manifest, but withdrawn; ruler of all creation, but appearing only to David and Solomon. The text, even with its common patterns, destabilizes that characterization even as it makes it. The destabilization occurs within each level of characterization. Yet the strains, tensions, and grinding between each level keep the reader off balance with 'God', unsure but looking, grasping but then revising in light of a constantly in-coming difference.

Perhaps that is the contribution that the characterization of the presence and activity of God in Chronicles grants us. On the surface, God in Chronicles comes with an apparent plainness, simplicity, even banality. Yet even in the plain language of sameness, when one speaks of God, 'God' necessarily comes as 'other'; and when God comes as other, our narrative world is disrupted, our rational moral–cultic–political order unsettled.

INDEXES

INDEX OF REFERENCES

OLD TESTAMENT

The Chronicler as Theologian

OTHER ANCIENT REFERENCES

INDEX OF AUTHORS

JOURNAL FOR THE STUDY OF THE OLD TESTAMENT
SUPPLEMENT SERIES